Paving the Third Way

PAVING THE THIRD WAY

The Critique of Parliamentary Socialism

David Coates - Editor

THE MERLIN PRESS

First published 2003 by The Merlin Press Ltd.
PO Box 30705
London WC2E 8QD
www.merlinpress.co.uk

ISBN: 0850365120

British Library Cataloguing in Publication Data
is available from the British Library

Printed in Great Britain by Antony Rowe Ltd., Chippenham

Contents

Acknowledgements

Chapters 4, 8, 9, 10, 11, 13 and 14 are edited versions of articles in various editions of *The Socialist Register*, to which the reader is referred for a fuller version. Chapters 1 to 3 and 5 are edited versions of part of R. Miliband's Parliamentary Socialism (first edition, 1961; second edition, 1972). Chapter 6 is an edited version of pp. 235-259 of L. Panitch, Social Democracy and Industrial Militancy (Cambridge University Press, 1976). Chapter 7 is an edited version of pages 130-176 of D. Coates, The Labour Party and the Struggle for Socialism (Cambridge University Press, 1975). Chapter 12 is an edited version of an essay of the same title, which first appeared in New Left Review, 219, September-October 1996, pp. 62-78. All chapters are reproduced here with the permission of the original publishers.

Introduction

The essays reproduced here – and indeed the idea for this collection – originated in the run up to a conference that was held in Manchester in the summer of 2001, a conference on the historiography of the Labour Party organized by the Labour Movements Study Group of the Political Studies Association. In preparing the statement on the legacy and importance of the work of Ralph Miliband in the field of labour studies for that conference, first I and then Leo Panitch was obliged to work systematically through sets of writings that we had known, and in some cases written, over years, indeed decades, past. Much of that writing first appeared in the pages of *The Socialist Register,* the annual journal of independent socialist thought initially edited by Ralph Miliband and John Saville, and subsequently by Leo Panitch and Colin Leys. Not all the writing that we re-read bore re-visiting! Certainly not all of it was of sufficient long-term value and relevance to warrant republishing; but in my view a remarkably large amount of it was. I say 'in my view' here because much of what is of value in these essays was actually written by Leo Panitch. So let me be clear from the outset. This is not an exercise in personal vanity on Leo's part. On the contrary, though the final essay in this collection is jointly written, the selection has been mine alone, as was the impulse to produce such a volume. While researching for that conference paper I came progressively to the view that many of the arguments on the nature of the Labour Party and the potential of Labour politics for the advance of left-wing causes that were developed by Miliband, Saville, Panitch and others sharing their general perspective still have a contemporary relevance and value. For this and the following reasons they are reproduced here.

The first is simply to set the historical record straight on what was actually thought, written and claimed by writers who other Labour Party scholars and commentators often link together as a Miliband 'school' or representing a Miliband 'approach'. Arguments within this 'school' are often reported by others in extremely misleading and hostile ways: a pattern of disagreement and distortion that has been there from the outset. In the 1995 *Socialist Register,* in an essay which looked back at initial reactions to Ralph Miliband's *Parliamentary Socialism,* John Saville reported at length on the earliest of those misleading and hostile responses – the 1961 review in *The New Statesman* by Richard Crossman, once a leading Bevanite and soon to be a major figure in the Labour Governments of 1964-70. In that review Crossman accused Miliband of 'a degree of tendentious distortion and misquotation which no journalist or politician would dare to use' – an accusation he was later unable to substantiate in extensive correspondence with Saville[1]. *Parliamentary Socialism* has long been out of print – accessible to a new generation of Labour Party scholars only in well-turned university library

copies or secondhand book shops; and many of the *Socialist Registers* that Miliband and Saville then edited from 1964 are even harder to find. So part of the
value of reproducing key sections of both the 1961 Miliband volume and later
Register essays is that it enables a new generation of readers to assess for themselves the adequacy of the description – and associated dismissal – of this way of
understanding Labour Party politics placed upon it at times by its critics.

None of that criticism would matter, of course, except to those criticised, if the
past of the Labour Party had no contemporary relevance. But it does. The return of New Labour to power has re-awakened interest in Labour politics more
generally, after the long 'wilderness years' of Thatcherism; and the fact that the
Labour Party returned to power claiming its own novelty (not simply against
Thatcherism but against its own past) has made the study of 'Old Labour' of
vital political concern again. Part of the New Labour appeal is its telling of the
Party's own history. But much of that telling is itself partial, misleading, self-
indulgent, and persistently distorting of the nature and limits of earlier Labour
leaderships. New Labour is not as new as it likes to think. If its politics involve
breaks with the party's past, other breaks have occurred before. And earlier and
current revisionisms have features in common, and operate within parameters
and logics that were evident long before the current leadership even joined the
Party, let alone led it. The limits of Old Labour paved the way for the limits of
New Labour, and therefore a full analysis of New Labour and its potential requires a full understanding of Old Labour, and of the process of transition from
the one to the other.

A number of such analyses are available: those inspired and influenced by the
work and politics of Ralph Miliband are simply an important part of an on-go-
ing debate. The premise of this collection is that the Miliband approach is still a
key element in that debate, as it has been now for over four decades. The collection of essays gathered here makes accessible again the best of the Miliband-inspired writings on the Labour Party. The writings have a freshness which comes
from their being written at the moment of, and as attempts to shape, the various
historical conjunctures they describe. Collectively they also constitute a new history of the post-war Labour Party, and as such are a powerful counter-weight to
more conventional tellings of that same tale. And though there is no 'party line'
here – all the essays here were individually written, and the views expressed are
those of their authors – nonetheless they are held together by a shared anchor-
age in the politics of *The Socialist Register* itself. Since not everyone reading this
collection will know *The Register* and its history, it is perhaps worth saying just a
little about *The Register*'s genesis and politics.

Ralph Miliband and John Saville (with the help of Edward Thompson and
Lawrence Day) conceived *The Socialist Register* in 1963 as part of the British New
Left's post-1956 attempt to mark out a political and intellectual space *between*
social democracy and communism. It is a space which *The Register* has occupied

ever since, albeit now intellectually more than in party political terms, given the de-radicalization of social democracy and the disappearance of communism. From the first volume of *The Register* in 1964, its editors sought constantly to encourage the emergence of a form of left-wing politics free of traditional parliamentarianism on the one side, and of the Stalinism of Communist (and the Leninism of Trotskyist) politics on the other. That remains *The Register*'s core political goal: which is why, given the weight of the Labour Party in Britain, its essays have regularly had to engage in a critical way with the illusions of Labourism. Indeed it is with those illusions that the first essays reproduced here are centrally concerned.

Notes

[1] J. Saville, 'Parliamentary Socialism Revisited', in L. Panitch (ed), *Why Not Capitalism: The Socialist Register 1995*, London, Merlin Press, 1995, pp.231-2.

Part 1: Labourism and Its Limits

Editorial Introduction to Extracts 1-3

When Ralph Miliband published *Parliamentary Socialism* in 1961 the text represented a very sharp break with normal histories of British Labour, and one that was not initially universally popular. It came out the same year as Henry Pelling's *A Short History of the Labour Party*, hard on the heels of Robert MacKenzie's *British Political Parties*, and soon to be followed by Sam Beer's *Modern British Parties*; so there was no shortage in the 1960s of more sympathetic treatments of Labour's record than that offered here. As John Saville, Ralph Miliband's long time co-editor of *The Socialist Register* noted later, the book quickly became 'a key text in the revival of socialist ideas in the 1960s and 1970s'; and it did so, as I can attest from my first reading of it as an undergraduate, in part 'because it offered for the first time an extended analysis of why the great hopes of 1945 had so quickly evaporated into the dull conservative record of the nineteen fifties', and in part because 'it fitted the great stirrings of political conscience that came with the nuclear debate at the end of the decade'[1]. The central thesis of *Parliamentary Socialism*, one which at the time seemed rather shocking to people in the mainstream of the labour movement, but which is now both well known and commonplace, was that 'of all political parties claiming socialism to be their aim, the Labour Party has always been one of the most dogmatic – not about socialism, but about the parliamentary system'[2]. Though subsequent analysts have always tended to treat *Parliamentary Socialism* as simply a left-wing history of the Party, its author didn't initially present it in that way. On the contrary, he was adamant that he had '*not* tried to write a comprehensive history of the Labour Party, much less of the Labour movement'[3], but had attempted instead primarily to document the early consolidation of the Party's commitment to the norms of the British parliamentary system, and to chart the impact of that commitment on subsequent party policy and performance. It was Labour's parliamentarianism with which Ralph Miliband was overwhelmingly concerned.

Yet in *Parliamentary Socialism* Ralph Miliband did write a history of the Labour Party. He just wrote it in a particular way. He set the Party's official policy positions and strategic concerns alongside those of three other elements of the wider labour movement: those of the Labour Left, the extra-parliamentary Left, and the national trade union leadership; and he did that the better to trace the inability of socialists inside or outside the party to hold the Party leadership to their periodically adopted socialist project. The pages of *Parliamentary Socialism* are clear on both the importance of that socialist project to the Labour Party's politics throughout the first six decades of the Party's history, and of the moderate nature of the project itself. Writing at a moment of revisionism inside the Labour Party – if Tony Blair's rise to power began the party's second period of revisionism, we do well to remember that Gaitskell's assumption of the party leadership a generation earlier began its first period – the Miliband text was sensitive to what was then (as now) being revised. As he put it,

> An older generation of Labour leaders had always set very definite limits, in their programmes and policies, to Labour's socialism. But they had also held out to their followers the promise that accommodation with capitalism was a temporary halt, however prolonged, on the journey to the Socialist Commonwealth…. In outward form at least, their quarrel with the Left … thus appeared as a quarrel about the pace of advance, not about the ultimate desirability of advance itself.[4]

Parliamentary Socialism treated Gaitskell's revisionism both as a move in the wrong direction and yet as an entirely intelligible response to the inadequacies of previous Labour programmes. For far from writing of Labour's performance in its first sixty years as some kind of 'glorious journey' or 'long march' in the then conventional manner, Ralph Miliband presented it as a series of missed opportunities for the development of more radical programmes after 1918, again after 1931, and even after 1945. Ultimately *Parliamentary Socialism* told the history of the Labour Party as a story of two linked failures: the failure by the Party leadership to transform capitalism into socialism as periodically they had promised to do, and the failure by successive generations of the Labour Left to prevent this leadership's retreat from radicalism. These were failures which *Parliamentary Socialism* explained by pointing to the subordination of the Labour Party leadership over the years to the norms and practices of the existing political and social order: to what *Parliamentary Socialism* briefly referred to as the 'integration' of the Labour Party into 'parliamentary politics' and 'the parallel … growing integration' of the trade unions 'into the framework of modern capitalism'[5]. They were failures explained by the commitment of the party leadership to what here was labeled 'the politics of labourism'.

This collection begins with three substantial extracts from the 1961 edition of *Parliamentary Socialism*. First, the much quoted introduction, then the last two chapters of the narrative, which carry the story of the party from the electoral landslide of 1945 to the internal party disputes triggered by the three successive electoral defeats of the 1950s. Together these extracts provide an accurate insight into the overall thesis of Ralph Miliband's first major statement on the Labour Party, and they constitute the first detailed Miliband account of postwar Labour's retreat from radicalism.

Notes

[1] J. Saville, 'Parliamentary Socialism Revisited', in L. Panitch (ed), *The Socialist Register 1995*, London, Merlin Press, 1995, p. 237

[2] R. Miliband, *Parliamentary Socialism*, London, Merlin Press, 1961, p. 13

[3] ibid, p.14

[4] ibid, p. 332

[5] ibid, p. 14

1. INTRODUCTION TO PARLIAMENTARY SOCIALISM (1961)

Ralph Miliband

Of political parties claiming socialism to be their aim, the Labour Party has always been one of the most dogmatic – not about socialism, but about the parliamentary system. Empirical and flexible about all else, its leaders have always made devotion to that system their fixed point of reference and the conditioning factor of their political behaviour. This is not simply to say that the Labour Party has never been a party of revolution: such parties have normally been quite willing to use the opportunities the parliamentary system offered as one means of furthering their aims. It is rather that the leaders of the Labour Party have always rejected any kind of political action (such as industrial action for political purposes) which fell, or which appeared to them to fall, outside the framework and conventions of the parliamentary system. The Labour Party has not only been a parliamentary party; it has been a party deeply imbued by parliamentarism. And in this respect, there is no distinction to be made between Labour's political and its industrial leaders. Both have been equally determined that the Labour Party should not stray from the narrow path of parliamentary politics. The main purpose of this book is to analyse the consequences which this approach to politics has had for the Labour Party and the Labour movement from the time the Labour Party came into existence.

Labour's devotion to the parliamentary system does not, of course, date from the formation of the Labour Party. The Labour Representation Committee in which the Labour Party originated was itself the product of a parliamentary view of politics which had been steadily gaining in strength over the previous decades. By the time the L.R.C. was formed in 1900, there were not many people in the Labour movement to contest the view that Labour's grievances and demands could only find solution through parliamentary action, and that the parliamentary method was ideally suited, not only to the achievement of immediate gains by the working classes, but also to the socialist reconstruction of society.

It was a view which, in the first years of the century, was coming to be more and more widely held by the leadership of all Western Labour movements. Parliamentarism in the British Labour movement was only unique in that it was so much more explicit, confident and uninhibited than its Continental counterparts, and that it met with so much less resistance.

However, the establishment of a distinctive Labour Party in the House of Commons marked more than the continuation of a well established parliamentary tradition in the Labour movement. For the creation of the Labour Party gave that tradition new forms and created problems which had not existed, or which had been far less acute, so long as the Labour movement did not have its own party in Parliament.

I must make it clear that I have not tried to write a comprehensive history of the Labour Party, much less of the Labour movement. I am particularly conscious of the fact that I have had to pay less attention than I should have liked to the multitude of activities at local level which, more than anything else, have made the Labour movement a living reality, indeed a way of life. I have proceeded historically, not only because my theme obviously requires detailed historical illustration, but also and more important because Labour's integration into parliamentary politics has been a process of growth, becoming more pronounced, assuming more specific forms, and producing new tensions as the Labour Party changed from a small pressure group in the House of Commons into a party of Official Opposition and of Government. Indeed, the recent controversies over the powers of the Labour Party's Annual Conference in relation to the Parliamentary Labour Party indicate that the process is even now by no means complete. Nor would the Labour Party's integration into parliamentary politics have taken place, or taken place in the same way, had it not had its parallel in the growing integration of the trade unions into the framework of modern capitalism. This integration has not been smooth, but it has been continuous; and the crucial influence it has had on the political ways of the Labour Party explains why its various aspects occupy so large a place in the following pages.

Throughout the history of the Labour Party, its leaders have had to contend with two different sets of critics and opponents on the Left. The first of these has been the Labour Left, whose purpose has always been two-fold: to push their leaders into accepting more radical policies and programmes, and to press upon them more militant attitudes in response to challenges from Labour's opponents. The Labour Left's own acceptance of the categories of the parliamentary system has been distinguished from that of the leadership by a continuous search for means of escape from its inhibitions and constrictions. What the Labour leaders have accepted eagerly, the Labour Left has accepted with a certain degree of unease and at times with acute misgivings.

This Labour Left has assumed a variety of political forms in different periods. From 1900 to 1932, its main political expression was the Independent Labour Party. When the I.L.P. ceased, in that year, to be a constituent body of the Labour Party, it was replaced, until 1937, by the Socialist League. In the fifties, it found expression, firstly in the Bevanite movement and then in such organizations as Victory for Socialism. But the Labour Left has always encompassed many more people than have actually joined any of its organizations. One of its main sources of strength, for instance, has always been in the trade unions, whose militant members have generally steered clear of the political organizations of the Labour Left. This left-wing activist element in the Labour Party and the trade unions

has always been in a minority. It has seldom been able to pose an effective challenge to the Labour leaders and it has never come near to capturing the Labour
movement's commanding heights. Even so, organized or unorganized, it has
been a force with which the Labour leaders have always had to reckon, and to
which they have often been forced to make concessions; in various ways, the Left
within the Labour Party has at least reduced the leaders' freedom of action.

The second set of opponents of the Labour leadership has been made up of
what might be called the extra-parliamentary Left, for whom parliamentary
politics has always been of secondary importance, if that. This extra-parliamentary Left too has been a permanent part of Labour's political landscape, though
outside the Labour Party. Until the foundation of the Communist Party after
the First World War, it was represented by a number of political groupings and
organizations, such as the Social Democratic Federation and the British Socialist
Party. After 1920, it came to be concentrated mainly in the Communist Party,
and its impact upon the Labour movement, notably in the trade unions, cannot
be discounted, despite the smallness of its numbers.

But the Labour movement is not a self-contained entity. It responds to, and
is deeply influenced by, external factors, historical, economic, social and political. It is, for instance, hardly necessary to stress how much, in their eagerness
to 'work' the British political system, the Labour leaders have been affected
by the strategy of the traditional parties. Thus, no analysis of Labour's role in
British politics would make much sense which did not include at least some
consideration of the politics of Liberalism before the First World War, and of
Conservatism after it. I hope that the analysis which will be found here of this
interplay of contending forces may throw some useful light on the true nature of
British politics in this century, as well as on the politics of Labour.

The assumption is often made in discussions of the present crisis in the Labour
Party that the latter's difficulties are of recent origin. This is not so. Like Hobbes
and fear, crisis and the Labour Party have always been twin – Siamese twins.
And explanations which begin with recent difficulties either mistake the symp-
toms of the crisis, or its aggravation, for the crisis itself. Much, for instance, has
been made in recent years of the Labour Party's supposed inability to 'adjust' to
the circumstances and demands of the 'affluent society'. This, it has been said,
explains the Labour Party's loss of appeal, as expressed in successive electoral
defeats. But such an explanation would surely carry greater weight if the Labour
Party had fared any better in the years of the not so affluent society, say in 1935,
when the Conservative Party, having carried the main responsibility for the conduct of affairs during four years of mass unemployment, was returned to office
with a parliamentary majority of well over two hundred. And what, to take another instance, is being said about the Labour Party's failure to act as an effective
opposition in the fifties, or of its ambiguity of purpose in the same period, has

also been said, with equal emphasis (and equal justification), ever since it came into being. In fact, what is so remarkable about the Labour Party is the similarity of the problems which have beset it throughout its history.

In suggesting the permanence and similarity of crisis, I do not wish to minimize its present gravity. Quite obviously, the Labour Party's difficulties in the last few years have been more acute than at any previous time, and it is at least unlikely that they will be resolved without causing profound changes in the Labour Party's whole character. But I do suggest that the present difficulties can only be properly understood by seeing them in the perspective of what has gone before. It is such a perspective that I have sought to provide.

2. THE CLIMAX OF LABOURISM (1961)

Ralph Miliband

During the Coalition the Labour members had learnt a great deal from the Conservatives in how to govern.
Herbert Morrison to King George VI, November 1945.

1. THE IMPACT OF WAR

July 1945, when the first majority Labour Government came to office, is generally regarded as marking the beginning of a new era in British history. In fact, the new era did not begin in 1945, but in 1940, and in the years of war. These years are not the prologue to the history of the Labour Government. They are an essential part of it. Without them, neither July 1945 nor what followed from it can be properly understood. For it was the experience of war which caused the emergence in Britain of a new popular radicalism, more widespread than at any time in the previous hundred years. It was of that popular radicalism that the Labour Party was, in 1945, the electoral beneficiary. And it was also the war which was responsible for the setting in place of an elaborate system of State intervention and control, which was of immeasurable help to the Labour Government in its first years of office after 1945.

In the first phase of the War, the new popular radicalism was submerged in the will to national survival, and in an intense national pride in Britain's lone struggle against the Axis Powers. But once survival seemed assured, the men who had imperilled that survival were remembered, as well as the class to which they belonged, and the Party whose label they wore. True, Churchill himself belonged to the same class and the same party, and his own prestige at the end of the War was no doubt worth many votes to the Conservative Party, but not enough to prevent the popular repudiation of Tory rule. The war leader was easily distinguished from the Conservative politician.

The rhetoric of war was itself an important element in the fashioning of popular radicalism. That the conflict was not only against Germany, or Italy or Japan, but against Fascism, gave it powerful ideological overtones, with an emphasis on democratic values and a celebration of the 'common man' which entailed an implicit (and often explicit) condemnation of the manner in which Tory Governments had treated him, and his family, in the inter-war years. With the entry of Russia in the war, and with the manner of her resistance to the German onslaught, these ideological overtones acquired an even sharper edge: to admiration for Russia, there was coupled an entirely new interest in the social and economic system under which the Russian war effort was organized. And it was not forgotten that pre-war Conservatism had been as eager to appease the Fascist aggressor as it had been loath to seek co-operation and alliance with Russia.

Nor was America's entry into the war a counter-balancing factor. On the contrary, America too helped to feed the growth of popular radicalism. For the American message during the war was the message of freedom rather than of free enterprise, of democracy and of opportunity, of the New Deal and of social equality: to millions of people, the embodiment of the promise which victory held was not Winston Churchill, or Clement Attlee, or Joseph Stalin, but Franklin Roosevelt.

As important was the fact that the war constituted an enormous exercise not only in military but also in social and economic planning and that it was a very successful exercise. Because of the demands of war, Britain's rulers were forced to give a convincing demonstration that economic planning and State intervention on a massive and, for Britain, quite unprecedented scale, not only worked but were the indispensable conditions of victory. Because of State intervention and control, millions of people found themselves better fed in wartime than they had been in peace time; and. through the agency of the State, they found their needs the object of more solicitude than any Government had ever before thought appropriate. Well before the war had come to an end, they had been officiallyassured that the State, which had been deemed capable of so little in the inter-war years, would, when peace came, guarantee them employment, welfare, security and greater opportunities for education. Nor were the millions of men and women who were winning the war disposed to regard these promises with the gratitude of the humble poor. With a new consciousness of their collective strength, and with a new confidence in their own worth, they regarded a new deal as a right which dare not be denied them.

In the political articulation of the experience of war, left-wing activists played a considerable part. In barracks and mess decks, in factories and air-raid shelters, in organized and even more in unorganized discussions and debates, the anti-Fascists of Popular Front days now found an audience receptive as never before to the message of socialist change.

Despite the Party Truce, there were already clear political signs of this groundswell in the later stages of the war. Indeed the continuation of the Party Truce itself was strongly disliked by the constituency activists; and the policy of giving Labour support to Government candidates of other parties was only endorsed at the 1942 Labour Party Annual Conference by 1,275,000 votes to 1,209,000. From early 1943 onwards, a new Party of the Left, Commonwealth, founded by a convert from the Liberal Party, Sir Richard Acland, had begun to contest by-elections in Conservative seats, and actually won two of them. As was later noted, 'the long series of Government rebuffs in the latter part of the war was a portent to which observers were curiously blind. Commonwealth candidates, Radical Independents, Scottish Nationalists, Independent Labour Party men, all sorts of political enthusiasts, had only to present themselves and they would either poll extremely well, or even win the seat.[1]

The Communist Party was prevented from sharing in these successes by its own ardent support for the Coalition after Russia's entry into the war. But neither this, nor its appeals for higher productivity and no strikes, prevented it from active political propaganda, or from campaigning for members – with conspicuous success. From around 12,000 in June 1941, membership leapt up to nearly 23,000 at the end of that year, and to nearly 60,000 by the end of 1942. This was a peak. But the Party's membership at the end of the war still stood at some 45,000, while its influence in the trade union movement was now greater than at any time since the Party was founded.

All this is not to suggest that the popular radicalism of war-time Britain was, for the most part, a formed socialist ideology, let alone a revolutionary one. But, in its mixture of bitter memories and positive hopes, in its antagonism to a mean past, in its recoil from Conservative rule, in its impatience of a traditional class structure, in its hostility to the claims of property and privilege, in its determination not to be robbed again of the fruits of victory, in its expectations of social justice, it was a radicalism eager for major, even fundamental, changes in British society after the war.

The Labour leaders also thought and spoke of the new social order that must follow the ordeals of war. But the impact of war upon them was very different from the impact it had on their supporters. Most of the major figures of the post-war Labour Government (Aneurin Bevan was the only important exception) held high office in the Churchill Coalition. For five years, they were deeply immersed in the business of government, and they acquired in those years an even more 'responsible' view of affairs than they had had in opposition. And they also forged in those years close and personal links with Conservative colleagues, with high civil servants and high ranking officers, collaboration with whom was also much more conducive to caution than to radicalism. 'I have,' Attlee later recalled, 'very pleasant memories of working with my colleagues in the Government. It was very seldom that any Party issue arose to divide us, until the last stage, when I think they were designedly fomented by certain persons. Usually applying our minds to the actual problems which faced us, we came to an agreement as to what was the best course.' And, he adds, in a significant phrase, 'quite naturally, in war, when the public good must take precedence over private interests, the solutions had a strong socialist flavour'.[2]

Differences of course remained, but there was also much common ground between Labour Ministers and their Conservative colleagues on the shape of the post-war settlement, the more so since the latter agreed, at least in principle, that post-war reconstruction would have to be geared to a 'high level of employment', and to extended provision for welfare and social security. Even on the issue of controls over the economy, most Conservative leaders agreed, before the end of the war, that many controls would have to be retained for some time after it. The difference was that Conservatives naturally laid the main emphasis upon a speedy restoration of a system of 'private enterprise', in which State intervention, though not wholly discarded, would play a marginal and mainly indirect role, while the Labour leaders wanted much more than this. The war had greatly reinforced their already strong interventionist bias and, haunted by the memory of what had happened at the end of the First World War, they were determined to see maintained in peace time the web of controls over the economy which they deemed essential to post-war reconstruction and full employment.

On the other hand, the now prevalent notion that they thought at the end of the war, of a fundamental transformation of the social order on the basis of common ownership is quite inaccurate, as is shown in the debates on a future Labour Government's programme in 1944.

By the time the Annual Conference of the Labour Party met in December 1944, the war with Germany was evidently drawing to a close, and a General Election, if not imminent, was at least in sight. In the previous two years, the Executive's Reconstruction Committee had issued a number of Reports, and those dealing with coal, transport, gas and electricity had recommended nationalization. However, the main economic resolution which the Executive presented to the Conference (under the rubric *Economic Controls, Public Ownership and Full Employment*) made no mention whatever of public ownership. It said that 'Full Employment and a high standard of living for those who work by hand and brain can only be secured within a planned economy, through the maintenance and adaptation of appropriate economic controls after the war, *and above all by the transfer to the State of power to direct the policy* of our main industries, services and financial institutions'.[3] In particular, the resolution said, a Labour Government, in order to sustain a high and steadily rising level of purchasing power would find it necessary 'to *control* the Bank of England, and the lending policy of the Joint Stock Banks, and to set up a National Investment Board'; secondly, it would be 'essential for the State to control the location of Industry' in order to prevent the re-emergence of local unemployment and depressed areas; and, thirdly, it would also be necessary, in order to encourage foreign trade and establish a more prosperous and secure economic system throughout the world, to 'enter into International Agreements with the Dominions, Russia, the United States and other friendly nations'.[4]

It was Emmanuel Shinwell who introduced this resolution on behalf of the Executive. 'The Socialist policy of the Labour Party,' he claimed, 'remains unchanged ... we stand, as always, for the abolition of a vicious competitive system and for the establishment of the highest possible standard of living based on collective organization and the ownership of indispensable national industries and services.' But 'naturally', he added, anticipating later re-thinkers, 'we have to bring our policy up to date and adapt ourselves to an ever-changing situation; that is a scientific procedure and in the nature of the case inevitable'. And in any case, he told the delegates, the resolution did not indicate a long term policy; 'it is a short term policy designed, and rightly designed, for those years in which a Labour Government will have assumed full power in this country'. However, he promised the delegates that 'if (sic) a monopolistic undertaking has reached that economic position when the commodity it produces or over which it has power is indispensable to the life of the community, that monopolistic undertaking must be taken over by the State in the interests of the community' [5]

On the basis of these remarkable formulations and, more important, of the Executive's resolution, it is evident that, after five years of war and twenty-six years after the Labour Party's adoption of its common ownership clause, not to speak of its inter-war programmes and resolutions, most members of the Executive would have been content to present to the electorate a programme altogether free from any commitment to the nationalization of anything at all, save for the half-nationalization of the Bank of England.[6] Not, as Shinwell had explained, that they were opposed to some few measures of nationalization; they merely did not think nationalization essential to the immediate purpose at hand, namely a post-war 'reconstruction' which did not entail major structural transformations in the economy. Nor in any case were they in the least convinced that the electorate was now ready for such a transformation.

The activists, both in the constituencies and in the trade unions, had very different ideas: Resolution after resolution on the agenda of the Conference demanded an extensive programme of common ownership. One of these came from the Transport and General Workers' Union and it asked that 'all vital services, Land, Banking, Coal and Power, Steel, Chemicals, and Transport (including Road, Rail, Shipping and Civil Aviation) shall be brought under a system of Public Ownership and Control'[7].

A composite resolution, moved by Ian Mikardo, asked the Executive to include in its programme 'the transfer to public ownership of the land, large-scale building, heavy industry, and all forms of banking, transport and fuel and power'; and to say that 'appropriate legislation' would be passed to ensure that publicly owned enterprises would be 'democratically controlled and operated in the national interest with representation of the workers engaged therein and of consumers'.[8]

For the Executive, Philip Noel-Baker asked that the resolution should not be pressed to a vote. 'Of course,' he said, 'we are in general agreement with it' but, he added, in a phrase which expressed well the leadership's hesitations, 'we think that the resolution should be neither accepted nor rejected today.' What they would undertake to do was to examine the various points of the resolution 'with great care'! But the resolution was pressed, and carried without a card vote, and some, but only some, of its provisions were embodied in *Let Us Face the Future*, the Programme on which the Labour Party went to the country in 1945.

Let Us Face the Future was published in April 1945, by which time it was certain that the days of the war-time coalition were numbered. Though Labour's spectacular electoral victory some months later, and developments since, have invested it with a quasi-revolutionary aura, it was, in its concrete proposals, a mild and circumspect document, which marked no advance on Labour's *Immediate Programme* of 1937. The Labour Party, it said once again, 'is a Socialist Party, and proud of it. Its ultimate purpose at home is the establishment of the Socialist Commonwealth of Great Britain – free, democratic, efficient, progressive, public-spirited, its material resources organized in the service of the British people'. But, it also warned, 'Socialism cannot come overnight, as the product of a week-end revolution. The members of the Labour Party, like the British people, are practical minded men and women'.

In regard to industry a careful distinction was made between 'basic industries ripe and over-ripe for public ownership and management in the direct service of the nation', and 'big industries not yet ripe for public ownership'; these, however, would be required 'by constructive supervision' to further the nation's needs. And there were, thirdly, 'many smaller businesses rendering good service which could be left to get on with their useful work'.

What this meant of course was that the largest part by far of British industry and finances would in fact remain in private hands, indefinitely, though subject, or so at least the intention was, to State direction and control. Furthermore, so 'ripe and over-ripe' for public ownership were the industries and services it was proposed to nationalize that this had in fact already been recommended, as Professor Brady has noted, 'by Conservative dominated fact-finding and special investigating committees'[9]. Save for iron and steel, of which more later, they had long ceased to occupy a strategic place in the system of capitalist power, and this, as later debates showed, was quite clear to Conservatives, more so than it was to most Labour supporters. This did not make their nationalization less necessary or desirable; it only made it a rather less revolutionary enterprise than was later claimed. The document itself made no such claim. It noted that, as a result of nationalization, other industries would benefit, that 'fair compensation' would be paid, and its emphasis was overwhelmingly on efficiency rather than power. Indeed, it is remarkable, in retrospect, how defensive some of the most prominent Labour leaders were even about these minimal proposals. Thus, Herbert Morrison, introducing the debate on *Let Us Face the Future* at the 1945 Conference, insisted that the case for nationalization must be argued out 'industry by industry on the merits of each case . . . in our electoral arguments it is no good saying that we are going to socialize electricity, fuel and power because it is in accordance with Labour Party principles so to do . . . you must spend substantial time in arguing the case for the socialization of these industries on the merits of their specific cases. That is how the British mind works. It does not work in a vacuum or in abstract theories.'[10]

The implication was that the case for nationalization must not be argued as part of a general socialist case against capitalist enterprise but in terms of a specific remedy for particular situations and applicable in purely functional and technical terms to particular industries and services. It is, however, doubtful whether Morrison's advice was much heeded by Labour candidates and speakers in the election of 1945.

Directly related to Morrison's view of nationalization was the Executive's refusal to commit itself to any kind of experiment in industrial democracy. At the 1944 Conference, Philip Noel-Baker had assured the delegates that 'we are all for the participation of workers in control and that discussions were proceeding with the Trade Unions as to the methods for workers' participation in control and management. *Let Us Face the Future* merely said that the workers should have 'proper status and conditions' in the nationalized industries. At the 1945 Conference, one composite resolution (later withdrawn) demanded a far more extensive programme of nationalization and also asked the Party to pledge itself 'to secure the democratic control and operation of these (nationalized) institutions by the workers and technicians'. This latter demand, Morrison said, did not 'demonstrate good socialization in its method of administration and management' For his part, Shinwell, replying to the debate, agreed that 'of course workers have a right to participate in industry', and so had technicians; 'but as to the form of participation, that is a matter that has to be worked out'. Much the same had repeatedly been said since 1918.

The nationalization proposals of *Let Us Face the Future* represented the least the Executive could present to the 1945 Conference without causing acute dissension in the Party. The Left was given a great deal less than it wanted (and less indeed than had been agreed by the 1944 Conference). But the Left, though more powerful at the end of the War than for many a year, was not an organized and coherent pressure group. Nor, given what they had been able to obtain, were left wing delegates disposed, on the eve of an election to challenge the leadership. The latter's proposals, on nationalization, on economic policy, and on social reforms were all unanimously endorsed. Outwardly, *Let Us Face the Future* united the Party as no document had ever done. In reality, the divisions within the Party were as profound as they had ever been, in some ways more; but they were, in 1945, sufficiently blurred to suggest a common purpose.

This was even more true in relation to foreign affairs, about which *Let Us Face the Future* said little, and said it in unexceptionable generalities. The main point it made was that it would be necessary, when peace came, to consolidate the war-time association between the British Commonwealth, the U.S.A. and the U.S.S.R.; and the British Labour movement, it claimed, came to the task of international organization 'with one great asset: it has a common bond with the working peoples of all countries, who have achieved a new dignity and influence through their long struggles against Nazi tyranny'.

At the 1945 Conference, both Attlee and Bevin, speaking for the Executive, only referred in very vague terms to the strains and stresses which the shape of the post-war settlement had already produced between Russia and her Anglo-American partners, and they both managed to convey the impression that Britain under a Labour Government would act as a bridge between the United States and the U.S.S.R. 'We have,' said Attlee, 'to have our own line and our own judgment as, Socialists.'

The delegates were even less prepared to press their leaders on foreign affairs than on home policy. But Denis Healey was certainly speaking for many of them when he insisted that 'the Labour Party should have a clear foreign policy of its own, which is completely distinct from that of the Tory Party'. The Socialist revolution, he said, had already begun in Europe and was already established in many countries in Eastern and Southern Europe; 'the crucial principle of our foreign policy,' he proposed, 'should be to protect, assist, encourage and aid in every way that Socialist revolution wherever it appears …. The upper classes in every country are selfish, depraved, dissolute and decadent. These upper classes look to the British Army and the British people to protect them against the just wrath of the people who have been fighting underground against them for the past four years. We must see that that does not happen.'

When he came to reply to the discussion, Ernest Bevin, in a long, rambling speech, made it obvious that, whatever other principles might inspire a Labour Government's foreign policy, help to socialist revolutions in Europe was not one of them. By 1945, both he and Attlee, as members of the Cabinet, had shared responsibility for policy decisions which, as for example in the case of Greece, were designed to achieve the precise opposite. As to relations with Russia, Bevin said that it would be the duty of the Labour Party, if returned to power, to remove the mutual fears and suspicions that existed between the Soviet Union and the 'Western Powers'. 'We have no bad past to live down,' he claimed, 'we never sent the Director of the Bank of England to deal with the enemies of Soviet Russia. We opposed it. We fought all the machinations. If we had been in power in 1939 we would have sent the Foreign Secretary to Moscow, and not just an official.'

However, fears that a Labour Government would be committed to foreign policies neither of its own making nor of its own inspiration remained, and were enhanced by Churchill's invitation to Attlee to accompany him to the Potsdam Conference due to begin the day after the Election. On the 14th of June, Churchill told the House of Commons that in the last few years, he and Attlee had 'always thought alike on the foreign situation', and that Attlee's attendance would show that '… although Governments may change and parties may quarrel, yet on some of the main essentials of foreign affairs we stand together'.

It was precisely this suggestion of bi-partnership that Laski, the Chairman of the Party, was concerned to dispel in a statement he issued on the 15th of June. Neither Attlee nor Labour, the statement said, should accept responsibility for agreements concluded by Churchill and which had not been debated either in the Party Executive or at meetings of the Parliamentary Labour Party. 'Labour,' it asserted, 'has a foreign policy which in many respects will not be continuous with that of a Tory-dominated Coalition. It has in fact a far sounder Foreign Policy.'[11]

Conservative leaders expressed deep alarm at this threat of Labour independence in foreign affairs. 'We believed', one leading Conservative spokesman said in a broadcast, 'that there was a measure of agreement between the Socialist Party and the National Government in carrying forward to a conclusion the policy of the great Churchill coalition ... We are now advised in plain terms that a continuing foreign policy is something we can no longer take for granted.' They need not have feared. As James Byrnes, then the American Secretary of State, later noted, 'Britain's stand on the issues before the (Potsdam) Conference was not altered in the slightest, so far as we could discern, by the replacement of Mr Churchill and Mr Eden by Mr Attlee and Mr Bevin. This continuity of Britain's foreign policy impressed me.' Indeed, Bevin's manner towards the Russians was 'so aggressive' that 'both the President and I wondered how we would get along with this new Foreign Secretary'[12].

This, however, was for later. Before the Election, the Conservatives not only professed alarm at the possibility that Labour might pursue a distinctive foreign policy; they expressed equal alarm, from Churchill downwards – at the possibility which Laski's statement was alleged to imply, that the election of a Labour Government would mean rule by a Party caucus, and the Government's subjection to its commands. Immediately upon the publication of the statement, Churchill wrote to Attlee to ask whether he proposed 'merely to come (to Potsdam) as a mute observer', which would, he suggested, 'be derogatory to your position as leader of your party'. In reply, Attlee wrote that 'there never was any suggestion that I should go as a mere observer', and added that he did not anticipate 'that we shall differ on the main lines of policy, which we have discussed together so often'. At the end of the campaign, Churchill again wrote to Attlee to say that 'the constitution (of the Labour Party) would apparently enable the Executive Committee to call upon a Labour Prime Minister to appear before them and criticize his conduct of the peace negotiations'. This, said Churchill, must entail the disclosure of confidential information and he asked for a statement 'signed jointly by yourself and the Chairman of the Executive Committee clarifying the position.' Attlee replied that the Executive had 'a right to be consulted' but denied that it had 'power to challenge (the actions) and conduct of a Labour Prime Minister.'

These last exchanges were only the dim echoes of a Conservative scare campaign with Laski cast as the main villain, and designed to convince the voters that, in the event of a Labour victory, Attlee, as some Conservative candidates put it, would be no more than 'a ventriloquist's dummy sitting on Laski's knee'. In the event, the image was found to have lacked force. As a bogey, 'Gauleiter Laski, about to play Lenin to Attlee's Kerensky, proved a poor successor to Zinoviev and Post Office Savings. Times had changed. Potential Labour voters refused to be scared off by Conservative assertions the Labour had irresistible propensities to totalitarianism, and that Labour victory would result in the creation of a 'Police State'. These charges, dismissed by Labour as typical Conservative stunts, only strengthened the view, fatal to Conservative electoral fortunes, that the Tories had learnt nothing and forgotten nothing. So did the latter's deliberate enlargement of the progammatic differences between the two parties.

At the end of the 1945 Labour Party Annual Conference, Laski had described the coming General Election as a 'straight fight ... a fight between private enterprise now expressed as monopoly capitalism, and socialism that realizes that the new age is born and that only through the establishment of a Socialist Commonweal can we realize the purposes for which we have been fighting the war'. At the time this had been said, neither Labour's programme nor certainly the pronouncements of most Labour leaders, remote suggested that this was the issue of the election. Nor, in reality, did it ever become the issue of the election. But it was made to appear the issue, not by the Labour leaders, but by the Tories. It was they who, from the start of the campaign, insisted that the electorate was confronted with a choice between 'free enterprise' and socialism, and it was also they who sought to create an image of the Labour leaders as red-blooded socialists, determined upon the strangulation of British capitalism, and much else besides. In the mood of that summer, the Tories could not have adopted a strategy more likely to enhance Labour's electoral chances.

After so many years of disappointments and defeats, a Labour victory, resulting in the first majority Labour Government, held an element of real drama. The victory was made the more dramatic by coming at the end of the war, and after a campaign in which socialism had been proclaimed to be the issue. But what made it most dramatic of all was the size of Labour's parliamentary majority. When the votes had been counted, it was found that 393 Labour candidates had been returned, and that Labour would have a majority of 146 over all other parties. The Conservatives had lost 172 seats and, with their allies, would number 213 in the new House of Commons. It may be incongruous that Sir Hartley Shawcross should have been the one to say 'We are the masters now.' But this was the feeling of countless men and women in the Labour movement who found in Labour's victory the vindication of their faith and the fulfillment of their hopes, and who believed that now at last was to begin the transformation of Britain into a socialist commonwealth. Nor was there now anyone to prevent the Parliamentary Labour Party from singing the Red Flag when the new House of Commons assembled.

In terms of votes cast, as opponents were quick to point out, the majority was less spectacular. Nearly 12,000,000 people (48.3 per cent of the votes cast) had voted for the Labour Party; the Conservatives and their allies had polled less than 10,000,000 votes (39.8 per cent) and the Liberals, who won twelve seats, polled 2,239,668 votes. The Communist Party, which put forward twenty-one candidates, increased its parliamentary representation from one to two, and polled 102,760 votes. The Commonwealth Party had twenty-three candidates, one of whom was elected, and it polled 110,634 votes. The I.L.P., with five candidates (three elected), polled 46,679. Taking the poll as a whole (76 per cent of the electorate, on an antiquated register) there was, as Cole notes, 'very little in it' as between Right and Left. Nevertheless, no one denied that Labour had scored a remarkable victory.

2. LABOUR'S SOCIALISM

In the first flush of victory, the hesitations and inhibitions of Labour's leadership in the year preceding the Election were easily overlooked. And indeed, the leaders themselves, as a result of a victory so great and so unexpected, found a measure of confidence they had previously lacked. They too now spoke of the social revolution they were about to initiate.

The mood was sufficiently strong to carry the Government forward to the achievement, in its first three years of office, of much that had been promised at the Election. By 1948, it had ensured an orderly transition from war-time mobilization to peacetime reconstruction. It had placed on the Statute Book the nationalization proposals of *Let Us Face the Future* – except for the nationalization of iron and steel. And it had brought into being a National Health Service and a new comprehensive system of social insurance. In housing, in education, in welfare, it could well boast to have done more than any Government had done before – and to have done it in the midst of acute economic difficulties. In a different context, it could also point to its ready recognition of the fact that there was no alternative to India's political independence, with which went the political independence of Burma and Ceylon.

These achievements were real, and of permanent importance, but even in those first years of social and economic reform, the Government's impact upon post-war Britain was profoundly ambiguous.

Of course, the very fact that a Labour Government had come to power, with an assured majority, was sufficient to give bourgeois England, and all those who identified themselves with bourgeois England without being part of it, a genuine sense of outrage at what was taken to be the country's capture from its traditional rulers, and at the proletarian threat which Labour's assumption of office was deemed to entail. Mr Evelyn Waugh may have been straining for effect when he wrote in 1959 that he had 'bitter memories of the Attlee-Cripps regime when the kingdom seemed to be under enemy occupation'.[13] But there was a vast and socially heterogeneous host which did then feel that the Government, if not the kingdom, was in enemy hands, and whose hostility fed as much on post-war scarcities and restrictions, for which the Government was held to be responsible, as on the welfare and nationalization measures of those years.

Yet, with the hostility went the realization that things could have been much worse. As *The Economist* wrote in November 1945, after the Government had announced its nationalization proposals 'an avowedly Socialist Government, with a clear Parliamentary majority; might well have been expected to go several steps further ... If there is to be a Labour Government, the programme now stated is the least it could do without violating its election pledges'.[14] The sentiments were apposite in regard to much more than nationalization. For if the social advances of the post-war years were substantial in comparison with the pace of earlier years, they were also modest by any more humane criterion. And if the Government further enhanced the sense of confidence and strength of the working classes, it also made it its business to moderate and discipline both their claims and their expectations.

As far as the trade unions were concerned, the coming to office of a Labour Government did not entail any substantial departure from a pattern of consultation on economic and social matters which the war itself had done much to enhance. The unions could of course rely on a sympathetic hearing from a Government, more than one third of whose members were trade union sponsored MPs; and one of the Government's first acts was to repeal the Trades Disputes and Trade Union Act of 1927. But in return, the Government expected, and received, from the trade unions a measure of co-operation in the maintenance of industrial discipline which was of inestimable benefit to it. And when industrial discipline did break down, the Government's interventions, as V. L. Allen notes, 'were not markedly dissimilar from interventions before 1926. Troops who moved food supplies were employed in the interests of the community, but in fact they were blacklegs who reduced the effectiveness of the strikes.... Whatever the motives of the Government, troops invariably appeared as strike-breakers and as protectors of the interests of employers'.[15]

In regard to nationalization, there was no ambiguity at all. From the beginning, the nationalization proposals of the Government were designed to achieve the sole purpose of improving the efficiency of a capitalist economy, not as marking the beginning of its wholesale transformation, and this was an aim to which many Tories, whatever they might say in the House of Commons, were easily reconciled, and which some even approved – with the exception of iron and steel.

By 1945, what really mattered about the nationalization measures of the Government was compensation and control. As to the first, the interests affected found the Government forthcoming and, as in the case of coal, for instance, did considerably better out of nationalization than they could conceivably have done had the industry remained in private ownership. In fact, one consequence of the Government's compensation policies was to release vast financial resources for profitable investment in the 'private sector'; another was to saddle the nationalized industries with a burden of debt which materially contributed to difficulties that were later ascribed to the immanent character of public ownership.

As for the effective control of the nationalized industries, the Conservatives found the Government much more than half way in their own camp. Though ultimate control was vested in the Minister and provision made for a measure of parliamentary accountability more formal than real, the Government's conception of public ownership ensured the predominance on the boards of the nationalized corporations of men who had been, or who still were, closely associated with private finance and industry, and who could hardly be expected to regard the nationalized industries as designed to achieve any purpose other than the more efficient servicing of the 'private sector'.

Most people in the Labour movement believed that the nationalized industries should be examples of a new socialist spirit in industry, islands of socialist virtue in a sea of capitalist greed. This would in any case have been difficult enough to achieve in a predominantly capitalist economy. But the Government's conception of the nature of public ownership did not even induce it to try. In fact, had the Government been determined that nationalization should make little appeal to the voters, it could not easily have managed the business better.

The T.U.C.'s Interim Report on Post-War Reconstruction had stated as 'fundamental to any plan for the organization of a public service that the workpeople have the right to a voice in the determination of its policy'.[16] But when it came to concrete applications, both the Government and most trade union leaders gave no sign that they wished to see brought about major changes in the pattern of 'industrial relations' in the nationalized industries. There was at hand a system of joint consultation, which had been extensively used during the war. The Government was entirely willing to extend this further and to make joint consultation compulsory in the public sector. But joint consultation was always confined to a narrow range of subjects.

In a famous speech in October 1946, Sir Stafford Cripps declared that 'there is not yet a very large number of workers in Britain capable of taking over large enterprises ... until there has been more experience by the workers of the managerial side of industry, I think it would be almost impossible to have worker-controlled industry in Britain, *even if it were on the whole desirable.*'[17] The doubt was certainly not unique to Cripps. But even those Ministers who expressed their fervent belief in industrial democracy, agreed that the difficulties were overwhelming and that much time would have to pass before anything could be done to overcome them. What is more notable is how little the Government tried to do to overcome them. It did introduce limited training and promotion schemes in the nationalized industries; like the trade union leaders, it wanted to encourage promising youngsters from the working classes to 'rise to the top', in industry as in other walks of life. But their rise to the top could hardly be said to bring any nearer that 'best obtainable system of popular administration and control of each industry and service' which the Constitution of the Labour Party had enshrined as one of the Party's major aims.

The prime concern of the Labour leaders, it has been noted earlier, was not to nationalize British industry, but to control it and to bend it to the Government's purposes. As has also been noted, the Government, when it came to office, found at hand a ready-made system of war-time controls, operated in close consultation with the industrial interests concerned – indeed, largely operated by representatives of these interests. These arrangements had been strongly criticized in the Labour movement during the war. The Government, however, relied at least as much as its predecessors upon the advice of private industry and finance and gave their representatives a major share in the operation of controls: if there was no workers' participation in those years, there was at least employers' participation.

This partnership between Government and private enterprise would no doubt have been much less easy had the Government sought to apply controls in a manner and for purposes irreconcilable with the purposes and profits of business. But the Government had no such wish, and it thus enjoyed the co-operation of private industry. Or, more accurately, private industry enjoyed the cooperation of the Government. And where co-operation did not suit industry, exhortations, appeals, inducements, and occasional muttered threats fell on very deaf ears.

There was of course Labour's much reiterated belief in planning. But the Government, when it finally came, early in 1947, to announce what it meant to do about it, drew a sharp distinction between 'totalitarian' and 'democratic' planning. The former, the *Economic Survey for 1947* said, 'subordinates all individual desires and preferences to the demands of the State'; a democratic government, on the other hand, must plan 'in a manner which preserves the maximum possible freedom of choice to the individual citizen'. This entailed much more freedom of choice than planning, particularly freedom of choice for private enterprise. 'Had shortages not existed,' Mr Rogow notes, 'planning under the Labour Government would have been largely confined to the compilation of economic information and of forecasts by the expert agencies in the Economic Section, the Central Statistical Office, and the Economic Planning, Staff – with the use of a small number of key controls to guide resources into the right places. In other words, the decisions as to the quantity and kind of industrial output required would have been left substantially to market forces.

And indeed, he adds, 'it was towards this goal of essentially liberal planning that the Labour Government was moving throughout its period of office and with considerable speed between 1948 and 1950.'[18]

Government intervention in economic affairs, though in some aspects irksome to private industry and finance, presented no serious challenge to the power of the men who continued to control the country's economic resources, the more so since they themselves played so large a role, directly or indirectly, in determining the nature and applications of Government intervention. This situation had its parallel in the field of politics and administration generally. If Labour's rule did not signify any notable diminution in private economic power and influence, neither did it represent nearly so striking a diminution in the power and influence of political Conservatism as the existence of a Labour Government was widely believed to entail. For the Conservatives, though expelled from the centre of the political stage, namely the Government, yet remained an important part of the play – and could always rely on the support of a noisy claque, led by a Conservative press eager to exploit every opportunity of damaging the Government.

There was, to begin with, the House of Commons itself. The Government was entirely safe from defeat, but it was also deeply concerned to placate the Opposition. Nor did the Conservatives in Parliament behave like a defeated party, expecting little and therefore receiving little. They could not hope to prevent the Government from enacting its main proposals. But they could hope, by unremitting pressure, to limit the import of those proposals. Seldom if ever has the House of Commons been so effectively used as in those years of Conservative opposition to denounce the Government and to erode its morale. 'I have not forgotten,' one of the least timid of junior Labour Ministers has recalled, 'the tension of rising to answer questions or conduct a debate under the cold, implacable eyes of that row of well-tailored tycoons, who hated the Labour Government with a passion and fear which made them dedicated men in their determination to get it out of office and to limit the damage it could do to the world which they saw as theirs by right.'[19]

There was also the House of Lords. *Let Us Face the Future* had done no more, despite earlier pledges of reform and even abolition, than 'give clear notice that we will not tolerate obstruction of the people's will by the House of Lords', and, at the 1945 Labour Party Conference, Herbert Morrison had also given 'their lordships notice that if we have any serious nonsense from them, they will have some serious nonsense from us – and we mean that'. That the House of Lords avoided any 'serious nonsense' in the first years of the Government's life, when the operation of the Parliament Act would in any case have overcome its opposition, is more often remembered than the steady pressure it exercised upon the Government. 'Though it almost never coerced the Government,' Dr P. M. Bromhead writes, 'it persistently obliged the Government to justify its decisions, and it sometimes persuaded the Government to be accommodating on matters with regard to which it had been adamant in the Commons.'[20] And when it came to the nationalization of iron and steel, by which time the provisions of the Parliament Act of 1911 had been amended to reduce the Lords' powers of delay from two years to one, the House of Lords fought a very different kind of battle than it had fought over earlier measures of nationalization.

But in their struggle to 'limit the damage' and to induce the Government to 'moderation', the Conservatives were not only able to rely on their political resources, inside and outside Parliament, or on the hostility to the Government of powerful industrial and economic interests. There were other more diffuse but no less persuasive influences also directed to the purpose of enhancing the Government's already well developed tendencies to 'moderation'.

One of these influences, which should neither be exaggerated nor too lightly discounted, was that of the King. The King, in the advice he gave to the Prime Minister, undoubtedly felt that he was doing no more than fulfilling his constitutional duty and that he was, indeed, helping the Government. But the fact remains, on the available evidence, that his advice was not calculated to stiffen the Government's boldness. 'On the subject of strikes,' Mr Wheeler-Bennett notes, the King 'was emphatic with his Prime Minister'.[21] As to nationalization, the King, as early as November 1945, expressed the view to Herbert Morrison that 'he was going too fast in the new nationalizing legislation'. 'I told Attlee,' he wrote in his Diary on the 20th of November, 1945, 'that he must give the people here some confidence that the Government was not going to stifle all private enterprise. Everyone wanted to help in rehabilitating the country but they were not allowed to'. In January 1947, he wrote again that 'I was doing my best to warn them that they were going too fast in their legislation and were offending every class of people who were trying to help them if they were asked to, but were swept aside by regulations, etc.'[22]

It is hardly likely that the King, had he tried to do so, would have been able to deflect the Government's course on any major issue. But it is a naive mistake, particularly in regard to the operation of so subtle an instrument as the British Constitution, only to look for the dramatic and, not finding it, to conclude that this exhausts the range of possibilities. As Mr Wheeler-Bennett notes, the King 'was aware that in his talks with Ministers he was not infrequently successful in presenting arguments which caused them to reconsider decisions at which they had already arrived'[23], and it would seem reasonable to suppose that the reconsideration was not in the direction of greater radicalism.

Mr Wheeler-Bennett's words might equally be taken to describe the Labour Government's relations with its professional Civil Service advisers. Lord Attlee has recalled that, when he returned to Potsdam, this time as Prime Minister, 'our American friends were surprised to find that there was no change in our official advisers and that I had even taken over, as my Principal Private Secretary,

Leslie Rowan, who had been serving Churchill in the same capacity'.[24] This pattern was substantially reproduced throughout the whole administration. The Government gratefully inherited from the war-time coalition, and from previous Conservative governments, a body of officials who, by social provenance, education and professional disposition, were bound to conceive it as one of their prime tasks to warn their Ministers against too radical a departure from traditional departmental policies. No doubt the experience of war had taught them to view with far less distaste than in the past the enlargement of State intervention and control and they were, at the end of the war, quite ready to serve the purposes of a Government pledged to positive State action. But they were equally ready to try and convince their political masters of the dangers of innovation. This did not involve the kind of administrative sabotage which the Left had feared likely in the thirties. What it entailed was the active discouragement of bold experimentation. Of course, Ministers usually had the last word. But the last word was likely to be greatly influenced by the cautious words that had gone before. Mr Shinwell notes that many of his officials at the Ministry of Fuel and Power were 'apathetic or antagonistic to nationalization'.[25] This would not prevent his leading advisers from executing the policy laid down for them; but neither would it dispose them to search for unconventional solutions to the problems it raised, or to press upon their Minister plans and ideas unhallowed by the routines and usages they knew.

Labour Ministers have often paid generous tributes to the loyalty and co-operation of their official advisers. This, however, may be less a comment on the conversion of those advisers to socialist principles than on the Government's failure to act upon these principles. It would have been odd indeed if Foreign Office officials had not given their wholehearted support to a Foreign Secretary whose views accorded so largely with their own, and with those of the Conservative Opposition; or if the Service Chiefs had refused to cooperate with a Ministry whose approach to military matters differed little from their own; and, in this last instance at any rate, Lord Montgomery has said enough to show that, where differences did arise between Ministers and their military advisers (colleagues would be a better word), it was not the Service Chiefs who had the worst of the encounter. The point is not that the Government's advisers should have pressed socialist policies upon their Ministers; the point is that they provided an additional and powerful reinforcement to all the forces in the land whose purpose it was to 'limit the damage' they feared even so moderate a Labour Government might do.

As against these pressures, but by no means of equal weight, there were the contrary pressures on the Government from within the Labour movement. These were not only incomparably weaker, less persistent and less organized, but Ministers, heavy with the responsibilities of office and invested with a new authority and prestige, were also better equipped to resist them, and much more determined to do so.

Although there was much in the Government's handling of affairs at home which worried the Labour Left, its greatest unease was with foreign policy. In its attempts to defend traditional imperial interests in the Middle East, the Government resolutely pursued the policies inherited from its predecessors. And in the developing conflict between East and West, it had also shown, even before the Cold War was properly under way, that it would unhesitatingly take its place as the most senior of the junior partners of the United States. Given its belief in a Russian military threat, and its economic dependence upon the United. States, there never was any question that it would explore any 'third way'.

British foreign policy after 1945 was soon under fire from the Labour Left, over specific issues such as Bevin's handling of the Palestine question, but also in regard to its general drift. At the 1946 Labour Party Annual Conference, the Government was attacked for, as one resolution put it, the 'apparent continuance of a traditionally Conservative Party policy of power politics abroad', and it was urged to return 'to the Labour Party foreign policy of support of Socialist and anti-Imperialist forces throughout the world'. Another resolution called upon the Government to 'maintain and foster an attitude of sympathy, friendship and understanding towards the Soviet Union' and to 'repudiate Mr Churchill's defeatist proposal to make the British Commonwealth a mere satellite of American monopoly capitalism, which will inevitably lead to our being aligned in a partnership of hostility to Russia'. A third also asked the Government 'to undertake a drastic revision of existing methods of recruitment to the Foreign Service' and to entrust the execution of a Socialist foreign policy 'to men who believe in it, rather than to those whose whole background and tradition have rendered them incapable of understanding the first principles of such a policy'. The first of these resolutions was withdrawn after Ernest Bevin had said he considered it a vote of censure upon him, and the other two were lost on a show of hands. But the unease they reflected endured: one of its expressions was an Amendment to the Address tabled by fifty-three Labour MPs in November 1946; another was *Keep Left*, the manifesto of a number of Members of Parliament, which appeared in April 1947. This document, though paying tribute to the Government's achievement, urged greater boldness upon it at home, denounced 'the fallacy of collective security against Communism', and repudiated the argument that 'the only way to stop Communism spreading is to organize the world against Russia'. 'It would be a betrayal of British and European Socialism,' said the document, 'if we meekly accepted Communist leadership. But it would be equally fatal to accept American leadership in exchange for dollars.'

However, the Keep Left group was never more than a fairly loose group of MPs, without any hard centre. Never in fact had the Labour Left so entirely lacked coherence and organization as it did after 1945. Nor did it now have any leader of any prominence: its standard bearer of the war years, Aneurin Bevan, was now safely busy, as Minister of Health, with the creation of the National Health Service.

As for the Parliamentary Party as a whole, it was not the body to deny loyal support to the Government, at meetings of the Parliamentary Party as well as in the division lobbies of the House of Commons. The Standing Orders of the Parliamentary Party were suspended throughout the lifetime of the Labour Government. But this was without prejudice to the right of the Party to withdraw the Whip from Members should occasion arise. And there was never any occasion when a decisive majority was not to be found for whatever policy the Government might decide, even though, as R. T. McKenzie notes, 'there was no question of the Government revealing in detail its parliamentary proposals or seeking formal approval for them in advance of their presentation to Parliament'.[26] From the first, the Government had easily established its supremacy. Even the earlier pattern of consultation with backbench MPs was now discarded. This time, there was created a Liaison Committee, composed of a Chairman and Vice-Chairman (a second Vice-Chairman was later added) elected by the Parliamentary Party, a Labour Peer, the Leader of the House of Commons, the Chief Whip and the Secretary of the Parliamentary Party, who was not an MP; but this body was much more a watchdog for the Government than a lever of pressure upon it.

Of course, backbench pressure was exercised upon Ministers either informally, or at the fortnightly meetings of the P.L.P., or through the latter's standing committees, and Ministers, as Mr McKenzie also notes, 'tended to take party feeling into account before attempting to make a case for a particular line of policy at the party meeting'; but, he adds, 'when an issue was forced to a vote (in the P.L.P.) the Government could rely on a solid block of votes composed of approximately seventy members of the ministry. In addition, of course, those who hoped to win promotion into the Government tended to take care not to carry any misgivings they might have concerning the Government's policies to the point of voting against them. And in any case the party's strong sense of loyalty to its leaders and its internal cohesion almost invariably sustained the Government'.[27]

Most of the rebellions which did occur in the course of the Government's existence only involved a small minority of Members. One issue which provoked a sizeable Labour backbench rebellion and forced the Government to a retreat which proved temporary was the length of conscription. When the National Service Bill, which proposed a period of conscription of eighteen months, was introduced in the House of Commons in March 1947, eighty Labour backbenchers signed an amendment asking the House to reject it, and seventy-two later voted against it. The Government then agreed to reduce the conscription period from eighteen to twelve months. The Bill was due to come into operation on the 1st of January, 1949. In October 1948, by which time the international situation had greatly worsened, Lord Montgomery, the Chief of the Imperial General Staff, 'assembled the Military Members of the Army Council ... and asked them if they were all prepared to resign in a body, led by me, if anything less than eighteen months National Service with the Colours was decided upon by the Government. They all agreed.'[28] The Government gave way in November, 'without serious parliamentary opposition,' and later extended National Service to two years.

What, in the present context, is notable about the relationship of the Government to its backbenchers is not only the Government's strength, but also the fact that its use of that strength was mainly devoted to the neutralization of one current of thought: that of the Left.

This was also true of the Government's relation to the Labour rank and file. The former's insistence on its prior constitutional responsibility to Parliament, and its concern that the Parliamentary Party (which meant the parliamentary leaders) should be free from Conference 'dictation' proceeded much less from some abstract model of parliamentary government, or from some preconceived notion of the desirability or otherwise of 'inner-party democracy' than from a desire to escape from the radical pressure of the rank and file. The debate on these issues, then and later, was firmly rooted in the ideological divisions between leaders and activists, and is only meaningful with reference to these divisions.

3. 'CONSOLIDATION'

By 1948, as Herbert Morrison pointed out to the Labour Party Conference of that year, the Government had, save for the nationalization of iron and steel, passed into legislation all the major nationalization proposals contained in *Let Us Face the Future*. In a crucial sense, the Labour Party had now, at long last, reached its moment of truth. What had now to be decided was whether it would go forward with a nationalization programme which, by eating really deep into capitalist enterprise, would be immeasurably more significant than the previous one, or whether it would stop at bankrupt industries and public utilities. The Government's predictable answer, though wrapped up in a vague promise of further public ownership, was that the time had now come for consolidation.

'Whilst in the next programme,' Morrison told the delegates, 'it will be right – and I can promise you that the Executive will do it – to give proper considera- tion to further propositions for public ownership, do not ignore the need, not merely for considering further public ownership, but for allowing Ministers adequate time to consolidate, to develop, to make efficient the industries which have been socialized in the present Parliament ... we must make the programme as attractive as we can to ourselves, but we must make it attractive also to public opinion ... *you must expect the new programme to be of a somewhat different character and a somewhat different tempo from the last ...'*[29]

The speech of the constituency delegate who followed Morrison[30] is worth quoting at some length, since it so clearly shows the gulf that divided most of the leadership from some at least of its following, and is also a succinct statement of the latter's case, then and ever since. Referring to Morrison's insistence on the need to make Labour's election programme not only attractive to themselves but also to 'public opinion', the delegate argued that 'the programme will be attractive to the public, not if it is something very wishy-washy and watered down but if it is bold and challenging. I want to see in the forefront of our General Election programme a declaration of faith in Socialism – not the approach the Liberal has to nationalization, that when two or three Royal Commissions have decided that in a particular case, for empirical reasons, an industry ought to be nationalized, then we will nationalize it. I want us to say we believe, as economic scientists and on the grounds of social justice, that the large resources of production in this country ought to belong to the common people. When Churchill says, "You Labour people are doing it for doctrinaire reasons," I want him to be quite right. I want us to be doing it from principle and doctrine ... When the present programme of the Labour Government has been completed some twenty percent of the industrial and economic life of this country will be publicly owned. At this speed it will take us twenty-five years to get to the stage when Socialism predominates. I want to see the present tempo maintained. I am not very happy about the suggestion that there is going to be some slackening off in speed. I do not feel that anybody can say that we are going too fast. Many of us think we are going too slow ... I would say that there are two ideas as to the next step. One is to increase the degree of public control, the other is to extend the area of publicly-owned industry. I do not believe that it is feasible, as a permanent basis, for a Socialist Government to control privately owned industry. Ownership gives control. The only way in which we can get control is by getting ownership. So I want it to be made quite clear in our programme that we stand for control through common ownership.'[31]

He was destined to be greatly disappointed. The Labour Party's Policy Statement, *Labour Believes in Britain*, published in April 1949, and endorsed by Annual Conference in June, proposed for nationalization industrial life assurance, sugar, cement, meat wholesaling and slaughtering, water and 'all suitable minerals'. In addition, if private enterprise should fail 'to act in the public interest', the Government would, 'wherever the need is clearly shown', start upon new public enterprises; secondly, the existing power to take over concerns 'which are woefully failing the nation' would be continued and, thirdly, the Government should be prepared 'to acquire suitable existing concerns where these are willingly offered for sale'.

Herbert Morrison, in commending the document to the delegates, had said that each nationalization proposal was 'carefully chose and fitted into the pattern'. But the programme, whatever its specific merits, quite failed to conceal the fact (save to many devoted Labour supporters) that Labour's leadership, should it be returned to power at the next election, was entirely prepared to postpone indefinitely any further attempt at the structural transformation of a predominantly capitalist economy, now increasingly and euphemistically labeled 'the mixed economy'. *Labour believes in Britain* in fact inaugurated a pattern that was to acquire ever more precise shape in the following years. Proposals for nationalization were not entirely eliminated; but neither were the proposals which appeared in Labour's programmes intended to make more than marginal inroads into the 'private sector'. They neither satisfied the activists nor made any marked impression on the electorate. But they also failed to pacify Labour's enemies or to attract that middle class vote, whose seduction had become a major obsession with Labour's electoral strategists.

'Consolidation' was intended to define the strategy and purpose of the next Labour Government; but it was already a reality when Herbert Morrison spoke of it at the 1948 Labour Party Conference. By then, the Government's reforming zeal was all but exhausted Doubts had even arisen in the Cabinet about the wisdom of proceeding with the outright nationalization of iron and steel and an attempt to find an alternative in greater State control only foundered because the proposals came up against strong opposition from some members of the Cabinet, including, so it was said, a threat of resignation from Aneurin Bevan.

Of all the Labour Government's nationalization measures, the nationalization of iron and steel was the only one which entailed a serious threat to the 'private sector'. Had the Government differently conceived its task in 1945, iron and steel, instead of being left last, would have been among the first to be taken over, at a time when opposition was likely to be least effective. And, had the Government differently conceived its task in 1949, it would have reacted with greater vigour to the pressure and threats of the steel interests, and made fewer concessions to them.

Neither these interests nor the Opposition could prevent the passage of the Bill through the House of Commons. But they could rely on the obduracy of the House of Lords. Under the procedure of the Parliament Act of 1949, the Government could have rejected the Lords' amendments and carried the nationalization Bill through all its parliamentary stages by the beginning of 1950. Instead, it agreed, in return for the House of Lords' withdrawal of its amendments to the Bill, not to make any appointments to the Iron and Steel Corporation until the 1st of October, 1950, and not to transfer properties to the Corporation until the 1st of January, 1951. This delay was of course intended to ensure that another General Election would intervene before nationalization could come into operation. In the meantime, the steelmasters, while preparing to defeat the eventual application of the Act, also embarked on a massive campaign in the country to persuade the electors that nationalization was unnecessary and fraught with disastrous consequences to the nation.

Their efforts were only part of a more general offensive by business and financial interests, now confident that they had the full measure of the Government, to discredit not only nationalization but also bulk buying, municipal trading, Government intervention and control. In the two years preceding the General Election, enormous resources, in money, skill and ingenuity, were deployed to sell 'free enterprise' and anti-Labour propaganda to the public. The most lavish of these campaigns were undertaken by Tate and Lyle, the sugar refiners, and by the insurance interests; by September 1949, the latter 'had set up 400 anti-nationalization committees up and down the country on which 4,000 employees were working after office hours to publicize their objections to the Labour Party's proposals. Insurance agents also constituted a ready-made army of canvassers, the great majority of them in favour of the preservation of the status quo.

Neither in resources, nor, it may be added; in energy and determination, was the Labour Party a match for the business interests and their public relations experts. What is even more notable, however, is that the Government itself was no match for them either. Its own information services were perpetually attacked in Parliament and in the Press as wasteful, costly and partisan. In actual fact, most Government information was deliberately and carefully 'neutral'; much of it was also couched in language both repellent and partly incomprehensible to the audiences to which it was addressed. This was not what the Opposition disliked: it simply wanted to reduce the Government's information to the public to the barest minimum. And, by October 1948, the Government was sufficiently defensive to appoint an official committee to make recommendations 'as to any direction in which economies may be desirable or the organization (of information services) could be improved'. The Committee reported that it regarded the expenditure as 'too high', and its recommendations for reductions were duly accepted – at a time when business expenditure against the Government was soaring.

From the end of 1949, with an election in the offing, Ministers did go as far as to warn business interests that the expense of their propaganda campaigns might well come to be added to the election expenses of Conservative candidates, how and with what effect was not made clear. The interests concerned replied that they were not attacking the Labour Party, but the threat of nationalization as such, and that they had an elementary right to defend themselves. Lord Woolton, the Chairman of the Conservative Party, was even more bland. 'Throughout these industrial campaigns,' he said after the date of the election had been announced, 'Conservatives have been completely dissociated from them ... The only thing I do suggest to these gentlemen is that to avoid confusion they should desist as soon as Parliament is dissolved ... At the General Election we shall fight nationalization tooth and nail and we want the ring clear for the politicians to fight.'[32] There spoke the voice of the true parliamentary democrat – of course after whatever damage could be done had been done.

The parliamentary battles over the Iron and Steel Bill and the business campaigns against the modest nationalization proposals of *Labour Believes in Britain* had their uses to the Government. For they helped to obscure the fact that, over the wider range of policy, there existed an ever more substantial measure of agreement between the Labour leadership and its Conservative counterpart, and most of all in regard to foreign policy. This bipartisanship was not due to any Conservative shift to a distinctive Labour foreign policy. There was no such policy. Winston Churchill was not vainly boasting when he said, as he often did, that the Government had consistently followed his own recommendations and proposals. With the setting up of NATO, of which Ernest Bevin was one of the main architects, agreement between the two front benches had became sufficiently explicit to cause serious embarrassment to the Foreign Secretary. With NATO, and for the first time in twentieth-century British politics save in time of war, the most important factor in foreign policy was now agreed to be above and beyond 'partisan' debate.

Nor, from the time Labour had taken office in 1945, had there been any serious disagreement over the management of the Colonial Empire. All that *Let Us Face the Future* had said on the subject was that the Labour Party would seek to promote 'the planned progress of our Colonial Dependencies'. Both parties were agreed on the need for 'Colonial Development' and Labour Ministers made no bones about the fact that the purpose of such development was to help alleviate Britain's economic and financial difficulties. As John Strachey, then Minister of Food, put it in 1948, to obtain, 'by one means or another, by hook or by crook, the development of primary production of all sorts', everywhere in and outside the Empire was 'a life and death matter for the economy of this country'; 'we certainly do not want to score any party points,' he also said, 'about which is the best of these forms of development … our national position is really too grave to warrant any indulgence'.[33] As to this, the Opposition concurred wholeheartedly, which is not very surprising since, as Conservatives were delighted to point out, the Government's plans were quite in tune with traditional Conservative colonial policy, however different the colonial rhetoric of each party might be.

Over most of the Colonial Empire, there were national leaders who did indulge in particular opinions on the methods of overseas development. The Government's response to the anti-colonial challenge it faced was a mixture of minimal constitutional reform on the one hand, and of repression on the other, including, as part of the defense of the 'free world' against Communism, the waging of a fierce colonial war in Malaya.

Even at home, there was, after 1947, less and less about the Government's economic policy that was really distinctive. With the rapid dwindling of the

American Loan, the Government had faced a major balance of payments crisis. This, to an appreciable extent, was the result of the Government's failure in effective planning and control. Yet, no sooner had the immediate crisis passed than the Government initiated a substantial reduction in physical controls and moved rapidly from 'democratic planning' to an even more democratic reliance upon appeals, particularly to wage earners, to produce more without seeking to earn more. In 1948, the policy of 'restraint' both on wage claims and dividend payments had found official expression in the Government's *Statement on Personal Incomes, Costs and Prices.* From then onwards, the Government was mainly concerned to preach 'austerity' to its supporters, who might have responded with greater enthusiasm had austerity been less obviously reserved for wage earners. The 'wage freeze' had been accepted by both the T.U.C. and the Labour Party Conferences in 1948. In 1949, the Government was again caught in a financial crisis and devalued the pound. In September 1950, the policy of wage restraint was rejected by the T.U.C. Conference, against the advice of the General Council. By then, the Government, returned in February with a majority of six, had given up the pretence that it was in control of economic policy. As *The Economist* wrote, the *Economic Survey* for 1950 was a 'humble document, meek almost to the point of being meaningless. There is nothing here of the notions of "democratic economic planning" as proclaimed in earlier Surveys, which presented a working pattern for the year's economic effort and left all men of good will to work for it. Indeed, the perplexing thing about the Survey for 1950 is its lack of plan.'[34]

It was not only the Government which was in retreat in the latter part of its period of office. The Labour Left was too. On the evidence of its first years of office, the Government would have retreated in any case. What above all caused the retreat of the Labour Left was the exacerbation of the Cold War, which, as *Keeping Left*, published in January 1950, made clear, greatly affected its attitude to a policy of alignment with the United States. The Labour Left only accepted that alignment with reluctance, with reservations, with the hope that the Labour Government would use its membership of the alliance to 'restrain' its American partners, and with the even greater hope that the time would soon arrive when Britain would become the leader of a 'third force' of democratic socialism. But it accepted the alliance all the same; and found much in Russian foreign policy which made any general challenge to Government policy much more difficult to sustain.

Root and branch opposition had in any case become a risky enterprise, particularly for the Labour parliamentarians. For the Cold War, and the anti-Communist climate it engendered, exposed the Government's critics to the now dread charge of 'fellow travelling', and to threats of punishment commensurate with the offence.

In this respect, the turning-point in the taming of the Government's parliamentary critics was the leadership's reaction to the telegram of good wishes for success in the Italian General Election which a number of MPs sent, in April 1948, to what the Parliamentary Report of that year called the 'Communist-dominated Nenni Socialists'. Twenty-one of the signatories were summoned by the Executive to undertake individually that they would cease 'acting as a group in organized opposition to Party policy', failing which they would be expelled from the Party. The assurances were given. This episode, and the subsequent expulsion from the Labour Party of a few MPs, notably Konni Zilliacus, were sufficient to discourage the expression of dissent on the fundamentals, as distinct from the specific applications, of the Government's foreign policy.

Even on home policy, the Labour Left's message was now uncertain. By 1950, there were many who found plausible the view that first attention should now be given to something like the consolidation of what had been achieved in the previous years. *Labour Believes in Britain* would have raised greater opposition had this not been the case. In 1947, the authors of *Keeping Left* had insisted that Labour would have to proceed with more measures of large-scale nationalization. In 1950, *Keeping Left* was 'less concerned about who owns a factory and more about who manages it and how, and whether it is working according to socialist plans … the next steps are not so obvious or so simple'. Indeed, *Keeping Left* now expressed the belief that *Labour Believes in Britain*, 'with its new proposal of flexible, multi-purpose competitive public enterprise, opens up a whole new field for national ownership'. This of course entirely missed the drift of the Government's proposal; and the insistence of the authors of *Keeping Left* that they still believed in an extension of public ownership, coupled with appeals to the Government to show greater boldness and imagination, was hardly likely to worry the consolidators.

It is very unlikely that, in July 1945, any Labour activist would have thought it possible for the next General Election to be called 'demure', as Winston Churchill called the General Election of February 1950. Any such Labour activist would have argued, in 1945, that, on the contrary, this election would be the most fiercely contested ever, since the Government, having by then negotiated the outworks of British capitalism, would be asking the electors to return it to power so that it might begin the investment of the citadel. No doubt, he would also have said, the leaders would need to be kept up to the mark by the Left; but he would have been confident that, under pressure, there would be further and more significant advances towards the socialist society.

The fatal flaw in the argument was the assumption that the differences between the activist and most of his leaders were differences of degree when they were in fact differences in kind. For the activist saw the Welfare State and the nationalization measures of 1945-8 as the beginning of the social revolution to which he believed the Labour Party was dedicated; while his leaders took these achievements to *be* the social revolution. Of course, they would readily agree that there was still much to be done to consolidate that social revolution. But, as far as they were concerned, the bigger part of the task had, by 1950, been completed. And they therefore were genuinely impatient with the argument that there remained a citadel to be conquered. They believed it to be already occupied. It is this, rather than economic difficulties, or the international situation, which explains why Labour's election programme was so barren and the campaign 'demure'.

Since it had few positive proposals to make, and was not very sure about those it had, particularly in regard to nationalization, the Labour Party was almost exclusively concerned to stress how much the Government had achieved since 1945, and how much these achievements, and particularly full employment, would be threatened if the Tories were returned. Conversely, the Conservatives dwelt on the miseries and shortages attendant, as they would have it, upon 'socialism', and stressed their own devotion to welfare and full employment and also quoted authoritative Labour spokesmen to suggest that, without American aid, there would have been mass unemployment in Britain. One of the main items in this titanic confrontation between the two parties was a broad Conservative hint that the abolition of petrol rationing might well follow the return of a Conservative Government, which Labour spokesmen denounced as a cheap bribe to the electorate.

The two parties would have found it even more difficult to find points of substantial disagreement over foreign affairs. And, over relations with Russia, there was an ironical demonstration of how the wheel had come full circle since 1945 in Labour's reaction to Churchill's cautious suggestion (coupled with a complaint that Britain did not yet have her own atomic bomb) of 'another talk with Soviet Russia upon the highest level'; 'the idea', said Churchill, 'appeals to me of a supreme effort to bridge the gulf between the two worlds, so that each can live their life, if not in friendship, at least without the hatreds and manoeuvres of the cold war'.[35] This was instantly dismissed by Labour Ministers as an election stunt. If it was, it is perhaps a pity that they had not thought of it themselves. Instead, Ernest Bevin was content to recapitulate his difficulties in negotiating with the Russians, and Herbert Morrison to note that 'these things would need careful preparation between us and the Soviet Union', that 'the United States would be involved', and that 'it could cause unnecessary friction if we suddenly took the issue out of the hands of the United Nations, for delicate discussions are taking place'.[36]

Defensive and hesitant though Labour was throughout the campaign, its achievements were sufficient for it to receive well over 13 million votes as compared with nearly 12 million in 1945, on a poll of nearly 84 per cent. However, the Conservatives, with a poll of 12.5 million votes, did substantially better than in 1945; their percentage of the votes cast had risen from 39.8 per cent to 43.5 per cent; that of Labour had declined from 48.3 per cent to 46.1 per cent. What made the election results appear much more dramatic than they were was the virtual disappearance of Labour's parliamentary majority. With 315 seats, Labour had an overall majority of six.

Labour's opponents immediately chose to interpret the result as a decisive rejection by the electorate of nationalization, particularly of the nationalization of steel. Nor had Labour's leaders any great wish to rebut the interpretation. After all, they themselves, while very willing to defend past measures of nationalization, had appeared almost apologetic about future ones. Indeed, such an interpretation had its use to the consolidators: for it made it appear that it was 'the electorate', rather than the leadership which was satiated with reform.

In the same sense, Labour's tiny majority usefully served to hide the fact that, on the evidence of the two previous years, the Government would have been seriously embarrassed with a larger one. For it would then have had to justify itself as a radical, reforming administration. And neither its programme, nor its mood, would have made this at all easy.

4. PROM CONSOLIDATION TO DEFEAT

What a Government returned to office with a majority of six could do to improve its chances of obtaining a more satisfactory result at the next election is, in the present context, a rather academic question. This Government, exhausted politically and ideologically long before it entered its second term, could only endure, to no distinctive purpose, and, by the manner of its endurance, improve the chances of its opponents.

The first casualty of the election was the nationalization proposals of *Let Us Win through Together*. The King's Speech of the first session of the new Parliament in March 1950 spoke tentatively of the possibility of legislation affecting water supplies but, for the rest, victory was implicitly conceded to the anti-nationalizers. Still, the Government's legislative programme did include such proposals as the breaking-up of roads by public-utility undertakings, changes in the constitution of the General Medical Council and the Central Midwives Board, and the placing of cattle grids along certain highways.

On the other hand, the Government had inherited one embarrassing legacy from its previous term of office, namely the nationalization of iron and steel, the vesting date for which was the 15th of February, 1951. In the intervening year, an unequal battle was fought out between a demoralized Government and steel interests (aided by the Conservative Opposition) ever more confident that nationalization would prove a temporary and easily reversible measure, but also determined that the take-over should be as difficult as, possible. In the House of Commons on the 19th of September, 1950, G. R. Strauss, the Minister of Supply, related how, having invited the spokesmen of the steel interests to submit the names of 'experienced men who would be acceptable to their fellow industrialists for inclusion in the Corporation', the Executive Committee of the Iron and Steel Federation refused 'on the grounds that in their opinion the Government had no mandate to carry out the Iron and Steel Act'. 'They warned me at the same time,' the Minister went on, 'that the Corporation, deprived of such people, would be unable successfully to plan the steel industry. Further, I was informed that every effort would be made to dissuade any important man I might approach from serving on the Corporation ... In short, these people decided to threaten, and indeed they did carry out, a political strike.' There was in fact, in the Minister's words, a 'gentleman's agreement throughout firms in the industry not to serve on the Corporation', and this, he complained, 'is concerted action by a number of people for the specific purpose of sabotaging an Act of Parliament'.[37]

Save for the nationalization of iron and steel from which it could not retreat, the Government's main ambition was to spin out an invalid existence until some such time as its electoral prospects might, somehow, improve. But the rapid worsening of the international situation after the outbreak of the Korean conflict in June 1950 shattered its hopes of a quiet life. From then until its demise in October 1951, it was involved in a succession of crises, its responses to which rapidly accelerated its decline.

As for the Labour Left, the Korean war was a further blow to its morale. There was no disposition to challenge the Government's support for American intervention in Korea, or to criticize Britain's own contribution to what the Labour Left generally agreed to regard as an exercise in collective security, to which it now felt committed. However, there were grave fears, by no means confined to the Left, that, as a result of American policy, the Korean 'police action' might come to involve war with China, which in turn might precipitate a world war; and there was also, on the Labour Left, much unease, which antedated the Korean war, but was much increased by it, at what was regarded as the British Government's failure to do more by way of restraining its American ally.

It is worth noting in how subdued a form this unease was expressed at the Labour Party Annual Conference in October 1950, where a resolution expressed 'alarm at the increasing danger of war', but was content to urge the Government to 'strive to end the differences between the five great powers, to which end a Conference should be called immediately', to renew its efforts 'to create friendly relations with the U.S.S.R.' and to pursue a number of other equally worthy aims. Supporters of the resolution insisted that it contained nothing to which the Government or the National Executive could object. However, the Executive and Ernest Bevin did object, and the resolution was defeated, though 881,000 votes were cast for it (against 4,861,000).

Unease and apprehension grew to much vaster proportions with General MacArthur's drive to the Chinese border and with the entry of Chinese troops into the Korean conflict in November. With President Truman's statement at a Press conference that the use of the atomic bomb was under consideration, the need for 'restraint' on the United States appeared greater than ever before, and brought Attlee to Washington at the beginning of December. From this visit grew the legend that it was the Prime Minister's intervention which prevented the use of the atomic bomb against China. What was not a legend, however, was the Government's commitment, in May and September 1951, to the possibility of military action against China.

It is equally worth noting, particularly in the light of later developments, how little Labour criticism there was of the Government's decision, announced in September 1950, to increase expenditure on rearmament to a total of £3,600,000,000 for the years 1951-4. Nor, despite acute misgivings on the Labour Left, was there any challenge to the upward revision of that figure in January 1951, under intense American pressure, to a total of £4,700,000,000. Indeed, Aneurin Bevan, speaking for the Government in February against a Conservative motion of no confidence, defended the new programme, and barely qualified his defence with ambiguous warnings of the dangers of too rapid a rate of rearmament. Two months later, however, the Budget was to lead to Bevan's resignation and thus provide the Labour Left with the leader it had lacked since 1945.

The Budget which Hugh Gaitskell (who had succeeded Cripps as Chancellor of the Exchequer the previous October) introduced on the 10th of April, 1951, was the logical consequence, not only of the rearmament programme, but even more of the Government's long standing policy of 'consolidation'. For the Government, having agreed to an enormous rearmament burden, also had to find ways of footing the bill. Its problem was in some ways similar to that which had confronted the Government of Ramsay MacDonald in 1931. And, like Philip Snowden before him, the Chancellor found it much easier to place the major share of the burden on the poor than on the rich. Snowden's economies on unemployment benefits had no relevance to the economic problem he faced; nor had Hugh Gaitskell's economies of £25 million on the National Health Service. Within a few months, Britain was again in the throes of a major balance of payments crisis, which the Government had entirely failed to foresee. As in 1931, it was the Conservatives who found most cause to rejoice in the Budget. 'Mr Gaitskell,' the *Daily Express* wrote, 'introduces a Tory Budget. He puts a charge of 50 per cent on teeth and spectacles. That is what the Tories would have done. Now the job is done for them.' *The Times* put the same point more elegantly: 'Mr Gaitskell,' it said, 'seemed to have resisted most of the temptations which beset a Socialist Chancellor of the Exchequer.'[38]

For the meagre consolation of his own side, the Chancellor did budget for an increase of 4s. a week in the pension of some categories of old age pensioners; and a casual compliment was also paid in the Budget to the old notion of 'equality of sacrifice' in the form of a higher tax on distributed profits. The City's embarrassing welcome for the Budget did not suggest that the burden would prove very great.

Initially, Bevan's objections to the Budget had been confined to the imposition of charges on Health Service patients. Had this been all, some compromise would no doubt have been found. But the Budget served to crystallize an accumulation of discontents over the general drift of the Government's policy. At the time, the Government's precarious majority prevented discontent from erupting into open rebellion. Though Bevan resigned from the Government (as did Harold Wilson and John Freeman), there was no challenge to it. As Bevan and three of his supporters on the National Executive (i.e. Barbara Castle, Tom Driberg and Ian Mikardo) wrote after his resignation, 'we are determined to do nothing that may impair this unity (of the Party), weaken the position of the Government in the House of Commons, or handicap the Prime Minister's exercise of his initiative in determining the date of the General Election'; even so, they added, 'we reserve our democratic right to debate freely issues of Government policy'.

However, what debate there was was cut short by the Prime Minister's announcement on the 19th of September that there would be a General Election on the 25th of October. Labour's Election Manifesto, drafted by a committee consisting of Hugh Dalton, Aneurin Bevan, Sam Watson and Morgan Phillips, and then approved by the National Executive, was an even woollier document than its immediate predecessor. This time, there was no specific pledge on nationalization. 'We shall,' said the document 'take over concerns which fail the nation and start new public enterprises wherever this will serve the national interest ... we shall establish Development Councils, by compulsion if necessary, wherever this will help industrial efficiency ... We shall associate the workers more closely with the administration of public industries and services.'

Nor, for that matter, was there any specific pledge on anything else. In the main, the Manifesto was content to stress Labour's past achievements, notably the maintenance of full employment, and to contrast these achievements with the Tories' dark pre-war record.

Much of the document's emphasis, however, fell, not surprisingly in the light of the world situation, on the issue of peace. Though it insisted that Britain 'must play her full part in the strengthening of collective defence', peace, it also said, 'cannot be preserved by arms alone.... As our armed strength grows, more attention must be given to the under-developed regions of the world'. Only a Labour Government would do this: 'the Tory still thinks in terms of Victorian imperialism and colonial exploitation'.

This last point was highly topical in the light of Britain's dispute with Persia over the nationalization of the Anglo-Iranian Oil Company. But in the light of the Government's policies in that dispute, it was a somewhat disingenuous point for the Labour leaders to make.

It was just before the General Election that the conflict over Persian oil had entered its most acute phase. For years past, the British Government had waged a tenacious battle against concessions to Persian demands for a greater share in the profits of the Anglo-Iranian Oil Company. It was only after the Majlis voted to nationalize the oil fields on the 15th of March, 1951 that the Company made an offer of a fifty-fifty share of the profits to the Iranian Government. The offer came too late to stem the tide of Persian nationalism and the assumption of the Premiership by Dr Mossadegh at the end of April directly posed the threat of .the Company's eviction from Persia.

There followed a summer of abortive negotiations, of appeals to the international Court of Justice and to the Security Council, of assertions that Britain would not leave Abadan, of economic pressure, and of displays of naval strength in the Persian Gulf. Nothing of all this was of any avail. On the 3rd of October, just before the opening of the electoral campaign, Abadan was finally evacuated. The day before, Winston Churchill had fiercely attacked the Government. The decision to evacuate, he said, 'convicts Mr Attlee and the Lord Chancellor of breaking the solemn undertaking they gave to Parliament . . . in August. . . . I do not remember any case where public men have broken their word so abruptly and without any attempt at explanation'.[39]

These and similar Conservative accusations provided Labour with one of its major electoral themes – the danger of war if a Conservative Government was returned. Speaking to the Annual Conference of the Labour Party on the 3rd of October, Herbert Morrison directly challenged Churchill to say whether Britain should have gone to war with Persia or not. 'I do not accuse the average Conservative of being a warmonger, of thirsting for the shedding of blood, or of wishing to be involved needlessly in a world war. I do not say that, and I advise you not to say that, because it would not be fair, and it would not be true. But it is their temperament; it is the background of their mental outlook – the old imperialist outlook. It is the semi-hysteria of the bulk of those Tory backbenchers that really alarms one as to what a Tory Government would do if a Tory Government were put in. Therefore if the country wants peace it had better vote for the people who can most surely be relied upon to preserve peace and, if I may say so, are the most competent to frame principles and proposals for the peace and well-being of the world.'[40]

Yet, the explanation of the Government's refusal to resort to armed intervention in Persia cannot be made to rest simply on its dedication to peaceful settlements. No doubt, a Labour Government would be less inclined than a Conservative one to contemplate armed intervention and would have found it much more difficult to persuade its backbenchers to support a military venture against Persia. But there were other factors. One of them was intense American pressure (by no means disinterested) against such a venture. Another was the danger of Soviet intervention. But there was also the fact that the Government was advised that the necessary resources for such a venture were not available. And Lord Morrison himself has recently revealed that, had the resources been available, a resort to force would have been by no means excluded.

At the time, however, Labour was able to argue that the Government's handling of the Persian dispute, as of its Egyptian difficulties, was a token, not of weakness, but of its abhorrence of force, and to charge its opponents with, at the least, powerful propensities to its use. This 'warmongering' theme, though partially qualified by most Labour speakers, and epitomized by the *Daily Mirror*'s headline on Election Day, *Whose Finger on the Trigger?* undoubtedly placed the Conservatives on the defensive, perhaps for the first time in any General Election in this century; in combination with Labour's warnings of the threats to full employment and the Welfare State which a Conservative victory were said to entail, it gave to Labour's electoral campaign a dynamic which its electoral programme alone could hardly have supplied. Without this, Labour might have fared much worse. As it is, Labour achieved its highest poll ever, with 13,948,605 votes, or 48.8 per cent of the total votes cast, while the Conservatives obtained 13,717,538 (48 per cent) It was not enough, however, to prevent Labour's loss of twenty-one seats to the Conservatives and the latter's return to office. In any case, the Government would have found another lease of life a burden rather than a challenge. By then, it had long fulfilled its limited purposes.

Notes

[1] R. B. McCallum and A. Redman, *The British General Election of 1945* (London, 1947) p. 268

[2] C. Attlee, *The Labour Party in Perspective* (Gollancz, 1937). p. 140. One of the most significant transformations brought about by the war was that of Cripps. 'He had worked,' Sir Stafford's biographer notes, 'with men of other political beliefs than his own, he counted them among his personal friends ... he appreciated the high principles and personal qualities of his Conservative friends'; however, Mr. Cooke also notes, 'their politics were not his, and their ideas of post-war government were not enough for him'. (C. Cooke, *The Life of Richard Stafford Cripps* , London, 1957. p. 326)

[3] Labour Party Annual Conference Report, 1944, p. 161. My italics.

[4] ibid, p. 161. My italics.

[5] Labour Party Annual Conference Report, 1944, pp. 161-3.

[6] The Bank of England, the Executive's Report on *Full Employment and Financial Policy* (1944) noted, was already 'no more than a section of the Treasury, subject to the direction of the Chancellor of the Exchequer and the Cabinet'. This, the Report said, would have to be made permanent; the responsibility of appointing the Governor of the Bank should be made to rest with the Chancellor of the Exchequer, whose approval should also be required for the appointment of members of the Court of the Bank; as to the joint-stock banks, the Report said, they must be 'required' to behave as a Public Service and to act in the interests of the community. (*Full Employment and Financial Policy*, p. 3.)

[7] Supplementary Report and Special Final Agenda, Labour Party Annual Conference, 1944, p. 36.

[8] Labour Party Annual Conference Report, 1944, p.163

[9] R. A. Brady, *Crisis in Britain, Plans and Achievements of the Labour Government* (London, 1950) p. 41.

[10] Labour Party Annual Conference Report, 1945, p. 90.

[11] K. Martin, *Harold Laski, 1893-1950*, London 1953, p. 169

[12] J. Brynes, *Speaking Frankly*, London, 1947, p.79

[13] The Spectator, 2nd of October, 1959

[14] *The Economist*, November 1945, p.139

[15] V.L.Allen, *Trade Unions and the Government*, London, 1960, p. 127

[16] T.U.C. Annual Conference Report, 1944, p. 409

[17] *The Times*, 28th of October, 1946. My italics.

[18] A. Rogow, *The Labour Government and British Industry 1945-51*, London 1955, p.25

[19] J. Freeman, 'The Old Look', *New Statesman*, 14th of November, 1959

[20] P. M. Bromhead, *The House of Lords and Contemporary Politics*, 1911-1957 (London, 1958) p. 176. In 1952, Lord Jowett, the Lord Chancellor in the Attlee Government, recalled that he had, in the conditions of 1945-51, been 'forced to be reasonable'. 'As many of your lordships well remember,' he said, 'I used to get them round to my room and we would thrash out our problems frankly and in the most friendly way. Very often I used to be able to meet them on all sorts of topics … If I could not, I explained why … Sometimes I used to go round to Ministers to try to get them to give way. The net result of all this was very satisfactory'.

[21] Wheeler-Bennett, *King George VI, His Life and Reign*, London, 1956. p. 652.

[22] ibid, pp. 651,662.

[23] Ibid, p. 653

[24] Attlee, op. cit. p. 149

[25] Shinwell, op.cit., p.174

[26] R.T.McKenzie, *British Political Parties*, London, 1960, p. 447

[27] ibid, p.447

[28] Montgomery of Alamein, *Memoirs*, London, 1958, p. 479

[29] Labour Party Annual Conference Report, 1948, p. 122. My italics.

[30] Hugh Lawson, of Rushcliffe Divisional Labour Party.

[31] Labour Party Annual Conference Report, 1948, p. 122.

[32] R.B. Nicolas, *The British General Election of 1950*, London, 1950, p.72

[33] R. Brady, *Crisis in Britain*, Cambridge 1950, p. 601

[34] *The Economist*, April 1, 1950

[35] Nicolas, op.cit., p. 103

[36] ibid, p.105

[37] H.of C., vol. 478, cols. 1834-5

[38] Both quotations are from *Tribune*, 20 April 1951

[39] D.E.Butler, *The British General Election of 1951*, London, 1952, p. 113

[40] Labour Party Annual Conference Report, 1951, p.129

3. THE SICKNESS OF LABOURISM (1961)

Ralph Miliband

1. FROM DEFEAT TO PARALYSIS

The Labour Party accepted its loss of office in 1951 with a certain complacency. This was partly due to a feeling that so much been accomplished since 1945 that a breathing space had become natural and inevitable. But it was also the product of two basic assumptions, then quite common in the Labour Party. The first of these was that opposition would restore its energies and it would therefore soon be ready for another period of office. The second assumption was that the Conservative Government would provide so disastrous a contrast to its predecessor that a majority of the electorate would wish to use the first available opportunity to return Labour to power with a comfortable parliamentary lead. Both assumptions were false.

The belief that Labour in opposition would soon regain its vitality not only failed to take into account Labour's steady degeneration of purpose in its last years of office, but also the fact that those who had been mainly responsible for that degeneration remained in secure control of the Labour Party after it had lost office. Even more important, it failed to take into account the fact that these men were determined, after 1951, that the course they had taken for the Labour Party in the previous years should not be reversed or substantially modified.

This was not because they were tired, or old, or stupid. They had adopted policies of consolidation at home and bipartisanship abroad because they were convinced that these policies were necessary and right, and they continued to believe in them after they left office. Unfortunately for the Labour Party, these policies made impossible vigorous opposition to the Government and the fashioning of a new and distinctive programme.

This, from a purely electoral point of view, might have mattered less had Labour's second assumption been true – had the Conservatives, that is to say, tried to undo all or most of Labour's achievements in the preceding years. But the belief that the Conservatives would do this was a bad misreading of the impact which the experience of war, the defeat of 1945, and the years of Labour rule had had upon them. By 1951, the Conservatives had come to be well aware that the minimal expectations of the larger part of the electorate now included regular employment and welfare services. Nor in any case was there any reason why they should seek to deny these expectations, since the denial, and the undoing of Labour's achievements, including most of Labour's nationalization measures, were in no way essential to their purposes.

Hence the Conservatives' refusal to act according to Labour's expectations. Hence also the problem for the Labour Party of maintaining, in concrete policy terms, a clear distance between itself and its political opponents. Given the political philosophy of Labour's leaders, this was (and remained throughout the fifties) an insoluble problem: for these leaders would not venture into territory where they stood no danger of being followed by their opponents, and their opponents would not beat a dramatic retreat from the territory which the Labour leaders felt to be their own.

Unlike the Labour leaders, the Labour Left did not find the problem insoluble. The solution, it said, lay in the adoption by the Labour Party of a new radical programme, with extensive proposals for further nationalization well to the forefront; and in an attempt to reverse at least some of the foreign and defence policies pursued by the Labour Government since 1945. Even before Labour had lost office, there had been increasing dissatisfaction on the Left with these policies. The return to opposition, coupled with the departure from the scene of two powerful figures, Ernest Bevin and Stafford Cripps, now revived, in a more acute form, the conflict between Right and Left which office had helped to contain.

For a long time after 1951, it seemed that the demands of the Left were particular to the parliamentarians associated with Aneurin Bevan, and to the constituency activists who supported them. But there is very little about Labour in the fifties which is more important than the fact that the opposition to the leadership's policies, at home and abroad, was at least as persistent in the trade unions as in the constituency parties.[1] Throughout the Bevanite controversies in the first years of the fifties, the Bevanites themselves rightly claimed that they not only spoke for the constituency activists, but for a large number of trade unionists as well.[2] Nevertheless, the conflict between Right and Left continued to be defined as one between the 'wild men' of the constituency parties and their parliamentary leaders on the one hand, and 'sober' trade unionists on the other.

There were a number of reasons for the persistence of this definition. It was the constituency parties which, from 1952 onwards, swept Bevanite candidates on to the National Executive Committee of the Labour Party. Secondly, the fiercest opposition to Bevan and to the Left generally came from the leaders of some of the largest unions who turned themselves into a knightly order for the defence of the political leadership of the Labour Party and, with the help of the block vote, ensured the regular defeat of the Left at T.U.C. and Labour Party Conferences. Their victories served to obscure the dimensions of the pressure of the trade union left for more radical policies. In fact, the orthodox trade union leaders never spoke for the whole trade union movement, just as there was always a substantial number of constituency parties who faithfully supported the Labour leadership against its critics on the Left.

In home affairs, the conflict in the Labour movement between Right and Left was soon focused on nationalization. As early as 1952, a resolution was moved at the T.U.C. which called upon the General Council to formulate proposals for 'the extension of social ownership to other industries and services, particularly those now subject to monopoly control', and for 'the democratization of the nationalized industries and services' so as to make possible 'the ultimate realization of full industrial democracy'.[3] The resolution was carried, against the wishes of the General Council, by 4,532,000 votes to 3,210,000.

At the 1952 Labour Party Conference a month later, the National Executive was faced with a similar demand that it should 'draw up a list of the key and major industries to be taken into public ownernship'.[4] Though the delegates were strongly warned against rashness by such speakers as Emmanuel Shinwell, Herbert Morrison, George Brown and Hugh Gaitskell, the Executive did not, after the vote at the T.U.C., offer outright opposition to the resolution, which was carried without a vote.

However, neither the General Council nor the National Executive had any intention of acting in the spirit of the respective resolutions with which they were saddled. Indeed, the manner in which both bodies dealt with the instructions they had received provided a good illustration of the fact that no such instructions, however imperative, could bind a leadership firmly determined to evade them. On this issue, both the General Council and the National Executive had plenty of room in which to manoeuvre, and to interpret their mandate in such a way as to nullify the expressed will of their Conferences.

The Interim Report on Public Ownership which the General Council presented to the T.U.C. in 1953 did not express opposition to further nationalization. On the contrary, it said that there was a 'clear case' for the complete public ownership of the water supply industry. Nor was there anything in the Report, as Sir Tom Williamson put it, 'which opposes or obstructs the approach to public ownership'.[5] All that the General Council asked was that the subject should be given the most careful reflection and study. Nothing, on the face of it, could have sounded more reasonable – indeed would have been more reasonable, had the plea for further study been inspired by a genuine wish to lay plans for a future nationalization programme of the kind envisaged in the 1952 T.U.C. resolution. But the majority of members of the General Council were not eager seekers for knowledge, the better to nationalize. They were opponents of further nationalization, who found it necessary to conceal their opposition behind pleas for thinking and planning. And, at the 1953 Conference, they won the day. A motion for the reference back of the Report was defeated, though no less than 2,640,000 votes were cast in favour of the motion.

The tactic of the General Council was also the tactic of the National Executive Committee of the Labour Party. The programme which it presented to the 1953 Annual Conference of the Party (*Challenge to Britain*) also displayed the passionate concern of its authors for further knowledge and research. It is unlikely that any document issued by any political party has ever proposed the setting up of as many committees of investigation and research as did *Challenge to Britain*; nor has any Party ever promised to set up more such committees if it was returned to office.

The document, James Griffiths, speaking for the Executive, told the delegates, reaffirmed 'that the general case for public ownership is overwhelming and remains a major objective and purpose of this great movement'. But when it came to concrete proposals, the Executive was rather less bold. A future Labour Government, it said, would restore to public ownership the steel industry, then in process of denationalization by the Conservatives; as for road transport, which the Government was also returning to private enterprise, Labour would take back into public ownership 'such road haulage units as are needed to provide a co-ordinated transport system'. Water supply would be nationalized; *where necessary*, the next Labour Government would take particular sections of the engineering industry into public ownership; it would also acquire, in the public interest, a number of the key machine tool firms; in regard to the aircraft industry, it would 'take powers to acquire any firm which falls down on the job'; for chemicals, a Labour Government would 'obtain from the industry itself such information and records as will enable it to determine the most appropriate sections to be acquired, and the most appropriate method of acquiring it'. And, more generally, 'where private enterprise fails to act in the public interest ... the state shall either build and operate new enterprises or acquire a controlling interest in existing enterprises or both'.[6]

It was in many ways extremely fortunate for the Labour leaders that the Conservative Government should have decided to denationalize steel and road transport. For however much they might be opposed to any serious extension of nationalization, these leaders could hardly do less than pledge themselves to the renationalization of either steel or road transport. This soon became the well-gnawed bone which the leadership regularly threw back to the hungry activists, as a token of the leadership's belief in public ownership. Together with the other proposals of *Challenge to Britain*, this at least partially blurred the fundamental division between the leadership and those in the Labour movement who believed that any talk of a socialist society must remain a feeble joke until a predominant part of the economy had come under public ownership.

As so often before in the history of the Labour Party, the Executive's programme, meagre though it was, served to neutralize the pressure from the Left. At the 1953 Conference, all attempts to strengthen the document were defeated with the help of the trade union block vote. Indeed, Arthur Deakin, who described the Plan for Engineering of the Confederation of Shipbuilding and Engineering Unions as 'just a mumbo-jumbo of meaningless words and phrases ... the worst abortion ever conceived in the mind of man', also warned the delegates 'not to drive us into the position of falling out and breaking with the Party on such an issue as this' (i.e. nationalization).[7] The threat was pure bluff. The fact that much of the opposition to *Challenge to Britain* had come from trade union delegates, and the vote at the T.U.C. a few weeks earlier, were sufficient proof that Arthur Deakin was not speaking for a united trade union movement. However, the endorsement of *Challenge to Britain*, which was to form the basis of Labour's next electoral programme, marked a major victory for the consolidators.

In opposing a bolder programme, these men had repeatedly invoked the prior need to improve the operation of the industries and services already national-ized – without ever indicating how they proposed to go about it. The advocates of further nationalization also wanted to improve the public sector, but insisted that so long as 'public ownership remained a marginal part of the economy, the full advantage of social ownership will be lost'.[8] And they also asked at the 1953 T.U.C. Annual Conference for 'greater participation in the management and control of nationalized industries of the workers employed in those industries'.[9] The resolution embodying this demand, which was moved by J. S. Campbell, the General Secretary of the National Union of Railwaymen, was opposed by the General Council, and was defeated.

A similar demand, also put forward by J. S. Campbell, was made at the An-nual Conference of the Labour Party a month later. The National Executive was also opposed to it. On its behalf. Harry Douglass, of the Iron and Steel Trades Confederation, explained that, as the resolution dealt 'specifically with workers' control – control by those employed in the industry', it was not acceptable.[10] The resolution was defeated by 4,658,000 votes to 1,488,000. On the other hand, the Executive had no objection to an innocuous resolution which said that a Labour Government, in conjunction with the Trade Union and Co-operative move-ments, would consider 'the formulation of proposals for closer association of workers and consumers with the management of publicly-owned industry and the supervision of privately-owned industry than at present exists'.[11] This was hardly likely to fire the imagination of those workers in the nationalized indus-tries who had told Arthur Deakin, as he reported to the Conference, that 'if you cannot get more out of this than we are getting at this time then on the next oc-casion we are going to vote Tory'. But the lesson Deakin drew from this was that the minds of trade unionists were not 'conditioned' to industrial democracy.[12]

Parallel to the demands in the Labour movement for the adoption by the Labour leadership of more radical policies at home, there was also pressure, much more insistent after 1951 than in the years of Labour's tenure of office, for different Labour policies in regard to foreign affairs and defence. The two main issues over which battle was joined between Right and Left were the size of the British rearmament programme, and the rearmament of Germany.

The Labour Government had left office committed to a programme of rearmament so unrealistic that the Conservatives themselves had found it necessary to begin reducing it. Former Labour Ministers were in a poor position to press for further reductions even if they had wished to do so. But a sizeable minority of the Parliamentary Party, and a considerable part of the Labour rank and file in the constituency parties and in the trade unions, felt no such inhibitions.

In March 1952, fifty-seven Labour Members (out of 295) defies the Whips and, instead of abstaining, as they were summoned to do, from voting on a Government motion asking for approval of the rearmament programme, voted against it.

At the 1952 T.U.C. Conference in September, the opponents of the leadership were badly defeated on the issue of rearmament mainly because of poor tactics; but at the Labour Party Conference a few weeks later, a resolution from the Shop, Distributive and Allied Workers' Union called for a 're-examination and reduction of the rearmament programme', and was only defeated by 3,644,000 votes to 2,228,000.

By 1953, it was German rearmament which had become the main issue of contention between Right and Left. At the Labour Party Conference of that year, the Executive itself presented a resolution urging 'that there should be no German rearmament before further efforts have been made to secure the peaceful reunification of Germany'. This was carried 'almost unanimously'. By February 1954, the Labour leaders decided that further efforts had been made, and justified them in now supporting German rearmament. Both the National Executive and the Parliamentary Party agreed, by slender majorities. When the T.U.C. met in September 1954, the French Parliament had just rejected German rearmament as part of the European Defence Community. Undeterred, the General Council put forward an emergency resolution which reaffirmed support for German rearmament. This was carried, but only by 4,077,000 votes to 3,622,000. With so narrow a majority at the T.U.C., it seemed very likely that, with the larger part of the constituency vote added to that of the trade union opposition, official policy would be defeated at the Labour Party Conference. And so it would have been, had not the delegation of the Amalgamated Society of Woodworkers switched, despite the mandate from its own Conference, from opposition to support of the platform, thus ensuring the latter's victory, by 3,270,000 votes to 3,022,000.

Throughout these controversies, on home and foreign policy, the limelight was held by the Bevanite parliamentarians, and particularly by Aneurin Bevan himself. These were the years in which Bevan was constantly and bitterly denounced, by his opponents in the Labour movement as well as by his opponents outside, as an unprincipled demagogue, whose sole impulse was personal power. At the same time, the assumption was easily made that 'Bevanism' was Bevan's own creation and that the really important battle was being fought in the Parliamentary Party and in the upper reaches of the Labour hierarchy. Both notions were false. Bevan did not create Bevanism: as a refusal on the part of a substantial minority of Labour's rank and file to endorse the leadership's drift of policy and as an affirmation of the need for different policies, it had existed in the Labour Party and in the trade unions long before Bevan gave it his name and his gifts; and it endured, and grew in strength, after he ceased to give expression to it. As for parliamentary Bevanism, its challenge to the leadership was crippled by inhibitions which made it, for all the interest it attracted, a great deal less significant than the opposition of the rank and file. This is worth examining a little more closely.

When fifty-seven Labour MPs defied the Party Whips in March 1952, there were powerful voices, notably that of Arthur Deakin, to press for their expulsion from the Parliamentary Labour Party. There were others to urge conciliation. It was this counsel which prevailed and the parliamentary leaders were content to place a veto on further rebellions by reimposing the Parliamentary Party's Standing Orders, suspended since 1945. This meant that only those MPs who could plausibly plead scruples of conscience would be allowed to abstain from voting in support of party policy, but that everyone who could not invoke a narrowly interpreted 'conscience clause' would have to fall into line with official policy. And since those who opposed official policy were only a relatively small minority of the Parliamentary Party, this meant obedience to policies with which they disagreed, failing which there would be the threat of expulsion from the Parliamentary Party, and from the Labour Party itself. To clinch matters, a resolution, clearly-directed at the Bevanite group, was moved by Attlee in the Parliamentary Party after the 1952 Labour Party Conference, banning all unofficial groups within the Party and demanding an end to all 'personal attacks'. This was approved by 188 votes to 51, and it meant the end of what degree of organized opposition there had been within the Parliamentary Party. Semi-organized activity did not altogether cease, but it never was very effective. As a parliamentary force, Bevanism had, by the end of 1952, been decisively checked.

This was somewhat masked by the success in 1952 of Bevanite candidates in the election to the constituency seats of the National Executive. In 1951, Aneurin Bevan, Barbara Castle, Tom Driberg and Ian Mikardo had shared these seven seats with Jame Griffiths, Herbert Morrison and Hugh Dalton. In 1952, Morrison aand Dalton were eliminated in favour of Harold Wilson and Richard Crossman.[13] Of the Old Guard, only James Griffiths managed to hold on, and the six Bevanites were again elected in 1953 and 1954.

To the Labour Left, this seemed a success of the first magnitude. This was a mistake. For the first result of the Bevanites' success was to impose upon the victors an acceptance of policies which they had no chance whatever of affecting in any significant way.

The Bevanite members of the National Executive might have found the constrictions of collective responsibility more difficult to bear had it not been for their belief that, by being members of the Executive, they would be able to make a difference to Labour's programme and policies. In fact, their membership of the Executive only made it more difficult for the Bevanites to give effective direction to the struggle against the Right. But their willingness, indeed their eagerness, to suffer the burdens of collective responsibility is not only to be explained in terms of an overestimation of how much could be achieved by a small minority of dissidents on a body like the National Executive. It also owed much to their high propensity to compromise. Though uneasy with the Labour Party's drift, they seldom found it possible (and where possible often did not find it politically desirable) to articulate their unease into clear alternatives. Thus, in the great controversy on the rearmament of Federal Germany, the leading Bevanites were severely limited by their reluctance to question the basic assumptions of Labour's foreign policy, of which the rearmament of Germany was a logical outcome. As for common ownership, they were ready enough to insist that there should be more of it. What they seemed unable to do was to offer an alternative analysis to the narrow Fabian view of its necessity and purpose. In other words, many of the political ambiguities of parliamentary Bevanism were but reflection of its ideological ambiguities. Throughout, parliamentary Bevanism was a mediation between the leadership and the rank and file opposition. The parliamentary Bevanites, while assuming the leadership of that opposition, also served to blur and to blunt both its strength and its extent. Themselves limited by their parliamentary and executive obligations, they fell back on the politics of manoeuvre, and were regularly out-manoeuvered in the process.

Bevan himself bore a double burden of responsibility without power. In addition to being a member of the National Executive, he was also elected to the Shadow Cabinet in November 1952, and was re-elected to it in 1953 and 1954. After two years of ineffectual opposition in the Executive and the Parliamentary Committee, Bevan finally resigned from the latter body in April 1954. However the circumstances of his resignation robbed it of much of its effectiveness. On the 13th of April, Attlee, speaking for the opposition, had given a qualified welcome to the Government's announcement that the establishment of a Treaty Organization similar to NATO was being considered for South East Asia. Bevan for his part, condemned the proposal, and thus appeared to disavow his Leader. Rebuked in the Parliamentary Committee, threatened with rebuke in the Parliamentary Party, Bevan, without consultation of any of his associates, chose to resign his membership of the Committee. Harold Wilson, who had been the runner-up in the 1953 election to the Shadow Cabinet, thus gained automatic admission to that body. But his acceptance of the vacant seat entailed a scarcely veiled disavowal of Bevan's action and completed the disintegration of a group whose inner cohesion had always been minimal.

However, Bevan's disengagement from official responsibilities was only partial. In June, he announced that, rather than gain easy re-election to the National

Executive in October as a representative of the constituency parties, he would be a candidate for the Treasuryship of the Party, for which post Hugh Gaitskell, with the strong backing of the most powerful trade union leaders, was already in the field. But Bevan remained a member of the National Executive until the 1954 Conference was over. As a result, Conference was treated to the unedifying spectacle of the leading Labour opponent of German rearmament remaining silent, as did the other Bevanite members of the Executive, in the debate which decided the issue. And when the Paris Treaties, incorporating German rearmament, were presented to the House of Commons in November 1954, six Labour MPs defied the parliament leadership's decision that the Party should abstain from voting, and challenged a division, thus ensuring that the Treaties would not be approved by the House without any opposition being recorded against them. The six (and a seventh Labour Member, Mr McGovern, who voted with the Government) were promptly expelled from the Parliamentary Party, but readmitted some months later.

After his expected defeat for the Treasuryship[14], Bevan announced that he would henceforth campaign among the rank and file trade unionists and seek their help in the defeat of the right wing trade union leaders. The announcement came three years too late. The time to have made it was 1951, if indeed not earlier. Nor, by October 1954, was there much in the project to cause any worry to those whom Bevan now belatedly challenged.

There was one final flicker of dissent within the Parliamentary Party before the General Election of 1955. In March of that year, the Government announced that it had decided to manufacture the hydrogen bomb. In its amendment to the Government's motion asking for the approval of the House of Commons for the Defence White Paper, the Labour Party approved the decision, while criticizing the deficiencies of the Services after a three-year expenditure of some £4,000,000,000. Despite a three-line Whip, sixty-two Labour Members, invoking the conscience clause, abstained from voting for the Party's amendment.

This opposition was too large to be disciplined. But Bevan's enemies (some of whom were by then little short of paranoid about him) thought that it might yet be possible to expel him from the Parliamentary Party, and from the Labour Party itself. In the course of the debate, Bevan had asked the Government whether it was contemplated that nuclear weapons should be used against an attack with 'conventional' weapons. But he had not only asked the question of the Government. He had also challenged Attlee to make Labour's position clear. On the ground that the embarrassment Bevan had caused Attlee was only the latest of numerous breaches of discipline, the Parliamentary Party agreed (by 142 votes to 112) to Bevan's expulsion from it. It only remained for a majority to be found on the National Executive to expel him from the Labour Party itself. Such a majority might well have been found had it not been for the storm of rank and file protest which the threat evoked, and had not a General Election been in the offing.

At the General Election of May 1955, the Conservatives, though they polled some 400,000 votes less than in 1951, increased their parliamentary majority from seventeen to fifty-eight. The percentage of votes cast for the Conservatives rose from 48 per cent in 1951 to 49.7 per cent in 1955. Labour's vote, on the other hand, showed a sharp decrease of some one and a half million, while its percentage of votes cast fell from 48.8 per cent to 46.4 per cent.

Labour's election manifesto, *Forward with Labour,* had marked a retreat even from the nationalization proposals of *Challenge to Britain.* Save for the inevitable inclusion of the renationalization of steel and road haulage, the manifesto only promised that 'sections of the chemical and machine tools industries' would be brought under public ownership; and, 'where necessary', a Labour Government would 'start new public enterprises'. These proposals gave Labour the worst of both worlds. They could not be presented (and the Labour leaders had in any case no wish to present them) as forming part of a thought-out socialist programme: and this, ironically, made it easier for the Conservatives to denounce them either as a token of Labour's 'doctrinaire' clinging to outworn dogma, or as the product of an uneasy compromise between Right and Left. But neither did these proposals arouse any enthusiasm among Labour activists, or much interest in the electorate at large. The same was true for the rest of Labour's proposals. These were apposite enough for a mildly reforming party,[15] but scarcely sufficient to bring the election to life.

As for foreign policy and defence, it was the H-bomb, *Forward with Labour* said, which 'loomed over mankind'. The Labour Party, it also said, would not approach the problem in a 'party spirit'. In fact, it did not approach the problem at all, save for suggesting that Britain should propose to Russia and the United States the immediate cessation of H-bomb tests.

Labour's main problem, from a purely electoral point of view, was that four years of Tory Government had not produced the catastrophies which had been confidently prophesied in 1951. The Government had brought rationing to an end, full employment had been maintained, the target of 300,000 houses a year had been reached and surpassed, the welfare services had not been dismantled, the Government had nursed with particular care its relations with the trade union leaders,[16] and there was very little in the Government's handling of foreign affairs to which the Labour Party, in the light of its own foreign policies, could have plausibly objected.[17] There was a powerful Socialist case to be made against the Conservatives, but it was not a case the Labour leaders were willing to make, or indeed would by then have known how to make.

It was to Labour's failure to put forward a bold socialist programme that the Left readily attributed electoral defeat. But there was little evidence to suggest that such a programme would have attracted greater support if it had been presented in 1955. The point has been made before: a socialist programme could only have enhanced the Labour Party's chances if it had been put forward, and fought for, in Parliament and outside, from 1951 onwards, and if all the resources and energies of the Party and the trade unions had been used to make it known and understood. As it is, the election of 1955 was the quietest of .the century. It was also the first election since 1918, save for the special circumstances of 1931, in which the Labour vote fell below the total recorded at the previous election.

2. PARALYSIS AS IDEOLOGY

The leaders of the Labour Party were even less prepared after 1955 than they had been after 1951 to listen to pleas from the Labour Left for the adoption of more radical policies – nor indeed was that Labour Left itself able to present either a clear diagnosis of the Party's troubles or a solidly-based argument for such policies as it wanted to see adopted. In consequence, there was ready agreement with the Executive that, as James Griffiths told the 1955 Conference, the Labour Party should 'go back to the classroom'. Over the next three years, he promised the delegates, a whole series of policy reports would be prepared, ranging from Equality and the Ownership of Industry to Agriculture and The Individual and Society. In addition, there would also be an investigation of the shortcomings of Labour's electoral machine.

The proposal that the Executive should engage in a prolonged 're-thinking' exercise, at the end of which the Labour Party would be equipped with brand new policies, had a wide appeal. But it was easily overlooked that the 're-thinking' would be directed by men who believed that it must also involve a great deal of 'de-thinking', particularly in relation to common ownership: the result of the exercise might be to provide the Labour Party with new policies, but the policies would reflect a further dilution of the Party's aims. What made this certain beyond any doubt was the election of Hugh Gaitskell to the leadership of the Party in December 1955.

By the time Attlee finally decided to resign, the only two likely contenders besides Gaitskell were hardly in the race at all. Herbert Morrison's star had long ceased to twinkle, and Bevan was wholly unacceptable both to powerful trade union leaders and to the vast majority of the Parliamentary Party. Hugh Gaitskell, on the other hand, had long enjoyed the support of the former and was also, *faute de mieux*, acceptable to the latter. So clear was his lead on the eve of the election that some of those who opposed him persuaded Bevan to withdraw in favour of Morrison if Gaitskell would do likewise. The latter refused and, was duly elected, by 157 votes to 70 for Bevan and 40 for Morrison.

Though the Labour Party's shift to the right had begun long before Hugh Gaitskell assumed the leadership, his election both accentuated the shift and helped to give it a much sharper ideological and political articulation.

An older generation of Labour leaders had always set very definite limits, in their programmes and policies, to Labour's socialism. But they had also held out to their followers the promise that accommodation with capitalism was a temporary halt, however prolonged, on the journey to the Socialist Common-wealth. And, cautious though they might be about common ownership, they had not been disposed to argue that it could be divorced from any meaningful interpretation of socialism. In outward form at least, their quarrel with the Left had thus appeared as a quarrel about the pace of advance, not about the ultimate desirability of advance itself.

In contrast, a new revisionism, to which the new Leader was ideologically and politically committed, claimed not only that nationalization was an electoral li-ability to the Labour Party, but that in a 'post-capitalist' society, it had actually come to be largely irrelevant.[18]

In political terms, there was much in revisionism which helped to obscure the retreat it signified even from that Labourism with which the Labour Party had made do since it had come into existence. There was the amplitude of its egalitarian rhetoric; and also the willingness of the revisionists to concede, in-deed to insist, that the frontiers of public ownership had not been finally drawn up: there would be cases where an industry or firm, having 'failed the nation', might be considered ripe for nationalization, or some diluted form of it.[19] But, whatever element of confusion these qualifications introduced in the debate on nationalization, they did not affect the essential difference between Right and Left, namely that the former envisaged as permanent an economic system in which the 'private sector' was to retain by far the dominant share of economic power, while the latter wanted precisely the opposite.

Just as Ramsay MacDonald had conceived it as one of his main tasks to edu-cate the Labour movement into the conventions and niceties of the parliamen-tary system, so did Hugh Gaitskell consider it one of his main tasks to educate it into a final acceptance of the 'mixed economy'. An important, though still intermediate stage in this process of education, was reached with the publica-tion in 1957 of *Industry and Society*, one of the 're-thinking' policy reports on the future of public ownership. Steel and long-distance road haulage, said that document, would be renationalized by the next Labour Government. 'Beyond that,' it went on, 'we reserve the right to extend public ownership in any industry or part of industry which, after thorough enquiry, is found to be seriously failing the nation.' Meanwhile, *Industry and Society* also proposed that 'the community (should) acquire a stake in the expansion of industry' through the acquisition of shares by the State. But such acquisition, it was made clear, 'will be guided solely by investment considerations and will not be aimed at securing control'.[20]

No one outside the Labour movement had the least doubt that the adoption of *Industry and Society* would constitute a major retreat from public ownership, and that the document owed its main inspiration to the Leader of the Labour Party. Nor was there much doubt on the Left as to the tendencies it represented.[21] On the other hand, the erstwhile Bevanite leaders of the Labour Left did not choose to challenge the new programme.[22] Instead, some of them argued that, provided it was properly interpreted, a bold nationalization programme could be extracted from it. Even if this had been true, the argument failed to take into account the fact that the interpretation of the document, when it came to the point, would not be left to those who wanted an extension of public ownership, but to those who did not.

It is notable that some of the most vigorous opposition to the spirit and to the practical proposals of *Industry and Society* came from within the trade unions. At the 1957 Labour Party Conference, it was a trade union leader, J. S. Campbell, who issued the clearest challenge to the Executive with a resolution affirming 'belief in the common ownership of all the basic industries and means of production', and deploring 'the present tendency to deviate from these accepted principles'. And the resolution also proposed the reference back of *Industry and Society* 'in order that a clear, unambiguous policy document can be prepared and issued indicating the industries to be brought under public ownership by the next Labour Government'. Another resolution, from the Hornsey Constituency Labour Party, took a leaf from the document and, while asking the Conference to reaffirm its belief in nationalization, also proposed that a Labour Government should, as a first step, 'seek to transfer to public ownership all the shares of a substantial number of the companies whose assets exceed £21 million'.[23]

In reply to the debate, Hugh Gaitskell assured the delegates that he and the Executive believed in equality, social justice, co-operation, accountability, and planning for full employment; and that, 'through public ownership and control we can achieve higher productivity'. But a future Labour Government, he reminded the delegates, was already committed to the renationalization of steel and road haulage, to a 'huge expansion of public ownership' in housing, to the repeal and replacement of the Rent Act, and to a new plan for superannuation. 'Believe me,' said the Leader, 'in these measures alone, together with all the other minor pieces of legislation, we have certainly more than enough to occupy the first two or three years of any Labour Government.'

'Those who wield the weapons of economic power, wherever they may be,' the Leader further told the delegates, 'should be accountable to the community for their actions.' It was therefore intended that, 'in order to plan this economy properly', the Government should know 'all we can about investment intentions', that it should have 'a fair degree of control over investment by private firms', that the latter, should present their accounts as did the nationalized industries, and that they should be prevented from avoiding taxation 'in various ways'. And there was also 'a strong case', the Leader believed, 'for laying down a code of conduct which these large firms must observe'.

In the light of these rather modest proposals, it was entirely appropriate that the Leader, notwithstanding his ardent commendation of Government share buying in industry, should have categorically rejected the Hornsey resolution. 'It commits us as a first step,' he said, 'to transfer to public ownership all the shares of a substantial number of companies. Frankly, I am not prepared to accept that. I think probably it is very much more important that we should renationalize steel and road haulage as a first step and I have already said we must have inquiries before we go further in that direction.'

Finally, there was the electorate to be considered, and particularly the 'so called marginal voters', who were not convinced socialists, but 'ordinary decent people who do not probably think a great deal about politics', and who would want to know the specific reasons for nationalizing any particular industry. The Executive, Gaitskell said, could have come to the Conference and presented a document with a long list of further industries to be nationalized without a new idea, and, 'very probably', this would have been received with acclamation. They had not done so 'because if we had done so we would have been putting something to you which in our hearts we did not believe we could carry out ... which in our hearts we believed the electorate was bound to reject ... we do not believe in that sort of leadership; we believe in leadership which is clear-eyed and clear-headed, which does not flinch from making the Party and the Movement face the facts of the day, both the economic and the political facts'.[24]

The Executive easily carried the day. *Industry and Society* was endorsed by 5,309,000 votes to 1,276,000. Support for the document was a great deal less enthusiastic than was suggested by these figures.[25] That it was carried by so large a majority was in fact due to a number of reasons which had little to do with the merits of the argument.

There were, in 1957, few people in the Labour movement who, did not believe that the sharp decline in Conservative fortunes after the fiasco of the Suez expedition would result in the return of a Labour Government at the next General Election. And the more likely a Labour victory seemed, the greater grew the desire to present the Labour Party as a united party, and the greater too the authority of its Leader – not least with potential members of his administration. By 1957, most leading members of the extinct Bevanite group had edged steadily closer to Hugh Gaitskell, and none closer, to all appearances, than Bevan himself.

Bevan's reconciliation with the Leader of the Party, and with many of his former enemies in the trade unions as well, had begun soon after his defeat for the leadership in December 1955. In October 1956, he had been elected Treasurer of the Party and had thus rejoined the National Executive as an ex-officio member. He was also re-elected to the Parliamentary Committee in November and was then appointed 'Shadow' Foreign Secretary by the Leader. It is in that capacity that he replied for the Executive at the 1957 Labour Party Conference to a debate on a composite resolution which asked the Conference to pledge that 'the next Labour Government will take the lead by itself refusing to continue to test, manufacture or use nuclear weapons, and that it will appeal to peoples of other countries to follow their lead'[26]

What is now remembered about that speech is Bevan's description of unilateralism as an 'emotional spasm' which would send a British Foreign Secretary 'naked into the Conference Chamber'. However, there was much else of interest in what he said.

'You may decide in this country unilaterally,' said Bevan, 'that you will have nothing to do with experiments, nor with manufacture, nor with use. With none of these sentiments do I disagree, none of them at all.' But this would mean, he told the delegates, 'that all the international commitments, all the international arrangements, all the international facilities afforded to your friends and allies must be immediately destroyed . . . The main difficulty we are in here is that in this way we shall precipitate a difficult situation with the nations that are now associated with us in a variety of treaties and alliances, most of which I do not like – I would like to substitute for them other treaties more sensible and more civilized and not chaos and a shambles. If any Socialist Foreign Secretary is to have a chance he must be permitted to substitute good policies for bad policies.'[27]

Despite its rejection of unilateralism, this was not an argument based on the proposition that the Labour Party was irrevocably committed to existing treaties and alliances, 'most of which I do not like'. Indeed, said Bevan, the purpose of a Socialist Foreign Secretary would be to prevent 'that deadly negative polarization that we have been fighting for years' and to interpose 'between those two giants (i.e. the United States and the U.S.S.R.) modifying, moderating and mitigating influences.' [28]

Whether Bevan was right or wrong in insisting that the possession by Britain of nuclear weapons was essential to a Socialist Foreign Secretary's purposes is not here the point. The argument had in any case become irrelevant three years later, when a Conservative Government had to admit that Britain would not, before many years had passed, have an independent nuclear deterrent at all. More important in this context is that, in his wish to inject a degree of flexibility in the foreign policy of a Labour Government, Bevan would have soon found himself at odds with many of his colleagues. For they, and most particularly the Leader of the Party, had none of Bevan's reservations about the treaties and alliances in which British foreign policy was enmeshed.

For the time being, however, these differences were entirely overshadowed by Bevan's support for the Executive and for the Leader of the Party. With his speech at the 1957 Conference, Bevan unambiguously removed himself from the leadership of the Labour Left and appeared to accept as final his position as Hugh Gaitskell's second in command. And with the massive endorsement by the 1957 Conference of *Industry and Society*, and the equally massive rejection of unilateralism, the Right seemed more firmly entrenched than ever, with a Leader of its own persuasion in unchallenged command of the Labour Party. All that was now required was for the Labour Party to seize the initiative from the Government.

Here, however, was the rub. For the initiative was not to be seized without far greater exertions than the Labour Party's policies and political attitudes made possible. This had already been demonstrated on the issue of Suez, and it was to be demonstrated again in the following years.

Though the Labour Party had failed to acquire clear and distinctive policies in regard to the Middle East from the time it left office in 1951, it did at least express opposition to the Government's actual resort to force in Egypt. On the 1st of November, 1956, a special meeting of the National Council of Labour had declared itself 'profoundly shocked' by the British Government's attack on Egypt and had called upon the Government 'forthwith to cease all military measures' against that country. The Council also decided to organize public meetings on the theme 'Law-Not War', but set a definite limit to its opposition by calling 'upon the British people to bring effective pressure to bear' on the Government 'through normal constitutional parliamentary methods' and 'to refrain from taking industrial action as a means of influencing national policy in the present crisis'.[29] British military operations did in fact come to an end within the next few days. No one, however, has so far seriously claimed that the Labour Party's opposition had much to do with this outcome.

Nor did the Opposition behave, after Suez, as if it really believed that the Government's conduct of affairs had robbed it of its title to govern, and that it must, at the least, seek a fresh mandate. Sir Anthony Eden's successor was as deeply implicated in the Suez venture as Sir Anthony himself, and so was the rest of Mr Macmillan's Government. Yet Labour's campaign came to an end as abrupt as the Government's military operations, and Labour pressure upon the Government soon subsided altogether. It is difficult to believe that a Conservative Opposition, in similar circumstances, would have been so obliging to a Labour administration.

The same pattern was repeated in every other field of policy. It was in fact the Conservatives who went on the offensive in the following two and a half years. Between June 1957 and September 1959, the Conservative Party spent £468,000 in a public relations campaign which, it has been observed, 'was altogether new to British politics',[30] while a variety of business interests sent an additional £1,435,000 between June 1958 and September 1959 in anti-nationalization campaigns.[31]

The most notable fact about these campaigns is not that they were undertaken, but that they largely went unanswered. It was inevitable that they should be left unanswered, since the Labour leaders were precluded by their own ideological predispositions from countering attacks on nationalization with arguments for it. Indeed, *Industry and Society* had itself conceded much of its case to private industry. 'The Labour Party recognizes,' it said, 'that, under increasingly professional managements, large firms are as a whole serving the nation well' and that 'no organization, public or private, can operate effectively if it is subjected to persistent and detailed interventions from above. We have therefore no intention of intervening in the management' of any firm which is doing a good job'.[32] It would have been unreasonable to expect the steel industry not to claim that these commendations applied to it as much as to other firms, and equally unreasonable to expect the Labour Party to put forward a convincing argument, on the basis of the narrow criteria it used, for making a special case of that industry: after all, it is not very likely that the nationalization of steel would have been an item of Labour's programme in the late fifties had steel not already once been nationalized.

It was not only a fundamental disbelief in the general case for common ownership which prevented the Labour leaders from countering Conservative propaganda. There was also the fear of the electorate, over this and most other issues. By the late fifties, the Labour leaders, obsessed as they were with the thought of electoral success, had come to be more convinced even than were their predecessors that the essential condition for that success was to present the Labour Party as a moderate and respectable party, free from class bias, 'national' in outlook, and whose zeal for reform would always be tempered by its eager endorsement of the maxim that Rome was not built in a day – or even in a century. Never indeed had Labour leaders been so haunted by a composite image of the potential Labour voter as quintessentially petit-bourgeois, and therefore liable to be frightened off by a radical alternative to Conservatism. But the paradox of this view was that it was both self-confirming and self-defeating: self-confirming in the sense that, the more the Labour Party geared its policies to suit those whom Hugh Gaitskell had described as 'ordinary decent people who do not probably think a great deal about politics', the less interest were they likely to show in the Labour Party; and self-defeating in the sense that the less interest they showed in the Labour Party, the less likely were its leaders to be electorally successful.

The late fifties were of course years of boom, in which a more prosperous population was invited to join in the apotheosis of 'free enterprise' and forget the deep economic, social and moral ills of a society sick with the impulse to private appropriation. The final impact on the electorate of Conservative claims that 'Conservative freedom works' is a matter of conjecture. But its impact on the Labour leaders is not. Well before the General Election of 1959, they had assumed a defensive, almost a plaintive, posture, and had repeatedly felt it necessary to minimize the threat Labour might pose to Conservative freedom.[33] They had no option but to propose the renationalization of steel and long distance road haulage. But only 'where an industry is shown, after thorough inquiry, to be failing the nation', said their 1959 electoral manifesto, did Labour 'reserve the right to take all or any part of it under public ownership if this is necessary'. And in the General Election itself, Mr Butler and Mr Rose have noted, the Labour Party, 'as in all recent elections ... played down any claim to stand, as a socialist party, for a radically different form of society ... it asked the voters to say that it could administer the mixed economy welfare state better than the Conservatives'.[34]

The adoption of *Industry and Society* by the 1957 Labour Party Conference had largely stilled the debate on nationalization within the Party. But the rejection of unilateralism by the same Conference had not ended the debate on foreign affairs and defence. In fact, the Labour leaders found themselves under increasing pressure in the following two years to depart from their rigid adherence to policies framed within the context of the Cold War. By the beginning of 1958, the Campaign for Nuclear Disarmament had been formed and the London to Aldermaston march at Easter had transformed unilateralism from an awkward word into something of a movement. It was a movement whose leaders (as distinct from many of its supporters) deliberately shunned some of the larger implications of unilateralism and sought to confine it to a purely moral protest against reliance on nuclear weapons. Nevertheless, the spread within the Labour movement of the unease the Campaign reflected was soon to pose a serious problem to the Labour leadership. In March 1958, the National Executive Committee of the Labour Party and the General Council of the T.U.C. made a first attempt to meet the problem.

In a joint document entitled *Disarmament and Nuclear War*, they now proposed that the British Government should 'at once suspend thermo-nuclear tests unilaterally for a limited period, in the hope that this will hasten permanent international agreement on tests and lead on to a general disarmament convention'. The statement also expressed support for an international declaration banning the use of all nuclear weapons, coupled with an agreement for the reduction of conventional arms and forces. As for the setting up of American missile bases in Britain, the document expressed the view 'not only that these bases must be effectively under British control, but also that no physical steps should be taken to set them up before a fresh attempt had been made to negotiate with the Soviet Government'. The British Government, it also said, had 'failed to show that it is necessary for British-based aircraft to carry nuclear weapons on either patrol or training flights'; these should therefore be 'limited forthwith to those necessary for the transport of weapon stocks'. Another statement, *Disengagement in Europe*, also proposed the 'gradual withdrawal under effective international control of foreign forces of all kinds from East and West Germany, Poland, Czechoslovakia and Hungary', and 'pending Summit talks', it also said, 'no steps should be taken towards the ultimate equipment of West

German forces with nuclear weapons'.

The retreat from previous policies which these cautious and mostly conditional proposals represented was more formal than real, save for the proposal for a unilateral ban by Britain on nuclear tests. Both statements avoided a direct answer to the question of what the Labour Party's policy would be, both in regard to the establishment of American missile bases in Britain and to the equipment of West German forces with nuclear weapons, if a Summit Conference produced no results. Nor did the statements indicate what a Labour Government would do if its allies rejected, as there could be no doubt they would reject, the proposals for disengagement in Europe. However, the answer was in fact quite clear: a Labour Government, whose proposals found no favour with its NATO allies, would not persist.[35] Nor could it have been otherwise, given the Labour Party's unqualified commitment to NATO. This gave the statements a somewhat academic air. What completed the effect was the announcement that the Labour Party and the T.U.C. had agreed to organize 'an educational campaign' on the subject of Disarmament and Nuclear War, 'consisting in the first instance of regional conferences within the Labour movement'. This rather suggested that the authors of the documents were at least as much concerned to wean the Labour movement away from dangerous thoughts as to influence the British Government on such issues as nuclear tests.

For the time being, the leadership's proposals served to suggest flexibility and movement. Though 102 of the 428 resolutions on the agenda for the Labour Party Conference in September 1958 asked for a unilateral renunciation of nuclear weapons by Britain, a composite resolution to the same effect was overwhelmingly defeated. Another resolution, calling upon the Parliamentary Labour Party 'to oppose under any circumstances the establishment of rocket missile bases in Britain' had a similar fate, after Hugh Gaitskell had told the Conference that it went 'too far in the direction of complete unilateral action'.

No more than the unilateralist defeat in 1957 did these Executive victories settle the issue. Not only was the second Aldermaston march at Easter 1959 a very much more substantial demonstration than the first; far more dangerous to the leadership was the growing opposition to official policy in the trade union movement. It was more than an accident that the National Union of General and Municipal Workers, hitherto one of the staunchest pillars of orthodoxy, should have actually passed a resolution in June 1959 (by 150 votes to 126, with 75 delegates not voting) asking that 'the next Labour Government should take unilateral action in ceasing to manufacture nuclear weapons and in prohibiting the use of all such weapons from British territories'.[36]

Nor was it fortuitous that the National Executive and the General Council should have put forward soon afterwards the proposal for the creation of a 'non-nuclear club', provided that an agreement could be reached with every country except the U.S.A. and the U.S.S.R. not to test, manufacture or possess nuclear weapons. In launching such an endeavour, the Labour Party-T.U.C. statement was careful to point out, 'we should in no way be weakening in our support for the NATO alliance or in our readiness to accept American bases in Britain subject to the veto which already exists concerning their possible use'. Furthermore, the agreement would also be subject, the statement said, 'to full and effective international control to ensure that it was carried out'.[37]

The 'non-nuclear club' sank without a trace after the General Election of October 1959, nor did it even figure prominently in Labour's campaign during the Election. Its only use was to provide a chance for the leaders of the National Union of Municipal and General Workers to recall their Conference and seek to reverse its unilateralist vote. At that recalled Conference, which met at the end of August 1959, the delegates were presented with a resolution from their Executive endorsing the Labour Party-T.U.C. statement, no amendment or alternative resolution being allowed. The Executive had its way: 194 votes were cast for the statement, 139 against. When the T.U.C. met in September, it had been announced that there would be an election in October, and the official policy was adopted by 5,214,000 votes to 2,690,000. However, the Conference also passed, against the advice of the General Council, a resolution protesting against the decision of the British Government to provide sites for the launching of United States ballistic missiles. The vote was 4,040,000, to 3,865,000.

None of these differences was allowed to appear in the Labour Party's election programme. The Party's campaign committee had concluded, Mr Butler and Mr Rose write, that 'it (the public) would be more swayed by a recital of the muddle in British defence policy than by an examination of the power-politics assumptions underlying British reliance upon NATO or the nuclear deterrent'.[38] As in the three previous General Elections, the Labour leadership, given its home as well as its foreign policy, had no choice but to trivialize the electoral debate and to help degrade the democratic process the Election was supposed to illustrate. In the end, after all the rethinking, the pamphlets, the statements and the debates of the previous four years, the proposal which most clearly emerged as the Labour Party's main contribution to the electoral campaign was the promise that a Labour Government would immediately raise the old-age pension by 10s. a week, coupled with a pledge by Hugh Gaitskell in the middle of the campaign that there would be 'no increase in the standard or other rates of income tax so long as normal peace-time conditions continue'.

The Labour Party had also set much store by its proposal for a comprehensive national superannuation scheme, and Labour candidates devoted much time and effort in explaining to their audiences the advantages that would accrue to them under the scheme once they had reached the pensionable age. Somehow, this failed to rouse great enthusiasm.

No sooner had the results been declared than a loud chorus of revisionist voices rose to proclaim that the Labour Party had lost the Election because of its attachment to nationalization. And indeed, it may well be that Labour's half-hearted presentation of a case in which most of its leaders did not believe lost the Labour Party some votes. But the revisionist interpretation of defeat was as arbitrary as would have been the claim, had Labour won, that its victory represented a vote for nationalization, let alone socialism. By 1959, Labour's image was much too blurred to give either defeat or victory so precise a political or ideological meaning. In 1951, 20 per cent of people, according to the Gallup Poll, had thought that it mattered little or not at all which party was in power; by the summer of 1959, the number had grown to 38 per cent. Indeed, of Labour's supporters, only 60 per cent recognized major differences between the parties.[39]

In fact, it was the 60 per cent who were right. In the kind of people whose vote they mainly attracted, in the reasons for the attraction, in the traditions they embodied, most of all in the aspirations of their respective activists, profound differences continued to divide the Labour Party from the Conservative Party. Nor could these differences have failed to find some reflection in a Labour Government's attitude to such matters as social welfare. At the same time, it was also entirely reasonable to believe that a Labour victory in 1959 would not have produced any substantial alteration in the shape of affairs at home, or in Britain's role abroad.

3. THE BATTLE FOR THE LABOUR PARTY

The battles which broke out in the Labour Party after the General Election of 1959 were not only about nationalization or nuclear strategy. These were the specific expressions of a more basic question, namely whether the Labour Party is to be concerned with attempts at a more efficient and more humane administration of a capitalist society; or whether it is to adapt itself to the task of creating a socialist one.

The question is as old as the Labour Party itself. But until the fifties, it was a question which could be evaded with a Labourist programme of social reform and the public ownership of basic utilities and services. It was after the fulfillment of that programme in the years of Labour's New Deal that Labourism revealed itself altogether inadequate as a basis of policy and action, and that it became increasingly difficult to evade the question of Labour's ultimate purposes.

Because of the inadequacies of Labourism, there is at least logic both in revisionist demands for the Labour Party's retreat, in practice if not rhetoric, from Labourism to a suitably contemporary version of Liberalism; and also in the demands of the Left for socialist alternatives to Conservatism, both in home and foreign affairs.

However, revisionist Right and 'fundamentalist' Left are not the only parties in the debate: there is also the Centre, whose main purpose is to keep the Labour Party within the bounds of Labourism, and whose main attribute is the invention of 'formulas' that might be all things to all men.

In a party like the Labour Party, and in an electoral system which greatly discourages political fission, appeals for unity through compromise are always likely to meet with much support, and to appear as the epitome of commonsense and political wisdom. At the same time, such appeals overlook the fact that genuine compromise between revisionism on the one hand, and socialist purposes on the other, is impossible; and that any verbal compromise which may be reached on the basis of ingenious formulas, not only perpetuates the paralysis of the last decade, but also ensures, in practice, the predominance of the policies favoured by a revisionist leadership.

Thus a compromise was reached in the controversy which Hugh Gaitskell initiated after the Election of 1959 with his proposal that Clause 4 of the ,Party Constitution should be revised. In face of the violent resistance this encountered, the proposal had to be dropped, but the 1960 Party Conference was also asked to accept, as a 'valuable expression of the aims of the Labour Party in the second half of the twentieth century', a lengthy statement of aims which was said to 're-affirm, amplify and clarify' the Labour Party's objects'. The statement expressed the conviction that the Party's 'social and economic objectives can be achieved only through an expansion of common ownership substantial enough to give the community power over the commanding heights of the economy'; and 'recognizing that both public and private enterprise have a place in the economy it believes that further extension of common ownership should be decided from time to time in the light of these objectives and according to circumstances, with due regard for the views of the workers and consumers concerned' [40]

The 1960 Conference agreed to this. But it is surely naive to think that these formulations provide the basis of genuine compromise between people who fundamentally disagree on the purpose, nature and extent of common ownership. All that such a compromise can do is to provide a temporary lull in a battle to be resumed so soon as actual programmes and policies come to be discussed. Yet, it is not the fact that a battle between Right and Left broke out in the Labour Party after 1959 which is remarkable; that battle has gone on uninterruptedly since the Party was founded. Much more remarkable are its dimensions. Had the opposition to the leadership's policies and tendencies been confined to the traditional Left, in the constituencies and in the unions, the neo-Liberals would have had very little difficulty in imposing upon the Labour Party an explicitly revisionist image, such as has now been assumed by the German Social Democratic Party; and the Left would have been equally powerless to affect the Labour Party's approach to nuclear strategy and related questions. Indeed, there would then have been no Centre to emerge as a political factor: the Centre, such being its nature, would have readily submitted to the Right. What has made all the difference and introduced new dimensions into the conflict is the massive trade union intervention against the leadership.

There have been occasions in the past when the trade union movement has been at odds with the Party leadership over this or that particular issue – most notably in August 1931, when the unions refused to accept Ramsay MacDonald's view of what the national interest entailed. But never in the history of the Labour Party has there been serious disagreement with the unions on its fundamental aims and purpose. This is why the Party leaders, protected by the crushing power which the Constitution of the Party attributes to the unions, were always safe from the challenge of the Left. It is the withdrawal of that protection after 1959 which has created a problem of unprecedented magnitude for the Party leadership.

Unlike constituency or parliamentary rebellions, and unlike 'ginger groups' of the Left within the Party, trade union opposition cannot be crushed or threatened with expulsion. Nor can its wishes, when translated into majority decisions at T.U.C. and Labour Party Conferences, be easily ignored by the Parliamentary Labour Party. It can be induced, by manoeuvre, verbal juggling and appeals for unity, to accept artificial compromises, as was the case in the Clause 4 controversy. It may be pacified by apparent concessions on specific issues of policy. And division among the unions may even ensure the reversal of Conference decisions to which the Party leadership is opposed. But nothing of all this resolves the real problem, which is that a leadership whose purpose it is to reduce the Party's commitment to socialist policies can no longer rely on the trade unions to help it in achieving its aims.

It would be wrong to see this trade union opposition as an ideologically cohesive and politically homogeneous force. But it would be equally mistaken to underestimate the genuine and stubborn radicalism which it expresses. In this context, much of its significance derives not only from its extent but from its persistence. Had the trade unions been single-mindedly committed to a consolidating Labour leadership throughout the fifties, their opposition since 1959 might more plausibly be interpreted as a sudden eruption of bad temper following Labour's third consecutive electoral defeat. But recent history suggests, on the contrary, that this opposition is only the latest manifestation of powerful currents which have been running in the trade union movement for ten years and more and which have produced a consistent pressure for more radical Labour policies, notably for more, and more democratically controlled, nationalization, and for new Labour initiatives in international affairs. Electoral defeat only increased an impatience which had been manifesting itself over the previous years.

The apparent paradox is that this groundswell has been gathering strength precisely in the years of the 'affluent society', which was deemed to have ushered in the era of what C. Wright Mills has called the 'cheerful robot'. But the paradox is only apparent. For the contradiction which is so often assumed between 'affluence' and radicalism leaves much out of account. It leaves out of account the fact that the long years of slump and mass unemployment were not years of trade union militancy and radicalism, either in industrial or in political terms. It also leaves out of account the fact that the social and economic changes which have occurred in Britain since the war have not been such as to eradicate the fundamental conflict of interests which continues to divide wage earners from their employers. But most important of all, it overlooks the fact that trade unionists have behind them two decades of increased confidence in their own strength – of increased confidence generated by the experience of war, by the achievements of Labour's New Deal after the war, and by the maintenance of full employment after 1951. That confidence has not only found expression, often against the wishes of trade union leaders, in a far less defensive attitude towards employers; it has also led to the rejection of that grand reconciliation between the Labour movement and contemporary capitalism which is the essence of revisionism.

At the Labour Party Conference of November 1959, Hugh Gaitskell, vigorously rejected the notion that the Labour Party should break with the trade unions. 'I have always looked upon the Trade Union Congress and the Labour Party,' he said, 'as part of the same great Labour Movement – and our close integration as one of our great strengths. I see no reason to change my mind. I hope our trade union friends feel likewise.'[41] At the same time, however, the Leader also complained that, even though the Labour Party in the House of Commons was 'a far better cross-section of the community than the Tories who are still overwhelmingly drawn from a single social class', yet 'somehow we let the Tories get away with the monstrous falsehood that we are a Class Party and they are *not*. We must now surely attend to this'.[42]

The two statements epitomize the crucial dilemma of those who wish the Labour Party to renounce its so-called fundamentalist principles. For alliance with the trade unions is not only one of the Party's great strengths; it is by far its greatest strength. And attending to the 'monstrous falsehood' that the Labour Party is a class party can only be achieved in one of two ways: dissociation from the trade unions, which Mr Gaitskell excludes, or an even greater dilution of Labour policy, to which the trade unions themselves are opposed.

In fact, it is not a monstrous falsehood for the Tories to claim that the Labour Party is a class party, however false it may be for them to claim that their party is not. But the Labour Party is also a party whose leaders have always sought to escape from the implications of its class character by pursuing what they deemed to be 'national' policies: these policies have regularly turned to the detriment of the working classes and to the advantage of Conservatism. Nor can it be otherwise in a society whose essential characteristic remains class division.

One of the reasons why Labour leaders have always repudiated the class character of the Labour Party has been their fear that to admit the fact, and to act upon it, would antagonize 'floating voters'. So in many cases it no doubt has. And so indeed it should. But there is nothing to suggest that a multitude of men and women, who are not of the working classes, have in the past found the class character of the Labour Party a bar to their support for it, or that support for it would wane if its leaders were to adapt their policies to that fact. The reverse is more likely to be true. For while Labour leaders have felt that the 'affluent society' required more urgently than ever that their Party should appear 'classless', profound unease with that society has grown apace far outside trade union ranks. If trade union radicalism in recent years is a sign of this unease, the radicalism to be found in a new generation is surely another. While lamentations have been loud at the supposed political apathy of youth, a multitude of young men and women have found in the threat of nuclear war and a host of other issues a basis of commitment far transcending the orthodoxies of Labourism. It is only in comparison with the mythical thirties that the fifties, or at least the late fifties, have been years of political disengagement. The comparison with the real thirties is not to the detriment of these past years. The real difference is that the fifties have often appeared to lack the political instrumentalities of radical change. And to this impression, a consolidating Labour Party, revisionist in practice if not in theory, has greatly contributed. If politics in the fifties have seemed a decreasingly meaningful activity, void of substance, heedless of principle, and rich in election auctioneering, the responsibility is not only that of the hidden or overt persuaders: it is also, and to a major degree, that of Labour's leaders.

Even if a socialist Labour Party had not, in the fifties, won more elections than did the Labour Party as it was, it would not have found defeat catastrophic: armed with genuine alternatives to Conservatism, it would have been able to take the longer view, and seen its electoral defeats, not as the occasion for retreat, but as a spur to greater efforts in its task of political conversion. And whether it would have won an election or not, it would certainly have provided a very different opposition to the Government in power, arnd made conversion more likely because of the opposition it would have provided.

If the Labour Party were to become such a party, it would be subject to attacks infinitely more fierce than it has had to endure for many a day, both from Conservative interests and a Conservative Press whose present yearning for a 'virile Opposition' would instantly vanish, and also from former members who would feel impelled to turn against it and denounce its policies and deeds. But against this, it would elicit and enlist the kind of devotion and support which a consolidating Labour Party now finds it increasingly difficult to engender. It is well to resist the urge to prophecy. But it does not seem unduly rash to suggest that the alternative to its becoming such a party is the kind of slow but sure decline which – deservedly – affects parties that have ceased to serve any distinctive political purpose.

Notes

[1] For a detailed analysis of the strength of trade union opposition to official policies from 1945 through the fifties, see M. Harrison, *Trade Unions and the Labour Party since 1945* (London, 1960) passim.

[2] See, e.g. Bevan: 'Do not let the union leaders think that they alone speak for their members. We speak for them as much as they do' (29th of September, 1954, in Harrison, ibid, p. 129).

[3] T.U.C. Annual Conference Report, 1952, p. 438

[4] Labour Party Annual Conference Report, 1952, p. 91

[5] TUC Annual Conference Report, 1953, p.390

[6] Labour Party Annual Conference Report, 1953, pp. 67 ff. My italics.

[7] Labour Party Annual Conference Report, 1953, p. 125. Bevan, for his own part, described the Executive's approach to nationalization as 'defeatism and treachery to the spirit of socialism' (*The Times*, 1st October, 1953).

[8] T.U.C. Annual Conference Report, 1952, p. 438.

[9] T.U.C. Annual Conference Report, 1953, p. 397.

[10] Labour Party Annual Conference report, 1953, p.129

[11] Ibid, p.130

[12] Ibid, p.132

[13] Immediately after the 1952 Conference, Hugh Gaitskell described the unseating of Morrison as 'not only an act of gross political ingratitude but a piece of blind stupidity which until it is put right must gravely weaken the party'. 'A most disturbing feature of the Conference,' he also said, 'was the number of resolutions and speeches which were Communist-inspired, based not even on the *Tribune* so much as the *Daily Worker* ... I was told by some observers that about one sixth of the constituency party delegates appear to be Communists or Communist-inspired. This figure may well be too high, but if it should be one-tenth or even one-twentieth it is a most shocking state of affairs to which the National Executive should give immediate attention.' However, the Conference, he felt, had 'come down firmly on the side of sanity and responsibility. The issues of foreign policy and defence are now settled. All the silly nonsense about withdrawing troops from Korea, breaking away from the Atlantic Alliance and going back on what the Labour Government stood for has been blown away. We are definitely opposed as a party to unilateral cuts in our defence programme, though we favour periodic re-examination with our allies ... Loyal members of the party must now accept all these decisions, including the new members of the National Executive'. 'It is time,' he also believed, 'to end the attempt to mob rule by a group of frustrated journalists and restore the authority and leadership of the solid, sound, sensible majority of the movement' (*The Times*, 6th of October, 1952.)

[14] Hugh Gaitskell was elected to the post by 4,338,000 votes to 2,032,000 cast for Bevan. The size of Bevan's vote should not be overlooked.

[15] E.g. proposals for a comprehensive schools system, for an improvement in the rates of national assistance, for the removal of taxes on sport and the living theatre, for the improvement of working conditions in shops and offices, and for the restoration of a free health service, including the abolition of all charges, amongst them those which Hugh Gaitskell had imposed as Chancellor of the Exchequer.

[16] Not that this presented any major difficulty: Immediately after the Election of 1951, the T.U.C. General Council had issued a statement referring to 'our long standing practice to seek to work amicably with whatever Government is in power and through consultation jointly with Ministers and with the other side of industry to find practical solutions to the social and economic problems facing the country. There need be no doubt therefore of the attitude of the T.U.C. towards the new Government.' (T.U.C. Annual Conference Report, 1952, p.300)

[17] 'I doubt,' Hugh Gaitskell had said in October 1954, 'if foreign policy will play a big part in the next Election – not because it is not important, but because Mr Eden has, in fact, mostly carried on our policy as developed by Ernest Bevin, in some cases against the views of rank-and-file Tories' (*Tribune*, 8th of October, 1954). It will be recalled that both Sir Winston Churchill and Sir An-

thony Eden had claimed, for their part, that it was Bevin who had followed Conservative policy.

[18] For the most articulate exposition of revisionism, see C. A. R. Crosland, 'The Transition from Capitalism', in *New Fabian Essays* (Ed. R. H. S. Crossman), pp. 33-68 (1952) and the same's *The Future of Socialism* (1956).

[19] For an exposition of this functional approach to nationalization, see Hugh Gaitskell, *Socialism and Nationalisation* (1956).

[20] *Industry and Society*, p.57

[21] See, e.g. the letter to *Reynolds News* of 32 Labour MPs expressing 'disappointment and dismay' at the document. (*Reynolds News*, 28th of July, 1957.)

[22] It was Harold Wilson, speaking on behalf of the Executive, who opened the debate at the 1957 Party Conference on *Industry and Society* with an ardent commendation of the document (See Labour Party Annual Conference Report, 1957, pp. 128-31)

[23] Labour Party Annual Conference Report 1957, pp. 131,133

[24] Ibid, pp. 157 ff.

[25] See, e.g. the speech of Frank Cousins (ibid, pp. 142-3). However, his union's vote was cast in support of the leadership

[26] Labour Party Annual Conference Report, 1957, p. 165. The resolution was defeated by 5,836,000 votes to 781,000 (ibid, p. 183).

[27] Ibid, p.181

[28] Ibid, p.182

[29] Ibid, p.9

[30] D. E. Butler and R. Rose, *The British General Election of 1959* (London, 1960) p. 17

[31] Ibid, p.252

[32] *Industry and Society*, pp. 48-9.

[33] In April 1959, e.g. the Secretary of the Labour Party felt obliged officially to deny Conservative allegations that the Labour Party intended to nationalize 500-600 large firms. Save for steel and long distance road haulage, his statement said, no industries or firms would be nationalized 'unless an official inquiry were to show (1) that they were seriously failing the nation and (2) nationalization was in fact the best remedy for the industry's problems' (Labour Party Annual Conference Report, 1958, p. 9).

[34] Butler and Rose, op. cit. p. 70.

[35] See e.g. Hugh Gaitskell: 'If the American Government do not accept this proposal (i.e. disengagement), the proposal will not be put forward on behalf of the West. Our object is to try to persuade the American Government to accept this proposal' (H. of C., vol. 600, col. 567, 19th of February, 1959)

[36] *The Times*, 5th of June, 1959.

[37] Ibid, 24 June 1959

[38] Butler and Rose, op. cit., p.70

[39] Ibid, p.19

[40] Labour Party Annual Conference Report, 1960, p.13

[41] Labour Party- Annual Conference Report, 1959, p. 109.

[42] Ibid, p.109, italics in text

Editorial Introduction to Extract 4

As is now perhaps clear, the explanatory framework deployed in *Parliamentary Socialism* was very much a buried and underdeveloped one. *Parliamentary Socialism* was written as a narrative informed by an argument, rather than as an argument informed by historical example; and as a result it was not easy then, and is not easy now, to find in this first major Miliband text the constituent elements of the underlying explanation. Those elements were trailed in the text, but they were never spelt out there with any clarity. Digging within the argument of *Parliamentary Socialism* opens up at least two such trails. One was the trail of something called 'labourism', a concept which was clearly vital to Ralph Miliband's 1961 understanding and characterization of the Labour Party's continuing moderation, but which remained undefined in the volume: indeed used more in chapter titles than in the text itself. The other trail was that of 'state constraints', with *Parliamentary Socialism* providing the first listing of what would later become powerful themes in Ralph Miliband's writings on the state constraints on Labour in power that came from the conservative impact of monarchy, civil service and business pressures. Yet these important concepts and arguments were only tantalizingly floated into the argument in *Parliamentary Socialism*. They were never developed there. Their development would come later. As we will see, (pp. **XX**) Ralph Miliband would give a full definition of labourism in his 1983 essay; and he would develop his theory of class containment in a series of major publications (notably *The State in Capitalist Society* and *Capitalist Democracy in Britain*) which later established him as a figure of international importance in political sociology[1]. But the first clear elaboration of these organizing ideas did not come from his pen, but from that of his collaborator and friend John Saville. It was Saville who produced essays – first in 1967, then in 1973[2] – that first put flesh on the bones of what then became the distinctly Milibandish understanding of why the Labour Party so regularly disappointed its supporters on the Left. The 1967 essay is reproduced here.

In it, Saville deploys an understanding of 'labourism' that he most clearly defined in 1973: namely the notion of

> Labourism as a theory and practice which accepted the possibility of social change within the existing framework of society; which rejected the revolutionary violence and action implicit in Chartist ideas of physical force; and which increasingly recognized the working of political democracy of the parliamentary variety as the practical means of achieving its own aims and objectives.[3]

In *Parliamentary Socialism* Miliband had argued that the general power of labourism understood in this way predated the creation of the Labour Party by at least several decades, and that indeed by 1900 'there were not many people to contest the view that Labour's grievances and demands could only find solution through parliamentary action, and that the parliamentary method was ideally suited, not only to the achievement of immediate gains by the working classes, but also to the socialist reconstruction of society'.[4] Saville then argued similarly that the acceptance by the Labour leadership of the appropriateness of parliamentary democracy (and of the associated Fabian-inspired belief in 'the inevitability of gradualism') was the key to why 'those who win elections with socialist phrases on their lips – and most are not conscious hypocrites ... then proceed to administer a capitalist society which they had previously denounced'[5]. The explanation of Labour backsliding lay for Saville, as arguably it had for Miliband when writing *Parliamentary Socialism*, in labourism's over-estimation of the autonomy of the state: in what Saville termed the Labour leadership's 'state of innocence'[6] about the class constraints on political power in capitalist societies. Labour politicians, Saville argued, simply failed to grasp the true 'nature of economic and political power in industrial Britain' and failed to understand the relationship between that power structure and the rules of the parliamentary game.

In his 1967 essay, John Saville then drew two main conclusions from the argument that 'the neutrality of the state ... has been accepted by Left as well as Right within the Labour Movement in the twentieth century'[7], conclusions that would soon become defining of the Miliband approach to the Labour Party. First he emphasized the functionality of the rhetoric and mythology of labourism to the stabilization of British capitalism at moments of crisis, singling out in particular the way in which after 1945 'Labour went on telling their own supporters that they were part of a great social revolution the like of which had never previously been seen in this country, and the Labour intellectuals kept on repeating the story in the years that followed...embellishing it with sophisticated theoretical constructs', at the very moment when the Attlee governments were seeking to win the active support of the business community for their policies, and were winning a degree of working class discipline, loyalty and restraint quite beyond the capacity of the Conservatives to mobilize. The result of this 'smokescreen of propaganda being put up by both Labour and Tories', Saville argued, was the de-radicalization and 'mystification' of 'the great majority of trade unionists' and the making of Britain safe again for 'the era of profiteering, capital gains and expense account rackets that followed the resumption of office by Britain's traditional rulers in 1951'[8]. And second – drawing on his Communist Party past and making explicit what in *Parliamentary Socialism* was only embryonic – he concluded that 'Labourism has nothing to do with Socialism; that the Labour Party has never been, nor is it capable of becoming, a vehicle for socialist advance; and that the destruction of the illusions of Labourism is a necessary step before the emergence of a socialist movement of any size and influence becomes practicable'[9].

4. LABOURISM AND THE LABOUR GOVERNMENT (1967)

John Saville

"Whoever is in office, the Whigs are in power."

The argument that all political parties in Britain, who style themselves reforming and progressive, behave like conservatives when in office and have done so far the past hundred years, has received increasing support from the evidence of the last few decades. In general terms, the behaviours of Liberal Governments before 1914 and of Labour Governments after do show remarkable similarities. Their administrations can usually be relied upon to lose their political nerve some time before they have to face the electorate once again: serious factional quarrels commonly develop between various ministerial groups and there are often resignations: the legislative programme of social reform is normally well below the expectations of their followers in the country; and above all, the foreign policy of their Conservative predecessors is never deviated from. These are not, in general, propositions to which members of the present Labour Party in Britain are likely to agree, whichever political wing of the Party they belong to. The Labour Party adopted a socialist constitution in 1918 and its members genuinely believe that Labour politics are concerned with some degree or other of radical change. It is a matter of sober fact that the left wing of the Labour Party have always assumed that the achievement of socialism will be possible through the Labour Party, as the only mass political organization of the British workers, and that the assumption of office by Labour will be the starting point for the advance to socialism. Here, for instance, is the editorial in *Tribune* – the leading journal of the Labour left – written immediately after the General Election of Spring 1966 which returned Labour to power with an unassailable majority:

> The argument now is about the implementation of Socialism in Britain. We believe that the leaders of the Government know that well; they know also that the whole Labour movement will support them in their efforts to establish socialism. But should they instead decide to take the path of compromise they can expect a sharp reaction from the whole Labour movement.

It is, no doubt, the long intervals between Labour Governments in Britain that have encouraged the illusions that encrust the movement concerning the socialist potential of a future Labour Government. It is worth emphasizing that after the establishment of the Labour Party in 1900 – in a country where manual workers have formed the majority of the electorate – it took 45 years, two world wars and the most serious economic crisis that industrial capitalism has ever experienced before a Labour Government was elected with a workable majority in the House of Commons. Not to put too fine a point on it, this is hardly a success story; and it is understandable that the long wait for the promised land has nurtured the fond hopes of a socialist initiative in those who have been tilling so patiently the stony soil of twentieth century Britain. So far, moreover, the experience of office has not been followed by skepticism or disillusionment on any extended scale. Despite their obvious incompetence, the two Labour administrations of 1924 and 1929 were minority affairs, and the long interval of time between 1931 and the majority Government of 1945 was sufficient to allow the magic of socialist rhetoric once more to rehabilitate itself. Political memories in most parties and political groupings seem to be a curious mixture of elephantine persistence and almost total oblivion, and certainly in the Labour movement memories of past follies of Labour administrations have had plenty of time to fade and grow dim, before the next shock is administered.

Myths and illusions form an interesting and often an extraordinary part of the political behaviour of many individuals who make up the Labour movement. If this were not so, the cultivation of private gardens would perhaps be carried on even more vigorously than is already the case; and nowhere is the matter of myth so pervasive than in the record of the Labour Government of 1945. This is the example often used to attempt to disprove the thesis about the generally conservative nature of self-styled reforming Governments. Even for those who do not accept the exaggerated views of social transformation the Labour Government was supposed to have brought about: "in my opinion the Labour Government between 1945 and 1951 did in fact appreciably modify the nature of British capitalism"[10] – the memory of a Government which broadly carried out its mandate from previous Labour Conferences and which established the Welfare State is still a very sympathetic one; and mention of the National Health service is usually sufficient to attenuate more critical views.

It is true that the Labour Government after 1945 broadly carried out the programme which Labour Conferences had agreed upon. By 1948, the nationalization proposals of *Let Us Face the Future* – except for iron and steel – had been placed on the Statute Book and the Government had brought into operation its universal insurance system and the National Health Service. Given the problems of transition from war to peace and the acute economic problems of post-war Britain, the Government was not unreasonable to claim credit for its achievements. It had kept faith with those who had voted it into power and it could make this claim with some justification. The real question remains: what was the nature of the social change involved? Did the Labour Government do any more than continue the line of social advance that the Liberals had begun in 1906? What is the historical assessment of the 1945 Government in post-war history, looked at as a whole? It is the answers to questions of this kind that provide a very different picture from that which is usually accepted of these two post-war

Labour Governments.

What remains in most people's minds is the social security legislation of the Attlee Government. The claims made by Labour apologists are that the system of welfare benefits introduced after 1945 were superior to those of any other advanced industrial country, and that this comprehensive system was complemented by a major re-distribution of income that had begun during the war and was continued in the years that followed. Neither claim is today acceptable. The belief that income and wealth were redistributed in favour of the working people has now been thoroughly exploded, and the intellectual constructs which the Labour intellectuals – Strachey and C. A. R. Crosland in particular – erected upon these supposed facts have now demolished themselves.... By the early 1960's acknowledgement of the inequalities of income and wealth began to be discussed in official Labour Party statements and the facts provided an essential part of the propaganda which the Labour Opposition used during the General Election of 1964. The other leg to the argument about the 1945 Government – that its social security programme represented a major achievement of universal application – has been undermined both by research into the facts of contemporary Britain was well as by the increasingly unfavourable comparisons of the British social services with those of other countries, in particular with the Common Market countries. Mr. Richard Crossman has recently noted that the Beveridge system of flat-rate contributions and benefits, which formed the basis of the national insurance scheme introduced after 1945 "was obsolescent years before it was introduced";[11] and there has grown up in the past ten years or so a body of literature which has analysed the welfare state policies of 1945 in terms of their greater material and financial benefits to the middle classes rather than to the working people. The middle classes, in fact, get a good deal more than their share of the public social services, in particular education: they draw as well special extra benefits from their occupations, such as sick pay, pension schemes, regularity and security of employment, substantial fringe payments in cash and kind; and in addition there are the concealed social services provided for by tax concessions of many kinds. The middle class tax payer can claim for children, for old age, for mortgage payments .... The fact that the middle classes do not think of tax allowances and tax concessions as social services is beside the point. They are. In 1958 children's allowances paid to every mother cost the State £120,000,000; child allowances on income tax were worth £320,000,000. Mr. Brian Abel-Smith summed up in *Conviction*: "The middle classes get the lion's share of the public social services, the elephant's share of occupational welfare privileges, and in addition can claim generous allowances to reduce their tax liability. Who has a Welfare State"?[12] A further and more recent comment is also worth quoting since it comes from one who has no prior sympathy with the general ideas of the Labour movement. Sir Roy Harrod in 1963 produced a volume for the Economics Handbook Series edited by Seymour Harris of Harvard

University. After discussing the social welfare measures introduced by the Attlee government, Harrod summed up:

> Whereas Labour should be given credit for enthusiasm and efficiency in putting through the necessary measures, it is not clear that there is much in the items, as listed above – apart, perhaps, from the free health service – that either constitutes a radical departure from pre-war British policy or is widely different from what the Conservatives would have done. Foreign ideas about all this have been very much out of balance.

The administration of Mr. Attlee that took power in 1945 had only the vaguest idea about the structure of the social services which it wanted to alter and improve. It took what was to hand, and the results were much more modest than was recognized, either by friend or enemy, at the time. The British legislation has been matched and in most respects improved upon by the development of social security schemes in Western Europe from about the middle 1950's onwards; and it is now clear, although hardly a novel analysis, that such measures are a necessary and essential part of the structure of advanced industrial societies. They serve a number of purposes. They help to take the edge off the harshness and insecurity which is a built-in characteristic of industrial life: they are the partial safeguards against the accidents of ill-health, sickness, disability or death of the wage earner and his family. From a strictly economic point of view it is inefficient to have large numbers of illiterate or semi-literate workers, since increasing degrees of skill are being demanded by the development of technology; and it is equally uneconomic to have a working force that is ill-fed or sickly. The differences in the scope of social welfare legislation in individual countries, between America for example, and Britain, are largely the product of different political environments and above all of the strength and vigour of the respective labour movement. It is certainly the pressures of the movement in Britain that have been responsible for much of what has so far been secured; but having made this general point, the basic similarities between countries of differing climates of opinion should also be recognized.

In other fields of economic and political life, the conservatism of the Attlee government was even more pronounced. The administration took office in the closing months of the war and when the war ended, in August 1945, it was confronted with the immense task of switching a war economy to a peace-time basis. Millions were waiting to be demobolised from the armed forces: there was widespread bombing destruction and the housing problem was acute. A traditionally export-orientated economy had to begin paying its way in international terms, a problem made more acute by the abrupt termination of Lend-lease at the end of the war. The Government inherited an economy whose pre-war record, in terms of its general rate of growth, industrial structure, productivity and the overall balance of payments, was unsatisfactory. The staple export industries of the pre-

1914 era – especially coal and textiles – experienced serious excess capacity and unemployment during the inter-war period, and were contracting too slowly. By the end of the thirties the British economy had only partially re-adjusted itself to the new world conditions. The share of British exports in world trade was falling steadily, and during the 1930's there were deficits in most years on the balance of payments current account. While during the war years there was some improvement in productivity in certain sectors of the economy, pre-war industrial productivity as a whole was probably not overtaken until mid-1947, after which time the increase was considerable. Exports had fallen in the later stages of the war to about one-third of the pre-war volume. In sum, Britain was faced with a major economic effort, but by 1950 the economy had made a remarkable recovery. Industrial production was rising fast, productivity was increasing at a faster rate than in the pre-war years and export volumes, above all, had shown a notable rise to 75 per cent above the 1946 level while import volumes were still below the 1938 figures. Looked at after twenty years there is no question that the transition from war to peace was accomplished much more successfully than after world war one, and in a number of respects certain of the structural deficiencies of the inter-war period were now being remedied.

The crux of the matter for socialists is, however, of a different order. What was it that was being remedied, and in whose interest? Did the Labour Government after 1945 do any more than effect a transition to normal peace-time functioning of an economy whose foundations and structure were basically unchanged? A decade or so after the propaganda smoke of the immediate part-war years had cleared, and economists and statisticians began once again to look carefully at the class structure, it was discovered that Britain in the early 1960's exhibited all the economic and social characteristics that had been the intellectual stock-in-trade of Labour propagandists of the 1930's and earlier periods. In particular, to quote Professor James Meade, "no less than 75 per cent of the personal property was owned by the wealthiest 5 per cent of the popoulation."[13] Full employment and the rise in living standards had not touched the basic divisions of society into the property-owning minority and the remainder of the population who worked for wages and salaries: for the concentration of income from property was even more marked than property ownership itself, with 92 per cent of income from property going to the same five per cent of the population. This was certainly not the result of the years of Tory "freedom" since 1951, although the Tories did their best; but since there had been no inroads of any fundamental kind in the ownership of wealth, all the Tories had to do was to manipulate the tax structure in the interests of the wealthy, to ease the pressures here and there, and to offer more possibilities of profit to private enterprise.

When we look back at the economic policies of the Attlee government it becomes only too plain there was never any intention, on anyone's part, to do other than pursue a line of economic and industrial orthodoxy. Of the indus-

tries which were nationalized, coal and the railways were virtually bankrupt, and
any Government would have been forced to provide massive financial support
for the large scale investment that was required to achieve some degree of efficiency.

Nationalisation was one possible method out of several, and the way it was
carried through in these two industries left unaltered the structure of industrial
relations, rapidly increased the burden of debt, which provided an increasing
rentier income to property owning individuals and corporate institutions, and
offered a cheap service to the capitalist sector of industry. The same considerations apply to gas and electricity, also nationalized by the Attlee government, but
coal and railways have a special place since the opportunity for a radical solution
could easily have been taken. There is now a considerable literature on what has
been called the "subordination" of the nationalized industries "to the short run
needs and interests of capitalist industry";[14] and it makes sorry reading indeed.
In their dealings with the private sector of industry the Attlee administration
just carried on the controls it inherited from the war. The machinery of consultation and control, involving a close relationship between industry and the
Government, had been fully developed during the war years, when not even Mr.
Crosland is anxious to claim that socialism was advancing steadily, and the system had been bitterly criticized both inside and outside the Labour Party. Those
who were involved in planning and the operation of controls continued to be
drawn mainly from private industry, as they had been during the war years. For
most of the period of the first Labour Government the principal industrial advisor to the Board of Trade was the chairman of the British Rayon Federation. The
Capital Issues Committee set up during the war was taken over by the Labour
Government: its functions were to approve or deny new issues on the capital
market, and it was composed of seven bankers, stockbrokers and industrialists.
The only representative of the Treasury, no doubt included to safeguard the
interests of his socialist ministers, was secretary to the Committee and took no
deliberative part in its discussions. So the list can be extended:

> The leather controller at the Board of Trade until later 1951 was an official of
> the United Tanners' Federation. The match controller in 1946 was an official of
> Bryant and May, Britain's largest producer of matchers, and for a time had his
> offices on the firm's premises. The paper controller was the Chairman of the larg-
> est paper manufacturing firms. The footwear controller was a director of the shoe
> manufacturing firm of Dolcis, and the hosiery, furniture and tobacco controllers
> or advisors were trade officials. Employees of Distillers Ltd occupied the top posts
> in the Molasses and Industrial Alcohol Control of the Board of Trade, and the
> Cotton Control according to a Government spokesman, was 'largely recruited
> from Liverpool's cotton firms'. The Board of Trade's largest control, through most
> of the period, the Timber Control, was almost entirely staffed by industry people,
> a number of whom, occupying senior position, were unpaid.[15]

What is good for General Motors...; but controls, even when your friends are administering them, do get in the way, and most of industry, while recognizing a good thing when it was presented to them, clamoured for the free, mostly uncompetitive market. The Government agreed with the business men, and from about mid-1948 there was a substantial dismantling of controls and a shift to the market system.

Through its controls and machinery of planning the Labour Government in the post-war years was giving administrative expression to the views of the war-time Coalition Government in its White Paper on *Employment Policy* of 1944. In this, the view was given that there would inevitably be a transition period in the first years of peace during which there would still be required the rationing of consumer goods, the allocation of raw materials and other types of control designed to ease the difficult problems of transition in a situation of scarcity. The bitter experience of the years which followed 1918 were in everyone's mind, and a free-for-all, with immediate removals of all controls, was not in the interests of business in general, and it carried unpleasant political implications. What was needed was an orderly progression to the point where scarcities had been largely overcome and where above all labour had come to appreciate the difficult nature of the economic problem; and then would come the time for private enterprise to flourish like the bay tree. The crux of the matter was the attitude of labour in general and of the trade unions in particular. There had taken place a notable radicalization in political opinion during the war, of which the rejection of Churchill and the Tories at the General Election of 1945 was the obvious expression. The Labour Government tried to win the support of business, and it did not wholly fail by any means; but it was crucial to ensure the acceptance of the trade union movement for its policy of austerity, wage restraint and no utopian nonsense. To cut a heated story short the Government, with the full co-operation of most of the trade union leaders, won the considerable propaganda battle for the peaceful transition to the years of the businessmen's bonanza in the 1950s. In the six years after 1918, and not including the year of the General Strike, some 187 million days were lost through strikes and lock-outs: in the comparable period after 1945 the figure was just short of 13 million. There were important differences in the climate of political industrial opinion in the two periods, but there can be no doubt that a Conservative Government in office after 1945 would have been unable to extract the high degree of industrial discipline and the general loyalty to the Government that the Labour Party was able to achieve. Britain in these years after 1945 was being made safe for the era of profiteering, capital gains and expense account rackets that followed the resumption of office by Britain's traditional rulers in 1951. The great majority of trade unionists were not aware, of course, of what was in store, and again it was the smokescreen of propaganda being put up by both Labour and Tories that contributed to their mystification. Labour went on telling their own supporters that they were part of a great social revolution the like of which had never previously been seen in the country; and the Labour intellectuals kept on repeating the story in the years which followed, and embellishing it with sophisticated theoretical constructs such as that provided by Mr. Crosland in the *New Fabian Essays* of 1952, in which he explained to any puzzled manual worker who happened to read the article, that he was no longer living in a capitalist but in "a qualitatively different sort of society".[16] Important though this mystifying discussion was, in inducing bewilderment in the minds of Labour supporters – since the facts of word-a-day life were in sharp contrast with what the workers were being told about the social revolution of which they were supposedly the beneficiaries – even more helpful in encouraging loyalty to the Labour Government were the screams of apparent pain coming from the other side of the fence. "I have not forgotten", John Freedom wrote in 1959:

> ... the tension of rising to answer questions or conduct a debate under the cold, implacable eyes of that row of well-tailored tycoons, who hated the Labour Government with a passion and fear which made them dedicated men in their determination to get it out of office and to limit the damage it could do to the world which they saw as theirs by right.[17]

What the ineffable Angela Thirkell called the Brave New Revolting World was hated with a fury that nearly knew no bounds by the British middle class. What Mrs. Thirkell put into the mouth of one of her characters – a university teacher – was echoed up and down the land by a middle class that thought itself surrounded by the enemy:

> What is interesting, though I must say even to a philosopher damnably galling and uncomfortably, is that we are living under a Government as bad as any in history in its combination of bullying and weakness, its bid for the mob's suffrages, its fawning upon unfriendly foreigners who despise it, its efforts to crush all personal freedom.[18]

The middle classes were being told by reputably sober journals like the *Economist* that "At least ten per cent of the national consuming power has been forcefully transferred from the middle classes and the rich to the wage earners".[19] Against the background of shortages, from which, of course, the ordinary working people suffered much more than the middle income groups, the British middle classes firmly believed in the hostility of the Government towards them. Most of the press said that same thing, and the unrelenting vigour of complaint and opposition against the Labour Government inevitably consolidated the ranks of its own supporters. There were many matters of policy upon which the labour militants disagreed with the Government, but the alternative? The way the Tories were carrying on in the closing years of the forties made it abundantly clear that they were of the same breed, in many cases the same personalities, as those of the years of Hunger Marches, appeasement and the betrayal of Spain. Fighting on two fronts is always a difficult exercise and to oppose the Tories *in toto and* the Labour Government on many counts was not a technique of class battle which appealed to many, or at which many were competent.

There were several fundamental issues on which there was profound disquiet. The wage freeze was one, but of greater significance was the foreign policy of the Labour Government taken over from the Conservative Party without change. The Foreign Secretary was Ernest Bevin, a shrewd, rough, parochially-minded trade union leader with a genuine ability for administrative work which he had showed to great advantage during the war years, but who was quite incapable of seeing through the sophistication of his Foreign Office officials. The Foreign Office, like the Canadian Mounties, always get their man, and they hooked Ernie Bevin very properly. Bevin in some matters was simply an unpleasant man: before a working class audience he was a demagogue; and he had an overweening arrogance that at times was unbelievable. What follows is a short extract from his speech at the Labour Party Conference in 1946, when he had already begun his virulent anti-Soviet propaganda and policy:

> I said to Maisky [The Soviet Ambassador] on one occasion: 'You have built the Soviet Union and you have a right to defend it. I have built the Transport Union and if you seek to break it I will fight you'. That was a proper position to take up. Both were the result of long years of labour. After that there was a slightly greater respect for my view. I think that is fair.[20]

The Foreign Office loved Bevin: so did the other Tories in Westminster. In Greece and Palestine, and in a hundred and one corners of the world where the British Empire continued its usual bloody if now tattered existence, Bevin was to be found pursuing straight Tory policies. He was a front runner in the Cold War and set the example for later Labour Foreign Ministers of acquiescence in American policy when the American State Department called their allies to order. Being economically beholden to America no doubt made it easier for Bevin to agree on behalf of Britain. The Cold War *was* a confusing phenomenon, and Stalinism inside Russia made it only too easy to sell the Cold War to the British Labour movement. Its consequences have been disastrous. Throughout the post-war era, Britain has remained a more or less happy, and usually quite docile, satellite of the United States. In a world ravaged by the struggle for colonial liberation, and by the fierce nationalisms of the under-developed countries, Britain has pursued consistently repressive policies towards the emerging nations; and in Europe she has underwritten the tensions of the Cold War. In Greece, Palestine, Malaya, Egypt, the Persian Gulf area, Guyana and today Vietnam, the name of Britain is the name of a country which has steadily fought alongside the old, decaying social and political forces which are obstructing and, where possible, strangling progress; and she has done this either on her own account or at the instigation or with the support of the United States. Viewed from afar, a Labour Government succeeding a Conservative Government is the change from Tweedledum to Tweedledee. There is no change.

The Labour Governments of 1945 to 1951 began these post-war policies. On a world scale, or looked at in historical perspective after twenty years, the social legislation of the Attlee Government is but the long overdue, and certainly modest, offering of a rich society to the majority of its population who are producing its wealth. The Attlee administrations engineered the change-over from a war to a peace economy with remarkably little social disturbance. In this matter and in this matter only there was a crucial difference between a Labour and a Conservative administration; and in the way that the transition was effected, the Labour Government disillusioned its own militants, encouraged a far-reaching cynicism among the more non-political workers, brought the name and ideal of socialism into disrepute, and, by its streamlining of the economy, provided a spring-board for the rich to take off into the profiteer's paradise that was the outstanding feature of the 1950s.

***

How it comes about that those who win elections with socialist phrases on their lips – and most are not conscious hypocrites – and then proceed to administer a capitalist society, which they have previously denounced, in as efficient a way as possible, is one of the central ironies of modern British history. For socialists who have struggled to put their leaders in power, it is tragedy.

Politics is about power: the sources of power and their political expression; and the leaders of the British Labour Party have always had a markedly narrow understanding about the nature of the problem. For them, power means Parliamentary power. They have been told by constitutional historians that there are no restrictions upon the ability of the British Parliament to legislate what it likes, in terms of individuals or things. Parliament is a sovereign body, and for the Labour Party leadership power means control of the Government, and politics is concerned with Parliament and the winning of majority government through the ballot box. The argument that the owners of property will not allow themselves to be legislated out of existence is not one that is meaningful to those who have been nurtured in this tradition. It is an attitude and a belief that in Britain amounts to an act of faith, and it antedates by many years the foundation of the Labour Party in 1900. It has, however been given a very special flavour by those in the Labour tradition since verbally at least the movement has been dedicated to transforming capitalism into something different. But long before the labour movement adopted an official constitution that was socialist, the British labour movement was already enveloped within the myths and illusions that the main path to social progress lay through Parliament. It is, indeed, one of the wry turns and twists of history that in the country where the demand for the vote first became a political issue of a radical-revolutionary kind for the masses – in the Chartist period in the first half of the nineteenth century – the successful achievement of the vote by workingmen has been accompanied by an adaptation to the Parliamentary system it was originally intended to transform. Before 1850 universal suffrage meant democracy, and democracy was understood to mean social-democracy. In the years of Chartism, not only in Britain but over western Europe as a whole, democracy had not the emasculated and anaemic meaning that it has today. When the working people referred to themselves it was as The Democracy: used by the ruling classes it had all the prejudices of Edmund Burke's "swinish multitude". When Engels wrote of the programme of the Chartist movement: "These Six Points ... harmless as they seem, are sufficient to overthrow the whole English constitution" he was only saying what his contemporary Macaulay was expressing specifically, that the enfranchisement of the proletarians would be followed by "great and systematic inroads" against property and the propertied classes. It did not happen. With the failure of the European revolutions of 1848, and the parallel decline of the Chartist movement in Britain, working class ideology became blurred and muddled, and working class aspirations, above the level of trade union activity, were diverted towards the achievement of the franchise in a now much narrower context. Increasingly, the politically conscious sections of the working class began to accept the Liberal Party as the party of progress, and parliamentarism on the national plane and town politics on the local, as the road to working class improvement. There is a good deal more to the working class tradition as it developed in the second half of the nineteenth century than this acceptance of the parliamentary road, and it was much tougher and called for greater stamina and self-sacrifice than is often recognized; but when all the qualifications have been made, parliamentarism as the way of political life did become a central part of the evolving labourist tradition.

It was the Fabians who articulated the labourist philosophy. Their philosophy, it needs to be emphasized, was grounded in an acceptance of historical inevitability as firmly as any of their Marxist contemporaries. Sidney Webb constantly emphasized what he later described as the inevitably of gradualism[21] and was always quoting historical examples to prove his point. He argued that the growth of an increasingly complex society would itself compel an increasingly complex interference by the State, and that this would be reinforced by the development of political democracy; by which he understood the growing consciousness among the working people that political power now resided in them as the majority of the nation. Inevitably, Webb argued, the workings of political democracy would curtail the power of property over the lives of ordinary people. Summarizing political developments in the decades prior to 1889, Webb wrote:

> The liberty of the property owner to oppress the propertyless by the levy of economic tribute of rent and interest began to be circumscribed, pared away, obstructed and forbidden in various directions. Slice after slice had been gradually cut from the profits of capital, and therefore from its selling value, by socially beneficial restrictions on its user's liberty to do as he liked with it.[22]

The fact that this extraordinary and quite wrong-headed claim by Webb reads like a press statement from the contemporary Liberty and Property Defence League, whose activities were devoted to exposure of the Jacobin tendencies of Mr. Gladstone and spoliators of that kind, must not obscure the general point that Webb is establishing. He was right to argue that the existence of political democracy would in time mean a growing response by the traditional political parties to the demands coming from below, and that unrestricted individualism could not provide acceptable standards of living for ordinary people. He called these reforming trends "unconscious socialism" which he was convinced were irresistible.

The Fabian theory of historical inevitability rests upon one major assumption: that the Government in a political democracy are in full control of the State and State power, and that upon the Government's ability to legislate there are no effective limitations. It is based upon the postulate of the State's neutrality: that any administration which takes power *ipso facto* is in full and complete control of its legislative programme. There is a famous passage which forms the conclusion to Bernard Shaw's *The Impossibilities of Anarchism* in which Shaw makes explicit the theory of the State underlying the Fabian confidence in historical inevitability:

> It is easy to say, Abolish the State; but the State will sell you up, lock you up, blow you, knock you down, bludgeon, shoot, stab, hang – in short abolish you, if you lift a hand against it. Fortunately, there is, as we have seen a fine impartiality about the policeman and the soldier, who are the cutting edge of the State power. They take their wages and obey their orders without asking questions. If those orders are to demolish the homestead of every peasant who refuses to take the bread out of his children's mouths in order that his landlord may have money to spend as an idle gentleman in London, the soldier obeys. But if his orders were to help the police to pitch his lordship into Holloway Gaol until he had paid an Income Tax of twenty shillings on every pound of his unearned income, the soldier would do that with equal devotion to duty, and perhaps with a certain private zest that might be lacking in the other case. Now these orders come ultimately from the State – meaning, in this country, the House of Commons. A House of Commons consisting of 660 gentlemen and 10 workmen will order the soldier to take money from the people for the landlords. A House of Commons consisting of 660 workmen and 10 gentlemen will probably, unless the 660 are fools, order the solder to take money from the landlords for the people. With this hint I leave the matter, in the full conviction that the State, in spite of the Anarchists, will continue to be used against the people

by the classes until it is used by the people against the classes with equal ability and equal resolution."[23]

This belief in the neutrality of the State – which for the Labour Party, as for Bernard Shaw, has always meant the House of Commons – has been accepted by Left was well as Right within the Labour movement in the twentieth century; and when things go wrong, as they invariably do, and the hopes of the reformers are liquidated, then there is added some simple conspiracy theory of a banker's ramp, at home or abroad, or in combination. What has never been understood is the nature of economic and political power in industrial Britain, where two fifths of all private property is in the hands of one per cent of the adult population: where the wealthy groups are linked by social background, marriage and top business positions: where the identity between the wealthy and the politicians of the Conservative Party is very close; and where all the leading social and political institutions mirror the dominance of the wealthy classes. Britain is ruled by an élite which has its main economic basis in industrial and financial capital but with the old landed classes still important: its younger members use the leading public schools and Oxford and Cambridge as their private educational establishments, and the Conservative Party, the administrative grade of the Civil Service and the top managerial positions in business and banking as their providers of earned income. Britain is a profoundly conservative society with a traditional institutional framework within which political decisions are taken. The limitations upon the real power of the House of Commons are such that to accept the conventions of Parliamentary Government means to accept the impossibility of change that is radical in any meaningful sense. No leader of the Labour Party has ever considered stepping outside parliamentary conventions or going beyond the constitutional proprieties of Parliament. When, as in the days of the 1926 General Strike, there was being revealed a naked confrontation of class interests, the Labour and trade union leadership fell over themselves to reach a compromise, which in the event became capitulation. As J.H. Thomas said at the time, and he was speaking for the Labour leadership as a whole: "I have never disguised that in a challenge to the Constitution, God help us unless the Government won" (3 May 1926); and since 1926 there has never been a challenge of any serious kind to the position of the ruling class.

When a Labour administration takes over the Government, they inherit a large bureaucratic apparatus that is continuing to administer the affairs of the country. The first thing a Labour Government does is to carry on, using the accepted and traditional practices and procedures. Its ministers slip into the seats just vacated by their Tory predecessors, and are served by the same Civil Servants whose social background is attuned to Conservative traditions. Socialists even of a moderate kind are rare in the higher reaches of the Civil Service: left wing socialists entirely absent. Labour ministers are for the most part men who have spent many years already in Westminster: Parliamentary practices and proce- dures are accepted as right and proper and fundamentally unalterable, including the fiction of the neutrality of the Civil Service. Assuming that the Government has some reforming intentions, the complicated processes begin of drafting new legislation and then getting it accepted: first, from within the Civil Service and then by Parliament. The pressures on a Minister from his Civil Servants, from outside vested interests, from the Tory opposition in Parliament are intense and continuous; and the more radical the measure the greater the weight of opinion and interest with which the Minister responsible will have to contend. In the case of legislation that is genuinely reforming in intention the pressures to nar- row its scope and limit its application will be unceasing and unrelenting: and the reform when it finally appears as an Act of Parliament will be a good deal more orthodox and limited than when it began its passage as a draft measure. There is, indeed, a general law of social change which can be applied to social and political reform measures in Britain. It is a law of delay, for to the conservative interests in society delay means life and an abundance of opportunities to trim, modify and limit reforming measures as they continue their long journey through political life. It is the density and tenacity of conservative institutions in Britain that de- feats the genuine reformer and when reform is finally granted, often after years of weary struggle, its significance is usually exaggerated. The Labour leaders are inhibited in a fundamental way by their parliamentarism: by the unshakeable belief that all the British are gentlemen and will play the Parliamentary game ac- cording to its rules. They have, it must be admitted, good reason for these beliefs since nothing has even been done by the Labour leadership to cause the gentle- men of England to abandon their acceptance of the rules; but the record of the same gentlemen in other parts of the world, and on occasion in their own coun- try, makes it abundantly clear that rules are adhered to simply because there is no point in abandoning a system that so far has provided satisfactory answers.

The Labour leaders, and even more their followers, are in a real sense still in a state of innocence. Most of them are not cynical about their ideas or their ide- als: they do genuinely believe that by winning a Parliamentary majority they can then proceed to construct a new kind of society without any serious hindrance from those whom existing society exists to benefit. The only trouble with this belief is that it never works. Labour Governments in practice have never altered anything of a fundamental kind: they use the existing administrative machinery through which to develop their policies and what emerges is recognizable only in conservative terms: they spend their energies attempting to woo the business community to more dynamic paths of growth; and their social reforming pro- gramme is easily adapted to the workings of traditional society. In all this there is one difference only between the Attlee administration and the present Wilson Government: the former at least began as a reforming administration, while the Wilson Government has not yet achieved this role but has moved from its earliest days along the straightest conservative path....

***

The record of the Wilson administration in the first two and a half years of its life makes dismal reading for those who believed, and they were many, that the labourist tradition was capable of genuine radical change, even of change in a socialist direction. Before he became Prime Minister, Mr. Wilson was consistently putting forward a radical programme which, had it been carried into effect, would have altered many aspects of our social life. It was never, of course, a propaganda for change of a fundamental kind involving an attack upon existing property relationships, but there was a sense in his speeches of the need to cast away much of the old lumber and refurbish some parts at least of the structure of British society. Mr. Wilson's brave words soon wafted away once office was achieved, and they have not been heard since. Abroad, the foreign policy of the Tories has been unchanged, with the qualification that when the Labour Party was in opposition there was at least some focus of active dissent in the left wing of the Party. Now there is very little. At home, the Labour Government has produced a more severe dose of deflation and wage squeeze than did the Tories in the past. Following the precedent of previous Labour Governments, and particularly that of 1945, the Wilson administration have drawn upon the business world for most of their new appointments outside the Civil Service, and they remain as influential as ever: the old mumbo-jumbo of tradition and ceremonial continues at every point in British society. The leadership of the Wilson Government have long abandoned the rhetoric which sustained their followers while they were in opposition, and today the feeling of and for change is absent. So far we have been given Toryism without dilution.

When the Wilson Government first took office, and after they had increased their own parliamentary salaries and allowances, they began to remedy some of the elementary abuses in social provisions which had figured so prominently in Labour's election appeal, although in some cases, unlike the increase in parliamentary salaries, the change did not come into effect immediately. The National Health charges were abolished: there was a modest increase in pensions and certain allowances, and some, but only some, of the worst features of the Tory Rent Act were removed. There was little more, and how limited were the social horizons of the Wilson Government was strikingly exhibited by the abortive National Plan. The Plan, like so many of the other initiatives of the Government, was an elaborate piece of window dressing. It was conceived in euphoric ignorance, and when delivered, was still-born. But its assumptions concerning the relationship between the public and private sectors, and its estimates of the future development of the social services, are worth noting, revealing as they do the limitations of public policy the Wilson Government were imposing upon themselves, even in theoretical conditions that were always much too optimistic.

The National Plan assumed in increase in the Gross National Product of just over £8,000 million in a period of six years to 1970. Of this total just over half was to go in personal consumption, with less than £1,000 million being allocated to social and public services, excluding housing and roads. This would mean in 1970 that 3.9 per cent of gross national product was devoted to housing and about 4 per cent to public health services. These figures are well below the average for the advanced societies of Western Europe, and in the case of public health the proportion spent in Britain has not changed for a twenty year period. The Labour National Plan assumed that both health and education would expand at a *lower* rate between 1965 and 1970 than in the previous five year period of Tory government. As Brian Abel-Smith comments somewhat tartly, given the official statistics of social services and their rates of growth in Tory and Labour administrations over the past decade "a man from Mars…might easily make a mistake in an attempt to identify the socialist party".[24] In one minor sphere the Wilson Government has, however, achieved a striking growth rate: the cost of the Wilson administration (that is, of all Ministers' salaries and allowances) in January 1967 was just about double that of Sir Alec Douglas-Home's administration in 1963-4 – and is now running at around £740,000 a year.

By no stretch of the imagination can the Wilson government be considered a reforming government, even of the moderate kind that was represented by the first three years of the 1945 administration. Mr. Wilson is, of course, a much more efficient and competent politician than Attlee ever was, and his political nerves are certainly much steadier. His abilities have been well demonstrated by the ways in which has reduced the Left within the Parliamentary Party to political impotence, first by including some of the obvious candidates for the leadership of the Left in his own administration, where their consciences are now safe in his keeping, and second, by confusing, bullying, cajoling and bemusing the back-benchers of the Parliamentary Left to the point where up to the time of writing (January 1967), there has never been any effective movement of opposition to Wilson's policies. While the record of the Parliamentary Left has not been much better than pitiful, it must be said at once that they have received only feeble encouragement from the Labour movement outside Westminster. The political side of the movement has been especially weak, as witness the absence of any sustained campaign against the support which Britain is providing for America's policies of mass destruction of the Vietnamese people. All along the line, but especially on foreign questions, the Left is either divided or ineffective, or more usually both. The political and intellectual degeneration that afflicted the British Labour movement in the 1950's is still exercising a powerful influence. Mr. Wilson's special brand of Toryism may in the end convince many of the incompatibility of Labourism and socialist policies, but there is so far no sign of a new political upsurge of protest, although these are movements which in their nature are often hard to foresee.

By the end of 1947 – two and a half years after the formation of the Labour Government – the political nerves of the Attlee administration were already beginning to crumble. The Tories were recovering fast from the effects of the election debacle of 1945 and their growing strength and confidence was being reflected in a marked sharpening of hostility to Labour among the parliamentary Conservative Party. That these things have not yet come to pass in the first two and a half years of the Wilson Government cannot be wholly ascribed to the ineptitude of the present leadership of the Conservative Party, although that has made its own contribution. More important is that Mr. Wilson has been able to convince many Conservative voters in the country that the leadership of Britain is safe in his hands. His tough record of dealings with the trade union movement and the essential soundness of his foreign policy are well appreciated by the business community as well as by large numbers of middle class voters in general. Mr. Wilson, it is well known, is playing hard for the center of British society. If his government manages to achieve a reflation of the economy and a higher rate of growth in the last two years of its life, a new range of social security benefits, on a wage related basis, may well be introduced to the Statute Book. Properly timed, and Mr. Wilson's mind is never empty of electoral considerations, the combination of full employment again with some improvement in social benefits will help to maintain the greater part of the working class vote, while a proportion at least of the middle class vote can be expected to remember the firm conservatism of Mr. Wilson's basic policies. The Labor Party could well break all traditions and come back to Westminster in 1970 with a thumping majority. If this happens we may indeed be on the threshold of a new era in British political life, when the permanent Labour majority, always theoretically possible in a country with a majority of manual voters, becomes a political fact and reality. Labourism will develop into a highly articulate philosophy and practice of the Scandinavian kind, although the class conflicts and social tensions in Britain are not likely to be so easily smoothed away as they are in Sweden. At least some things should become clearer as time moves along: that Labourism has nothing to do with Socialism: that the Labour Party has never been, nor is it capable of becoming, a vehicle for socialist advance; and that the destruction of the illusions of Labourism is a necessary step before the emergence of a socialist movement of any size and influence becomes practical.

In 1960 it was estimated that there were between seven and eight million persons living *below* a specially defined "national assistance" standard. The numbers of these poor are almost certainly growing, and have continued to grow during the lifetime of the present Labour Government. The minor reforms which the Wilson Government have introduced are no more, says Peter Townsend, "than hot compresses on an ailing body politic".[25] It cannot be too strongly emphasized that Britain does not need economic growth in the future to remedy its present basic inequalities. It is today a richer country than ever before, and the large and growing gap between public squalor and private affluence can be bridged without any further economic growth. We need, here and now, a major shift in the proportion of the national income devoted to public services of all kinds: to health and welfare services, to public housing, to education in all its aspects. Economic expansion will help, but only if this shift in the allocation of national income has already taken place: otherwise we reproduce the American situation of increasing public decay and abomination.

These things have nothing to do with socialism: that is an order of change of quite a different magnitude. They are radical policies well within the political comprehension of a Government determined to introduce a genuine programme of reform. They fit comfortably inside the assumptions of any reforming Government concerned to honour its pledged to the electorate...but not those of the present Wilson administration. Mr. Wilson himself has no aspirations along this road: nor, presumably, have his ministers. From social reform to social conservatism: this is the measure of the present-day degeneration of the Labourist tradition in Britain. "when they desire to place their economic life on a better foundation, they repeat like parrots, the word "productivity". So Tawney wrote in 1920,[26] and he went on to ask the central question: productivity – for what purpose? Now it is his party, the Labour Party, that is shouting the word again, hoping to persuade their own people that it is productivity, and not how wealth is distributed, that is important. And the former socialists who are now ministers in the Wilson government will continue to tell themselves as well as others that dribbling out monies for the Arts, or improving transport facilities, or introducing American technical know-how to British industry, has something to do with the movement along the socialist road.

And in the meantime, the poor and needy – the millions of them – drag out their drab and dismal lives.

Notes

[1] R. Miliband, *The State in Capitalist Society*, London, Weidenfeld and Nicolson, 1969; and R. Miliband, *Capitalist Democracy in Britain*, Oxford, Oxford University Press, 1982.

[2] J. Saville, 'Labourism and the Labour Government', in R. Miliband and J. Saville (eds), *The Socialist Register 1967*, London, Merlin Press, 1967, pp. 43-72; and J. Saville, 'The ideology of Labourism', in R. Benewick et al, (eds), *Knowledge and Belief in Politics*, London, Allen and Unwin, 1973, pp. 213-226

[3] J. Saville, 'The ideology of Labourism', op.cit, p.215

[4] R. Miliband, *Parliamentary Socialism*, Lonbdon, Merlin Press, 1961, p. 13

[5] J. Saville, 'Labourism and the Labour Government', op.cit., p. 53

[6] Ibid, p.57

[7] Ibid, p.56

[8] Ibid, p.50

[9] Ibid, p.68

[10] John Strachey, "Tasks and Achievements of British Labour" *New Fabian Essays* (1952), p. 182.

[11] Richard Crossman, "The Lessons of 1945" *Towards Socialism* (1965), p. 153.

[12] B. Abel-Smith, "Whose Welfare State" *Conviction* (1958), p. 63

[13] J. E. Meade, *Efficiency, Equality and the Ownership of Property* (1964), p. 27.

[14] John Hughes, *Nationalised Industries in the Mixed Economy* (Fabian Tract 328), p. 1; and the literature there cited.

[15] A. A. Rogow and P. Shore, *The Labour Government and British Industry, 1945-1951* (Oxford, 1955), pp. 62-3.

[16] op. cit., p. 38.

[17] Quoted in R. Miliband, *Parliamentary Socialism* (1961), p. 291.

[18] Quoted in D. Pryce-Jones, "Towards the Cocktail Party", in *Age of Austerity* (eds. M. Sissons and P. French, 1963) p. 218.

[19] *Economist*, 3 January 1948

[20] Quoted in K. Zilliacus, *I Choose Peace* (1949), p. 113.

[21] The earliest comprehensive statement by Sidney Webb is his contribution to *Fabian Essays* (1889), "The Basis of Socialism: Historic".

[22] Ibid, pp. 78-9

[23] G. Bernard Shaw, *The Impossibilities of Anarchism* (Fabian Tract, No. 45), pp. 26-7.

[24] B. Abel-Smith, *Labour's Social Plans* (Fabian Tract 369), p. 6.

[25] P. Townsend, *Poverty, Socialism and Labour in Power* (Fabian Tract 371), p. 31.

[26] *The Sickness of an Acquisitive Society* (1920), p. 5.

Editorial Introduction to Extract 5

A second edition of *Parliamentary Socialism* was published in 1972 – the original volume plus an extensive postscript (which is reproduced here). By 1972, in the wake of the dismal performance of the first Wilson Government of 1964-70, the Miliband position had hardened. The opaqueness of the conclusions of the 1961 volume – with the implicit option of a transformable party still there in the text – had long gone. What was offered instead was fully in line with the 1967 Saville argument: that the Labour Party was not a route to socialism in Britain, but rather an important mechanism for the incorporation of the British labour movement into an untransformed British capitalism. By 1972, according to Ralph Miliband, the British Labour Party was no longer even reformist. Its reformist period was behind it, and could not be recaptured. On the contrary, those on the Labour Left who thought it could be so captured, were here written of (and written off) as trapped in an illusory strategy, one capable only of generating periodic and ephemeral revolts with no lasting consequences. By 1972 it was with the functionality of Labour Party moderation – and with the empty radical rhetoric of its leadership in moments of class militancy – that Ralph Miliband chose to close his postscript to what had by then become the definitive left-wing study of British Labour. The postscript is worth reading again: for its description and explanation of the failure of the first Wilson Government; for its sense of the Labour Party being, at most, a 'party of modest social reform in a capitalist society within whose confines it is ever more firmly and by now irrevocably rooted'; and for its closing observations on the functionality to the long-term stability of British capitalism of the leadership's periodic 'radical sounding noises'. By 1972, after the half decade of hot summers that followed the uprisings of 1968, it was Ralph Miliband's view that capitalism needed such a party, to 'play a major role in the management of discontent and…to keep it in safe bounds'. It was also by then his view that the British Left needed a very different kind of party.

5. POSTSCRIPT (1972)

Ralph Miliband

I

The last chapter of *Parliamentary Socialism* was written in 1960 at the height of the struggle between Gaitskellite 'revisionists' on the one hand, and an unstable coalition of their opponents in the Labour Party and the trade unions on the other; and the concluding section of the book left open the possibility that the Labour Party might yet become an adequate agency for that radical transformation of British society to which it had for so long been formally committed.

This, clearly enough, is not what happened in the following years. The groundswell of militancy to which I then referred did grow throughout the Labour movement and well beyond it in the sixties. But this found no reflection in Labour's policies and activities, least of all during the six years in which the Labour Government was in office; or rather, this militancy produced policies and activities designed to curb and subdue it.

The natural tendency, in discussing Labour in the sixties, is to focus on the Labour Government's record between 1964 and 1970. But that record needs to be seen as the consequence of attitudes and decisions which had been adopted well before the Government came to office. The key to its performance in office is to be found in the Labour leaders' basic approach, while still in opposition, to the purposes and tasks they assigned to a Labour Government. Directions were then assumed, or rather confirmed, which fundamentally determined the course of subsequent events.

The most important of the decisions that were made in the years which immediately preceded Labour's electoral victory in 1964 was that a Labour Government, when it next came to office, would not seek to extend public ownership in any really significant way[1]. This, in effect, was the outcome of the struggle around Clause 4 in 1959-60; and though the episode is now ancient history, it was sufficiently important in its long-term implications for its more salient aspects to be reviewed here.

Hugh Gaitskell, it may be recalled, had not specifically asked for the excision of Clause 4 from the Party Constitution, or even for its amendment.[2] What he had proposed was a new 'declaration of aims', which would become part of the Constitution of the Labour Party alongside Clause 4. The draft 12-point declaration which he had presented to the National Executive Committee of the Labour Party in March 1960 had invited the Party to affirm that 'its aim is a classless society from which all class barriers and false social values have been eliminated'; that it stood for 'democracy in industry'; that it rejected 'the self-ish acquisitive doctrine of capitalism'; and that it wanted instead 'to create a socialist community based on fellowship, cooperation and service in which all can share fully in our cultural heritage'. The reference to public ownership in the declaration went as follows: 'It [the Labour Party] is convinced that these social and economic objectives can be achieved only through an expansion of common ownership substantial enough to give the community power over the commanding heights of the economy'. This might have been taken to signify a far-reaching commitment. But the text then went on virtually to qualify it out of existence. 'Recognizing,' it said, 'that both public and private enterprise have a place in the economy it [the Labour Party] believes that further extension of common ownership should be decided from time to time in the light of these objectives, and according to circumstances with due regard for the views of the workers and consumers concerned.' Given the known attitude of the Labour leaders to the extension of public ownership, this evasive formula amounted to a commitment that nothing much would be done about it. Nor, for that matter, would a less evasive formula have made much difference in practice. What mattered was what the Labour leaders wanted, or, as in this case, what they did not want.

The proposal that the declaration be included in the Constitution of the Labour Party was accepted by the Executive. At this point, however, a difficulty arose. As one writer with strong sympathies for the 'revisionists' has noted, 'the trade union delegates to the NEC had provided him [i.e. Gaitskell] with the necessary support, but they had acted individually and without reference to their unions. The union conferences in the spring and summer of 1960 refused to ratify the decisions of their delegates, and what in March had appeared as an agreed solution had by the autumn turned into a defeat for Gaitskell'.[3] Faced with the certain prospect that his attempt to write the declaration into the Constitution would be turned down at the 1960 Labour Party Conference, Gaitskell agreed to an Executive resolution which decided to leave the Constitution as it stood, but which also declared that the statement which it had accepted in March was a 'valuable expression of the aims of the Labour Party in the second half of the twentieth century', and which it therefore 'commended' to the Conference. The Conference duly agreed to this, and the battle of Clause 4 was thus brought to an end.

It suited the contestants to proclaim (and as far as much of the Labour Left was concerned probably to believe) that the battle had ended without a decisive victory for either side. But save in purely formal terms, it was not an accurate view of what had happened. For all practical purposes, Labour's 'revisionist' leaders had had their way. Moreover, they remained firmly in control of the day-to-day decision-making apparatus of the Party. Such verbal concessions as they had been compelled to make – and they had been compelled to make very few, merely served to pacify the Labour Left, and thus even to strengthen the leadership.

In 1961, the Annual Conference adopted *Signposts for the Sixties*, the document which formed the basis of Labour's electoral programme in 1964, and this too is worth a brief mention.

This document called attention to the fact that 'the economy is still dominated by a small ruling caste. For years the Tories have talked about a property-owning democracy. Yet the top one per cent of the population owns nearly half of the nation's private wealth and property …. But these men are not only wealthy: they are also powerful – a small and compact oligarchy …, in private industry the directors of a few hundred great combines determine between them what Britain should produce. As their power increases, these men, together with the directors of leading insurance companies, are usurping the functions of a Government which is theoretically responsible to the whole people.'[4] In the same vein, *Signposts for the Sixties* called attention '

> to the menacing growth of private monopoly and the consequent concentration of power in irresponsible hands. The giant corporations or private financial empires which dominate so much of the British economy, and which decisively influence its total performance, grow each year larger, fewer and yet more closely interlocked.[5]

This analysis, it might have been thought, unmistakably pointed to the conclusion that major measures of public ownership must form an essential plank of Labour's platform. But this was precisely the conclusion which the document quite deliberately failed to reach. Having located the 'commanding heights', the Labour leaders showed that they had no intention of climbing them. *Signposts for the Sixties* committed a Labour Government to the re-nationalisation of steel, which had become an unavoidable pledge; and to the creation of an 'integrated and publicly owned transport system', which, however commendable, was hardly dramatic, since so much of public transport was already publicly owned. For the rest, the document was resolutely hypothetical, and spoke of public ownership, not as a means of capturing the "commanding heights', but, 'most important of all', as a means of 'helping to fulfil our national plan for economic growth'. There was very little about this economic, 'pragmatic' emphasis, that the 'small and compact oligarchy' which was said to dominate economic life need be unduly troubled about.

By 1963, Harold Wilson was explaining to the readers of *The New York Times* ('Wilson Defines British Socialism') that 'our plans to extend the public sector – to occupy the "commanding heights" consist mainly in the creation of new industries'. Even this was qualified: 'We shall not be dogmatic or doctrinaire about the ownership of the new industries. Some will be privately owned, some publicly owned – the important thing is to get them established'.[6]

By the time this was written, Wilson had become Leader of the Labour Party. Much, as a result, then seemed to many people to have been thrown back into the melting pot. To the Labour Left in particular, this utterly unpredictable turn of events appeared to suggest that the new chapter which was about to be written in the Labour Party's history would be very different, and much more attractive to the Left, than could have been anticipated had Gaitskell lived. From having been permanently exiled to the outer fringes of the Labour Party's apparatus of power, the Labour Left now felt itself to be represented at its very centre. After all, Wilson had challenged Gaitskell for the leadership of the Labour Party in 1960, and had therefore appeared, willy nilly, to ally himself with Gaitskell's opponents on the left. Nine years earlier he had resigned from the Attlee Government with Aneurin Bevan and John Freeman; and although he had been careful, in the following years, to keep his distance from the Bevanite group, he had also been even more distant from the Gaitskellite faction, indeed in personal terms much more so. The constituency parties had regularly returned him to the National Executive on what was generally regarded as a left slate. In short, he appeared in 1963 as the answer to the Labour Left's prayer for a sympathetic leader of the Party.

This view of the prospects unfolded by Wilson's accession to the leadership unfortunately overlooked a great deal that was known about him, and which should have been obvious from his pronouncements and conduct over the years – notably the fact that neither over foreign affairs, nor over home policy, including public ownership, did he materially differ from Gaitskell. Their views might not be identical over this or that policy issue, but such differences as there were could in no basic sense be said to place the new leader outside the ideological spectrum in which Gaitskell moved. What separated him from Gaitskell and the latter's friends (apart from the dislike, distrust and even contempt which they felt for him) was a matter of tactics and a certain style. Wilson had an infinitely greater sense of the complex strands which make up the political culture of the Labour movement, and he realised far better than did the 'Hampstead set' that the 'unity' of the Party, which meant in effect the neutralisation of the Left, could be achieved at a very small price, indeed at next to no price, provided the leadership was willing to wrap up whatever policies it thought suitable in language which would appeal to the Left. A small but significant episode may serve to illustrate the point. Shortly after Wilson's accession to the leadership of the Party, a Tory backwoodsman sought to embarrass him in the House of Commons by referring to Clause 4. Wilson defiantly interrupted him and answered him that it was 'the position of the whole Party'.[7] It was not the kind of thing which Gaitskell would have handled well, but which Wilson could take in his stride, and gain credit for from the Labour Left, even though what he said did not actually mean anything. There was to be much of the same kind in the following years.

However, Harold Wilson said much, in the eighteen months after he became Leader of the Labour Party, which appeared to provide an answer to Labour's search for the kind of positive 'message' which it had failed to find ever since the collapse of the Attlee Government in 1951.

His most insistent and persuasive theme was the need for change, renewal, modernization and reform in every area of British life, most of all in economic life. Much of what he said sounded radical enough, as for instance when speaking for the first time in the role of Leader of the Party to its annual conference, he told the delegates that 'for the commanding heights of British industry to be controlled today by men whose only claim is their aristocratic connections or the power of inherited wealth or speculative finance is as irrelevant to the twentieth century as would be the continued purchase of commissions in the armed forces by lordly amateurs'.[8] It needs to be understood, however, that what Wilson was attacking was not British capitalism as a system, but some facets of it, the 'old boy network', 'candy-floss commercialism', 'parasitic speculators', the 'grouse-moor mentality', and that what, in effect, he counter-posed to this was not the vision of a socialist society, but of a renovated capitalism, freed from its aristocratic and gentlemanly accretions, dynamic, professional, entrepreneurial, numerate and efficient.

Two things may be said about this. The first is that Wilson's apparent conviction that it was possible to make a clear separation between 'patriotic' and 'unpatriotic' enterprise altogether ignored the degree to which those forms of it to which he objected and those forms of it which he approved were in fact intertwined. Secondly, that even if some such separation was possible, the kind of capitalism which appeared to meet with his approval was as socially irresponsible and greedily exploitative as any other kind. It is in this perspective that such radicalism as forms part of Harold Wilson's philosophy has to be seen. It is too simple to suggest, as has often been done in the light of subsequent experience, not least by many of his erstwhile admirers, that when he spoke before 1964 of the need for radical change, he was merely engaged in an astute public relations exercise, designed to appeal to a widespread mood of impatience with a decrepit economic and social order. No doubt, the public relations aspect of the matter was there. But there is no need to deny Mr Wilson's interest in reform. To do so is to miss the much more important point that his reforming zeal was deliberately set, for all its verbal edge, within the context of an economic system whose *basic* features were accepted by him and his colleagues as given; and that all their proposals for change had therefore to be adapted to the nature and requirements of that system. But 'adapted' is too weak – 'subordinated' would be more accurate. Whatever deficiency and dereliction Harold Wilson touched on – and he touched upon many – was directly or indirectly related to the prevailing economic system: and it followed that the changes of which he spoke, if they were to be as far-reaching as he proclaimed to be necessary, would require precisely the kind of challenge to that economic system which his whole approach precluded. Given the context which he assumed, namely one in which the 'commanding heights' of the economy would remain under private ownership and control, and in which public enterprise would continue to remain an adjunct of capitalist enterprise, the 'modernization' for which he asked could only mean the more efficient operation of the capitalist system; and this would include that ever-greater concentration of private economic power, which he denounced, but which the Labour Government was in fact to encourage. He spoke of allying 'science to socialism': all that this could mean was the more effective harnessing of science to the purposes of capitalism. He appealed for an end to the 'system of educational apartheid' and proclaimed the need for careers to be open to talent. But what this meant, given the context, was that more talent should be channelled into the service of the going system. Nor did the Labour Government make any notable indent into the system of educational apartheid; and in the field of tertiary education, it even managed, with the adoption of the 'binary' system, to give it new institutional forms. Wilson comprehensively denounced the 'conservatism' of British life: but the only 'conservatism' he and his government tried to do much about was that of the trade union movement, which did indeed want to conserve hard-won rights of self-defence against the attacks of the Labour Government.

The fact is that, in order to acquire effective meaning, Wilson's radicalism needed to include the determination to mount an assault upon the 'commanding heights' of the economy. But he had no more wish than his erstwhile 'revisionist' opponents to do anything of the kind. This being the case, his radicalism was bound to remain mere verbiage. Without the control provided by the public ownership of strategic sections of the economy, he and his colleagues could only try and persuade those who did control the 'private sector' to cooperate with them. But they could only succeed in doing so by pursuing policies which corresponded with the purposes of capitalist interests. These purposes did not happen to include the radical aspirations by which the Labour leaders proclaimed themselves to be driven.

The attitude which the leaders held towards the question of public ownership had a significance which went far beyond that issue itself. The battle of Clause 4 had not only been about public ownership. Behind that issue, there was the determination of the Labour leadership to force upon the Labour Party the final acceptance of a economic system predominantly based upon private ownership and control, and its abandonment, for all practical purposes, of the alternative vision which Clause 4 embodied. In this crucial sense the argument had not at all been about 'theology' as Harold Wilson had found it convenient to claim at the time. On the contrary, it had vast political implications not only in terms of the Labour Party's ultimate purpose, but also in terms of its approach to immediate problems. A leadership as thoroughly reconciled as this one was to the permanence of British capitalism could also be expected to be easily reconciled to its requirements, and to the acceptance of its particular rationality. That this was so was richly confirmed by the experience of Labour in government.

The reconciliation was all the more likely to be achieved – or at least sought for by the Labour leaders – in that they had, like their predecessors, a profound sense of their 'national' vocation. It has been said about Gaitskell that he had a 'philosophic predilection for "class harmony" as opposed to "class division" or "class war"; and that this partly explained 'his desire to make Labour a "class-less party" and his intense emotional reaction against the Conservative Party's claim that they represented all social classes whereas Labour was tied to a single class.[9] This is no doubt quite accurate. The trouble, however, is that the search for class harmony could only be successful on two conditions: the first was that the Labour Party should not attempt to do much about the evils which its leaders were so ready to denounce on Labour platforms, since to try and do much about them involved a radical challenge to those forces which profited from their perpetuation. Secondly, it required that the Labour leaders should do their best to demobilize their own supporters and, where occasion demanded, to turn against them. Provided they were prepared to meet these conditions, and they were, there was no reason why they should not achieve a reasonable rapport with the best people.

Harold Wilson shared to the full this concern for class harmony. Indeed, his wish to cut a 'national' figure, particularly after he had assumed office, often seemed to be an almost obsessive preoccupation, only previously matched in its intensity by Ramsay MacDonald. At the 1966 Annual Conference of the Labour Party, following Labour's resounding victory at the polls, he explained the significance of that victory, as it appeared to him: 'It proved', he said, 'that the British people accepted that Labour could govern, that we had the means and the measures that the country knew were necessary. It proved that Labour could give national leadership, that we rejected the Conservative concept of cynical conflict between class and class'.[10] Of course the 'Conservative concept' was precisely the opposite, namely that there was no inherent conflict, cynical or otherwise, between class and class, and that where conflict did occur, it should be attributed to the machinations of ill-intentioned men seeking to exploit long-outmoded attitudes unfortunately still prevalent in the working class. This view, though in itself absurd, is a necessary part of Conservative thinking, since it serves important self-legitimating as well as propaganda purposes. Faced with class conflict and bent on class harmony, Wilson and his colleagues soon adopted the same Conservative view, and acted in accordance with it. The Labour Party's Manifesto for the General Election of 1964 was boldly entitled *The New Britain*. But the contents of the document hardly matched the promise of the title. The prospectus was breathless enough – obviously the brainwork of the public relations wizards which the Labour Party had called to its help: 'The country needs fresh

and virile leadership. Labour is ready. Poised to swing its plans into instant operation. Impatient to apply the New Thinking that will end the chaos and steril-
ity ... restless with positive remedies for the problems the Tories have criminally
neglected.' The prospectus was fraudulent. The Manifesto comprised a useful if
modest list of reforms, notably in the field of welfare, which Labour promised to
carry out. But what was being offered in 1964 was not a 'new Britain': rather, and
at the most, a more efficient and more 'compassionate' management of the old
order. The Manifesto mentioned 'socialist planning': but what this amounted
to was the promise to set up a Ministry of Economic Affairs 'with the duty of
formulating, with both sides of industry, a national economic plan'. But, the
document asked, suppose production falls short of the plan in key sections of
industry? The New Thinking had the answer ready: 'Then it is up to the Government and the industry to take whatever measures are required.'

Public ownership was dealt with perfunctorily: steel would be re-nationalised,
and existing nationalised industries would be encouraged to move into new
fields. A Labour Government would also establish new industries: but it would
do so 'either by public enterprise or in participation with private industry.' In
the election campaign itself, Butler and King have observed, 'Labour spokesmen played down the issue [of public ownership]; they tended to concentrate
on the monopolistic inefficiency of the steel industry and, defensively, to deny
any plans for the large extension of public ownership.[11] By 1966, the reference to
public ownership in the Labour Manifesto had come to be included in a section
significantly entitled 'Helping Industry' and had even less to say on the subject
than in 1964.[12] Four years later, still less. In effect, the issue had been relegated to
as low a place on Labour's agenda as Hugh Gaitskell and his friends could ever
have wished. Given the weakness of political formations on the left of the Labour
Party, this meant in effect that it had been removed from serious political debate
altogether. This was a major contribution of the Labour leaders to the nature
and substance of contemporary British politics, for which capitalist interests had
good cause to be grateful. In thus disposing of public ownership, in thus turning
it into a great non-issue, the Labour leaders had provided these interests with a
guarantee against the one threat they had most reason to fear. Wherever else the
consensus between the parties might break down, all was safe so long as it endured here; and those who controlled the Labour Party were wholly determined
that it should.

What has been said so far should help to explain one feature of Labour's affairs
which might otherwise seem puzzling, namely its lack of 'preparation' for office,
which was in some crucial respects as marked in 1964 as it had been on previous
occasions. The 1964 Election Manifesto had referred to Labour's readiness to
'swing its plans into instant operation'. But as one writer has accurately noted,
'detailed work had been undertaken on social security, land, higher education
and regional planning, but on the central problem of the balance of payments

and the modernization of the economy only sketch plans were available.[13] This lack of preparation, after thirteen long years in opposition, was in no way accidental. For, as the same writer also explains, 'in order to make proper preparations, a number of different and divisive issues would have had to be raised: Any thorough examination of overseas defence expenditure, for instance, would have called into question Britain's relations with NATO and the United States. Any serious examination of the tools available to the Government in economic planning might have led to the conclusion that the amount of control which was to be exercised over privately owned firms is strictly limited. Any real attempt to work out the machinery for new public ownership might have transformed this from a useful flag to wave at Party Conferences into a positive commitment to extend the frontiers of public ownership.'[14]

This is right. But Mr Pryke goes on to say that the reason such commitments were avoided was that to try and spell them out would have shattered the 'new-found unity' of the Party. 'The Labour leaders had no wish to reopen the acrimonious debates of the early 1960s. What they were usually trying to discover in their discussions was not a policy for the future but a form of words for the present. In this way Labour was able to fight the 1964 Election as a united party. If it had been disunited it would have lost.'[15] This would suggest that the lack of preparation of more radical proposals was due to the need for compromise between left and right in the top echelons of the Party. But there is no evidence that anyone among the policymakers in the Labour Party seriously pressed for a more radical programme, least of all that Harold Wilson himself wanted such a programme, and that he had to be satisfied with less for the sake of 'unity'. On the contrary, the evidence suggests that the leaders of the party, however divided they might be on personal grounds, were fundamentally at one in ideological and programmatic terms. Left and Right in relation to them are terms devoid of any really serious meaning. The real reason why more radical plan had not been prepared is very simply that the leaders had no intention of carrying out any such plans. Nor did the Labour Left, still bemused by the thought that Harold Wilson was really on their side, have either the will or the capacity to press for more radical policies. Those who belonged to it also accepted the argument that, particularly before an election which the Labour Party stood a good chance of winning, unity was all: what they gladly overlooked was that this unity had been achieved at their expense.

The point has an obvious bearing on the present, now that the Labour Party is once again in opposition. The call is again heard that the Party must address itself more seriously than in the past to the task of preparing its plans for office. But this ignores the fact that the men who will control the next Labour Government are just as determined not to be saddled with embarrassingly far-reaching plans as were the men who assumed office in 1964. There may be much to be said for working out detailed socialist policies. But then is nothing to be said for the notion that they will be taken up by Labour in office. This is not what the Labour leaders are ABOUT.

The point will be discussed further in the concluding section of this Postscript. For the moment, what needs to be stressed is that the basic pattern of the Labour Government's conduct was firmly set in the preceding years. What happened between 1964 and 1970 was not due to the unfavourable economic circumstances which the government inherited; or to the entrenched conservatism of top civil servants; or to the machinations of speculators and the hostility of capitalist interests at home or abroad. It was above all due to the particular ideological dispositions which the men who ran the government brought to their tasks. It was these dispositions which allowed all the adverse factors they faced in office to weigh upon them as heavily as they did. No doubt, these factors would in any case have had to be tackled: but they would have been tackled very differently had these men had a genuinely more radical approach to affairs. Not only would the solutions have been different: the problems themselves would have been differently perceived. At the 1966 Labour Party Conference, Harold Wilson told the delegates that 'we cannot afford to fight the problems of the sixties with the attitudes of the Social Democratic Federation, nor, in looking for a solution to these problems, seek vainly to find the answers in Highgate cemetery'.[16] But the trouble with Mr Wilson and his colleagues was that their own answers to the problems they faced were of such a kind as to involve the betrayal of their promises and the reinforcement of the system to which they declared themselves opposed.

II

Harold Wilson has described his apologia for his years of office as 'the record of a Government all but a year of whose life was dominated by an inherited balance of payments problem which was nearing a crisis at the moment we took office; we lived and governed during a period when that problem made frenetic speculative attack on Britain both easy and profitable.[17] Five years, however, is a rather long time for a government to be dominated by an inherited balance of payments crisis, however acute; and the fact that the Wilson government was thus dominated says much about the narrow framework of orthodoxy within which it chose to operate. It had been no secret to its leading members that a Labour Government would, in 1964, inherit a massive balance of payments deficit. What they did not seem to have anticipated was the run on the pound which occurred soon after the Government was installed. When it did occur, the Prime Minister and his colleagues firmly rejected the one measure which, in the short run, would have given them some respite, namely devaluation. In August 1965, Harold Wilson explained in an interview to the Guardian why he had decided against it: 'Although this would have given us a year or two breathing space free from all anxiety about foreign balances, we felt that, whatever the temptation from the party point of view, the national interest was one hundred per cent the other way ... I do not deny it would have made life more tolerable with our narrow majority; that it would have enabled us to carry through our positive generous programmes of social reform, but it would not have been right.' Indeed, it would have been 'totally wrong', since 'there are many people overseas, including governments, marketing boards, central banks and others, who left their money in the form of sterling balances, on the assumption that the value of sterling would be maintained. To have let them down would have been not only a betrayal of trust, it would have shaken their faith about holding any further money in the form of sterling.'[18]

These sentiments suggest a very revealing order of priorities for Labour Prime Minister. For in choosing not to 'let down' Britain overseas creditors, he was also choosing to 'let down' the people whose votes had brought him to office and to sacrifice 'our positive generous programmes of social reform'.

No doubt, as Mr Wilson has subsequently argued, devaluation was 'not an easy way out'. But, as experience was to show, it could scarcely have been harder than the decision to 'defend the pound' which was in any case unsuccessful. It was above all a political decision, intended to establish Labour's credentials with the international 'business community', and reinforced by the fear, as one well-informed writer has put it, that devaluation, to which the United States was then opposed, 'would cloud prospects for future Anglo-American cooperation which Wilson hoped would form the backbone of his foreign policy.' [19]

Having rejected devaluation, the Government resorted to international borrowing to shore up sterling: in November 1964, it mounted the first of the many international 'rescue operations', to the tune of 3000 million dollars, which marked its years of office Yet, it was only a month before coming to office that the Prime Minister himself, in words which have often been quoted, told the Trades Union Congress that 'you can get into pawn, but don't then talk of an independent foreign policy, or an independent defence policy'.[20] In actual fact, the Labour leaders had no intention pursuing an independent foreign or defence policy, so that being in pawn made no great difference. At the 1965 Labour Party Conference, Mr Wilson indignantly repudiated the charge that his support of the United States in Vietnam had anything to do with economy dependence. 'At no time – and I say this categorically – has the been any attempt to link economic cooperation with any aspect of foreign policy ... there have never been, whether in White House talks, in telegrams, in ambassadorial approaches, or even on the hot line, any attempts to link Vietnam with any aspect of economic monetary cooperation ...'[21] This is hardly conclusive: the Prime Minister did not have to be told that there would be retribution to be aware that it might occur, if anything he said or did proved to be a serious embarrassment to the American Administration. Still, the point need not be argued: it may well be that Mr Wilson and his colleagues were sufficiently committed to the 'Anglo-American alliance' to support American aggression in Vietnam without being forced to do so by financial necessity. More relevant are some other remarks which Mr Wilson addressed to the 1964 TUC: 'There is a warning here,' the Prime Minister had gone on to say. 'If you borrow from some of the world's bankers you will quickly find you lose another kind of independence because of the deflationary policies and the cuts on social services that will be imposed on a government that has got itself into that position.'[22] At the end of the General Election campaign, he had made the same point more specifically: 'You cannot go, cap in hand, to the central bankers of Europe as they [the Tories] have now been forced to do and maintain your freedom of action, whether on policies maintaining full employment here in Britain or even on social policies.'[23]

This was very well said and describes admirably what happened throughout the life of the Government. As Mr Maudling, the previous Chancellor of the Exchequer, put it in 1964, 'it is true the Labour Government have inherited our problems. They seem also to have inherited our solutions.'[24] It was entirely symptomatic of the climate in which the Government chose to operate that the Chancellor of the Exchequer, Mr Callaghan, who had in 1963 proposed an annual tax on all wealth over £20,000, and who had had the proposal endorsed by the Labour Party's Annual Conference of that year, should have declared in December 1964 that 'in view of the major reforms I have already announced to modernize the tax system and make it more fair, I have no plans for proceeding with this proposal'.[25]

The Government had come to office on a pledge to end the 'Stop-Go' policies of the Conservatives. It had proclaimed itself to be 'the party of growth'. But it quickly turned into, and remained throughout, a government of deflation and economic stagnation; and before long, it had come to preside over a level of permanent unemployment unknown in Britain since the war. In his book, Mr Wilson recalls that, on being pressed in November 1964 by Lord Cromer, the Governor of the Bank of England, for all-round cuts in expenditure, 'I asked him if this meant that it was impossible for any Government, whatever its party label, whatever its manifesto or the policies on which it fought an election, to continue, unless it immediately reverted to full-scale Tory policies.' On being told it it was so, 'because of the sheer compulsion of the economic dictation of those who exercised decisive economic power', the Prime Minister retorted that 'if that was the case, I was not prepared to accept it.'[26] What this means, on the record, is that Mr Wilson was not prepared to go as far as Lord Cromer wished. There is a Tory way of carry out Tory policies; and there is a Labour way of carrying out Tory policies. It may readily be granted that the Government carried out Tory policies in a Labour way, with heart-searching, qualifications, exceptions and so forth. But carry them out it did, all the same, and thereby cleared the way for the more drastic application of Tory policies by their Tory successors.

In 1965, the Government presented with much flourish its National Plan for economic growth. This proclaimed a series of targets which if reached, would have achieved a 25% increase in G.N.P. by 1970. In fact, the targets were no more than forecasts and Government had not much more control over their fulfilment than the Meterological Office has over its weather predictions. For it was no position to 'plan'. The planning endeavours of the Attlee Government after the war had been meagre enough. But compared to those of the Wilson Government, they were positively heroic. In any case the government was forced into policies of further deflation soon after the National Plan was announced, which made even greater nonsense of its forecasts. The Plan was dead even before the echoes of its promise had been stilled. Edward Heath was quite right to describe it as 'the biggest publicity gimmick which the Government has so far produced'[27] – not that he was by any means the most suitable person to issue the indictment.

There was one policy which the Labour Government pursued with great consistency throughout its period of office, namely an 'incomes policy'. This had been a fixed part of the Labour leaders' purpose long before the Wilson Government was formed, as it had long been a fixed part of the purpose of Conservative governments. What that policy amounted to, stripped of verbiage, was a state-imposed curb on wage increases: a matter of people earning £1000 a month more telling people earning £1000 a year (or less) that they must stop being greedy. On the other hand, an incomes policy badly required verbiage, and this certainly was not wanting. As so often in the past, when wage-earners had been asked to show 'restraint', the old and spurious cry of 'equality of sacrifice' was again raised. In 1963, Harold Wilson had warned that 'we shall have to ask for restraint in the matter of incomes', but, he had added, 'when we say incomes we mean all incomes. That means not only wages and salaries, but profits, especially monopoly profits, distributed dividends, yes, and rents as well …'[28] Once again, the rich were to be asked, without much effect, to defer cashing in their profits and dividends, while wage earners were to be pressed, with much greater determination, to forego 'unreasonable' wage increases altogether.

At the TUC in September 1964, Harold Wilson told the delegates that: 'we have the right to ask for an incomes policy because we are prepared to contribute the three necessary conditions. First, an assurance of rising production and rising incomes, so that the sacrifice, the restraint for which we ask is matched by an assurance that it will result in increased production and increased rewards. Second; an assurance of equity and social justice, in that our policies will be directed to the benefit of the nation as a whole and not to the advantage of a sectional interest. Third, an assurance that what we ask for in wages and salaries will apply equally to profits and dividends and rent (Applause). We shall not create a free-for-all for the speculator, and land profiteer and the landlord – and then ask wage and salary earners alone to show a concern for the national interest that others are not required to show.'[29]

Whatever else Mr Wilson might claim for his government, even he could hardly claim that any of these conditions had been fulfilled three months after the election of 1964. However, it was then that the Government persuaded the TUC as well as the CBI to sign a Declaration of Intent which endorsed the establishment of a new body, which became the Prices and Incomes Board, entrusted with the responsibility to 'examine particular cases in order to advise whether or not the behaviour of prices or of wages, salaries and other money incomes is in the national interest as defined by the Government after consultation with management and unions'. When this 'treaty' was signed, George Brown, then Minister of Economic Affairs, declared that 'history was being made', and announced, somewhat prematurely, that 'the document heralded the end of the class war'.[30]

This kind of exercise was not, however, nearly sufficient to ensure effective 'wage restraint'; and as the need for further financial help from abroad became acute, so did foreign pressure grow, notably from the United States, for an incomes policy 'with teeth'.[31] By the summer of 1965, the Government had set about persuading 'both sides of industry' to accept a 'compulsory early warning system'. The representatives of business duly agreed to do their patriotic duty, possibly encouraged by the fact that the system would above all bear upon wages. The TUC was much more reluctant, despite George Brown's dramatic announcement to the members of the General Council that 'he had just heard from Washington over the transatlantic telephone that President Johnson had authorised US participation in the vital support operation, based on the "package" proposal which included the new assurances about Britain's income policy'.[32] In the end, and after much arduous arm-twisting, the TUC did agree.

This was by no means enough either. Stronger measures were required, and the Government was fortified in its resolve to adopt them by its decisive victory at the polls in March 1966. For *Tribune*, which had earlier made the remarkable discovery that the Labour election manifesto was not only an 'interesting and stimulating document' but 'also in essence, a socialist one,' Labour's victory was taken to signify that 'socialism is right back on the agenda.'[33] What was in fact right back on the agenda was a more resolute attack on wage-earners.[34] An often-quoted remark of Harold Wilson's was that 'the Labour movement is a crusade or it is nothing'. But the crusade which the Prime Minister was about to launch was directed at the men and women who had given him his electoral victory.

A useful opportunity to display 'toughness' with recalcitrant trade unionists was soon provided by the seamen's strike, which began in May 1966. In a television broadcast, the Prime Minister made it clear that the 'toughness' was not least intended to impress Britain's foreign creditors. 'What is at issue here is our national prices and incomes policy. To accept the demand [of the seamen] would be to break the dykes of our prices and incomes policy .... Our determination to insist on these principles when the cost is great will be taken by everyone at home and abroad as a proof of our determination to make that policy effective.[35] Finding that the NUS Executive was unwilling to back down, despite intense pressure, blandishments, minor concessions and promises of future improvements, the Prime Minister announced that the fault did not lie with the union's leaders, but with a 'tightly knit group of politically motivated men' who, for their own nefarious purposes, were 'forcing great hardship on the members of the union and their families, and endangering the security of the industry and the economic welfare of the nation.' A few days later, he 'named names', i.e. some members of the Communist Party. This invocation of the Red Menace worked: the strike was called off the following week. The national interest was safe. Not quite, though. For even before the seamen's strike, the pound had again come under pressure, and the government was again faced with a by now familiar crisis. In July, the Government announced the most drastic measures of deflation since the war, and coupled them with a legally binding wage freeze, which was to operate for six months, and be followed by a period of 'severe wage restraint'.

The Prime Minister's justification of his wages policy to the trade union movement is worth noting, since it illustrates so well the ideological miasma which dominated his administration. Speaking to the TUC in September, he expressed the hope that it would not be necessary to invoke statutory powers and that his policies would work by voluntary means. But if they did not, he warned, 'if there is breakaway action, whether in wages or prices, or by any other challenge *by any section of the community see seeking to secure a privileged position for itself,* the Government will, reluctantly, have to replace voluntary action by operating the statute.'[36] Phrases of this sort have become so common a part of the vocabulary in which political debate is conducted that their double-think quality tends to be overlooked. For there were sections of 'the community' which had no need whatever to seek a privileged position, since they fully enjoyed it already. Mr Wilson spoke as if he was presiding over a society which was already roughly egalitarian, or at least one which was well launched on that road. Any such notion was of course absurd. But this did not prevent the Prime Minister from asserting that this was indeed the case. 'An incomes policy, the planned expansion of incomes to which we are pledged', he also told the TUC, 'could only be developed by a Government which by its social and taxation policies created the necessary climate of social justice. *This we have done ....*'[37] So well had a 'climate of social justice' been created that four years later, at the time of the 1970 General Election, it could cogently be argued that poverty under the Labour Government had actually increased; [38] and the best that Government spokesmen could do to counter the argument was that it had, at most, been marginally alleviated. Whichever the case, massive deprivation remained a permanent feature of life in Britain. As far back as 1959, before the General Election of that year, Harold Wilson had said that 'given a Labour victory, the test is this: will there be, twelve months from now, a narrowing of the gap between rich and poor, quite apart from any general upward movement there may be as a result of increased national production? The answer is, quite simply, that there will be.'[39] The Labour victory had been delayed; and six years after it, never mind twelve months, the answer, quite simply, was that Mr Wilson's government had badly failed the test. What was soon created by the July measures was, inter alia, the return of chronic unemployment. By the following summer, unemployment figures had risen well over the half million mark, and stayed there for the rest of the Government's period of office.

In November 1967, the Government was finally forced to devalue the pound. This was linked with yet another 'rescue operation', the terms of which included the pledge that the Government would continue with its deflationary policies. In January 1968, it was announced that there was to be a reduction of public spending to the tune of £300 million in the next financial year, and a further reduction of over £400 million the year after. This included economies in health services, education and housing, the deferment of the raising of the school-leaving age from 1971 to 1973, the end of free milk in secondary schools, and the re-introduction of prescription charges and an increase in dental charges. Once again, however, Tory policies were applied in a Labour way: there were exceptions for those most in need. In addition, the 'package' included defence cuts, and a decision, which the Primer Minister had resisted since he had come to office, to withdraw from Singapore, Malaysia an the Persian Gulf by the end of 1971. In March 1968, the Chancellor of the Exchequer, now Roy Jenkins, presented a Budget which imposed tax increases of £923 million. This time, 'equality of sacrifices' took the form of a special levy for one year on investment income, which was expected to yield £100 million. However, Mr Jenkins explained in a television broadcast that 'he had decided it was better not to raise income tax but to impose heavy increases on goods and services so that incentive would not be impaired at a time when the economy must be made to work.'[40] A Conservative Chancellor could not have put it better.

This was the 'climate' in which the Government decided to proceed with what was commonly described as 'the reform of industrial relations', which meant in effect the further curbing of wage demands and new limitations on the right to strike. It was then that began the long drawn out struggle between the Labour Government and organized wage-earners, which was to end in the Government's retreat in June 1969.

The attempt to deal more firmly with labour 'indiscipline' followed naturally from the Government's approach to the management of a capitalist economy. The tone of its approach to 'industrial relations' had been set as soon as the Government was installed in 1964. The then Minister of Labour, Ray Gunter,

had inaugurated his tenure of office by proclaiming that the threat of an unofficial strike of dockers 'could only lead to anarchy'. As *The Guardian's* Labour
Correspondent noted, 'this is the first time for at least thirteen years that a Government has, on its own initiative, anticipated an unofficial strike with a public
warning to the men . . . Mr Gunter, on the first day at his desk, has served notice
that this Government intends to pursue a forward policy in labour relations.'[41]
. Ever since then, the Government had indeed pursued a 'forward policy in labour relations', whose main characteristic had been to try and impose 'restraint'
upon wage-earners, coupled with the shrill denunciation of their resistance to it,
as when George Brown told the delegates to the 1965 Labour Party Conference
that 'we have been operating the law of the jungle ourselves while condemning
it for every other purpose'.[42] What presumably trade unionists should have done
was to abjure the 'law of the jungle', meekly accept sacrifices while everybody
else continued to act according to that law, and find consolation in its occasional condemnation by Labour ministers. The Government could have had all
the support it required from trade unionists, had it been seen to be genuinely
engaged in the creation of a society marked by greater social justice. Only the
Prime Minister and his friends believed that the Labour Government was. So it
did not get the cooperation of wage-earners; and it was therefore logically driven
to move from unsuccessful restraint to statutory constraint.

Its target was not primarily the unions themselves but rank and file trade unionists, who showed a deplorable propensity to by-pass their unions and resort
to unofficial strikes, which now acquired a new and more suitably sinister name,
'unconstitutional strikes'. The Government had no objection to strong trade
unions, on the contrary, provided their strength was used to contain and discipline their members. Mr Wilson and his colleagues did want good 'industrial
relations': but what they meant by this was that wage-earner should forego, save
on the rarest occasions, the one form of action which their employers had ever
found persuasive.

In the end, the Government was forced to give up its Industrial Relations Bill,
and it had to be content with a 'solemn and binding undertaking' from the TUC
that it would itself intervene in the matter of 'unconstitutional strikes'. Most
trade unions leaders no doubt shared the Government's wish to 'routinise'
industrial conflict and to contain militancy: what they opposed, and were compelled by rank and file pressure to oppose, was the means whereby the Government sought to implement the policy. Still, the failure was qualified: it had paved
the way for legislation by the Conservatives.

A few weeks after Labour's victory at the polls in 1964, Harold Wilson went to
Washington. John Freeman, then Editor of *The New Statesman*, and later British
Ambassador to India and the United States, reported the visit as follows:

'Wilson, Gordon Walker [then Foreign Secretary] and Healey [the Minister of Defence] have established the right of Labour ministers to be treated as well by Washington as their more familiar Tory predecessors. It is not very important – though true – that the talk took place in an atmosphere of sound professional cordiality. Far more important is Wilson's success in allaying many of the original doubts about him in the US Administration. These doubts never concerned his good will or ability. They arose partly from the Washington experience of dealing with a Tory administration, and the inevitable inscrutability of new faces, and partly from uncertainty about the soundness of Wilson's views on both defence and economics. There is still doubt about the correctness of some of his policies in the sense that they are not all acceptable at face value to American policy-makers. But any idea that he is a flighty politician peddling irrelevant formulae in response to domestic pressures, has been dispelled …. The acceptance of Wilson as a responsible international statesman is the first achievement of this week's talks'[43]

What this meant was the 'new men' could be relied on by the American administration to continue with the foreign policy which had inspired all British governments since the war; there would be no departure from unswerving support of the United States as the leader of the Western conservative coalition. So indeed it was. Mr Paul Foot has suggested that, as far as Harold Wilson was concerned, it was the advent of John Kennedy to the Presidency in 1960 which had wrought a transformation of his attitude to the United States. 'Suddenly', he writes, 'all Wilson's inherent anti-Americanism, dating back to the 1949 devaluation crisis, passed from him. In his speeches both as Shadow Chancellor and as Shadow Foreign-Secretary, the former citadel of capitalism and militarism became the bright land of purposive dynamism'.[44] This would seem to make rather too much of superficial sentiments, and too little of the fact that Mr Wilson was always as basically committed to the 'Anglo-American alliance' as any other leading politician in Britain, Labour or Conservative. At any rate, the Prime Minister was in all likelihood not exaggerating much when he told the House of Commons at the end of 1965, after another visit to Washington, that 'we have reached a clearer understanding than probably at any time since the Second World War'.[45]

At the time this was said, the United States had long been involved in Vietnam, and its involvement assumed even more murderous forms in the following years. There was growing opposition in the Labour movement to the Government's support of this American enterprise. This was a source of some embarrassment to Mr Wilson and his colleagues. The Prime Minister dealt with the problem by way of a series of 'peace initiatives'. It was, or should have been, obvious that these exercises were doomed to failure by the determination of the United States to maintain a client regime in South Vietnam. The only purpose they served was to help pacify the Labour Party, or at least the parliamentary Left.

But the Government's policy on Vietnam was not an aberration: it was entirely consistent with its approach to all other issues of foreign policy. In all such issues, its bias was authentically conservative. Even the long delayed abandonment of its 'East of Suez' policy represented no change in its general approach and outlook. It did finally abandon, for reasons of economic necessity, the maintenance of a permanent military 'presence' East of Suez. But as the Prime Minister told the House of Commons in January 1968, 'we have assured them both [i.e. the Governments of Malaysia and Singapore] and our other Commonwealth partners and allies concerned, that we shall retain a general capability based in Europe (including the United Kingdom) which can be deployed overseas as, in our judgement, circumstances demand, including support for United Nations operations.[46] In other words, Britain would remain, to the limits of its reduced powers, in the business of imperialist intervention. The Government's enduring purpose was well illustrated by the fact that, at the time of the General Election of 1970, British forces were being lifted in a vast and costly exercise to the Far East, in order to demonstrate their capability to intervene in the area, notwithstanding the abandonment of permanent military bases. At no point in its six years of office was there any serious indication that the Government had any distinctive Labour policies in regard to foreign affairs.

III

What, then, is it reasonable to expect from the Labour Party in the years ahead?

There are two entirely opposed ways of answering this question. The first proceeds from the view that the Labour Party, whatever its past and present shortcomings, can eventually be turned into a socialist party, genuinely committed to the creation of a radically different social order, which would be based on, though certainly not exclusively defined by, the social ownership and democratic control of a predominant part of the means of production, distribution and exchange, including of course the 'commanding heights' of the economy. The second view is that it cannot be turned into such a party. Of the two, the second seems to me much the more realistic. The remainder of this Postscript is largely concerned with setting out the reasons for this.

To begin with, the point needs to be stressed that the Labour Party is no longer even a 'reformist' party. 'Reformist' socialism is the belief that a socialist society will be brought into being by way of a gradual series of structural and social reforms. This conviction lay at the core of Fabianism and it inspired, however tepidly, a long line of Labour leaders. With the adoption of a new Constitution in 1918, it became the officially sanctioned perspective of the Labour Party and it remained its official perspective until some such time as the late forties. The question is not here whether 'reformist' socialism is or is not a realistic socialist strategy. The point is rather that it is no longer the perspective which, however theoretically, informs the Labour leaders' approach to affairs.

This is not to say that reforms are no longer on their agenda. They obviously are. But such reforms as these leaders may support do not form part of any kind of coherent strategy, designed, in however long a perspective, to achieve the socialist transformation of British society. The leaders of the Labour Party have no such strategy and, except for merely rhetorical purposes, want none of it. They may occasionally prattle on about socialism, but this, on any serious view of the matter, lacks all effective meaning. The 'revisionism' which dominates their thinking does not represent an alternative but an adaptation to capitalism.

There are many people in the Labour Party who, broadly speaking, accept that this is so, but who nevertheless insist that their party can be turned into a suitable instrument of socialist change. They do so on a number of different grounds, which must be examined in turn.

The first such ground is that the Labour leaders can be persuaded, or if not persuaded, compelled to adopt socialist policies, and to implement them in office.

This must surely be reckoned to be a very weak argument. For it enormously underestimates the strength of the Labour leaders' ideological and political commitment to the positions they hold, and which do not include the perspectives which animate their socialist followers. These leaders are not socialists who for some reason or other have lost their way and who can be brought back to the true path by persuasion or pressure. They are bourgeois politicians with, at best, a certain bias towards social reform. They have no intention whatsoever of adopting, let alone carrying out, policies which would begin in earnest the process of socialist transformation in Britain. On the contrary, they must be expected to resist with the utmost determination all attempts to foist such policies upon them.

No doubt, they may, in opposition or even in government, occasionally be prevented, as happened with the Wilson government's proposed legislation on trade unions, from taking up or carrying out measures which closely affect the trade unions and which the latter find particularly obnoxious. But this of course is hardly the point.

It is also true that Labour leaders may have to accept this or that Conference resolution, pledging them to carry out some measures of policy to which they are opposed, or about which they have serious doubts. But neither Labour Party Annual Conferences nor Trade Union Congresses can, in practice, effectively impose such policies on their leaders, and these leaders may safely be relied upon to ignore the wishes of their activists once they are in office, with arguments such as that circumstances have changed, or that the time is not ripe, or that there is so much else to do, or that the issue requires much more thought, and so on. Alternatively, they must be expected, given their cast of mind, to defuse whatever explosive charge the policies concerned may carry – in other words, to de-radicalise their application to the point where they lose much if not most of their significance.

But even these considerations, important though they are, do not quite touch the core of the matter. The really crucial point has to do with the fact that the business of challenging British capitalism at the roots, which also implies a challenge to international capitalism, is bound to be arduous and exacting enough, even for a leadership utterly determined upon the enterprise. There cannot be much in the notion that it could really begin to get under way with leaders who do not really believe that it should begin at all, which is precisely the case with the people who now control the Labour Party.

It is at this point that many socialists in the Labour Party tend to part company with the argument, on a second ground, namely that if the Labour Party's present leaders cannot be persuaded or compelled to respond to the pressure for socialist policies and actions, they will eventually be replaced by others, who would be determined upon the enterprise, and who would offer the kind of leadership which it requires.

After all, the case goes, the Labour leaders are not the Labour Party, much less the Labour movement; and already, much has happened in the last ten years or so to change significantly the balance of forces in the Labour Party itself, as a result of changes which have occurred in the Labour movement. Most obviously, the trade union leadership, which traditionally acted as a strongly anti-left wing force, and whose command of the block vote at Labour Party conferences insulated the Labour leaders from serious challenge, has undergone a substantial shift to the left; and this must eventually bring about the emergence of a new and different kind of leadership in the Labour Party. ....

This expectation (it can hardly be called a strategy) strikes me, for many reasons, as altogether illusory.

Of course, the shift to the left which has occurred in the trade union movement is in many ways significant, most of all because it reflects a rank and file militancy which is indeed important. But the evidence is entirely lacking that the new Trade Union left has the slightest inclination to bring about sweeping changes in the leadership of the Labour Party, or that it would be able to do so if it had. In 1966, when Frank Cousins resigned from the Wilson Government, Ken Coates, as he recalls, wired him his congratulations 'and wrote to him appealing for him to begin to organise the socialist opposition'. Mr Cousins replied that he had no wish to become a 'focal figure' of the left, and that his main, purpose was 'to try and help find a more reasonable understanding towards the removal of our economic problems than is possible under the proposed Bill for Prices and Incomes'.[47] The reply was fairly typical of the limited role which trade union leaders, including left wing ones, see themselves as playing in the Labour Party, namely that of representatives of organized labour, involved in a bargaining relationship, notably over industrial and economic issues, with their political colleagues in the Labour Party, and not in the least as political rivals intending to capture control of the party for purposes radically different from those of the men who now control it. Some left wing trade union leaders may develop political ambitions: if so, they would most likely seek to carve a place for themselves among the leaders of the Labour Party and as members of a future Labour Government. But this can hardly be regarded as a matter of great political significance.

The kind of sweeping changes at the top which a good many socialists hope to see one day brought about in the Labour Party, and which would signify a major ideological shift to the left, would presumably, given the nature of the political system, have to be engineered from within the ranks of the Parliamentary Labour Party. But to say this is surely also to indicate how unrealistic that hope is. It is unrealistic because it ignores the perennial weakness of the parliamentary left. That weakness is not accidental but structural, which is why the indignation so often manifested by left activists at the derelictions of Labour Left MPs is futile. The derelictions are real enough, but they are built into the system of which these MPs are a part. Left parliamentarians operate within the rules of a game designed to limit their capacity and indeed their willingness to challenge their leaders. They are required to behave 'loyally' and to accept compromise in order to help maintain the 'unity' of the party. They must not give aid and comfort to the other side, most of all when Labour is in government, but also when it is in opposition. Accommodation is in any case made easier by virtue of the fact that the members of the parliamentary left are, and always have been, characterized by a marked uncertainly as to what, in basic ideological terms they are really about. This too is not accidental: it is a necessary condition of their becoming parliamentarians in the first place. Political success, in this respect, and even political survival depends on an early ability to blunt the edge of one's dissent and to minimize the gulf which separates the would-be socialist dissenter from his leaders. There have been some exceptions: a few Labour MPs have, so to speak, slipped through the net. But they have remained isolated and often pathetic figures, bitterly at odds not only with their leaders but with that large and permanent majority of the Parliamentary Labour Party which entirely shares its leaders' orthodox modes of thought. Most left parliamentarians, for the part, have learnt, more or less easily, to adjust to their ambiguous situation; and very few, when the chance has occurred, have been able to resist co-optation into the Labour Establishment, at whatever cost to their proclaimed commitments: the ministerial career of former Bevanite parliamentarians provides ample testimony to the fact.

The Labour Left in Parliament can mount episodic 'revolts' on this or that issue, though with dubious effect; and it can act as pressure group upon the Labour leaders, with equally uncertain impact. But more than this it cannot be expected to do.

What this means is that the Labour Party will not be transformed into a party seriously concerned with socialist change. Its leaders may have to respond with radical-sounding noises to the pressure and demands of their activists. Even so, they will see to it that the Labour Party remains, in practice, what it has always been – a party of modest social reform in a capitalist system within whose confines it is ever more firmly and by now irrevocably rooted. The system badly needs such a party, since it plays a major role in the management of discontent and helps to keep it within safe bounds; and the fact that the Labour Party proclaims itself at least once every five years but much more often as well to be committed not merely to the modest amelioration of capitalist society but to its wholesale transformation, to a just social order, to a classless society, to a new Britain, and whatever not, does not make it less but more useful in the preservation of the existing social order.

It is very likely that the Labour Party will be able to play the highly 'functional' role for some time to come, given its overwhelming preponderance as 'the party of the left' in the British political system. There is at present no party or grouping which is capable of posing an effective challenge to that preponderance; and this helps to explain why so many socialists in the Constituency Labour Parties, in the trade unions (and for that matter in the Communist Party) cling to the belief that the Labour Party will eventually be radically transformed. But the absence of a viable socialist alternative is no reason for resigned acceptance or for the perpetuation of hopes which have no basis in political reality. On the contrary, what it requires is to begin preparing the ground for the coming into being of such an alternative: and one of the indispensable elements of that process is the dissipation of paralysing illusions about the true purpose and role of the Labour Party.

Notes

[1] This, incidentally, is not to be taken to imply that a vast extension of public ownership, least of all in the forms in which it was undertaken after 1945, is a sufficient condition for the transformation of a capitalist society into a socialist one or that it constitutes an instant remedy for all economic or social ills. The point is rather that it is a necessary condition for the transcendence of capitalism in socialist directions; and that the much more modest ambitions of the Labour leaders also depended, as they themselves were soon to argue, on their capture of the 'commanding heights' of the economy.

[2] Clause 4 reads: 'To secure for the workers by hand or by brain the full fruits of their industry and the most equitable distribution thereof that may be possible, upon the basis of the common ownership of the means of production, distribution and exchange, and the best obtainable system of popular administration and control of each industry and service.'

[3] S. Haseler, *The Gaitskellites* (1969) p. 170

[4] *Signposts for the Sixties*, pp. 9-10.

[5] Ibid, p. 17.

[6] The article is reprinted in H. Wilson, *Purpose in Politics* (1964).

[7] House of Commons, 18 February 1963, Vol. 672, Col.106

[8] Labour Party Annual Conference Report, 1963, pp. 134

[9] Haseler, op. cit. p. 164

[10] Labour Party Annual Conference Report, 1966, p. 162.

[11] D. E. Butler and A. King, The British General Election of 1964, p. 135 (1965).

[12] In *The British General Election of 1966* (1967), the same authors also note that 'one of the supreme ironies of the 1966 election was that the final emphasis of the Conservative leader was on the need for radical change and of the Leader of the Labour Party on the need for patriotism and stability' p. 124.

[13] R. Pryke, 'The Predictable Crisis' in *New Left Review*, No. 39, Sept.-Oct. 1966. p. 3. It may even be doubted whether work which had been undertaken on social security, land, higher education and regional planning was as 'detailed' as is here suggested – not to speak of the degree of 'radicalism' which the work, detailed or not, exhibited

[14] Ibid

[15] Ibid

[16] Labour Party Annual Conference Report, 1966, p. 163.

[17] H. Wilson, *The Labour Government 1964-1970. A Personal Record* (1971) p. xvii

[18] *The Guardian*, 6th of August, 1965

[19] H. Brandon, *In the Red*, (1966), p.44

[20] TUC Annual Conference Report, 1964, p. 383.

[21] Labour Party Annual Conference Report, 1965, p.197

[22] TUC Annual Confernce Report 1964, p.38

[23] *Sunday Telegraph*, 11 October 1964

[24] Butler and King, op.cit., p.5

[25] *The Times*. 16th December 1964

[26] Op. cit, p.37

[27] *The Times*, 17th September 1965

[28] *The Times*, 9th July, 1963

[29] TUC Annual Conference Report, 1964, pp. 384-5

[30] *The Guardian*, 17th of December 1964

[31] See H. Wilson, op. cit. pp. 131-2.

[32] Brandon, op. cit. p. 103.

[33] Tribune 8th of April 1966.

[34] This is how Wilson explains his decision to have a General Election in March 1966: '... to yield incontinently to strike threats would mean the end of any meaningful prices and incomes policy, with serious effects abroad. Nor would the legislation to which we were committed make things any easier. Sooner or later there would be a confrontation, with the likelihood of a prolonged and damaging strike. It was not a welcome prospect with a majority of, at most, three whether we were going for early legislation or not' (op. cit. p. 199).

[35] Quoted in P. Foot, *The Politics of Harold Wilson* (1968) p. 173. For the Government's handling of the strike, see also P. Foot, 'The Seamen's Struggle' in R. Blackburn and A. Cockburn, Eds., *The Incompatibles* 1967

[36] TUC Annual Conference Report, 1966, p. 398. My italics.

[37] Ibid, p. 398. My italics

[38] See Child Poverty Action Group, *Poverty and the Labour Government* (1970). For a detailed survey of Labour's record in social policies, see P. Townsend and N. Bosanquet Eds., *Labour and Inequality* (1972).

[39] *New Statesman*, 3rd October, 1959, quoted by Foot, op. cit. p. 145.

[40] *The Times*, 20th of March 1968

[41] *The Guardian*, 20th of October, 1964.

[42] Labour Party Annual Conference Report, 1965, p. 227.

[43] J. Freeman. 'Wilson at the White House' in The New Statesman, 11th December, 1964.

[44] Foot, op. cit. p. 207.

[45] Ibid. p. 214. Similarly, he stressed the 'complete agreement in Washington with the British Government's decision to continue to maintain a world-wide defence role, particularly to fulfill those commitments which, for reasons of history, geography, commonwealth association and the like,

we, and virtually we alone, are best fitted to undertake' (ibid.).

[46] House of Commons, 16 January 1968, vol. 756, col. 1581

[47] K. Coates, *The Crisis of British Socialism* (1971), p.131

Editorial Introduction to Extract 6

As we have now seen, Ralph Miliband chose to close his 1972 postscript with a limited set of observations about the functionality of Labour Party moderation to the longevity of British capitalism. But what was a closing paragraph to the *Postscript* was by then the central point of Leo Panitch's opening essays on British Labour. Against those who emphasized the recent origins of Labour Party moderation and unease with its class image, Panitch argued as early as 1971 for the importance of 'that strain in its ideology which has *throughout its history* been aggregative and has minimized the party's class role'[1]. Against those critics who saw the Milibandian perspective as always treating the Labour Party as a failure (because of its backsliding on its radical/socialist promises when entering office), Panitch's sensitivity to the 'party's own contribution to the political socialization of the working class'[2], led him to insist that, when measured against different criteria, the Party must be seen as a success. In the revised and published version of the Ph.D. thesis which he prepared under Miliband's supervision (*Social Democracy and Industrial Militancy*, the conclusion of which is reproduced here), Panitch argued that because of 'Labour's performance of its integrative role against the continued expression of industrial class conflict in the post-war period' it was best to realize that, to a very large extent, what are often seen from the Left 'as Labour's failures are really its successes'. 'The function of the Labour Party in the British political system', he wrote, 'consists not only in representing working class interests but of acting as one of the chief mechanisms for inculcating the organized working class with national values and symbols and of restraining and reinterpreting working class demands in this light.'[3] Central to his 1976 argument was the view that 'the missing link between industrial militancy and the development of a revolutionary political consciousness' within the British working class was at least partly to be explained by 'the trade unions' ties with the integrative Labour Party'[4]. Central to his argument too was a particular view – shared with Miliband – about the weakness of the Labour Left, the difficulties of transforming the Labour Party from within, and the manner in which 'a necessary pre-condition for the development of a revolutionary political consciousness in the working class would appear to be a break between the trade unions and the Party'.[5] These were arguments which, as we will see later, he would elaborate in a Socialist Register debate with Ken Coates on 'Socialists and the Labour Party'.[6]

6. SOCIAL DEMOCRACY AND INDUSTRIAL MILITANCY: CONCLUSION (1976)

Leo Panitch

This study of the Labour Party's relationship with the trade union movement since 1945 has endeavoured to show the extent to which the Labour Party has performed the functions of an integrative party in the British political system. The integrative element of its ideology, while by no means ubiquitous throughout the Party, has had its concrete expression in the economic and industrial policies of Labour governments, suggesting that this is in fact the effective and dominant ideology of the Labour Party. Labour's frame of reference is not primarily focused within the orbit of the working class's subordinate position in British society, involving questions of how to increase that class's solidarity, extend its economic and political power, defend it against loss of limited gains already made. These considerations are not absent from Labour's conception of its role, but they are confined within a national frame of reference – a concern for national unity shared in common with Britain's dominant classes – in which the aim of making the British economy viable is paramount. It is, to quote Tom Nairn, the 'nationalization of class',[7] from which Labour, wearing the twin hats of both national and class leadership, presumes to claim that its national concerns embrace the needs of the working class as well.

Analyses which begin with the premise that Labour is primarily a socialist party and a channel of working class representation and aspirations, and confine themselves to the attempt to explain Labour's consistent 'failure' to be 'socialist' when in government – whether in terms of the entrenched powers of the ruling class, or opportunist and middle class leadership, or even the limitations of a parliamentary strategy – must inevitably fall wide of the mark. For to a very large extent, what are seen as Labour's failures are really its successes. The function of the Labour Party in the British political system consists not only of representing working class interests, but of acting as one of the chief mechanisms for inculcating the organized working class with national values and symbols and of restraining and reinterpreting working class demands in this light. The Labour Party, in other words, acts simultaneously as a party of representation and as a major political socialization and social control agent, mediating between nation and class. In a generalized way, by upholding the values of the nation, parliament, responsibility, against the values of direct action, revolution or 'sectional' interests, it is performing a socializing role which both legitimates existing society and militiates against the development of a revolutionary political consciousness on the part of the working class. In this respect, it is not so much transforming values as acting to maintain values to which the working class has already been exposed, and usually absorbed, from other institutions of political socialization such as the family, the educational system, the church, the media, and even the Conservative Party; although the credibility of the Labour Party as 'our' institution in working-class consciousness, gives it certain advantages in this regard. But when the Labour Party mobilizes popular support in the name of these values in a particular instance by portraying the demands of a union or group of unofficial strikers as 'sectional' and contrary to the 'national interest', it is acting as a highly effective agency of social control against the objective expression of working class dissent.

Labour's performance of its integrative role against the continued expression of industrial class conflict in the post-war period has an important bearing on those analyses which explained the 'deradicalization' of social democracy in terms of the emergence of a new political culture of consensus produced by the security of the welfare state and post-war affluence. These analyses were characterized by a crude determinism which argued from the premise that if the superstructure (the Labour Party) changed, the causes must lie in the economic base (the effect of broad socio-economic changes on the values of the working class). What they did not consider, apart from vastly exaggerating the egalitarian effects of post-war development in terms of income and power redistribution between the classes, was the possibility that the Labour Party itself might be an independent factor in inculcating the working class in general and the trade union leadership in particular with national values consistent with consensus. Rather than merely assume that political culture determines political structures, one must examine the extent to which political culture is formed by political structures. Frank Parkin has observed of social democracy:

> To see the party simply as a receptacle for the political views of its supporters is really to underestimate its potential influence in shaping the social consciousness of the subordinate class and in providing its members with a distinctive moral framework for interpreting social reality. If, as so many observers suggest, there has occurred a marked decline in working class radicalism in the post-war period, this may be due at least as much to changes in the nature of the party as to changes among its supporters.[8]

This insightful view of social democracy's socializing role has become somewhat current in recent years.[9] But our study suggests that it is important not to fall into the error, as Parkin himself seems to have done, of accepting the view that the post-war period does in fact constitute a fundamental break with the past either in terms of any basic change in the nature of the Labour Party or in terms of any real success in closing the fissures of class conflict. Indeed, as we have argued elsewhere,[10] one of the main failures of many post-war analyses of British social democracy was their insufficient understanding of the Labour

Party's ideology in the pre-1945 period. For although the Party's integrative ideology was certainly strengthened and enhanced after 1945, it was by no means a new development. It was previously seen not only in the Party's rejection of the concept of class struggle at its founding conference, not only in the national posture of both the ill-fated Labour Governments in the inter-war period, but even in Labour's programmes in opposition which repeatedly reaffirmed that Labour was a national rather than simply a class party, a view which we have seen was proclaimed with the full authority of the Party's general secretary at the height of Labour's victory in 1945. Informative in this regard is Tawney's view of the Labour Party in the earlier period: 'It soothes the dog when it ought to be educating him to know burglars when he sees them, and to fly at their throats.... In a party which appeals to men, not to follow habits, but to break them, such an attitude is fatal.'[11] The complex factors which would explain what led the organized working class to align itself with an integrative party in the first place, cannot be examined here. But if the political consciousness of the trade union leadership at the turn of the century let it forge an alliance with a political party inclined to promote class harmony rather than class conflict, what must be appreciated is that in its turn that political party has helped to maintain that political consciousness throughout this century. In placing such emphasis on the guiding ideology of the Labour Party, it has not been our intention to minimize other factors which are often employed to explain Labour's integrative orientation, such as the Michelsian organizational and psychological explanation of the 'iron law of oligarchy' which divorces leaders' interests from the followers, or the reliance on leaders from middle class background or the independence of the parliamentary party from conference. But these factors are of greater value in explaining the deradicalization of working class parties with a revolutionary Marxist ideology than the integrative Labour Party, and even then they cannot explain the profound differences in ideology and programme which continue to separate social democracy from Communist Parties in the West.

If Labour's integrative orientation was enhanced in the post-war period, this did not reflect so much a basic change in the nature of the Party, but rather related to the fact that its greater electoral success gave the Party more opportunity of putting its effective ideology into practice at a time when changes in post-war capitalist generally provided social democracy with a larger and more obvious role in administering the society. What must be understood in this regard is that the integrative functions of the Labour Party, in terms of their precise content, are not determined by the Party alone, but by the capitalist system within which it is content to operate (and, to be fair, change somewhat from within) and its needs at a particular historical moment. What exactly is deemed to be 'in the nation interest' and what sacrifices the working class is asked to bear in its name is conditioned by the state of the British economy and the perceptions of correct national policy widely accepted by industrial financial and political leaders of the British upper classes with whom the Labour Party seeks to find a basis for cooperation, as well as by the process of 'non-decision' whereby possible alternative policies are not even considered by either working class or upper class leaders. And, to a very large degree, the extent as well as the precise nature of the contribution the Labour Party is able to make to national unity, economic viability, and working-class integration will be determined by these factors as well; so that, if Labour's national integrative posture was more fully elaborated in the post-war period, it is in this context that we discover why.

It was British capitalism's continual need for respite from wage pressure in the post-war period which underlay the Labour Party's enhanced integrative role. Beset by large sections of industry which were undercapitalized and highly inefficient, by a comparatively slow rate of economic growth, by a marked dependence on external trade and thus susceptible to pricing itself out of international markets and to recurrent balance of payments deficits, British capitalism has been particularly vulnerable to increased labour costs. Since mass unemployment is both an inefficient and politically dangerous solution, an incomes policy involving the trade unions voluntarily engaging in wage restraint is greatly desirable, if profit margins, the motive force for economic growth, are not to be unduly squeezed between labour costs on the one hand and international competition on the other. Increased state intervention in the economy, in the form of social welfare reforms, indicative economic planning, the extention of trade union representation in national decision making arenas, was undertaken as we have seen, from Beveridge on, by both Conservative and Labour Governments with the consideration of inducing union cooperation in wage restraint always an uppermost factor in the policy equation. This was a form of state intervention not opposed by capitalist interests, but promoted by them, although particular groups might quibble about the necessity or extent of certain elements of this intervention. Given the fact that the ideological basis of this 'new group politics' rested on a 'harmony of interests' conception of society, it might have been thought that the Conservative Party was best suited to introduce it. Yet it was Labour which repeatedly proved the better candidate for the operation.

  This was partly because Labour, unlike the Conservatives, was not encumbered by a tradition of laissez-faire and an explicit bias towards business, which badly got in the way of Conservative forays into the kind of state intervention needed by modern capitalism. Moreover, Labour found itself in the post-war period in a political climate which appeared to allow it to give programmatic effect to its own ideology of class harmony without apparently contradicting the ideas of state intervention and economic planning which informed its socialism. In the pre-war period the class cooperation principle had always rested uncomfortably with Labour's socialist programme. As Beer has pointed out, public ownership in the pre-1945 period had been 'advocated on various grounds: to equalise wealth, to eliminate the political power of private wealth, to promote democracy in industrial life. But the principal case for it was the need for public control of the economy.'[12] Yet the burning question of how this was to be introduced with the agreement of the capitalist class, as the ideology of class cooperation, and the gradualism and parliamentarism which rested on it, required, was largely avoided (although the answer was implied in party programmes which proposed nationalization of only select industries or parts of industries which for the most part were failing and thus which the capitalist class as a whole could be relied upon to give up). In the post-war period, however, Labour found the capitalist class generally prepared to accept state intervention and planning and to cooperate in it. Labour's ideology and its programme could now be fused. In the context of indicative planning and the welfare state, it was no longer necessary for a party such as Labour to continue to emphasize nationalization: indeed it appeared that to do so was not only to confuse means with ends, but to miss the opportunity of putting Labour's class cooperation ideology into practice The problem with doing this before had been seen to lie in the mis-conceived self-interested, rather than community-oriented, views of the capitalist class. These views had now apparently changed, at least in the eyes of Labour leaders who as early as the late 1940s, as we have seen, thought they saw around them an efficiency-oriented managerial capitalism which had come to understand the evils of the unrestrained market and the need for cooperation with the state and with the unions. No doubt, not only the economic vicissitudes of the British economy, but also Labour's own moderate attack on its unplanned nature, made some contribution to the more open reception on the part of Britain's traditional ruling classes to ideas of state intervention and planning. As such, Labour leaders might well believe that the long-standing Fabian goal of educating the ruling classes to socialism was at hand. In any case, the system had changed (or so it seemed), the goal of class harmony in the national interest could now be grasped ('we are all socialists now'), and the Labour Party, unencumbered by an outmoded laissez-faire, could meet the challenge.

It was in this way that the logic of Labour's traditional, integration ideology, which remained fundamentally unaltered in the post-war period, carried the Party into an enhanced integrative role in British capitalism. The key to its playing this role of course remained the allegiance of the organized working class. That is, at the same time Labour was elaborating its integrative functions through its promotion of indicative planning and incomes policy, seeking to effect compromise between the various classes by promulgating a high national interest, its very successes in this regard depended primarily on its structural ties with the trade unions. In the expectation that under a Labour Government the interests of the working class would take precedence over the interests of other classes, in the hope that the influence of the trade union leadership in economic decision-making would become not only formal but effective, as well as out of sheer emotional loyalty to the political arm of the labour movement, the trade unions were prepared to participate directly in developing and operating an incomes policy. Despite the fairly common expectation in the 1950s and early 1960s that declining working-class allegiance was the foundation of Labour's elaborated integrative posture, it was in fact the continued salience of working class political identification which facilitated the Party's performance of its integrative role. Conversely, a significant element in Labour's appeal to other classes lay not so much in jettisoning commitments to increase the state's role in the economy as in Labour's ability to retain working class loyalty and promise wage restraint at no greater cost than the Conservative Government had itself proposed to incur in its unsuccessful attempt at economic planning and incomes policy. Labour's structural ties with the unions were not an electoral liability, but an electoral asset, particularly for a Party whose commitment to state intervention seemed to provide a better fit with the needs of modern capitalism than that of the Conservatives.

With a virtuosity that only comes with practice, the Labour Party leadership in the early 1960s played both possible interpretations of the planning and incomes policy theme, one to each audience. They proved their mettle as integrative politicians in this period, performing with much greater finesse and aplomb than they had when, moved by much the same ideological and economic exigencies, they had rather stumbled into indicative planning and wages policy in the late 1940s. But once in Government again, they had to actually write the score, not just interpret the theme. The story is largely told in the disappointment of trade union expectations of extensive influence in the framing of economic policy; in the operation of incomes policy as wage restraint in the context of the abandonment of even indicative planning; in the extreme reluctance of the Labour Government to engage in price and profit controls; in the readiness with which the Government dropped the voluntary principle upon which the incomes policy was founded and thus challenged the unions' view of themselves as free agents in collective bargaining. Labour's incomes policy of 1964-70, like the wages policy of 1948-50 before it, was not designed to facilitate the planning and redistribution of incomes as part of a larger design to transcend the existing economic system, although as such it was likely to have been able to draw on the support of significant sections of the trade union movement. It was concerned rather to further the integration of the trade unions into the existing political and economic system by obtaining from the trade unions a more explicit acceptance of their responsibilities to society; to induce them to control their members more competently and, to a large extent, to define the unions' role as 'legitimate' interest groups and guide by statute their actions 'in the national interest'.

An overview and a contrast between Labour and Conservative success in restricting the growth of working class incomes since 1948 may be seen from the following table from the work of H. A. Turner and Frank Wilkinson, who have themselves come to the conclusion that 'it almost appears . . . as if the objective economic-historical role of the British Labour Party is to do (no doubt despite itself) those things to the workers that the Conservative Governments are unable to do'.[13]

Rates of growth in gross money, real and net real income, men manual workers

Annual compound rate of growth	Gross Money Income	Net real income (b)
1948-52	6.9%	0.7%
1952-56	7.2	3.5
1956-60	5.0	2.1
1960-64	5.5	1.3
1964-68	6.6	0.5
1968-70	10.0	1.3
1970-74 (a)	12.5	1.8

Notes
estimated a) Gross Money income discounted by price inflation and the effect of direct taxation (b) computed for the average wage earner married with two children

SOURCE: 1948-70: *Do Trade Unions Cause Inflation?* (see n.13), Table 2, p.66. 1970-74: Frank Wilkinson, 'The Outlook for Wages', in Cambridge Economy Policy Group, *Prospects for Economic Management*, 1973-77, Ch. 8, Table 2, pp. 8-12

In the period of the 1948-50 wages policy, the major factor in reducing the growth of working class incomes was rising prices as the Labour Government undertook its flight from economic planning in the 'bonfire of controls'. But this was complemented by an explicit decision by the Labour leadership that it could not compensate for this by a redistributive fiscal policy of 'fair shares' without damaging the incentive to invest on the part of the capitalist class, on which the 1945 Labour Government increasingly relied to achieve economic growth. Under the LabourGovernment of 1964-70 both price inflation and fiscal policy combined to restrict working class incomes, with an even sharper effect despite an average annual growth in industrial productivity of over 3% in 1964-9. The stagnation of workers' real incomes, as contrasted with the increases when the Conservative Party was in office was essentially the product of the Labour Party's greater political resources in terms of socialist and planning rhetoric and the traditional loyalty of the working class to the Party, so that it was able to secure union cooperation in wage restraint. This did not have to entail lower money wage increases per se, although in particular crisis years like 1948-9, 1956-7, 1961-2 and 1966-7, a Labour Government was far more likely to secure wage restraint than a Conservative Government. What it essentially involved was ensuring that the trade unions refrained from developing an adequate industrial response (in the absence of an adequate political response) which would involve wage demands large enough to compensate for the effects of inflation and taxation on working class living standards.

The source of this distortion between promise and performance in the operation of the new group politics under a Labour Government essentially lies in the fact, that contrary to the claims by pluralist theorists like Beer that a 'new balance of power between the classes' had been established in the post-war period,[14] the pivot of power in British society continued to rest with Britain's capitalist class. Beer identified three sources of the 'unrecognizably transformed power position of the unions'[15] – the state's need for their expert advice on the formation of policy, for their acquiescence or voluntary agreement to administer state policies, and for their approval and legitimation of state policy in the eyes of their members. Yet what we have seen as characteristic of the new group politics was how governmental policies were repeatedly framed either without first securing the advice of the unions, or after having explicitly rejected their advice. This was seen in the Cripps wage freeze of 1948, in the Conservative pay pause of 1961, and throughout the various phases of Labour's statutory incomes policy from August 1965 on. It was not their advice, but their acquiescence and approval which were studiously courted, usually after the fact. The advice on which Labour acted in introducing deflation and statutory wage restraint and abandoning the indicative plan for economic growth was that of the CBI, the City and Britain's foreign creditors, in light of the latter's immediate concern to protect the pound against devaluation. Indeed, even when the advice on which Labour acted proved faulty in the extreme as devaluation eventually was forced on the Government, Labour had to continue to promote private business incentives to foster economic growth. For insofar as the logic of class cooperation ruled out command planning, it also largely ruled out a redistributive fiscal policy. The orthodox fiscal policy of the Government was not forced on it, therefore, but rather was produced by an interpretation of the national interest which was common to both Labour and business leaders.

As Cripps had done in 1948, the architects of Labour's economic policy in 1964-70 repeatedly made the rather simple point that redistribution of the national wealth would not itself produce a high standard of living for the whole of the British working class. Yet this in itself cannot stand as an argument against a much more egalitarian society. What ruled out the latter was the necessity for inequality within a society which needs economic growth indeed, but seeks to achieve it within capitalist structures. To have raised questions about the extent to which this indicated that British capitalists were still self-interested rather than community-oriented, would have entailed however, a major shift of direction of which Labour Governments have proved ideologically incapable throughout this century. And the consequence of operating within the dominant interpretation of the national interest is the grotesque distortion of Labour's social reform policies. This was seen in our study as Labour orthodox fiscal policy underlined the innately conservatizing effects of incomes policy, which by its very nature in tying wage increases to productivity growth, seeks to remove the question of inter-class income differentials from the concern of the unions, the main economic force for redistribution within capitalism. Wage claims based on comparability and profitability by definition raise questions about equality in the social structure, while productivity bargaining eliminates this. The distorting effect all this produced in terms of Labour need to be seen to pursue social reforms for the working class, was not the abandonment of the equality theme altogether, but the transference of it, in the context of incomes policy, to a concern with narrowing income differentials within the working class. This is what we have called the doctrine of socialism in one class – seeking to concentrate workers' concerns with inequality, not on the highly privileged, but on others in a similar class situation to their own. And even this policy was in turn distorted by its operation in a capitalist society. For except in the case of intra-firm differentials, the wages foregone by well organized workers in high profit and high productivity firms and industries are not transferable in the absence of a directive economic plan to workers in low paid, low profit and low productivity firms and industries. Thus the final result of Labour's 'national' policy of linking the theme of equality to that of economy growth within capitalism was to proclaim the existing distribution of income between the classes as legitimate, while declaring illegitimate the infinitely narrower differentials within the working class about which neither the trade unions nor the Labour Government were able to do much via an incomes policy.

There can be little doubt that Labour's historical envelopment in a national, integrative ideology has been oriented towards making the achievement of social reform easier, given the traumas and difficulites entailed in social revolutions. It would be invidious and misleading to suggest that individual Labour leaders would not prefer a more equal distribution of wealth and income or a society somewhat less subject to the need to promote business incentive. The problem, however, is that when Labour's nation-class synthesis is translated into concrete policies in a class stratified society, both the concepts of national interest and of social reform become highly problematic. In terms of Labour's paramount concern to find a basis for compromise between working class and ruling class interests, the latter's position of dominance in the economy as well as its preponderant influence in the civil service, the judiciary and the media, inevitably comes to structure Labour's own definition of the national interest and to distort its aim of social reforms. What is primarily missing in both Labour's integrative ideology and pluralist theories of British society such as Beer's (which indeed bear a very close resemblance to each other), is an understanding of how the location of integration and the new group politics within a capitalist society inclines state interventionism towards policies that accord with the inner dynamic of such a society – the profit motive – to the enhancement of the class from which this dynamic stems and to the detriment of the working class. The 'new social contract' in this context is a contract not only between unequals but one in which the guarantor of the contract – the state, even under a Labour Government – is not and cannot be disinterested and neutral between the classes ....

It has been a central argument of this study that one of the crucial factors in explaining the 'missing link' between industrial militancy and the development of a revolutionary political consciousness has been the trade unions' ties with the integrative Labour Party. When the leader of the political arm of the labour movement laments the translation of industrial militancy into a wider political conflict, he is manifestly continuing Labour's traditional tendency to see the organized working class as a sectional interest group without claim to ruling the society, and to reinforce the working class's conception of itself as a subordinate class rather than a hegemonic one. Yet to point out the failure of the Labour Party to change fundamentally its role in this respect, ...is not in itself to deny the possibility that the Party can change. It has in no sense been the argument here that the integrative ideology has been ubiquitous in the Labour Party. Indeed, to say that it is dominant necessarily implies that it dominates over something else. That something else is the Labour Left, which has repeatedly challenged the integrative premises and policies of the Labour leadership. It simply will not do, as Tom Nairn has done in his otherwise brilliant examination of Labour's national orientation, to dismiss the Labour Left as merely the soulful, Christian conscience of the Party, 'which opposes the right, not in the name of class, but in the name of the true nation', as a weak moral force consumed by 'pious delusions' of a New Jerusalem, recoiling from power lest it sully its 'religious nature (laicized as "ethical socialism" or not)'.[16] This characterization may apply to Cripps who could subsist on 'radish tops and orange juice' and expect British workers to do the same, and is clearly intended to apply to Michael Foot. But it is a ridiculous caricature of the Labour Left as a whole. The Tribune MPs in 1964-70 were in no sense a group of frustrated parsons: over half were militant ex-trade unionists. One cannot ignore Eric Heffer's belief that: 'There can be no neutrality in the class struggle. Either one is for the workers or against them.' And when Heffer urges that the Labour Party 'becomes a class party at every level', and that 'the theory of class struggle should be a cornerstone of our ideology',[17] he may be deluded about the likelihood of this transformation, but his premises are nevertheless in sharp contrast with the integrative ideology.

It is not surprising that many who reject the dominant ideology should work to change the Party from within. The Labour Left is in this respect at least not far different from the British Communist Party, which continues to see Labour as the main political vehicle of the working class, and but for the refusal of the Labour leadership to allow it, would have long ago met its goal of affiliation to the Labour Party. Thus while the political socialization of union leaders like Jones and Scanlon was also influenced by the Communist Party and Marxism, the Communists' own view of Labour has played a reinforcing role in tying such union leaders to social democracy, especially as the Communist Party's waning political (although not industrial) influence was felt in the post-war period and no other real alternative was available outside the Labour Party. It is not being suggested here that the Labour Left is ideologically indistinguishable from the extra-Labour Left, but that the former finds its strength in a social base not unknown to the latter. As evidenced by their repeated success in constituency balloting for NEC positions, the Labour Left has a real base among party activists. Moreover, militant trade unionists have historically gravitated towards and made common cause with the PLP Left. There was a direct correlation between the Bevanite struggles in the Labour Party and the opposition inside the trade unions to the union bureaucracy in the 1950s And the main link between left-wing trade union leaders and the PLP during the 1964-70 period was the Tribune Group not their sponsored MPs.

Having said all this, what distinguishes the Labour Left from the extra-Labour Left, and how do we explain its failure to recast the Party's orientation? Two main factors are operative here, both of which have served to tie the Labour Left, against its will no doubt, to the dominant ideology of the Party. The first is the Left's acceptance of the doctrine of Parliamentarism. On this Labour has indeed been extensively united from its inception. It is true that during the 1930s the Labour Left through the Socialist League questioned the assumption that a parliamentary majority was enough to secure a socialist transformation, but the question was largely forgotten in the context of the war and Labour's 1945 victory, and virtually sunk without trace among the concerns of the Labour Left in the post-war period. For the Right, this complete acceptance of a parliamentary strategy is a natural corollary of the belief in class harmony. Parliamentary government represents the highest pinnacle of achievement for the British nation, the institutional expression of rational debate within the rules of the game, and the setting for Labour's aim of defining the national interest in conjunction with Britain's dominant classes. For the Left, however, the total acceptance of parliamentarism involves a direct contradiction with the view of irreconcilable class conflict. It stands as a barrier to fostering alternative forms of action, even when they are taken up in the trade union movement, and acts as a counter to the development of a coherent theory of the state in a capitalist society. Without such a theory, not only the Labour Left's supporters, but even those leaders of the Left who attain Cabinet positions themselves, are unprepared for the disappointments which regularly attend purely electoral victories in a capitalist society. We have observed in this study how the Tribune Group's primary occupation with parliamentary victories and defeats led it to take upon itself the task of preserving the unity of the PLP rather than force that responsibility on the Labour leadership. Similarly, the Left's unwillingness to embarrass the Party on the principle of opposition to direct action incapacitated it for providing much support, let alone leadership, to mass demonstrations against *In Place of Strife*. This was repeated again in the context of the Conservatives' Industrial Relations measures. Thus while Eric Heffer has indicated his belief that the political strikes were justified and the main source of effective opposition to the Act, the inconsistency between his responsibility to the PLP and direct action led him, in his own words, to 'duck the issue', although it 'embarrassed' him 'no end'.[18] The concern with parliamentarism has also affected the left-wing union leadership's ability to undermine the control of the parliamentary leadership over the Party. In an important speech at the time of the 1971 Party Conference, Jack Jones indicated his union's concern with ensuring that its parliamentary panel contained more MPs with active union backgrounds, but he emphatically rejected the notion that the unions should instruct their MPs on how to vote.[19]

A second, and even more important factor in the Labour Left's lack of success in changing the Labour Party, lies in its refusal to come to terms with the deep-rootedness of the class harmony orientation. The Left has generally seen this orientation as an aberration from the Party's origins: the Party and its leadership are not basically misdirected, but just not socialist enough, or reformist enough, or prepared enough, or close enough to the grass roots. The Left's task is to fill in the missing quantities by reminding the leadership of the Party's socialist traditions. The acceptance by the Labour Party of the mixed economy in the 1950s is seen by Eric Heffer as a period of 'utter folly' caused by the opportunist casting about for middle class support by non-socialist middle class leaders.[20] Any direct link between the Party's original rejection of the concept of class struggle and the policies of the 1950s is omitted. The great victories for the Left have been associated mainly with purely symbolic issues such as retaining Clause 4 or electing a leader who is prepared to dot his speeches with socialist rhetoric or quotations from Nye Bevan. The fact that these victories turn into even greater disappointments rests on the Left's failure to realize that it is, as Eric Hobsbawm has put it, 'quite as easy to justify a moderate policy in socialist as it is in liberal or conservative phrases: the former may be even more effective'.[21] The rhetoric of socialism or public ownership or even industrial democracy, as has now become all too obvious, does not necessarily have much in common with a commitment to bring the working class to power. In this sense, the Right has understood the 'basic principles' of Labour far better than the Left. Anthony Crosland correctly noted that Labour's founders had not seen the Party as an 'essentially proletarian and one-class party', and he drew inspiration from Labour's 'fundamental socialist principle' that 'a "classless" society will never be achieved through a wholly class-orientated instrument. The object must be to present ourselves as a broadly-based national people's party.'[22] Indeed; in any battle cast in terms of Labour traditions, the Right has far more to draw on than the Left. By treating the problem before it as merely one of bringing the Party to its original principles, the Labour Left has mistaken its task and under estimated the difficulty of achieving it. For the task involves recasting fundamentally the ideological basis of the Party by wrenching Labour out of its tradition rather than glorying in it. 'Until the Labour Party recognizes it is not Socialist', Tawney wrote after the 1931 debacle, 'it is not likely to become Socialist'.[23]

Given the problems of the Labour Left and the tremendous difficulty of changing the Labour Party through it, a necessary pre-condition for the development of a revolutionary political consciousness in the working class would appear to be a break between the trade union movement and the Party. But while such a break is not out of the question, should the conditions of the late 1960s repeat themselves, it would certainly be unwarranted to look forward to an immediate rupture. It could conceivably come about 'MacDonald style', that is, at the instigation of an integrative leadership this time able to retain the support of the parliamentary Party. But despite some wishful glances in this direction by certain Gaitskellites in recent years, the leadership has remained united behind Wilson's sanguine understanding that this would leave the Party 'uneasily poised between the Liberals and the Bow Group' without a mass base. It could come about through the union leadership following Briginshaw's action of 1968, and calling for a 'new political alignment', but this is unlikely at present for a number of reasons. First of all, the whole of the union leadership is by no means united in opposition to Labour's integrative policies vis-a-vis the unions, let alone the ideology on which these are based. Secondly, such a break would not take place in a political vacuum in which calculations with regard to the Labour Party alone are relevant. The unions are faced with a party system in which the Conservative (or Liberal) threat is constantly present. And the unions' ability to secure from a Labour Government the repeal of Conservative measures harmful to union interests (even if this carries the unions no further than they were before these measures were introduced) is an important factor to be taken into account in any calculation of advantages and disadvantages in breaking with the Labour Party.

The most important factor militating against a break, however remains the depth of loyalty of the union leadership, and indeed most union activists, to the Labour Party. The role that the Party has played as the major political socialization agent of union activists has nurtured the view of the Labour Party as the unique political expression of the British working class. These activists created the Labour Party, and without their support an effective alternative party cannot be maintained. Indeed, the long history of Labour's retention of working class political allegiance, despite open and bitter conflicts, suggests that once electoral mass mobilization of the working class occurs, is institutionalized in the configuration of a political participation through a social democratic party, and crystallizes itself over a period of a half-century, as it has in Britain, a political mould is formed which becomes exceedingly difficult to break. Even under conditions of industrial militancy and economic crisis, the possibilities of working class remobilization seem quite limited in the face of loyalties formed at a crucial phase

of working class political development and the inertia which inevitably attends
their perpetuation over a significant period of time. In his speech at the time of
the 1971 Party Conference, Jack Jones told a story of a man who was asked after
50 years of marriage if he had ever considered divorce: 'Divorce – never. Murder
– often.' This, Jones explained, was how the trade unions felt about their marriage to the Labour Party.[24]

Nevertheless, to point out the difficulty of remobilization is not in itself a
sufficient argument against the attempt insofar as the possibility of changing
Labour from within seems even more daunting. Certainly the magnitude of the
task is obvious – the whole history of the Party has to be overcome. And the fact
that fewer and fewer revolutionary socialists now enter the Labour Party even
further lessens the chances of change from within. At the same time, it is fairly
clear that Labour's integrative role will only continue to be performed with an
intensification of the attendant strains and conflicts which the Party's ties to the
organized working class have repeatedly produced. To the end of re-establishing
its credibility as a working class as well as a national party, Labour has adopted a
more radical programme for social reform within capitalism. But the capacity of
British capitalism, and the willingness of its dominant classes, to sustain such a
programme is highly questionable, and the trade union movement has recently
shown itself averse to undertaking limitations on its bargaining freedom without concrete evidence that extensive social reforms are in fact forthcoming. In
a situation of class conflict in the industrial sphere and severe weakness in the
economy it has proved difficult, in other words, for Labour to re-establish effectively the basic condition of its success, that ideological synthesis in which it
appears as the true expression of the nation as a whole as well as of the working
class. This is a situation of real crisis for the Labour Party. And in view of the
functional role Labour has played in the integration of the working class, to
speak of the crisis of the Labour Party is, to a significant extent, really to speak of
the crisis of British capitalism itself.

Notes

[1] L. Panitch, 'Ideology and integration: the case of the British Labour Party', *Political Studies*, vol.
XIX, no. 2, 1971, p. 187

[2] Ibid, p.199

[3] L. Panitch, *Social Democracy and Industrial Militancy: the Labour Party, the trade unions and
incomes policy 1945-74*, Cambridge University Press 1976, pp. 235-6

[4] Ibid, 253-4

[5] Ibid, p.257

[6] The Ken Coates article, 'Socialists and the Labour Party' was published in the 1973 Register. The
Panitch response, 'Socialists and the Labour Party: a Reappraisal' was published in 1979, and is
reproduced here as chapter 8

[7] T. Nairn, 'The Left Against Europe', *New Left Review*, no. 75, 1972, p- 43

[8] F. Parkin, *Class Inequality and Political Order*, London 1971, p. 99.

[9] In addition to Parkin see Tom Nairn (n. t above); and Barry Hinders, *The Decline of Working
Class Politics*, London 1971.

[10] Panitch, 'Ideology and Integration: The Case of the British Labour Party', *Political Studies*, vol. XIX, no. z, 1971.

[11] R. H. Tawney, *Equality*, 4th edn, London, p. 19

[12] S. H. Beer, *Modern British Politics*, London 1965, p. 190.

[13] D. Jackson et al. *Do Trade Unions Cause Inflation?*, Cambridge 1972, p. 76.

[14] Beer (n. 12 above), p. 216.

[15] Ibid, p.211

[16] Nairn (n. 7 above), pp. 48-9.

[17] Eric Heffer, *Class Struggle in Parliament*, London 1973, pp. 272, 279, 283.

[18] ibid, p.232

[19] 'Trade Unions and the Labour Party', speech to the Fabian Society Meeting, Brighton, 4 October 1971

[20] .Heffer (n. 17 above), p.232

[21] E. J. Hobsbawm, 'Trends in the Labour Movement', in *Labouring Men*, London 1964, p. 330

[22] .A. Crosland, *Can Labour Win?* Fabian Tract 324, 1960, p. 20

[23] 'The Choice Before the Labour Party', *Political Quarterly* (1932), quoted in Royden Harrison,. 'Labour Government: Then and Now', *Political Quarterly*, vol. 41, no. 11 1970, p.78.

[24] Trade Unions and the Labour Party', speech to a Fabian Society Meeting, Brighton, 4 October 1971.

Editorial Introduction to Extract 7

Leo Panitch's conclusion to *Social Democracy and Industrial Militancy* opened with the observation that analyses which 'confine themselves to the attempt to explain Labour's consistent "failure" to be "socialist" when in government.... must inevitably fall wide of the mark'[1]. One of the studies which, implicitly at least, was vulnerable to that criticism was my own, equally Miliband-inspired 1975 study – *The Labour Party and the Struggle for Socialism* – sections of whose explanatory chapter are reproduced here. Written long before I had fully come to terms with Labour's inability to act as an effective counter-hegemonic political force, my first 'go' at the Labour Party was in effect what Bernard Crick rather tartly dismissed as 'a kind of technicolour remake of Ralph Miliband's black and white (polemic against) Parliamentary Socialism'[2]. The book added three explanatory 'colours' to Miliband's analysis of the limits of Labourism. The first was nothing more than a re-emphasis of the by then standard arguments on the deleterious consequences on Labour Party radicalism of the Party's consistent over-estimation of the class neutrality of the state, and of the failure of socialists within the Party to recognize the constraints that Labour governments necessarily face when entering office. In *The Labour Party and the Struggle for Socialism*, the regular backsliding of Labour governments from their opening set of radical electoral promises was partly explained by the interplay of policy constraints generated from within the state machinery itself, by the persistent pressure of business and financial interests for policy orthodoxy, and by the particularly low tolerance for social reform characteristic of privileged circles at those moments of economic difficulty which alone propel Labour into office. The book was in consequence very much exercised with what Rosa Luxemburg long ago had characterized as 'parliamentary cretinism' – now more prosaically described as 'the impossibility of the parliamentary road to socialism'[3].

The Labour Party and the Struggle for Socialism was exercised by two other issues as well. It was exercised by the limited capacity of the Labour Party's electoral politics to shape the consciousness and self-confidence of the party's working-class base. In this regard it noted and emphasized the party's unwillingness to use parliament primarily as an agitational platform of the kind that might have radicalized its electorate, the paucity of its ideological resources relative to those of its opponents, its electoral dependence on 'floating voters' of a necessarily moderate kind, and the way in which its own under-performance in government eroded its long-term credibility and capacity for electoral mobilization. It was not just that the Labour Party had no strategy for implementing socialism, no matter what it promised. It was also that it had no mechanism for creating mass support for socialism; and because it did not, so the argument ran, the role and position of socialists within the Labour Party was a particularly forlorn one. As its third extension of the original Miliband corpus, *The Labour Party and the Struggle for Socialism* documented and explained the socialism of the Labour Left as a form of politics that was *necessarily* trapped between a capitalist rock and an electoral hard place. It had the Labour Left necessarily caught between, on the one side, party leaderships understandably cautious in relation to existing concentrations of power as they approached office, and on the other, electorates whose capture required the subordination of radicalism to the more conservative sensibilities of independent 'floating' voters – a subordination which inevitably sent the Labour Left into silence at the very moment of electoral battle when in principle their voice could most effectively have been heard. This 'position of structured impotence' was then seen as preventing the Labour Left from creating the mass base of support outside the party which alone could bring it long-term success within the party. It left Labour Party socialists 'wrapped in the rhetoric of the labour movement' while unable 'to act in any way which might have turned this rhetoric into a reality', and in consequence, trapped into 'a dismal and unbroken record of failures'[4].

7. THE FAILURE OF THE SOCIALIST PROMISE (1975)

David Coates

At the heart of Labourism, as we have seen, has been a faith in the autonomy of the State machine, and in the reforming potential of a Parliamentary majority – a faith that by winning a Parliamentary majority the Labour Party could 'then proceed to construct a new kind of society without any serious hindrance from those whom existing society exists to benefit'.[5] The trouble with such a set of beliefs is that it seriously overestimates the power of the Parliamentary State to change class relationships in the wider society. It was as if the Labour Party – in its reformist period at least, and on its left wing throughout – believed that the lines of class cleavage in a modern industrial society could be translated into the confines of a legislative assembly, and converted there into a question of majority votes between competing teams of Parliamentarians.

The inordinate importance which even the Labour Left has given to Parliamentary ritual and to the Parliamentary career of individual MPs suggests that they deluded themselves into thinking that a ruling class can be persuaded to voluntarily surrender its powers and prerogatives (presumably because its members hold more rigorously to the norms of Parliamentary procedure than they do to their own class interests). Certainly the essence of the Party's 'gradualist' perspective was that the privileged and powerful within a capitalist society would allow their power and privileges to be eroded bit by bit, whilst being persuaded that their experience of this gradual erosion (with its promise of more erosion to come) should be accepted out of a wider commitment to the good of the community as a whole. Yet State power cannot be used to undermine class power in that way, and ruling groups have rarely if ever surrendered their power so voluntarily. But the whole theory and practice of the Labour Party at its most radical expected them to do so. It was as though, committed to Parliamentary procedures and constitutionality themselves, Labour politicians failed to see that other groups need not prove so committed; and that the power structure that they faced when in office would not hesitate to use its extra-Parliamentary power to defend its class interests if these were threatened, and in so doing, seriously reduce the freedom of manoeuvre of the Parliamentary State in which the Labour Party had placed so much of its faith.

There have been occasions of course on which the Labour Party has publicly discussed this question of ruling class response. This was particularly so in the 1930s when the collapse of Weimar Germany, the spread of Fascism, and the ignominy of the Labour Party's ejection from office in 1931, combined to prompt a brief consideration of the likely response of industrial and financial capital to a socialist political party in Parliamentary power. Sir Stafford Cripps in particular, in his pamphlet *Can Socialism Come by Constitutional Means?* came as near as any Labour Party leader to questioning the validity of Labourist assumptions on the ability of the Parliamentary State to operate unconstrained by the distribution of class power in the wider society:

> We must face the fact, [he wrote] that those who at present hold the economic power will refuse their support to any Labour Government. The idea that if the Labour Party is gentle and well behaved it will persuade the capitalists to hand over the economic power to the Government is quite fantastic.

On the contrary, he anticipated that 'the ruling class [would] go to almost any length to defeat Parliamentary action if the issue is the direct issue as to the continuance of their financial and political control'.[6] His solution, though radical, was characteristically a constitutional one: not the counter-mobilisation of the working class but rather the passing by a Labour Government, immediately on taking office, of an Emergency Powers Act under which rapid socialist transformation could be introduced before the capitalist counter-attack could get under way. Similar doubts were raised by Labour Party intellectuals Tawney and Laski in the 1930s, and even Clement Attlee discussed it at some length in his writings in that decade. Here too the solution proposed was a radical but constitutional one: namely that 'the Labour Government must be armed with emergency powers for taking land and buildings without waiting for elaborate enquiries as to compensation',[7] and the House of Lords, at least in its present form, must be abolished.

These early doubts do not however appear to have troubled either Attlee or Cripps in office, and the question of the class constraints on the Parliamentary State was kept alive thereafter only in the most sporadic fashion. For the years of the Attlee Government removed this issue from the agenda of Labour Party politics for two decades, as the young Labour politicians who were to dominate the years of Opposition drew an extremely optimistic lesson from the events of 1945-51. They noted the Labour Party achievements of those years and the lack of visible and sustained ruling class offensive, and concluded both that the constraints had been negligible (and that the fears of the 1930s had been alarmist and unwarranted) and that the Labour Party could have done even more had it so chosen....In fact, the young Labour MPs left office optimistic about the potentiality of State power. As Crossman put it,

> We now know that the power of the State is not in the hands of any class. It is a power in itself, and once you hold that power, once you control the Army, once you control the instruments of coercion, and the instruments of thought control through mass communication, through radio and newspapers – once you control those you have power greater than any Capitalist under the sun.[8]

And yet he would have been more perceptive if he had noted how little the Labour administration under Attlee threatened the existing distribution of social and economic power, and how closely it co-operated with the representatives of industrial and financial capital; and if he had then concluded that this was the reason that the Labour Government met so little opposition. It was not the power structure that had changed from the 1930s so much as the Labour Party itself. Indeed when the Attlee Government began, however reluctantly, to make inroads into the profitable sectors of British capitalism (with its proposal for steel nationalisation in 1948) then the opposition which it met was sustained and ultimately effective.

In choosing to ignore the question of class constraints on the Parliamentary State, the Labour Party after Attlee turned away from the basic weakness of its whole politics. It ignored the insights of the prewar generation, just as they had ignored the criticisms made of Parliamentarianism even earlier, in the European sections of the pre-First World War Labour International. For the problem of 'bourgeois democracy' and the consequences of involvement within it, were argued out fully within the Second International just as the Labour Party was being formed. But, shut off from the world of Marxist socialism, the early Labour Party leaders either failed to hear or chose to ignore the dangers of 'Parliamentary cretinism' as these were laid out there. For as Rosa Luxemburg noted then, a preoccupation with Parliamentary politics has always encouraged an over-estimation of the prospects of peaceful reform and of the co-operation between classes. 'The illusion,' she wrote, that 'parliament is the central axis of social life and the driving force of world history ... cannot see beyond the complacent speechification of a few hundred parliamentary deputies ... to the gigantic forces of world history, forces which are at work on the outside ... and which are quite unconcerned with their parliamentary law-making'. The Labour Party has never been short of this illusion.

II

In their illusion of Parliamentary 'power' the Labour Party leaders have repeatedly overestimated both the degree of class neutrality that they could legitimately expect from the various sections of the State machine (the civil service, the judiciary and the armed forces) and underestimated the extent to which the close connections between the civil service and the senior managerial hierarchies of private business reduce the availability of the civil service for use in programmes that seriously challenge the social power and class prerogatives of these well-organised and class-conscious groups. The Labour Party on taking office has made no sweeping changes in its senior civil service personnel, and so when it was at its most radical (in 1945) it found itself facing civil servants who were 'apathetic and antagonistic to nationalisation' and who 'by social provenance, education and professional disposition, were bound to conceive it as one of their prime tasks to warn their Ministers against too radical a departure from their traditional Depart mental policies'.[9] Not that the Party in power experienced administrative sabotage. Their policies were insufficiently radical to invite that; Rather they experienced an administrative inertia that reflected the close personal, social and ideological interconnections between the State machine and the senior personnel of those private industrial and financial organisations that the Labour Party programme ostensibly challenged.

Nor, as far as we can tell, was this 'administrative inertia' restricted to the 1945-51 Labour Government. Barbara Castle reported exactly the same kind of problem as Minister of Transport from December 1965. As she wrote later:

> I remember Andy Cohen, the Permanent Secretary, trying to wear me down. He used to come in on policy points and things like appointments. He would be in my office about seven times a day saying: 'Minister, I know the ultimate decision is yours, but I would be failing in my duty if I didn't tell you how unhappy your decision makes me'. Seven times a day. One person against the vast department.[10]

For senior civil servants and businessmen shared in the 1940s, and in the main continue to share, similar social backgrounds, similar educational training, and similar social status and life-styles; and though none of these guarantee a total empathy of interests between the two groups, they do mean that senior civil servants are 'part of a specific milieu whose ideas, prejudices and outlook they are most likely to share'. More important even than this is the ever-growing interpenetration of State and business hierarchies which brings senior civil servants into daily and close contacts with the problems, needs and wider social and political orientations of the world of corporate capital, and establishes between them and the senior managerial strata a community of common interests which leaves the civil servants less and less open to political orientations that are at variance with the imperatives and class prerogatives of private financial and industrial institutions.

But it must not be thought that the relationship between civil servants and Labour Ministers are always those of mutual hostility. Or, the contrary, as far as can be seen from outside, many Labour Ministers have proved vulnerable to the inertia of civil service conservatism and to the orthodoxy of civil service routines. Indeed the more radical the Minister, the greater that the pressures of that orthodoxy will be, and few Ministers have been long able to withstand it, let alone been able to bend the civil service to their initial will. As Richard Crossman reported after six years in high government office, 'Departments are resistant. Departments know that they last and you don't. Departments know that any day you may be moved somewhere else, and they can forget you. It does not pay you to order them to change their minds on everything. There's a limit to the quantity of change they can digest'.[11]

Yet the constraints on the Labour Party in power run much deeper even than this. For it is not simply that Labour politics never challenge the interconnections between the State machine and the capitalist order. It is rather that the Labour Party in power invariably strengthens those interconnections. For each of the post-war Labour administrations has relied heavily on the expertise and information of private business, and has drawn many senior business executives into the planning and control agencies that it has established. Far from transforming capitalism, the Labour Party in power has established intimate working relationships with that system's managerial personnel. So the complex system of industrial controls that the Labour Party inherited in 1945 was left in the hands of senior industrial managers, and in 1964-70 the new State agencies of 'purposive' socialism (the N.B.P.I, the revamped N.E.D.C., the I.R.C. and the Land Commission) were placed in the hands of men drawn from the next generation of those same senior managers, and even (in the case of the N.B.P.I) in the hands of an ex-Conservative Minister. With such a State bureaucracy, it is hardly surprising that twelve years of post-war Labour Government have left the personnel and institutions of the private sector largely unaffected, and have failed to dent the legal and cultural superstructure within which that private sector maintains its economic and social dominance. Nor, with such a close set of connections between the State bureaucracy and senior managerial personnel from private industry and finance, is it surprising that twelve years of post-war Labour Government have totally failed to change the imperatives (of profit maintenance and capital accumulation) under which a capitalist system functions.

Yet it is no accident that the interconnections between the State and the private capitalist sector are strengthened whenever the Labour Party takes office. For in such a situation, the Labour Party faces more than anything else – the need to ensure the smooth running of the economy over which it formally presides and on which its electorate depend for their material subsistence. And the Party in power faces only two social groups to which in principle it could turn for detailed and regular assistance: a radicalised trade union and working class movement on the one side, or the existing hierarchies of command on the other. Yet the whole tradition of Labourism has done nothing to create the former, and has indeed fought hard against its creation whenever (as in 1926) the possibility of a radicalised proletariat arose. So the Labour Party in power has left itself with no choice but to seek the cooperation of the ruling groups that it faces in industry and finance, and the appointment of their personnel to State agencies is but one visible sign of the close contacts which the Labour Ministers must establish if they are to achieve even their minimum stated programme of economic growth and full employment. The pattern of appointments is also one crucial indication that, in the process, the Labour Government actually strengthens the very economic system and ruling groups that its rhetoric suggested it would control and weaken.

For though it is easy to be misled by the press-coverage, the glamour and the rhetoric of electioneering into thinking that political parties are powerful entities *sui generis*, in reality they are nothing of the kind. The Labour Party in power is some three hundred MPs (technically white-collar workers and normally a collection of ex-trade union officials, lawyers, teachers and academics) who assemble in Westminster, talk to one another in public, and issue documents which we call 'legislation'. These documents, embodiments of Labour Party decisions, are in no sense self-enforcing. True, they have an immense legitimacy and an authority which helps to make them so, though that would not long survive in certain quarters if they proved too radical. And it is the case that they are buttressed by the administrative and coercive mechanisms of the State. But even if a radical Labour Party could rely whole-heartedly on those administrative and coercive mechanisms (and we have just suggested that this is unlikely) even then it could not literally dominate all the private structures of command in a capitalist economy. Instead the Labour Party in power has to win the voluntary co-operation of the power groups that it faces, and that co-operation will be forthcoming only on certain terms. There is thus a general truth in Mannie Shinwell's despairing outburst in 1947: 'We do not produce coal at the Ministry of Power. People seem to think we do. Coal is not produced by statistics, or by Government Departments, or even by speeches, however eloquent they may be. Coal is produced by miners working underground[12], and if they won't produce it, nobody else can.

It is not that the Labour Party in office faces a unified, centralised power structure, which leaves the Party as the passive tool of an unseen elite. It is not a situation of capitalist conspiracy – even less, one of trade union domination. Doubtless there are, particularly at moments of crisis, elements of conscious co-ordination between the senior managerial personnel of the various financial and industrial institutions that the Labour Party faces. But it is more significant for Labour Party politics that the men who may or may not conspire are capitalists than that capitalists may or may not conspire. For the reality of power in a modern industrial society is an infinitely more complex and subtle entity than any simple conspiracy theory can allow. It is rather that the Labour Party, on taking office, faces a complicated matrix of interlocking class relationships which set limits on its freedom of manoeuvre, which effectively limit its ability to redistribute class power and G.N.P., which possess the power to negate the impact on the distribution of class power of any Labour Party initiative, and which on occasions impose upon the Labour Party in power demands for the redistribution of resources away from the Party's working class electorate. For in that complicated matrix of class relationships are concentrations of social power, institutions whose monopoly of certain material and ideological resources both gives to the men who head them leverage against the State and provides those men with a set of private imperatives which they must defend against a reforming Government if they are to maintain their own class privileges and power.

No one institution is totally dominant. Indeed it is a feature of the social tensions and inherent instabilities of capitalism as a system that it generates no one centre of power. Rather the Labour Party in power faces an industrial process dominated by large (and of late, increasingly multi-national) corporations, whose viability ultimately turns on their ability to maintain a sufficient level of profits to sustain reinvestment and research, and who can reasonably be expected to press for the social and economic conditions that will make that possible. A Labour Government also faces a set of financial institutions that are committed to the free movement of international currencies and to the stabilisation of exchange rates around a strong pound sterling. And it faces an organised working class with a vested interest in the retention and extension of its previously achieved degree of wage levels, job security and job control. At every stage in this matrix of class relationships, the Labour Party meets blockages, obstacles and power centres which have to be ameliorated and cajoled. Precisely because the Labor Party in power has to win the voluntary co-operation of these private power groupings by harnessing their self-interest to its own, so it finds that the ways in which individual and institutional self-interests are structured by the class imperatives of a capitalist society constitute the ultimate level of constraints with which its Parliamentary leadership has to come to terms.

III

There is no doubt that the major blockage on the ability of the Labour Party to reform capitalism into socialism by the Parliamentary process or even to sustain major programmes of social reform, comes from the institutions and representatives of corporate capital – both financial and industrial. The immediate needs which these institutions have of the State set the terms of reference within which the Labour Party in power has to act, since they determine the conditions on which Labour policies of economic growth can be achieved and co-operation with business ensured. These terms of reference have been variously described. Corporate business certainly requires of the State 'a "reasonable" attitude to key industrial and financial interests; a willingness . . . to preach to the trade unions the virtues of moderation in wage demands; a "sensible" attitude to tax reform; and a sympathetic appreciation of the general requirements of an economy geared to the profit motive'.[13] Financial institutions, and the Bank of England in particular, have shown a persistent preference for fixed exchange rates, and for the free movement of international currencies, and have argued strongly for both before Conservative and Labour Governments alike.

But let us be clear on what is being argued, and what is not. By arguing that the Labour Party in power has to operate within the terms of reference set by the general requirements of an economy geared to the profit motive, this is not to deny that the Labour Government has its own power-resources, which it can use, and which give it leverage against individual firms and industries. On the contrary: many firms and industries, especially those selling large parts of their product to Government agencies, and those in need of investment grants and capital loans, will experience the Labour Government as a senior partner, able to shape their own patterns of profitability and growth directly. Moreover it is clear that the general set of relationships between a Labour Government and industry are affected, if only at the margin, by the degree of unity within the Labour Party, by the size of its Parliamentary majority, by the length of time it has been in office and by its chances of defeat at the next general election. And all Governments, including Labour ones, possess a wide range of controls that directly affect firms, industries and even multi-national concerns But the danger of stopping the analysis at this point, which is precisely where most Labour MPs stop when talking of what 'they' will do to business and finance when in power, is in sliding from the recognition that all Governments have some power to the assumption that that power is unlimited. It is also to forget that the Labour Party, in its more radical periods at least, is promising not simply to manage the economic and social system, but to change it. As a result, if its own experience between 1945 and 1951 is any guide, a Labour Government is likely to meet opposition 'at every point at which power interests, rather than property interests'[14] are threatened. As Rogow put it, in a classic understatement of the power reality faced by every reformist Labour Government, in such a situation, 'the continued co-operation vested power groups in measures of social change designed to reduce their power and influence can no longer be taken for granted'[15]

Moreover, even if that opposition were miraculously to be absent, any Labour Government would still inevitably experience a tension between its reforming aspirations and its related search for co-operation with senior managerial personnel in a common drive for sustained economic output. For there are real limits to what a Labour Government can do, and to the type of policies it can actually pursue, limits that are rooted in the general requirements of capitalist private enterprise as a system, and these limits eat away at precisely those aspects of Labour policy that the Party periodically has offered to the electorate as a way of transforming capitalism gradually into a more socialist system. It cannot equalise incomes and wealth without destroying the basis of private profit and corporate endeavour. It cannot take over vast areas of profitable private industry without alienating future private investment and therefore economic growth. It cannot introduce major changes in the distribution of control within industry without inviting major ideological counter-attacks from the organs of private capital, and without driving major sources of future plant, machinery and output away to 'safer' political climates. It cannot even sustain exchange controls for any substantial period without provoking a hostile response from international financial agencies and without running the risk that the big multinational corporations will be driven to redirect their internal resources towards its competitor economies. And as the Labour Party found in the 1960s, with the dwindling international competitiveness of British industry, it cannot avoid taking an interest in cost-effectiveness within industry and in general wage rates and earning levels in the economy as a whole. That is, it cannot avoid playing a role in the control of the working class at the point of production.

For if the Labour Party is to achieve a sustained rate of economic growth from which to pay for greater social welfare programmes, educational expansion and the like, it has to provide when in office that economic and social environment in which private corporate profits can flourish, and in which the class prerogatives of senior managerial personnel can remain unchallenged. It is in this sense that the freedom of manoeuvre of the Labour Party power is constrained by the 'health' of the economy in capitalist terms by its cost-competitiveness, its overall profit rate, its productivity and its degree of re-investment. And here, as the politics of 'Catch-22' for the Labour Party, the paradox occurs: that the maintenance of such 'health' invariably strengthens the very capitalist class the Labour Government was supposed to control, and brings the Party in power into conflict with its own industrial wing and its own working class electorate, who then appear as a secondary blockage on the Party's freedom of manoeuvre.

For at the heart of the capitalist system lies the tension between the political economy of Capital and that of Labour, a tension which throws into fundamental doubt the Labour Party's traditional commitment to social unity, a national interest, and the gradual change of class society by consensus. That tension takes many forms: of wages against profits, of managerial prerogatives against working class job control, of capitalist exploitation against alienated labour, of the rich against the poor in a society divided by the class allocation of wealth, income, life chances and power. With a Labour Party experiencing and demonstrating the real limits on its freedom of manoeuvre imposed by corporate capital, it is hardly surprising that the working class and its trade unions have come (albeit slowly in its official voice, more rapidly in sections of its rank and file) to act as a secondary limit on the freedom of the Labour Party in power, by being reluctant to surrender easily any of its hard-won industrial control and living standards in a new Labour Government-inspired social contract.

The consequences of this for the internal stability of the labour movement have been enormous. For the very failure of the Labour Party to deliver its more radical promises has eaten away at the relationship between itself and its working class base. That relationship has never been very strong. Organisationally the Party structure has never made any direct connection with the worker at the point of production. Socially, its leaders have increasingly shed (or never had) any working class experience or roots. And ideologically, the long-standing separation of industrial activity from political activity in the Labourist tradition has sustained a central ambiguity in the relationship between the two wings of the labour movement. But even so, by 1945 the connection between the working class and the Party was close indeed. Yet the failure thereafter of the Labour Governments to shift substantial degrees of power and resources away from corporate capital has left its working class electorate still subject to capitalist instability, still dependent on its own industrial efforts to achieve that degree of affluence, job security and job control that the Labour Party could not guarantee, and still subject to marked inequalities of power and wealth. And as such the working class electorate is left increasingly as, at best, a reluctant ally of a Labour Party whose response to repeated pressure from international and national industrial and financial capital has been to adopt a 'managerial' attitude to the trade union movement and its activities that bodes ill for the continuing close relationship between the two wings of the labour movement.

IV

Before probing the consequences of this for the Labour Party's own development, we should note how it is reinforced by a secondary and related feature of Labour Party politics, namely by the Party's relationship with its electorate. For the utter dependence of the Labour Party in power on the voluntary co-operation of senior managerial personnel in private industry reflects the absence of any alternative power base within the labour movement itself to which the Party, in any confrontation with Capital, could and would be willing to turn. It reflects the absence, that is, of a radicalised proletariat able and willing to buttress Labour Party policy initiatives by industrial action at the point of production, and of a trade union movement prepared to take on that role. There have been moments, certainly, when events external to the Party have produced signs of mass political radicalism in the British working class; and it has been at these points, and only at these points, that the Labour Party has found a radical programme both electorally vital and politically viable. But it is hardly too much to say that the 'reformism' of the Labour Party before 1970 was a temporary consequence of two wars and a prolonged depression, rather than something endemic to its whole mode of politics. For the Labour Party has never set out to create such a radicalised proletariat. On the contrary, such a radicalised proletariat has always been anathema to the Labourist tradition.

Instead the Labour Party has been committed to a theory of party-class relationships which gives the Party an educating role (between the wars, for example, as a socialist propagandist) but which restricts the Party programme at any stage to a point commensurate with existing levels of political consciousness in the Labour electorate at large. Indeed, its whole mode of politics, Parliamentarianism, has made this essential, as we shall see. And in its preoccupation with Parliamentarianism, the Labour Party has not even used Parliament, as many revolutionaries have used equivalent institutions elsewhere, primarily as a stage upon which to make agitational and propagandist statements that could connect with, generalise, and intensify the growing conflict between the classes at the point of production. On the contrary, Labour Party pronouncements on even industrial disputes have been uniformly hostile to mass radicalism, and have sought always to emasculate the class struggle by restricting it to constitutionally sanctioned channels. This is as true of its hostility to the General Strike of 1926 as it is of its reaction to working class industrial opposition to the 1971 Industrial Relations Act: that the working class should not challenge the legal powers of the State by extra-constitutional industrial means, even if those legal powers were visibly class-biased and even if the alternative is to surrender and wait for the next Labour Government. To the extent that the Labour Party has had any impact at all on patterns of consciousness in its working class electorate, it has been to constantly reinforce the illusion of the untrammelled sovereignty of the democratically elected Parliamentary State.

But in fact the Labour Party has had far less impact on the general level and type of consciousness in its working class electorate than have its political opponents. There are a number of reasons for this. In part, it reflects the control which private capitalists have retained over the mass media, and their willingness to use that control to defend their class privileges by sustained propaganda against Labour radicalism. The campaign against the nationalisation of steel, sugar and chemicals at the end of the Attlee Government is a case in point. Much more importantly, it also reflects the fact that the gap between Labour promises and Labour performance in office always provides such propagandists with an enormous stick with which to beat the Party. This was particularly important in the 1950s, when the very failure of the Attlee Government to transform capital-ism into socialism via public ownership, state planning and welfare provision left even Labour voters sceptical of the Party's pre-occupation with the further creation of public corporations. For the Party had promised working class eman-cipation and a qualitative change in human existence. It had created instead a bureaucratised public sector and a strengthened capitalist class. Here the limits of State power under a 'reformist' Government left, as an electoral legacy to the next generation of the Party, a generalised antipathy to nationalised industries and State planning, and a concomitant faith in a private enterprise system which had been strengthened by the Attlee Government's nationalisation policies. It left, that is, a 'conservative renaissance'[16] to which the Party leadership increas-ingly succumbed, and against which its counterpropaganda was increasingly defeatist and hesitant.

Yet the Labour Party could ill afford such listlessness in its propagandising, for the scales of history were, and remain, against it. It inherited a predominantly conservative electorate, with a popular culture rooted in a liberal-imperialist past. Admittedly, two world wars and the inter-war experience of capitalist in-stability had moved that electorate towards political radicalism, but still with a culture that contained within it the anti-socialist notions and aspirations of Vic-torian imperialism. It inherited also a class structure riddled with internal, sub-sidiary status divisions between occupational groups, and one which since 1945 has witnessed a substantial shift out of manual employment into white collar occupations that were traditionally less closely identified with 'the working class' and the Labour Party. It would have taken – and still requires – a massive ideo-logical effort on the part of the Labour Party to have shifted that legacy. But, in the event, this was an effort which the Labour Party undertook only sporadically and with limited effect. All too often, the Party surrendered to existing levels of prejudice in an undignified search for votes on any terms, so reinforcing tenden-cies in popular culture that were inimical to radical social change on socialist lines. This has weakened the Party profoundly, as Anderson has observed:

> The real criticism to be made of them is . . . that they cannot gain power as long as they sacrifice principle for the sake of winning elections. They may well win, but under these conditions 'power' is simply permission to operate the status quo. It has no purchase whatever on the statute of the society. There is no 'mandate' for changing this. Social-democracy is thus trapped in the closed circle of electoralism. It restricts its own freedom to win a partial power which is then further curtailed by its initial restriction. The result is a profound impotence and demoralisation.[17]

The precise manifestations and consequences of this varied over time. Between the wars, when the Labour Party faced an electorate shaped by political forces stronger than itself, it encouraged the Party to tone down the radicalism of its 1918 programme, until the severity of the Depression and the rigours of war presented to it an electorate demanding radical change. In the specific conditions of capitalist prosperity in the 1950s, the repeated evidence of electoral skepticism and hostility towards public ownership that the half-heartedness of the Attlee Government had itself created, was a major force pulling the Party leadership away not simply from its old 'reformist' trilogy of nationalisation, planning and welfare, but from any 'reformist' aspirations at all. And even in the changed conditions of the 1970s, when capitalist instability has undoubtedly created again a more generalised dissatisfaction within the Labour Party's potential electorate, the Party leadership are still under 'electoral' pressures to moderate their promises.

Of course, this attempt to moderate the Party's image partly reflex the leadership's realisation of how little they can actually do in power (though Labour politicians in the past have tended to forget this all too easily as the years of Opposition have lengthened). What the Party leaders cannot forget are the electoral pressures for moderation in the programme. For the Party's Parliamentarianism effectively isolates it from the points of working class struggle, and militates against effect propaganda work by the Party there. And yet this same Parliamentarianism makes the Party totally dependent upon an electorate (whose support it must win to be able to do anything in Parliamentary terms a all) – an electorate subject to waves of ideological pressure from the Party's political opponents. Indeed, the Labour Party's passivity and impotence before the electorate is even greater than this, for it is dependent if it is to 'win' State power, not simply on the generalised support of the electorate, but on the support of critical smaller electorates in a series of marginal constituencies. It must win these, and by definition these are the very constituencies in which party radicalism runs the greatest risk of voter-alienation and consequent electoral defeat. The massive Labour vote of Ebbw Vale would doubtless tolerate radicalism from the Party. Indeed the Labour Party's problem now is that its traditional vote in places like the Welsh valleys is being eroded by the Party's conservatism in office. But it dare not be more radical, lest its critical marginal vote be lost. Of course, there are those in the Party who argue that it should gamble, and educate its electorate in a radical alternative. But even they have to concede that it is a gamble, and they have invariably gone along with a toning down of party programmes at election times that is commensurate with the political sympathies of the marginal seats. Even in power, as between 1964 and 1970, it was this sensitivity to the electoral proclivities of marginal sea and marginal voters which reinforced the tendency of the Party leadership to conservatism and moderation.

V

This twin experience, of the limits of State power and the logic of electoral politics under capitalism, is the source of the growing conservatism of the Labour

Party's chosen agency of social change, the Parliamentary Party and its leadership. Together, they had effectively destroyed that Parliamentary Party by 1970 as an agency of anything but its own desperate search for government office. This twin experience had whittled away the radicalism of earlier party programmes, and in the process had transformed the Parliamentary Party into a mechanism for mediating the immediate needs of the capitalist system to the working class, rather than one that could lead the class to transform capitalism, or even one that could effectively impose up the capitalist system social reforms of sufficient scale to make a qualitative difference to the life experience of its electorate. And it has done this by educating the Parliamentary leadership into a definition of the 'realistic' in politics that was coterminous with the maintenance of the existing distribution of social power and had in the process generated a set of leaders whose hypersensitivity to the imperatives of that realism left them as only pale reflections of their more radical younger selves. As a result, we are left, as Tom Nairn has observed, with a situation in which

> realism turns, in Labour leaders into mere cowardice, a kind of timid hypnosis in the face of events; practicality turns into willful short-sightedness, a ritual pragmatism wielded to exorcise the sort of theoretical thinking socialism requires; [in which] dignified reverence for the past becomes a depraved fetish-worship of idols which seem to change into dust at the very torch of such falsity.[18]

Now when faced with such a set oaf Parliamentarians, it is conveniently easy to restrict the explanation of Labour Party conservatism and failure in office to an analysis of the personalities that make up the leadership. The 'sell-out' thesis... has a long pedigree in Labour Party polemic and analysis. So the Labour Party is explained and excused because some of its leaders found personal advantages in sucking up to the rich (the theory of 'aristocratic embrace'). Or it is criticised because its constituency parties have proved too fond of selecting MPs from middle class occupations (the theory of leadership 'embourgeoisification'). Or it is excused because some of its leaders, isolated from the rank and file, found solace in excessive sensitivity to Parliamentary procedures (the theory of 'parliamentary socialisation'). Or the Party is condemned because a good number of its leaders, overworked and overawed, fell victim to the dictates of their civil servants, (the theory of 'poor quality Ministers'). Clearly Labour Party history is rich in examples of all these, and no explanation of Labour Party politics can ignore them. J. H. Thomas was undoubtedly under the domination of his Permanent Secretary, Sir Horace Wilson, whom he knew affectionately as 'Orace'.[19] Herbert Morrison was clearly passionately committed to Parliamentary procedures and norms. Ramsay MacDonald clearly accentuated the trend to conservatism by his personal foibles and growing empathy with aristocratic ladies. But the trend existed in any case, and it is no accident that the Parliamentary leaders of the Labour Party have succumbed to these tendencies. For the logic of their conservatism is rooted in the general character of Labour Party politics.

For what characterises that politics is that it generates sets of leaders who, in office, experience particular problems, and particular possibilities of success and failure. To achieve power at all, as we have seen, they require the support of marginal voters. Then, when in power, they need the co-operation of the hierarchies of private capitalism that surround them. They both daily experience the potential offered to them when that co-operation is forthcoming, and the frustration and impotence that follows its withdrawal. And in both cases, their daily experience of office, and their observation of it from afar when in Opposition, underline how essential it is for the Labour Party leadership to establish their 'respectability' in the eyes of the power-groupings that they face. So the desperate search for 'respectability' and the repeated attempts to 'prove their fitness to rule' which characterise the speeches and policies of Labour Ministers are no accident of Ministerial personality (though they may be accentuated by that). They are rather rooted in the Labour Party's need for co-operation. They are the visible admission by the Party's leaders of the limits of State power. And given the Labour Party's pretensions to be a party of social reform, this 'respectability' is always in doubt. Business co-operation is something on which the party's leadership can never automatically rely, since it is something which the party's radical rhetoric in Opposition has invariably done much to put in jeopardy. And so paradoxically, the stronger the Labour Party politically, the more radical its programme, and the louder its left wing, the less secure will organised capital feel, and the more that it will demand of the Labour leadership as 'proof of the Party's 'soundness' and suitability for co-operation. Only the peculiar situation of post-war mass radicalism eased this corporate pressure in 1945, and even then it was fully back in evidence as early 1948.

This is the paradox at the heart of Labourism – what Michael Foot has called 'the fundamental and fatal contradiction of the Labour Party'. It was a dilemma clear to Aneurin Bevan as early as 1931, that

> In opposition, the Labour Party is compelled, by the nature of the class struggle, to take up an alignment which hamstrings it when in office. A Party climbing to power by articulating the demands of the dispossessed must always wear a predatory visage to the property-owning class . . . although all the time its heart is tender with the promise of peaceful gradualism. It knows that the limited vision of the workers will behold only its outward appearance, but it hopes that the gods of private enterprise will look upon its heart. In either case, one must be deceived. To satisfy the workers the Labour Party must fulfill the threat of its face, and so destroy the political conditions necessary to economic gradualism. To calm the fears of private enterprise it must betray its promise to the workers, and so lose their support.[20]

When in power, the pressures on the Labour Party leadership to take that second option, 'to betray its promise to the workers', are enormous. As we saw, senior managerial personnel in the major private industrial and financial agencies possess a number of potent sanctions against a recalcitrant Government which in the past they have been prepared to use. So even in the Labour Party's modest history, its leaders have known strikes by senior managerial personnel, ideological offensives against certain of its policies, flights of capital out of the country, and dictation of domestic and foreign policy terms by those in control of international lending agencies. Indeed, the very international competitive weakness of British capitalism and the legacy of a Imperial past have left every post-war British Government particularly dependent on these last mentioned financial agencies. This has given British finance capital a particular leverage on the Labour Party in power, precisely because its co-operation has been vital to stem the short-term net export of funds that would otherwise send the economy into a payments deficit with the usual crippling effects on domestic interest rates, economic growth and manufacturing investment. Yet it is significant that the Labour Party in power has only rarely experienced these breakdowns of co-operation between its leadership and the well-organised representatives of industrial and financial capital. Instead and more normally, as we have seen, the relationship between the State and the capitalist sector has been strengthened under Labour. For the threat that a radical Labour Party poses to the existing distribution of class power has been neutralised over the years far less by class coercion and lack of co-operation, far more by the *incorporation* of the Labour Party leadership into the command structures and world view of the ruling groups that the Party once existed to bring down.

Two sets of relationships experienced by Labour politicians are particularly significant here. Their experience of Parliamentary procedures and atmosphere is clearly one force incorporating many MPs into less radical ways. As Bevan said, the radical MP must really be on his guard:

> To preserve the keen edge of his critical judgment he will find that he must adopt an attitude of scepticism amounting almost to cynicism, for Parliamentary procedure neglects nothing which might soften the acerbities of his class feelings. In one sense the House of Commons is the most unrepresentative of representative assemblies. It is an elaborate conspiracy to prevent the real clash of opinion which exists outside from finding an appropriate echo within its walls. It is a social shock absorber placed between privilege and the pressure of popular discontent.[21]

Yet Parliamentary socialisation can be, and has been, resisted – at least by those few MPs for whom the Commons was never more than an arena in which to make propaganda for the class struggle going on outside. Far more insidious, and ultimately more crucial, is a second set of relationships of incorporation between Labour Ministers on the one side and their senior advisers in the Ministries on the other. This seems to have been, and to remain, the major and most potent mechanism by which Labour Party politicians are absorbed into the rul-

ing ideas of the day. It is the ability of private capitalism to dominate the definitions and policy options perceived by a Labour Government which holds the
key to the absence of more frequent and more open withdrawals of cooperation
by various sections of the British ruling class whenever the Labour Party is in
power. For the Labour Party in office is enveloped in the 'conventional wisdoms'
of the day, operating in a 'reality' defined for it by the civil servants of the public
and private bureaucracies that it faces (in the Treasury, the C.B.I, the Bank of
England and so on). Because the Labour Party coming into power inherits a
situation in which there is a close inter-penetration of personnel, institutions
and attitudes between the State bureaucracy and the private bureaucracies of
industry and finance, so it inherits a government machine which offers it only a
limited range of policy options, and which tells it repeatedly that only a limited
range of 'solutions' are possible to 'problems' that are themselves defined by civil
servants operating within a world view a set of class interests shared with the
senior echelons of private capitalism.

To this enmeshing of the Labour Ministers in the ruling ideas of day, the
Labour Party makes its own contribution, by repeatedly failing to generate alternative definitions, detailed policies, and the social forces on which to break
through the material and ideological domination of this class of men at the top
of the industrial, financial and public bureaucracies. As a result, so all pervasive
are these orthodoxies, so united are these bureaucracies in their definition of
'important problems', 'policy alternatives' and 'desirable solutions' that the Labour Party in power faces a body of ideas that appears not as the embodiment
of the interests of the ruling class alone but as the embodiment of the interests
of the society as a whole. The Labour Party in power, that is, faces a truly 'hegemonic' power structure, before which Labour Party politicians find themselves
helpless, lacking as they do a counter-definition of reality of the same force and
any alternative power base on which to put that counter-definition into practice.
And so their very impotence without the co-operation of this hegemonic power
structure only persuades them, on a day to day basis, that they really do face only
the set of policy alternatives that they are offered by their civil service.

In such a situation, it is no accident that the 'class' content of the Labour
leadership's aspirations should drain over time, not least because it is the manifestations of working class aspirations which create problems for them in their
dealings with the City and with organised business. As politicians in power they
depend for their success on their ability to find the common ground between
opposing class forces; or failing that, on their ability to ally with the stronger
class. For the alternative for them as Parliamentarians is total ineffectiveness and
likely electoral defeat. So, out of their daily experience, the Labour Party leadership are driven to a view of 'reality' which defines as 'the problem' those working class forces which make more difficult the establishment of close working
relationships with the senior manage; strata of private industrial and financial

capital. Out of the logic of their own politics Labour leaders are drawn away from their class perspectives and their class roots, and emerge highly sensitive to the requirements of the capitalist structure that they face, increasingly socialised in the norms of Parliamentary gradualism, increasingly prone to define reality from a managerial standpoint, increasingly reluctant to mobilise or radicalise their own working class base, and increasingly willing to use State power (at times of class crisis) directly against the material interests of the working class that they claim to represent.

Nor is it an accident that the Labour Government in 1931, in 1948, and in 1964-70 seriously weakened itself defending the parity of the pound sterling that the Conservatives calmly abandoned immediately on taking office. For the hyper-sensitivity of international financiers to Labour plans, and the capacity of flights of money abroad to cripple production at home, leaves the Labour Party leadership necessarily sensitive to the City's demands. For the financial institutions of the City actually possess a series of material sanctions whose short-term impact on Labour Government policies is considerably greater and more immediate than anything that industrial capital or the organised working class can muster. Indeed these moments of capitalist crisis demonstrate the bankruptcy of the Labour tradition, as the leaders of the Party are driven to turn the power of the State machine against their own plans and against the living standards and industrial power of their own working class electorate. For in a very real sense the Labour Party leaders have no choice, if they are to win the co-operation of organised capital, if they are to create the economic conditions in which organised capital can afford to co-operate, and if they are to 'prove' that they can be trusted to rule. Or rather, precisely because they have failed to mobilise any alternative source of political power in their own working class electorate, they have no choice. It is from the logic of their own politics that they find themselves isolated from their own rank and file, under the intense personal pressures of office, and with ideological defences that are inadequate to repel conservative orthodoxies. And so ultimately Labour Party leaders find themselves in this ludicrous situation: formally socialist MPs, but in reality, dependent for their definition of the 'national interest' on the specifications of the central institution of British finance capital. The bankruptcy of Labourism could nowhere be more clearly demonstrated than in this.

Notes

[1] L. Panitch, *Social Democracy and Industrial Militancy*, Cambridge University Press, 1976, p. 235

[2] B. Crick, 'After the Fall', *The Guardian*, July 24, 1980

[3] D. Coates, *The Labour Party and the Struggle for Socialism*, Cambridge University Press 1975, p. 229

[4] ibid, p.208

[5] J. Saville, 'Labourism and the Labour Government', in R. Miliband and J. Saville (eds) *The Socialist Register 1967*, London, Merlin, 1967, pp.57-8

[6] Quoted in R. Miliband, *Parliamentary Socialism*, London, Merlin, 1961, pp.197-8

[7] C. Attlee, *The Labour Party in Perspective*, Lobdon, Gollancz, 1937, pp. 115-23

[8] Quoted in F. Bealey (ed), *The Social and Political Thought of the British Labour Party*, London, Weidenfeld and Nicolson, 1970, p.182

[9] Miliband, op.cit., pp. 293-4

[10] B. Castle, 'Mandarin Power', *The Sunday Times*, 10 June 1973, p. 19

[11] R. Crossman, *Inside View*, London, Cape, 1972, p. 72

[12] Quoted in M. Sissons and P. French (eds), *Age of Austerity 1945-51*, Harmondsworth, Penguin, 1964, p. 258

[13] R. Miliband and J. Saville, 'Labour policy and the Labour Left', in their *The Socialist Register 1964*, New York, Monthly Review Press, 1964, pp. 152-3

[14] A Rogow, *The Labour Government and British Industry*, Oxford, Basil Blackwell, 1955, p. 179

[15] ibid, p.176

[16] T. Nairn, 'The nature of the Labour Party', in P. Anderson (ed), *Towards Socialism*, London, Fontana, 1965, p. 179

[17] P. Anderson, 'Problems of socialist strategy', in *Towards Socialism*, op. cit, p. 237

[18] Nairn, op. cit., p. 179

[19] R. Skideslsky, *Politicians and the Slump* Harmondsworth, Penguin, 1970, p.112

[20] M. Foot, *Aneurin Bevan, Volume 1: 1897-1945* London, Four-Square Illustrated, 1966, pp. 227-8

[21] A. Bevan, *In Place of Fear*, London, Heinemann, 1952, pp.6-7

Part 2: From Old Labour to New Labour

Editorial Introduction to Extract 8

In the quarter century that followed these early extensions of the thesis under-pinning Miliband's *Parliamentary Socialism*, scholars influenced by the writings of Ralph Miliband and John Saville produced a string of articles and a series of monographs on different aspects of what is recognizable now as the movement from Old Labour to New. I published two such monographs: in 1980 *Labour in Power?*, a study of the Labour Government of 1974-79; and in 1989, *The Crisis of Labour*, an examination of industrial relations and the state in the post-war UK that traced the growing strains between the industrial and parliamentary wings of the old labour movement. Leo Panitch, writing with Colin Leys, would much later (1997) produce *The End of Parliamentary Socialism*, a study in which the move from Old Labour to New is linked to the rise and fall of the Bennite Left. And throughout that period, primarily within the pages of successive *Socialist Registers*, Miliband, Panitch, Leys and others documented and commented upon each stage of what became for them an increasingly depressing saga.

This set of essays on the move from Old Labour to New, begins with one by Leo Panitch, first published in the 1979 *Socialist Register*. 1979 was, of course, the beginning of 'the wilderness years' for the Labour Party; but that was not obvious then. In 1979 the debate on the British Left was still set against the backcloth of fifteen years in which the Labour Party had been in government for all but three. The debate was still all about Labour in power. Indeed the movement of policy within the Labour Party in the middle of those years – the three in which it was not in power – had rekindled the confidence of sections of the British Left in the potentiality of the Labour Party as a vehicle for socialism. The rise of a strong left-wing current in the trade unions, and the weakening of right-wing political forces towards the end of the first Wilson Government, had persuaded a number of leading left-wing intellectuals that Ralph Miliband was wrong to argue that 'the belief in the effective transformation of the Labour Party into an instrument of socialist policies' was 'the most crippling of illusions to which socialists in Britain have been prone'[1]. Ken Coates (*no relation of mine, but a source later of endless confusion in carelessly constructed footnotes!*), who would later become a leading leftwing Euro-MP, led the charge, arguing in an earlier *Register* that the Left must work within the Labour Party, given the paucity of meaningful alternatives, the important defensive work to be done there, and the genuine possibilities for change still evident in Labour Party politics[2].

By 1979 such a hopeful scenario for the Labour Left within the party had to be set against the experience of Labour in power between 1974 and 1979. Leo Panitch drew on that experience to reassert the counter-case. His 1979 article documented what *Labour in Power?* had termed 'not so much the power of the trade union leadership over this Labour Government, but rather their subordination and loyalty to that government and their willingness to play a role which inevitably brought them into conflict with the aspirations of at least a significant section of their own rank and file'.[3] Picking up themes from his earlier *Social Democracy and Industrial Militancy*, Panitch charted how the Labour Government had defused working-class militancy early in its period of office, and later laid the groundwork for what would become Thatcherism. He used that experience to challenge Ken Coates' faith in the socialist potential of left-wing unionism and parliamentary pressure within the Labour Party. He conceded that struggle within the party would go on – that 'to be sure, the battle is not over', that it was in 'the nature of the Labour Party that the battle lines will continue to be drawn up to and including the Day of Judgment'[4]. He just insisted that 'the problem with the Labour Party is not that it has sought to bring the working class to power by peaceful means. Rather the fact that it has not seen its task as bringing the working class to power has determined the kind of parliamentarianism which it practices'[5]. That parliamentarianism then blocked the political remobilization of the working class vital to socialist advance in Britain. In the 1979 *Socialist Register* article reproduced here, Panitch conceded the huge difficulties involved in that remobilization. He just refused to concede the ease of the alternative parliamentary route. 'Where', he asked, 'are the examples of a transformed social democratic party?'[6]

8. SOCIALISTS AND THE LABOUR PARTY: A REAPPRAISAL (1979)

Leo Panitch

In the 1973 Socialist Register, Ken Coates produced a timely and brilliant defence of socialists working within the Labour Party[7]. The argument was largely cast in terms of the absence of any alternative agency capable of maintaining a full scale political presence outside the Labour Party. But at the same time Ken Coates provided a positive case for working within the Party, stressing the critical role it plays in defensive struggles, the importance of parliamentary activity, and the possibilities for change in the Party contained in the radicalization of the unions in the late sixties and early seventies. The article was notably free of illusions on the radicalization of the parliamentary leadership of the Party, but it contended that the cardinal tenets of late fabianism have been refuted by events and therefore that the ideas of the leadership could no longer dominate the labour movement, 'since the integrating force of their dogma has rotted away'. The changing balance of forces in the movement would come to be reflected in its political councils: the Parliamentary Party would have to elect a new leader acceptable to the unions or face a 'shattering rift', indeed, 'a candidate with the insight and skill to present a platform of socialist change (was) very likely to win'. The idea that the status quo pragmatism of Wilsonism 'might be botched along for another parliamentary term [was] not completely absurd', but the consequences of this for Labour would be immense:

> Another Wilsonite government would split the labour movement into irreconcilable camps, the vastly larger of which would be in sharp opposition to it ... if this scenario is plausible, where must the socialists engage themselves? There can hardly be a moment's doubt. Another Labour Government offers socialists the chance to do well the work they botched up last time: to force the imposition of socialist policies, or to isolate and defeat those who oppose them. While external critics might aid in this process in its essentials it will either be an inside job or it won't get done.

The challenge Coates presented to socialists outside the Labour Party has not stood alone. Despite the actual emergence of another 'Wilsonite' government similar arguments directed to, or at least against, the extra-Labour left have continued to be advanced, most notably by Geoff Hodgson, Peter Jenkins and Frank Ward[8]. And most recently, Lewis Minkin's monumental study of *The Labour Party Conference*, while meticulously uncovering the organizational bases of leadership control over the Party, has also sought to challenge the orthodox view that intra-party democracy is ineffectual or inconsistent with parliamentary government, and to show that the unions' policy commitment to extensive public ownership never waned, but was only temporarily concealed by the Party leadership. On both counts he clearly identifies the Labour left of the 1970s with the forces 'which Party tradition nourishes' and contends, albeit more circumspectly than Ken Coates, that the alignment between the left and the unions on the floor of the Party Conference which emerged in the late 1960s was 'bound to have long-term consequences for the distribution of power in the Party as a whole'.[9]

Taken as a whole these writings may be seen as a regeneration in the 1970s of what Ralph Miliband has called 'the belief in the effective transformation of the Labour Party into an instrument of socialist policies (which) is the most crippling of illusions to which socialists in Britain have been prone'.[10] It is the purpose of this article to reassess the case for working within the Labour Party not only in the light of the record of the 1974-9 Labour Government, but of the behaviour of the trade unions and the Labour left since the late 1960s. As the labour movement moves into a period of opposition against a clearly reactionary Tory Government, as the actions of the Labour Party leadership against the working class recede from centre stage, as the appeal for defensive solidarity re-emerges with urgency and cogency, the pull to join the Labour Party will gain renewed strength. And with it the illusion that Labour can be transformed will cast its shadow over many dedicated socialists. As it does the argument that there is no viable alternative to the Labour Party is liable to take on the hue of a self-fulfilling prophesy.

1

It has always been its unique relationship with trade unions that has drawn socialists to the Labour Party. To a large extent this has simply reflected the perception that it is necessary to locate one's political work on that terrain where the working class is itself engaged. But more than this is involved. Precisely because the Labour Party is part of the labour movement, this means that the development of class struggle even if not initiated by the Party, is bound to affect it considerably from within. The great paradox of the Labour Party, and the source of the continued renewal of the belief that it can be changed, lies in this fact. The 'class harmony' ideology which has dominated the thinking of the leadership since the founding conventions rejected the concept of class struggle, is consistently challenged not merely by external events and by socialist currents in the Party, but by the direct expression of working-class struggle within the Party, above all on those occasions when the trade unions act as immediate agencies of working-class defence against the actions of Labour Governments.

The central factor underlying the belief in the 1970s that the Labour Party was ripe for socialist change may be located in the specific manifestation of this contradiction in the late 1960s. The action of the 1964-70 Labour Governments, not just in terms of disappointing the promise on which they had been elected, but in terms of directly challenging the basic material and organizational interests of the trade unions, would itself have strained considerably that 'bond of mutual confidence between the Parliamentary leaders and a preponderant part of the trade union leadership which is the essential key to the understanding of the functioning of the Party'[11] and the mechanism whereby the contradiction had been contained for most of the post-war years. But it was combined with developments within the union movement which strained the relationship further. The broadening and deepening of militancy at the base and the increasing decentralization of collective bargaining began to come to fruition in the mid 1960s and resulted in a greater radicalization of union conferences and delegations to TUC congresses and Labour Party conferences, and in the election of left-wing leaders in some major unions. After the enormous political loyalty and material sacrifice shown by the union movement from 1965 to 1967, and as a direct reaction against it, there ensued a period of sustained conflict within the Labour Party which was unparalleled in the Party's history. To Minkin these developments proved that '"the bond of mutual confidence" was a contingent and not an endemic feature of the pattern of power within the Party'.[12] Coates was more emphatic:

Wilson injected an unprecedented scepticism about Labour politicians into nearly all the unions, which serum took effect from top to bottom. At the same time, the reaction produced a notable democratization of the main unions, which process has adamantly resisted the Industrial Relations Act, and shows not the slightest sign of recession. No new leader of the Party can avoid coming to terms with this profound development, which already carries the problem of accommodation far beyond the scope of the kind of bureaucratic intrigue which was open to leaders of the Gaitskell era. Unlike Lawther and Williamson, whose capacity to uphold conservative policies rested on widespread mass lethargy, Jones and Scanlon can only lend their weight to policies which carry support in an active and self-assertive rank and file. Of course, they could always theoretically abandon the rank and file; but if they ever did, they would be of little value to the establishment without it. All this means, quite plainly, that the unions will not be easily diverted from the pursuit of serious social change.[13]

Indeed, in the 1970-74 'interregnum' the unions supported policies which, while not amounting to a socialist programme, certainly went as far in proposing to test the limits of reforms within capitalism as any in Labour Party history. Suffused in the spirit of the greatest period of class confrontation in Britain for fifty years and encouraged by the alliance between the TGWU and AUEW and the Labour left forged in the late 1960s, Party Conferences breathed the rhetorical fire of socialism with uncharacteristically little intake of the reformist smoke that is inevitably present on these occasions. The National Executive Committee's 1973 Programme, while going nowhere near as far as some successful conference resolutions of 1971 and 1972, nevertheless promised a major extension of public ownership and control, above all through the proposed National Enterprise Board's acquisition of 'some twenty-five of our largest manufacturers', and through a system of Planning Agreements with the top 100 companies, both backed up by extensive compulsory powers in a new Industry Act. When combined with the commitments established in the TUC-Labour Party Liaison Committee's 'Social Contract' on repealing the Industrial Relations Act, 'real moves' towards industrial democracy, extensive wealth and income redistribution, and statutory price controls, socialists in the Party could with justification claim to have made major gains. It was all summed up in Coates's challenge to sceptics: 'If the unions decide to support real socialist options, why should the socialists need to split away?'[14]

Yet if the events of 1968 to 1974 were indicative of the extent to which the Party is internally affected by major periods of class struggle, they by no means disposed of the question of whether the Labour Party can actually be transformed into a socialist party by struggles on its own terrain. On the contrary the intra-party conflicts of this period were subject to specific limitations which considerably undermined their potential for change. In the first place, the shift to the left in the unions was not nearly as pronounced as was sometimes imagined. As Minkin himself has shown ' ... in spite of the move to the left evident in the resolutions submitted and votes cast there was no major change in the leadership of the largest unions between 1970 and 1973. Those changes which did take place in fact reinforced the position of the right ... thus it was still the case in 1975 that most of the senior officials of the ten largest unions were to the right of the Party's political centre of gravity.'[15] Secondly, the extent of the rift between the left-wing union leadership and the Party leadership was often exaggerated. Both the left-wing union leaders and the Parliamentary left had a consistently great regard for Harold Wilson's 'tolerance' of minority opinion in the Party and a marked tendency to put real stock in the (re)conversions of their erstwhile Bevanite colleagues. This did not apply to the Jenkinsites both because they showed less tolerance and less readiness to employ socialist rhetoric to conceal their orthodoxy, and because they never fully appreciated as did Wilson (and Callaghan) that without the unions the Party would be 'uneasily poised between the Liberals and the Bow Group' without a mass base.[16] To be sure, the establishment of the Liaison Committee and the absorption of Michael Foot into the leadership specifically to act as what Tony Benn called 'the link and buckle with the industrial wing of the movement'[17], greatly facilitated the accommodation between Jones and Scanlon and the leadership. But apart from the stipulation that a Labour Government never again impose statutory penalties on collective bargaining, this accommodation was much more 'endemic' and much less 'conditional' than Coates or Minkin allowed.

Thirdly, the force of union solidarity and tradition, which had been a source of the cleavage regarding the issue of state intervention in collective bargaining, was at the same time a source of continuity and conservatism. in terms of maintaining the dominance of the Party leadership. Again as Minkin admirably has shown, even the left-wing unions continued to cast their votes for the Conference Arrangements Committee and the NEC largely on the basis of traditional arrangements and understandings, leaving right-wing sitting tenants in place. Although these committees were more responsive to delegate pressures in the early 1970s, it was significant that CLP resolutions which would have required MPs to abide by conference decisions were either kept off the Agenda or remitted to the Executive. Similarly left-wing union leaders refused to countenance the idea of instructing their union's sponsored MPs on how to vote. The Party leadership were still able to draw substantially on the union leadership's feeling, gained from experience in managing their own union conferences, that a 'good conference' was one that did not go too far towards divisiveness, and their sensitivity that unions should not be seen to be 'running' the Party. All this was reflective of the 'typically limited role' which Ralph Miliband identified the union leaders as playing in the Party, whereby they see themselves as 'representatives of organized labour, involved in a bargaining relationship, notably over industrial and economic issues, with their political colleagues in the Labour Party, and not in the lead as political rivals intending to capture control of the Party for purposes radically different from those of the men who now control it'.[18] This is not so much a matter, as Ken Coates seemed to think in challenging this view in his 1973 article, of union leaders failing to put themselves forward from time to time as political leaders or even acting as policy initiators; it is rather the unions' maintenance of traditional practices *vis-a-vis* the party leadership which inhibits them from throwing the full weight of their organizational strength in the Party behind the forces for change, even when their differences with the leadership on major policy issues is significant.

But far the most important factor prohibiting change in the Party, what in fact reproduces the unions' 'limited role', is the very commitment of the unions to maintaining the Labour Party as a 'viable' political force, both out of immediate defensive and electoral considerations and out of overwhelming loyalty to the Party as an institution. The very process that suggested to Coates that the Party 'might possibly recover from a whole succession of Wilsons' – the threat of a Conservative Government to the interests of the working class and the lack of any ready alternative to Labour's political machine – is the same process which all but guarantees that the Party will actually have to face a whole succession of Wilsons, however 'implausible' Coates finds this prospect. For to carry intra-party conflict to the point of forcing the imposition of socialist policies, or isolating and defeating those who oppose them, entails too great a risk to Party unity in terms of the primacy of immediate electoral and defensive campaigns. It is Party unity, not change, which is ultimately paramount from the union's perspective when intra-party conflict emerges. There may be some good defensive reason for this, but it is not the basis for the kind of transformation entailed in changing the Labour Party.

What Coates called the 'barely concealed civil war' between the Party and union leadership in 1968 and 1969 is particularly illustrative in this regard. The 'Solemn and Binding Agreement' between the TUC and the Government, which resolved the immediate controversy over *In Place of Strife*, may be seen from one perspective as a sterling victory by the labour movement over a Labour Government. But from another perspective, the long and abrasive negotiations between Wilson, Barbara Castle and the General Council was not only about avoiding the proposed legislation, but about avoiding an actual 'civil war' in the Party. The union leadership, no less than the Party leadership, were reaching for some political formula to heal the immediate scission and were for that reason anxious that 'extraneous' issues (such as those which were at the source of the division) should not be raised. What stood out about the victory over *In Place of Strife* was its purely defensive character: it involved neither a change in Party leadership, or ideology, indeed it did not even address the question of the Government's continuing commitment to a statutory incomes policy. Although it did not by any means re-establish a consensus between the unions and the Government, it certainly left the latter in a much stronger position vis-a-vis the Labour Party than it had been a year earlier. Whereas the leadership had been defeated in five major policy issues at the 1968 conference, the 1969 Conference left the TGWU and AEU in virtual isolation amongst the unions in opposing the leadership on incomes policy, and the delegates were treated to the sight of Hugh Scanlon moving fulsome support for the Government, without the reservations he had insisted on (and obtained) a year earlier.

It can, of course, be said of 1968 (as Coates said of 1973-and is being said of 1979) that the 'battle-lines are just beginning to form'. But in the 1970-73 period again the very factors that Coates identified as ensuring that 'the whole alliance did not fall apart – the common struggle against the Tory Government and the necessity of maintaining Labour as a viable political force to fight the next election – also ensured that the battle would not go so far as to risk Party unity. This was most critically evident with regard to Harold Wilson's successful opposition to the NEC's '25 companies' proposal. As Minkin has put it, the 'triumvirate' of Foot, Jones and Wilson 'acted as a reconciling force between the Party's factions and a restraint upon the leftism in the Programme. Thus in 1973, the advantages of this link went to the Party as both large union delegations responded to the call for moderation and pre-election unity. There was no concerted attempt to push the more radical interpretation of the role of the National Enterprise Board.[19] In these circumstances, Harold Wilson did not actually have to use his threatened 'veto' by the Shadow Cabinet against including this proposal in the Manifesto. But his view that 'it was inconceivable that the party would go into a general election on this proposal, nor could any incoming Labour Government be so committed',[20] was overwhelmingly confirmed by the 1973 Conference.

The result was that the Labour Party emerged out of its period of opposition with a most ambiguous programme. The NEC's Programme itself had already exhibited considerable ambiguity by noting that the proposed Planning Agreements System as 'developed from those already in operation in France, Belgium and Italy', thus inviting the question of whether this was in fact to be the center-piece of a socialist economic strategy or of a modernized state capitalism. Similar questions could have been raised about the resemblance between the NEB and Italian state holding companies. Precisely because it could have been argued, however, that the way that these new policies would be used by a Labour Government would depend on the balance of forces in the Party and the State, Wilson's pre-election victory on this question was so significant. For it indicated how easily openings for change in the Party are closed in the face of immediate pressures of Party unity. Insofar as the unions were concerned in 1973, the battle-lines for change were hardly being drawn. On the contrary, the hatchet was being buried.

2

The limitations which the requirements of defensive and electoral unity place upon changing the Labour Party entail consequences which by no means can simply be measured in terms of the ambiguity of Labour's Election Manifestos or even the failure of Labour Governments to implement those reforms which the Manifestos do explicitly promise. For the problem with the Labour Party is not simply that in the absence of a better alternative, the working class has to make do with a reformist rather than a revolutionary party. It is that the Party itself plays an active role as an agency of social control over the working class. Ken Coates was indeed right to explain the importance of Parliamentary politics and the stability of the Labour Party on the grounds that no alternative socialist grouping can become an alternative vehicle 'for the development of the outlook of a whole social class until they can be seen to have the potential to enable that class to speak for itself at every political level on which its interests are, the object of contention. Even the corporate interests of the subordinate class cannot be safeguarded without organization on this scale.' But when he immediately went on to maintain that 'it is manifestly silly to speak about "hegemonic aspirations" developing within such a class unless it has safely passed the point at which its self-defence is relatively assured'[21], it was he who was being unrealistic. This is not only because self-defence entails a constant struggle and is never 'assured'; but more importantly because continued subordination may be inscribed within the very process of self-defence. In the case of the Labour Party, self-defence takes place at the expense of the hegemonic development of the working class.

This is not just a matter of Labour Governments introducing reforms which are specifically structured to integrate the working class in the existing social order, reforms which constitute real gains for the class – but are designed to close rather than open room for further struggle.[22] Nor is it just a matter of leaving a Party leadership in place which proclaims and maintains those 'national' values which prescribe subordination of the working class and which treat the whole class as a mere sectional group in the society. (In periods of mass quiescence this may not entail misrepresentation; but it certainly will greatly reinforce the quiescence.) It is also a matter of Labour Governments employing the loyalty and solidarity inherent in the movement actually to demobilize the working class at critical junctures in its development and to secure real material sacrifices from the working class at those very moments when economic militancy threatens profitability. The very self-confidence and self-awareness of an active working class, which is the force behind the election of Labour Governments, becomes the very object of the attempt to subdue and extirpate this energy. Although these attempts are only partially and temporarily successful, they nevertheless mean that it is never quite a matter of just picking up where one left off when class conflict re-emerges again.

The 1974-9 Labour Government has to be seen precisely in this light. It was composed of a Party leadership which in Coates's words, 'inspires no sacrifice, blazes no trails, bodes no fundamental changes, and meets no spiritual needs'. But this is too negative a view. It was a leadership which continued to see itself playing, and did play, an active and indispensable role in the British political system – above all the role of tempering, containing and channelling into 'responsible' outlets the industrial militancy of its time. The Labour leadership's part in the defensive campaign against the Industrial Relations Bill was not merely that of fighting the battle in Parliament, but of urging the unions not to take the very industrial-cum-political action which in the end scuppered the Act. A prime basis of Wilson's opposition to the Act was that it fostered revolutionary tendencies in the working class, that it was a 'militants' charter', that it treated industrial relations as part of 'a wider political conflict'. Throughout its years in opposition the Labour leadership remained committed, moreover, to one fixed ideal – resurrecting union agreement to wage restraint. Wilson and Callaghan did come to appreciate that a statutory incomes policy was unacceptable to the unions; indeed, this was the one genuine 'conversion' they experienced while in opposition, the one real lesson they learned from Michael Foot and Jack Jones. But this did not dampen their enthusiasm for wage restraint. On the contrary, they continued to hold to the view, first elaborated in the early 1960s, that the Labour Party's ability to promise this was its major electoral asset. Although they could not obtain from the unions the kind of fulsome commitment to incomes policy than they had engineered in 1963, they continued to press for it via the Liaison Committee and in the drawing up of the Manifesto, right through the industrial crisis of December 1973 and January 1974. The Labour left were able to convince themselves, as they had done from 1959 to 1964, that what was involved was a 'socialist incomes policy', in which wage restraint was not the object of the exercise but an inevitable part of socialist planning. The Labour leadership, however, clearly accepted the more radical elements of the Social Contract only to the extent that unions insisted that, as the February Election Manifesto put it, 'only deeds can persuade ... that an incomes policy is not some kind of trick to force [the worker] ... to bear the brunt of the national burden'. If it turned out that such persuasion was possible without too many such deeds, so much the better.

And what happened? Within a year of the February 1974 election, incomes policy became the center-piece of the Social Contract, and the unions responded with an exercise in voluntary wage restraint unparalleled in modern British history. Increases in gross money earnings for the average worker fell from 25.5 per cent in 1974-5 to 12.4 per cent in 1975-6 to 8.8 per cent in 1976-7. As the rate of inflation fell more slowly (from 25 per cent to 14 per cent over the three years) real wages fell considerably. Even taking into account the compensatory tax concessions offered by the Government, real wages fell by 5.5 per cent, 1.6

per cent and almost 1 per cent in the three respective years. The real weekly net income of the average male worker, married with two children, if calculated in terms of October 1978 prices, had stood at £68.90 in September 1970, risen to £74.50 in September 1972, and maintained that level until September 1974; it fell by September 1977 to £68.10-i.e., by over £6 per week. In 1977-8, with a less restrictive pay norm, a rate of inflation of 8 per cent, additional tax concessions, and the first instances of breakdown of union co-operation, real net earnings recovered substantially (increasing by 9 per cent). But this still left the average worker with a real weekly take home pay in September 1978 which was £3.50 less than in 1974 and almost £1 a week less in terms of real net weekly income (i.e., taking account of increased transfer payments of 1977-8).[23]

It would of course be absurd to attribute these losses to the Labour Government's wage restraint policies alone in abstraction from the economic crisis. But the sacrifice entailed in wage restraint would have been one thing had it been inspired on the basis of Tony Benn's promise to the 1973 Conference (broadly incorporated into the 1974 Manifesto) that 'the crisis we inherit when we come to power will be the occasion for fundamental change and not the excuse for postponing it'.[24] Instead the crisis became the basis for maintaining the existing balance of wealth and power in British society by increasing the exploitation of the working class. Wage restraint was secured and maintained: while the statutory price controls and food subsidies introduced in 1974 were weakened and phased out; in the context of massively deflationary budgets and an increase in the unemployed, once school leavers were included, by almost one million; and while public expenditure programmes were cut and subjected to cash limits so that instead of the promised 13 per cent growth there was no growth at all in real terms from 1974 to 1978. As Stuart Holland put it in commenting on the Thatcher Government's Budget of 1979: 'Certainly, the edge of Mrs Thatcher's axe was first ground and then fell under successive Healey Budgets.'[25]

As for the Industrial Strategy, the true basis of the case for a 'socialist incomes policy', the wage restraint programme was launched after Tony Benn had been dismissed from the Department of Industry, an act which Jack Jones, speaking for the TUC as a whole, warned at the time would constitute 'a grave affront to the trade union movement'." The Industry Bill was shorn of its compulsory dimensions, and the singular Planning Agreement entered into with a private company occurred in the context of the Government sanctifying in this way the bail-out of Chrysler. As for the NEB, it was largely absorbed into the role of traditional state fire-fighting on closures and in any case operated, as its intellectual progenitor put it with great dismay, 'purely on commercial rather than public, or social criteria'.[26] In these circumstances, the locus of the Industrial Strategy shifted back to the NEDC and the tripartite sectoral working parties established under its auspices in 1975. It was all summed up in 1977 by Jack Jones: 'Somehow, somewhere, the Government's objectives seem to have been hijacked off

course, and I mean "hijacked"... an industrial strategy which relies only on delib-
eration of sectoral working parties, on polite talks with industrialists and trade
associations ... is not a strategy at all, but an excuse for one. '[27]

Why then did the unions display such loyalty? One explanation, which is fairly
common on the Labour left, was expressed in Ian Mikardo's early admission
to the 1975 Conference: 'We were all conned'[28] – with the implication that the
unions were simply conned for a longer period. This is an attractive explanation
for the Labour left for it carries within it the premise that you can't fool all the
people all the time and that at some point the party will rise up against the char-
latans. But this will not do as an explanation of the unions' loyalty. Jack Jones's
own account of the Government's behaviour, that they were 'hijacked', already
indicates a very different perspective: the Government were themselves unsus-
pecting 'victims' of the 'hijack'. This was indeed the dominant view among the
union leadership and was reflective of the strength of the 'bond of confidence'
established in the pre-1974 period.

This bond was in fact strengthened by the precarious parliamentary position of
the Government and the constant spectre of another Tory Government (which
would have of course acted as even less of a buffer against the worst effects of
the crisis than Labour was doing). And no less important was the fact that this
Government, far more than had been the case in 1964-70, showed a sanguine
understanding of the unions' own priorities – that when push came to shove,
the unions would insist on those policies in the Social Contract 'that pertained
directly to industrial relations, and would exert less pressure when it came to the
economic strategy. This order of priorities stemmed not only from narrow organizational interests, but also from the unions' own fears and frustration with
the effects of economic militancy and high inflation on real wages and employment. It also stemmed from the union leadership's own lack of confidence in
the alternative economic strategy they and the Labour left advanced in the face
of the harsh 'economic realities' put forward by the Government, the Treasury
and foreign 'experts' from the IMF. The fact that Michael Foot allowed the TUC
to write its own ticket on industrial relations legislation served, in terms of the
unions' own priorities, to cement the ties between the unions and the Government at the same time as reactionary economic policies were pursued. Moreover, the Government proved amenable to introducing wage restraint in the form
advanced by Jack Jones, i.e., the £6 across-the-board norm so that the low paid
would suffer less. And the very fact that the Government was seen to be resisting
strong Treasury pressures to institute a statutory policy,[29] confirmed the unions'
resolve to meet their 'obligations' to the Government.

The *defensive* priorities of the union movement in the context of the crisis
were secured, in other words, at the expense of insisting on alternative, let alone
socialist, economic policies. The question remains, however, of whether the
defensive gains were so great as to be worth the sacrifice. The egalitarian thrust

of the £6 norm, such as it was, certainly struck a responsive chord in the labour movement, at least temporarily. But this cannot obscure the fact that it mainly concerned redistribution within the working class (involving Labourism's new twist on socialism – what I have called before its 'socialism in one class'[30]) in a context of a policy which reduced the proportion of the national income going to the class as a whole. Much more of a case can be made for the industrial relations legislation of 1974 to 1976. Yet it is certainly questionable how much the unions have benefited from this in concrete terms. The Tory Industrial Relations Act had before its repeal been rendered more or less impotent by the unions. The role that ACAS has been able to play in extending union recognition under the legislation has been very limited, particularly when conciliation has failed. As a number of long and futile recognition strikes have shown, moreover, employer intransigence and an anti-union judiciary are able to render the new procedures useless. In other areas – disclosure of information, job security, equal pay for women – the laws are not only deficient in certain respects, but are only effective when unions are already strong enough to advance their members' interests beyond minimum legal guarantees. Above all, there is a real danger, that litigation of issues (e.g., unfair dismissal) undermines shop floor struggle and saps the time and energy of officials who become embroiled in the legalistic procedures. In two internal TUC reassessments of the legislation at the end of 1978, all this was being admitted, although little was said publicly lest it be used by the Conservatives to remove the advantages the laws do give. But this should not conceal what the TUC's own counsel, Lord Wedderburn, has called the unions' own

> ... self-doubt as to the degree to which the trade union movement should in future come to rely upon machinery provided by the State to achieve that which in the past it has collectively won largely without the help of – often despite – the State's laws. Already the movement has been disillusioned by the operation of some of 'its' laws and has realised afresh the limitations that inevitably fall upon trade unions who trust in the regulation of industrial relations by the law. Even the floor of individual laws is often found to be ineffective without industrial strength to support them, especially in the case of equal pay for women. What the law gives the law can take away.[31]

The point to be drawn from this, however, is that the Labour leadership can hardly be accused of 'conning' the unions on this question – they were fulfilling 'their side' of the Social Contract. Indeed what Ken Coates did not foresee in predicting the scission that another Wilsonite Government would produce in the movement was that this was another Wilsonite Government with one major difference from the last ones – it was bent on ensuring that it was not the Labour leadership that would become isolated from the union leadership, but the Labour left. (As indeed occurred over public expenditure cuts and wage restraints in 1976.) To this end, the Government even maintained the form of the rest of the Social Contract while violating its spirit in most respects. Unlike the 1964-70 Government's abandonment of the Economic Plan, this Government never rejected the Industrial Strategy. All its constitutive elements – the Industry Act, statutory prices controls, the NEB, even the concept of Planning Governments – were retained. Even the public expenditure cuts were defended, both by Labour and union leaders,[32] in terms of the industrial strategy, as freeing resources for investment in manufacturing industry. Even while union leaders recognized that the brunt of policy was in the opposite direction from what they had intended, the fact that the formal structures were in place (as was also the case with the Royal Commission on Income and Wealth and the Bullock Inquiry on Industrial Democracy) allowed them to expect that a new spirit might be injected into them once the immediate crisis passed. Above all the Government did maintain close consultation with the union leadership. The accommodation between them, which Ken Coates believed could be secured only on the basis of socialist policies, was in fact reached on the basis of corporatist ones. Only occasionally did a union leader admit the reality of the situation to the movement, as did Alan Fisher at the time of the TUC's twenty-to-one endorsement of wage restraint in 1976:

> ... we in the movement should understand the nature of bargaining at the national level between the TUC and the Government ... it is possible that we will become mesmerized by the process itself rather than considering the results that it achieves ... capital will not hold back from using its power to influence these negotiations. One example we have is by pushing down the value of pound. In that context, it is dangerous for the movement to accept incorporation in the apparatus of the State, articulated through what may be a loyalty to a Labour Government and the test for the trade union movement is to develop effective bargaining power at this level, if necessary through new procedures and new institutions, and not to regard the State as in some mysterious way a neutral body. It never has been and it never will be.[33]

The big question, of course, remains why the rank and file went along with the leadership. Coates's confidence rested after all on the 'active and self-assertive rank and file' without whose continuing support Jones's and Scanlon's 'theoretically possible' about-face would be of little worth to the establishment. It was in fact worth a great deal. As Steve Jefferys has pointed out ' ... "left" union leaders either led or were prominently placed in four of the five most strikeprone industries. Despite the fact that the five only employed 6 per cent of the total labour force, they accounted for 47 per cent of the working days lost in 1969-74; by 1975-6 this figure had declined to 22 per cent, in a period of falling strike statistics.'[34] The level of resistance to Phases I and II of the Social Contract was simply minimal. Both the deep reserves of loyalty to a Labour Government among activists and the same fears and frustrations that beset the union leadership must surely have been factors in this. Just as there was a mistaken tendency among some of the Trotskyist left in the early 1970s to assume that the shop stewards of today are the revolutionary vanguard of tomorrow, so it must be said that many on the Labour Left vastly overestimated the staying power of economic militancy and the political effects which an 'active and self-assertive rank and file' would have as a force for change within the Labour Party. In order to forestall criticisms of being wise after the fact, it might be permissible in this instance to quote something I wrote in 1974:

> It is true that industrial militancy does have a clear political character. The dissatisfaction with existing social relations is inherent in wage claims of 25, 30 or 40 per cent; in the expectation by dockers or car workers or miners that they be paid as much or more than groups high above them in the status hierarchy; in occupations of factories shut down in accordance with the law of profit; in the large number of strikes challenging managerial prerogatives. But this militancy retains a nonpolitical veneer by virtue of the fact that it arises from separate segments of the working class at different times, and arises moreover in the absence of a generalized and explicit rejection of the economic and political structures in which these social relations are embedded. This is indeed an inherent limitation of trade unionism; demands for a 40 per cent increase in the income of the working class as a whole, and for workers' control over production, cannot be effectively expressed industrially but only politically, and although we have seen in recent years a number of overt and official political strikes for the first time since the TUC left Trafalgar Square for Whitehall in the aftermath of the General Strike, these actions have been hesitant, sporadic and defensive. Without a political party which would maintain and give focus to industrial militancy, it is not unlikely to be dissipated in yet another phase of quasi-corporatist policies, or, if not, to be met by a more fully authoritarian challenge than the British labour movement has yet faced.[35]

That this militancy was indeed dissipated from 1975 to 1977 has a great deal to do with the inability of the Labour left, no less than the various socialist groupings outside of it, to capture the political imagination of rank and file activists. The fact that the Labour vote continued to drop in 1974 despite Labour's more radical programme was proof of this, and suggested that the 'unprecedented skepticism about Labour politicians' which Coates identified, was by no means highly discriminating between right and left and not necessarily an entirely positive force for social change. Steve Jeffery's admission, from an IS/SWP perspective, that 'in the face of the crisis there appeared to be no "practical" alternative' as far as most workers were concerned, and that 'when the general conviction was that there was little you could do, you just had to put up with the Government's pay policy; then this is what the shop stewards generally felt as well,'[36] is a damning testament to the ineffectiveness of the IS/SWP in the previous period. It is even a more damning testament to the failure of the Labour left, whose alternative might be thought more 'practical', to touch the roots of the movement for all its visibility at the national level in the 1970s.

Of course the forces that originally produced this militancy were not themselves dissipated during this period, and, as had been the case with the wage restraint policies of both the 1945 and 1966 Labour Governments, the breakdown of restraints occurred not after Labour was defeated at the polls, but before. This indicated once again that while Labour remains able to foreclose class struggle for a certain period, it is unable to quash for too long the class antagonisms of British society. Callaghan's cynical manipulation of the 1978 Congress, encouraging it to pronounce its opposition to the 5 per cent guidelines only in faint whispers by giving it the impression that a general election was imminent, may have looked like a brilliant political manoeuvre at the time, but it proved to be a major blunder. For the union leadership by this stage could simply not hold back the rising tide of economic militancy that had begun to surface spontaneously as early as a year before. (Indeed to some extent they may have encouraged it, despite their effective cooperation in wage restraint until 1978, by their verbal recommitment to full collective bargaining and by their more open criticisms of the Government's policies from 1977 onwards.) As a result the class collaboration dogma of social democracy faltered again on its own terms: Labour's claim that it was the governing party of 'consensus' while the Tories were the party of 'confrontation' lost a good deal of its electoral credibility.

The resurgence of economic militancy in the winter of 1978-9 certainly reflects the resilience of the working class and its continuing ability to impose severe barriers to the strategic options of capital and the state. But in terms of the question of changing the Labour Party, there is little comfort to be drawn from it. It most certainly does not conform to Coates's scenario of an irreconcilable split between the vast proportion of the labour movement and the Labour leadership. There has been renewed friction, but what is remarkable is how the conflicts within the movement were politically contained in the last years of the Government. Both the NEC and the Party Conference were certainly much less the mouthpieces of the leadership throughout this Government, but their ability to control or even influence its actions showed no marked increase. On the contrary, the existence of the Liaison Committee has allowed the leadership to by-pass conference resolutions without openly flouting them by promising to work out policy disagreements at a higher level. The Liaison Committee's policy statements have invariably turned out to be much less radical than those of the NEC or than conference resolutions. And even when conflict with unions broke into the open, as they did on the first day of the 1978 Conference, when the unions defeated the leadership on both the 5 per cent guidelines and economic policy as a whole, the unions refused to widen the conflict. On the very next day, enough union votes were available – including the TGWU's – to defeat the constitutional amendment for an electoral college, encompassing both the extra-Parliamentary and Parliamentary Party, to elect the leader. The fact that this was combined with the defeat, on the basis of Hugh Scanlon miscasting the AUEW vote, of mandatory reselection of MPs, made Coates's burial of 'bureaucratic intrigue' in the Party look very premature indeed.

Nor did matters change as the industrial conflict of the winter gained momentum. In order to protect the Government, as far as they could, from the electoral consequences of the media rampage against its 'weakness' in the face of anarchy, the General Council was drawn into producing, with indecent haste, a new Solemn and Binding Agreement, the so-called 'Concordat', in which they agreed to undertake voluntary control on picketing, the closed shop, inter-union disputes and (eventually) wage demands. Even seen as a symbolic electoral exercise pure and simple, it was nevertheless significant how purely defensive a document it was. It was accompanied moreover by a policy statement by 'moderate' union leaders which endorsed the economic policies of the leadership. With no little justification, and in the midst of the winter's industrial strife, Shirley Williams could observe that the unions were 'moving clearly back to the centre' and scorn earlier suggestions that the social democrats in the Party were politically 'dead'.[37] Not surprisingly, the hopes of the Labour left in the fall of 1978 that the postponement of the election would give them the chance to avoid the Election Manifesto 'watering down' the NEC's 1976 Programme, were entirely frustrated.

3

To be sure, the battle is not over. It is in the nature of the Labour Party that the battle-lines will continue to be drawn up to and including the Day of Judgment. But given the experience of the last dozen years, what foundation remains for the argument that the Party can be changed? The NEC has once again put the issues of the election of the leader and mandatory reselection on the Agenda of the 1979 Party Conference, and despite considerable noise from 'moderate' union leaders against friction in the Party, it is by no means certain that these proposals will be defeated. But even if these proposals were carried, would they constitute an effective basis for changing the Party? It was certainly clear from Callaghan's election that a leader who is 'acceptable to the unions' is not necessarily one who is committed to socialist policies. And if a Michael Foot or even a Tony Benn were elected, and setting aside all doubts as to their socialist 'credentials', how fundamentally different a tack could they take, given the fine array of upstanding gentlemen that numerically dominate the PLP?

The mandatory selection procedure is presumably designed to obviate this problem. But the Parliamentary left is itself divided on this issue; the unions are concerned about its effects on sponsorship; and it is unlikely that those constituency parties that are presently moribund will suddenly spring to life just to turn out a sitting MP. As a theory of an inevitable fall from grace of socialist parties, the 'iron law of oligarchy' may have little to recommend it. But as an account of how MPs will be able to use considerable organizational and psychological resources to maintain their position *vis-a-vis* their constituency parties, mandatory reselection or no, it is discounted only by the naive.

But what about 'forcing the imposition of socialist policies'? This, as Coates made clear, will depend on the unions. Minkin's identification of a steady undercurrent of union support for public ownership, despite the revisionist machinations of the Party leadership, says nothing about the efforts they will make to force its imposition on the Labour leadership. If anything the 1970s provide rather strong evidence that too much stock should not be put in union conference resolutions on public ownership.

This may be especially seen with regard to the unions' reaction to the NEC's 1976 statement on 'Banking and Finance', which proposed taking over the biggest four clearing banks, a merchant bank, and the top seven insurance companies. Like all NEC proposals of this kind, it was primarily defended as a means of facilitating investment in manufacturing industry and specifically drew its inspiration from the publicly owned financial institutions of Britain's capitalist competitor countries (in this case, France, Japan and Italy). Nevertheless for the Labour Party it was a very radical proposal indeed. Although it drew screams of anguish from the City and strong public opposition from Callaghan and other Labour Ministers, it did not come out of the blue (having stemmed from a Conference resolution passed in 1971 and revived in 1975). Nor was it without apparent support from the unions directly involved – at least those affiliated to the Labour Party. USDAW's annual conference, which Minkin describes as 'that weathercock of the British trade union movement', passed resolutions in 1973 and 1974 proposing to 'eliminate the capitalist system' and specifically endorsing the takeover of the banks, the Stock Exchange and the insurance companies." But while the 1976 Party Conference endorsed the statement by an overwhelming majority of 3,314,000 to 526,000, it turned out the unions weren't too keen on the idea. The total votes cast already indicated a substantial number of abstentions; the TGWU had reservations about 'timing'; and the unions in the field of banking and insurance demanded 'further consultation'. When nine relevant TUC unions were consulted by an NEC working party, they were found to be 'to varying degrees, hostile to the proposals on nationalization'. Fears of redundancy and loss of overseas earnings were apparently involved, but most interesting was the fact that both USDAW and ASTMS, while agreeing that 'some reform was necessary … questioned the conclusion that ownership was the best means of exercising control'.[38] Despite the conference decision, it was clear that the issue was now a dead letter. The 1978 Liaison Committee Statement, 'Into the Eighties', and the 1979 Election Manifesto made this abundantly clear. It will be less easily resurrected than mandatory reselection.

This critical episode suggests that a concerted push by the unions *against* the

Party leadership on socialist policies is less of a possibility than the Labour left would like to think. There remains, however, one other prospect suggested by Coates (although he was none too keen on the idea): that if the Party could not be won over, it might be divided with the left retaining a considerable hold over 'the apparatus ... necessary to meet the demands of full participation in political life'.[39] Yet the likelihood of such a division being initiated by either of the major groupings on the right or the left must be counted as remote in the extreme. The leadership as a whole understands only too well the importance of retaining their hold over this apparatus; a Prentice or a Taverne may go from time to time, but attrition at this rate is not going to matter much. A resurrection of 1931 is perhaps more likely, but this would leave the Party composed of much the same forces as before. One would still have to ask whether, apart from a temporary hiccup, the Party could be changed against 'those who helped to sustain Mac-Donald's supremacy and Snowden's economics to the eleventh hour of the last day',[40] but who had the sagacity to stay.

As for the Labour left, it must surely be recognized that whatever else it is about, it is not about dividing the Labour Party. Precisely because it identifies itself with Party Tradition, the thought of dividing the Party is particularly abhorrent to it. (It must be said that to the extent it makes this identification unambiguously. it is either hypocritical or mistaken. In terms of the class harmony ideology, the policies effectively pursued, and the absence of mass socialist education via the Party at the base, the task of changing the Labour Party surely involves wrenching it out of its tradition.) The left has always taken the burden of Party unity on its shoulders and has been far more ready than the right to compromise its principles to this end.

What then *is* the alternative for Socialists? In a number of respects, Coates cannot be faulted. The issue is not about 'parliamentananism versus insurrectionism'. The question of whether Parliament can be the effective vehicle for implementing a socialist programme will indeed 'only be answered when it has been tried' (which it never has in Britain or any other major capitalist country), and tried, moreover, on the basis of the crystallization of the kind of socialist consciousness 'in the whole active part of the subordinate class' which Coates envisages[41]. The point about the Labour Party is that it has always been dominated by a leadership which, with the support of most of the movement, has not only been unable or unwilling to develop a coherent socialist programme, but has not seen its task as one of instilling such a consciousness. It has lived off the existing consciousness of the working class, it has even represented it, but rather than attempting the difficult task of securing working-class support by undermining those values of national unity and moderation which encapsulate class subordination, it has chosen the easier route of engaging working-class allegiance by associating itself with those values. The problem with the Labour Party is not that it has sought to bring the working class to power by peaceful means. Rather the fact that it has not seen its task as bringing the working class to power has determined the kind of parliamentarianism which it practices.

Coates was also right in his assessment that existing revolutionary groups will not stand serious scrutiny as viable alternatives to the Labour Party, not least because of their doctrinaire refusal to allow any 'equivocation' on a parliamentary strategy.[42] And however one might applaud certain changes in the Communist Party, the vast historical weight under which it staggers, no less than the transparency of its illusion that the Labour Party might be remotely interested in an alliance with it, suggests that it will continue to fail to make much progress as a viable alternative.

To sum up: the Labour Party will not conveniently fall apart; a good measure of parliamentary success is indeed essential; the present alternatives hold out little hope. It is scarcely surprising that many socialists cling to the illusion that the Labour Party can be changed although one might expect from them greater candour about the costs involved – i.e., that by continuing to work within the Labour Party, they necessarily do their bit to sustain Labourism's strangling hegemony over the politically active working class. But given the Sisyphus-like task they appear to be engaged in, it is by no means inappropriate to ask whether it is not indeed worth the candle for socialists in Britain to come together to 'try again' in the 1980s: to make a start at building a mass socialist party. Certainly such a party would have to detach many activists, and perhaps eventually some major unions, from the Labour Party. But it need not inherit by this token the same structure or all the burdens that come with the Labour Party tradition. With different leaders, a different ethos and with a positive attitude to Marxism, these elements would necessarily combine in a different way. Even if a federated structure were adopted, it need not carry with it the same separation between parliamentary and extra-parliamentary activity, and the same division of labour between industrial and political leadership. One important reason for making the attempt is that even a remotely viable alternative would act as pole of attraction for those socialist elements within the Labour Party to break out of the vicious circle of both trying to change the party and maintain its defensive unity, and put their energy, their talents, and the respect and legitimacy they enjoy in the eyes of many trade unionists to more positive use.

The fact that what is entailed in creating a mass socialist party today is not a political mobilization of the working class, but its remobilization, is indeed what makes such an attempt seem so Herculean. That there is little historical evidence for such a successful re-mobilization is true. But where are the examples of a transformed social democratic party? With no less justification, indeed with rather more in light of the experience of the past six years, one might indeed launch such an attempt at remobilization by quoting Coates's own concluding call to arms: 'The work will be arduous and intricate, daunting indeed. It will need all the socialist forces we can muster, and, indeed, it needs them now.'[43]

Notes

[1] R. Miliband, 'Moving On', *The Socialist Register 1976*, London, Merlin Press, p.128

[2] K. Coates, 'Socialists and the Labour Party', in R. Miliband and J. Saville (eds), *The Socialist Register 1973*, pp. **XX**

[3] D. Coates, *Labour in Power?*, London, Longman, 1980, p. 205

[4] L. Panitch, 'Socialists and the Labour Party: a Reappraisal', in R. Miliband and J. Saville (eds), *The Socialist Register 1979*, London, Merlin Press, 1979, p. 69

[5] Ibid, p.71

[6] Ibid, pp. 72-3

[7] Ken Coates, 'Socialists and the Labour Party', *The Socialist Register 1973*, p. 174.

[8] Geoff Hodgson, *Socialism and Parliamentary Democracy*, Spokesman, 1977: Peter Jenkins, 'The Labour Party and the Politics of Transition', *The Socialist Register 1977*; Frank Ward, *In Defence of Democratic Socialism*, Rye Express, 1978.

[9] Lewis Minkin, *The Labour Party Conference*, Allen Lane, 1978, p. 322.

[10] Ralph Miliband, 'Moving On' *The Socialist Register 1976*, p. 128.

[11] Robert McKenzie, *British Political Parties*, London, 1963, p. 505.

[12] Minkin, op. cit., p. 321

[13] Coates, op. cit., pp. 176-7.

[14] Coates, op. cit., p. 176.

[15] Minkin, op. cit., p. 344.

[16] Harold Wilson, quoted in *The Financial Times*, 16 and 31 May 1968.

[17] Tony Benn,. *A New Course for Labour*, IWC, 1976, p. 10.

[18] Ralph Miliband, *Parliamentary Socialism*, Merlin, 1972, p. 375.

[19] Minkin, op. cit., p. 344.

[20] Quoted in Michael Hatfield, *The House the Left Built*, Victor Gollancz, 1978, p. 199.

[21] Coates, op. cit., p. 156

[22] When Hodgson (op. cit., pp. 60-61, 129) and Jenkins (op. cit., pp. 21-2) use the examples of the New Deal to argue that legislative reforms are possible even in a period of capitalist crisis and can have a 'galvanizing effect on large numbers of workers', they ignore the longer-term role that industrial relations legislation has played in the United States in containing, juridifying and deadening autonomous working-class struggle. The 'right to belong to a union' sanctioned by the state against the wishes of the employers in the 1930s was by no means an entirely unmixed blessing given the package it became enveloped in.

[23] The quarterly figures for real weekly income from 1970-78 at October 1978 prices, are presented in tabular form in Written Answers by Robert Sheldon in H.C Debates, Vol 960, 15 December 1978, and 19 January 1979, cc. 519-20 and cc. 969-70.

[24] Labour Party Annual Conference Report (LPACR) 1973, p. 187.

[25] 'Budget That Sells Seed Grain For a Decade', *The Guardian*, 18 June 1979.

[26] Stuart Holland, 'Planning Agreements: A Case Study of Industrial Suicide', *Tribune*, 19 September, 1978, p. 3.

[27] . TUC, The Trade Union Role in Industrial Policy, report of a conference of Affiliated unions, October 31, 1977, p. 33.

[28] LPACR, 1975, p. 323.

[29] See Joe Haines, *The Politics of Power*, Jonathan Cape, 1977, ch. 3.

[30] See my *Social Democracy and Industrial Militancy*, Cambridge University Press, 1976, p. 124.

[31] Lord Wedderburn 'The New Structure of Labour Law in Britain,' *Israel Law Review*, Vol. 13, No. 4, October 1978, p. 457.

[32] See Scanlon's speech in LPACR 1973, p. 457.

[33] TUC, The Social Contract 1976-77, Report of the Special Congress, 19 June 1976, p. 39.

[34] . Steve Jeffreys, 'Striking into the Eighties,' *International Socialism*, Series 2, No. 5, Summer 1979, p. 33.

[35] *Social Democracy and Industrial Militancy,* op. cit., p. 253.

[36] Jeffreys, op. cit., pp. 33,35.

[37] *The Financial Times,* 21 February 1979

[38] LPACR 1978, Appendix II, pp. 450, 453

[39] Coates, op. cit., p. 171.

[40] Michael Foot, *Aneurin Bevan,* Vol. I, Paladin, 1975, p. 136.

[41] Coates, op. cit., p. 158.

[42] .See Duncan Hallas's reproach to Ralph Miliband in 'How can We Move On?', *The Socialist Register 1977,* p. 10.

[43] Coates, op. cit., p. 177

Editorial Introduction to Extract 9

To the question that Leo Panitch posed at the end of his 1979 essay – where are the examples of a transformed social democratic party?' – the Labour Party itself offered one kind of answer in the four years that followed. For between 1979 and 1983 – under the impact of the Bennite Left – the Labour Party came as close as it ever did to fundamentally resetting itself as a socialist political formation. Ralph Miliband, among others, was sufficiently sensitive to the importance of the Bennite struggle as to mellow his hitherto adamant assertion that the Labour Party was not for turning. As late as 1976, in his 'Moving On' essay in that year's *Register*, his position had still been that 'the belief in the effective transformation of the Labour Party into an instrument of socialist politics is the most crippling of illusions to which socialists in Britain have been prone'.[1] It might be otherwise, he put it, 'if there was any likelihood that the Labour Party could be turned into a socialist formation; but that is precisely the premise which must, on a realistic view, be precluded'.[2]

But by 1983, as will be seen in the next essay, the tone (and indeed the argument) that Miliband developed was more nuanced than that. By then he was prepared to lay out two scenarios – in one of which at least the Left do capture and transform the Party. In the light of that possibility, Miliband wrote this.

> I must enter a personal note at this point. I have for more than ten years written that this hope of the left to transform the Labour Party ... was illusory and that, far from representing a short cut to the creation of a mass socialist party in Britain (which has never existed), it was a dead end in which British socialists have been trapped for many decades – in fact, since the Labour Party came into being. It was this view which led me to advocate the formation of a new socialist party able to do all the work of socialist advocacy and agitation that the Labour Party had been prevented by its leaders from doing. I am far from convinced that I was mistaken. For it is by no means evident that the new activists can realize the 'scenario' I have just outlined: on the most optimistic scenario, they have a long way to go, with many large obstacles on the way. But it is obvious that I underestimated how great was the challenge that the new activists would be able to pose to their leaders; and how limited would be the capacity of those leaders to surmount the challenge. I now take it that the question whether the activists can push matters further is more open than I had believed.[3]

But sadly if didn't stay open for very long; and the first, rather than the second, of the two scenarios painted by Miliband in this essay came to prevail. The Labour Party found in Neil Kinnock what Miliband thought in 1983 they might not: namely a leader 'able to combine a vocabulary that would please the

Left on the one hand with a sufficient degree of flexibility over policy on the other to reassure the Right and the Centre'[4]. That scenario – even in this 1983 essay otherwise so sympathetic and open to the Bennite Left – would, according to Miliband, if successful oblige 'socialists in the Labour Party ... to decide whether the time had finally come to leave the Labour Party to labourism and its devotees, and to seek a realignment of the left by way of a new socialist party'[5]. Either way, the task before the Left, whether in a new political formation or a transformed old one, was, according to Miliband in 1983, everywhere the same: to create a majority in the electorate for a socialist programme (since visibly one did not exist in 1983), and to do so by building on that portion of the 8.5 million people who had voted Labour in 1983 who remained, in his terms, in a 'state of de-subordination'.

9. SOCIALIST ADVANCE IN BRITAIN (1983)

Ralph Miliband

To speak of socialist advance in Britain a short time after the General Election of June 1983 may seem rather strange. For the election was a major defeat not only for the Labour Party but for all socialist forces; and while that defeat may eventually turn out to have had beneficial political effects, in that it may help to break the mould in which the labour movement has long been imprisoned, such a blessing is hypothetical whereas the immediate effects of Labour's defeat are very tangible. The election results have conferred a new legitimacy upon an exceptionally reactionary Conservative government; and they have also served to demoralize further a movement that was already in bad shape well before the election. It may be said – and indeed it should be said – that the Conservative Government only obtained 30.8 per cent of the total vote and 42.2 per cent of those who voted; and that its vote was less than in 1979. But the system is designed to put the main emphasis on the number of seats won rather than on votes cast; and the fact that the Government obtained a majority of 144 seats in the House of Commons makes it possible for it to claim, however spuriously, that it has a 'mandate' for the policies it chooses to put forward.

The extent of Labour's defeat has another long-term consequence which is clearly important, namely that it would require a net gain of well over 100 seats for Labour and a swing from Conservative to Labour of over 12 per cent to bring about a majority Labour Government. This kind of swing (to the Conservatives) has only occurred once in this century, in the exceptional circumstances of 1931, when a former Labour Prime Minister, Ramsay Macdonald, was leading what was in effect a Conservative coalition against the Labour Party. It is useless to speculate on how things will turn out in a General Election which is some years off: but it is nevertheless reasonable to believe that the extent of Labour's defeat, leaving aside all other detrimental factors, greatly reduces Labour's chances of being able to form a majority government for many years to come.

What adds further to the demoralization of defeat is that the election results – as is agreed by everybody in the labour movement right, left and center – are not the product of some extraordinary set of events whose impact will soon be dissipated, at which the Labour Party will be restored to its former vigour, but rather the most dramatic manifestation of a deep-seated, long-term crisis for which no immediate remedy is at hand. My purpose here is to discuss the nature of this crisis, in the light of Labour's election defeat and to link this with the problem of socialist advance in Britain.

I

Of all the reasons which have been advanced for Labour's defeat, two have obtained the most currency. One of these is that changes in the composition and character of the working class have been such as to erode drastically the support which the Labour Party might expect from its 'natural' constituency; and the other one is that the Labour Party presented the image of a party so deeply divided as to inspire no confidence in its capacity to govern. Other reasons which have found favour include the lack of credibility of much of Labour's electoral programme; the dangerously 'extreme' nature of some of its proposals, notably on defence; the mismanagement of the election campaign, to which may be linked the personality of Michael Foot; the 'Falklands factor'; and so on. But it is upon the changes in the character and composition of the working class on the one hand, and the divisions in the Labour Party on the other, that most attention has come to be focused. I will argue that the first of these explanations is misconceived; and that the second is inadequate because it does not explain why divisions, which are nothing new in the Labour Party, have been so much more significant, intractable and damaging than in the past.

II

It is perfectly true that the Labour Party has suffered a steady loss of electoral support since its peak achievement of nearly fourteen million votes in the General Election of 1951, with 48.8 per cent of the votes cast. By 1983, this had fallen to 27.6 per cent, the lowest percentage share of Labour's vote since 1918, when the Labour Party did not contest over one third of the seats. In 1951, the Labour Party also had an individual membership of around a million: by the early eighties this had dropped to not much more than a quarter of that figure.

It should first be said about the explanations which have found most favour to account for this loss of support that they have a strong ideological purpose: for thirty years now, a shoddy sociology has been invoked by anti-socialist politicians and commentators in the Labour Party and outside as part of an endeavour to rid the Labour Party of those of its commitments which ran counter to their own 'moderate' positions. A certain code language has grown up over the years to obscure the nature of these endeavours. After Labour had lost office in 1951, despite its remarkable electoral performance, it was widely said that the Labour Party must 'rethink' its policies- and who could be against 'rethinking'? After the electoral defeats of 1955 and 1959, it was widely said that the trouble with the Labour Party was that it was saddled with commitments that belonged to an earlier age, and that it must come to terms with a new 'age of affluence': Labour *must* lose, so long as it refused to renew its image and its message, meaning that it must shed what formal socialist commitments it had. After the defeat of 1983, it has been said that the Labour Party must 'learn to listen' to what 'ordinary' people were saying – and who could be so unreasonable as to refuse to listen? When all the verbiage and coded language is cast aside, however, what is left is the insistence that the Labour Party must dilute its policies and programmes, and adopt more 'moderate' positions. This was the whole burden of the battle which Hugh Gaitskell waged in the fifties to change the Labour Party, to 'adapt it to the modern age', to 'bring it up to date', and so forth. The attempt focused on Clause Four of the Labour Party Constitution: unless there was a clear repudiation of this preposterous commitment to nationalize everything in sight, including street corner shops and garages, it was said, the Labour Party was doomed to electoral disaster and annihilation. The attempt failed. Clause Four remained in the Party Constitution (with as little effect as ever before); and notwithstanding the 'age of affluence' which was supposed to have anesthetized the working class, Labour won the election of 1964 on a platform not markedly less 'radical' than previous ones; and it went on to win the election of 1966 with a majority of 97 seats. Nor did the 'radicalism' of Labour's electoral platform in February 1974, with its pledge to bring about 'a fundamental and irreversible shift in the balance of power and wealth in favour of working people and their families' prevent Labour from winning the election then, or the one in October of that year, again with a much increased majority.

Nothing of this is to suggest that the fact of decline in popular support is not very real: it is simply to note that explanations for it usually advanced by anti-socialist commentators are highly suspect and an intrinsic part of the battle which has been waged against the Left in the Labour Party and outside ever since World Way Two – indeed ever since the Labour Party came into being. So too has it been waged since Labour's electoral defeat of May 1979. Once again, it has been said from many quarters that the working class, in so far as it could still be thought of as a class at all, was no longer what it was, and could not be expected to support a Labour Party which obstinately refused to come to terms with these changes (read: 'refused to dilute its policies').

Here too, the point is not to deny that changes in the working class have oc-curred. 'Traditional' occupations and industrial production have declined, and their decline has been accelerated by the Conservative Government's policies; white collar and public service employment has grown and those engaged in it form a larger proportion of the working class than heretofore. It is also possible, but by no means certain in the light of the history of the working class, that 'sec-tionalism' has grown; and it is unquestionably true that unemployment and the fear of unemployment have reduced the willingness of many workers to engage in strike action. The question, however, is what impact these and other changes in the working class may have on its political attitudes and allegiances; and it is here that instant sociology turns into special pleading and bad faith.

To begin with, a very large fact needs to be recalled about the political attitudes of the working class, namely that a very substantial part of it has never supported Labour at all, even in the inter-war years of depression, mass unemployment, the Means Test and Tory retrenchment. Instant sociology often seems to imply that there was a time of depression and poverty when the working class *of course* supported Labour: but that in the age of affluence, of home ownership (a new favourite in the explanation of working-class 'de-redicalisation'), a car in every garage, consumerism, video cassettes and holidays in Spain, no such automatic support could be expected. This conveniently overlooks the fact that, even if one leaves out all general elections from 1918 to 1935, when the Tory and Liberal Parties obtained a vast preponderance of working-class votes against the Labour Party, the General Election of 1935 returned the 'National' Government (in ef-fect a Tory Government) with a majority of well over 200 seats.

This betokens an enduring conservatism in large sections of the working class; and it was this conservatism (which does not necessarily betoken allegiance to the Conservative Party) which was greatly shaken – but not overcome – by the traumas of war. As a result, the Labour Party, after forty-five years of existence, two World Wars and a Great Depression, was at long last able to win a major-ity of seats in the House of Commons – 146 – with 48.3 per cent of the votes cast. Even then, the Conservative Party was still supported by nearly ten million voters (39.8 per cent) and the Liberal Party by nearly two-and-a-half million. Twelve million people had voted for the Labour Party. In other words, the pro-Labour and the anti-Labour votes were more or less evenly divided. Nor can it be assumed that the majority of those who did vote Labour, then and later, were fired by particularly strong radical sentiments. Many perhaps were. But many Labour voters, in 1945, were probably doing no more than expressing a general sentiment that the time had come for a new deal for the working class in Britain, and that the Labour Party was the party to bring it about. Nevertheless, and for all its limitations, the victory of 1945 was a great advance: but instead of being enlarged, that basis was steadily narrowed in subsequent years. I will argue that the main responsibility for this shrinkage lies with Labour leaders and the 'labourism' which provided their ideological and practical framework. But it is at any rate clear, on the historical evidence, that neither the deprivations and sufferings of the 'old' working class, not the 'affluence' of the 'new' (in any case always grossly exaggerated) provides an adequate explanation for the support or lack of support which Labour has obtained: here is vulgar economic determinism indeed, whose inadequacy is further confirmed by the fact that Labour's loss of support has continued through the last ten years of economic crisis, retrenchment and retreat.

III

What has sometimes been called 'Labour Socialism'[6] is a loose amalgam of many different strands of thought – Christian ethics, Fabian collectivism, a radical and democratic tradition of reform, based on age-old notions of social justice, equality, cooperation and fellowship. Even so, 'labourism' seems a better label for the ideology which has moved Labour's leaders – and many others in the labour movement – for a hundred years past. Labourism has never been turned into a systematic body of thought; and it adherents and practitioners have frequently made a virtue of their 'practical' sense, their rejection of 'theory', and their freedom from all 'isms' (and they themselves have never adopted 'labourism' as a label for their views). But it is nevertheless ideological promptings suitably called by that name which have guided their practice.

Labourism is above all concerned with the advancement of concrete demands of immediate advantage to the working class and organized labour: wages and conditions of work; trade-union rights; the better provision of services and benefits in the field of health, education, housing, transport, family allowances, unemployment benefits, pensions and so on. These demands may be clad in the garb of 'socialism' but most leaders of the labour movement, however much they might believe in some vague and remote socialist alternative to the present social order, have in practice only had a very weak concern – in so far as they have had any concern at all – with large socialist objectives. The reforms they have sought have never been conceived as part of a strategy for the creation of a fundamentally different kind of society, but rather as specific responses to immediate ills and needs. Their horizons have been narrowly bound by the capitalist environment in which they found themselves, and whose framework they readily took as given; and it is within its framework and the 'rationality' it imposed that they sought reform.

This acceptance of capitalist 'rationality' helps to explains some notable features of their politics: for instance, why the reforms they sought were generally so modest in scope and substance, and so geared to what 'society' could afford; why Labour governments so quickly and so regularly moved from being agents of reform to being agents of conservative retrenchment, more concerned to contain pressure from below than to advance labour's demands; and also why these leaders were so ready to collaborate with Labour's class enemies. Trade-union leaders steeped in labourism might have to fight the class struggle, and occasionally fought it hard; but neither they nor certainly Labour's political leaders thought of society as a battlefield upon which the working class was engaged in a permanent and irrevocable struggle against the domination and exploitation to which it was subjected by a rapacious ruling class: or if they thought in those terms, they did not let it affect their political practice. But for the most part, they thought of 'society' as presented with 'problems' whose solution mainly required the kind of good will, intelligence, knowledge and compassion which their Conservative opponents somehow lacked.

Given these perspectives, labourism readily accepted the political system that was in existence when the labour movement assumed definite shape in the second half of the nineteenth century. Labour leaders might demand some reforms in this realm too – for instance, the extension of the suffrage, or the reform of the House of Lords or of local government. But they took the system as a whole more or less for granted and capitalist democracy on the British model to be the most accomplished form of democratic government conceivable – hereditary monarchy and hereditary peers in the House of Lords included. They mainly thought of the political process in parliamentary terms, and of grassroots activism and extra-parliamentary activity as party work at local level for the purpose of supporting local and parliamentary representatives and helping to fight local and parliamentary elections. The notion that a local party might be a focus of struggle, agitation and education fell outside their ideological spectrum. Nor have Labour leaders ever shown much concern to bring about any large reform in the organization of the British state so as to change the closed, oligarchic and profoundly conservative character of its administrative, judicial, police and military branches.

Finally, Labourism has always had a strong national vocation. The Labour Party has regularly been accused by its Conservative opponents of being 'unpatriotic', heedless of British interests abroad, unconcerned with British 'greatness', etc. Nothing could be further from the truth. Labour governments have always pursued foreign and defence policies (and in an earlier epoch colonial policies) which did not greatly differ from those of Conservative Governments – not perhaps very surprisingly since Labour Governments relied on the civil servants and military advisors they inherited from the Conservatives. Of course there have been some differences: it may well be, for instance, that a Conservative Government, had one been elected in 1945, would not have accepted without much bitter struggle the inevitability of Indian independence; and divergencies between Labour and Conservative defence policies have widened in recent years and were manifested in the General Election of 1983. It is permissible to doubt how far these divergencies would have been maintained, if a Labour government had been elected, given the lukewarm support, at best, which senior Labour figures gave to major items of Labour's defence programme, but the divergencies were nevertheless evident. On the other hand, it has to be remembered that, beyond these divergencies, all senior Labour figures, without exception, continued to be committed to the American alliance and NATO, which have been the cornerstones of the defence and foreign policies of *both* the Conservative and Labour Parties since the war years.

These being the main features of labourism, it is reasonable to see it as an ideology of social reform, within the framework of capitalism, with no serious ambition of transcending that framework, whatever ritual obeisances to 'socialism' might be performed by party leaders on suitable occasions, such as Labour Party or trade-union conferences, to appease or defeat their activist critics. Labourism, in other words, is not, like Marxism, an ideology of rupture but an ideology of adaptation.

It is this ideology which has been overwhelmingly dominant in the labour movement for a hundred years and more, whatever 'socialist' label might be given to it. Marxism, as a main alternative to labourism, has not been a negligible strange of thought among activists and its influence has been greater than the proclaimed number of its adherents might suggest. But it has nevertheless been marginal in comparison with labourism. For it is labourism which slowly made its way in the working class and became an acceptable perspective to a substantial part of it; and it is labourism which, from the peak which it reached in 1951, has been losing support in the working class. The question I now turn to is why.

IV

An explanation of this growing alienation has to begin with the long-standing economic decline of the British economy, and with the aggravation and acceleration of this decline by virtue of the world capitalist economic crisis from the early 1970s onwards; or rather, an explanation has to begin with the response of the Labour Governments of the sixties and seventies to decline and crisis. The chronic British economic malady and the recurring emergencies which it produced presented these governments with a challenge that they always promised to meet but which they always failed to meet. Instead, and well in line with their labourist ideology, they consistently pursued economic policies which were broadly acceptable to the capitalist forces at home and abroad on whose help and cooperation they relied. In so doing, they were also and naturally compelled to turn themselves, as I noted earlier, into agencies of retrenchment and containment.

The failures, derelictions and betrayals of the Wilson and Callaghan Governments of 1964-70 and 1974-79 have been amply documented and need no retelling here.[7] The point that does need to be made is that these governments did, to a quite remarkable degree, act in ways which were bound to alienate masses of actual or potential Labour supporters in the working class, and not only in the working class. It was the Labour Governments of those decades which inaugurated the 'monetarist' policies which the Conservatives pushed much further after 1979. It was these Labour Governments who launched repeated attacks on public expenditure by central and local government for collective services whose level is of crucial importance to the large majority of people who cannot pay for private health, education, housing, transport and amenities; and it was also they whose budgets turned into tax exercises much more calculated to hit lower incomes than high ones. It was the Wilson and Callaghan Governments which made war on industrial activists, and who persistently sought to curb wages under the guise of income policies, wage norms, social contracts and national agreements. Nor even could these policies claim any measure of success: after a combined period of eleven years of Labour governments from 1964 until 1979, with a Conservative interruption of only four years, there was no major improvement in the British condition to which Labour could point. Meanwhile the rich prospered, and so did a Labour state bourgeoisie loud in its denunciation of militants and wreckers who were spoiling their enjoyment of the pleasures of office.

This record alone would be perfectly adequate to account for the progressive alienation of masses of potential Labour voters from the Labour Party. The argument is not, of course, that the working class wanted more socialism and turned away from Labour because Labour Governments did not give it to them. That is indeed nonsense. The point is that Labour supporters wanted, and voted for, programmes of economic and social betterment, but that the betterment they got from Labour Governments was easily overshadowed by the negative side of the record. As a result, many of them abandoned Labour in 1983, as more and more of them had been doing in previous elections, and did so all the more readily as there now appeared to be a plausible alternative to both Labour and Conservatives, namely the Social Democratic and Liberal Parties. Furthermore, many of them simply did not vote: one of the significant facts about the General Election of 1983 is that 47 per cent of the unemployed young people between the ages of 18 and 22 did not bother to cast a vote at all.

Even so, eight-and-a-half million people did vote Labour. This is really very remarkable, when account is taken of the relentless and quite unscrupulous assault to which working-class – and other – voters were subjected during the election campaign and for many years before the campaign. The assault had two obvious objectives. One of them was to get voters to overlook the viciously regressive character of the policies of the Thatcher government. The other was to persuade them that the Labour Party had been taken over, or was in imminent danger of being taken over, by political perverts and lunatics. Not the least persuasive element in that assault was the contribution which senior and respected figures in the Labour Party made to it, by joining in the chorus of vilification which united all anti-socialist forces, including of course the ex-Labour renegade leaders and parliamentarians of the Social Democratic Party. In the circumstances, and given the intensity of the assault, the wonder is not that Labour lost, but that so many people resisted the propaganda, overlooked Labour's condition and record, and still voted for it. That so many did constitutes a precious asset, to whose significance I will return later.

V

The second main reason advanced to account for Labour's defeat, I noted earlier, is that the Labour Party was, and had been for a long time, so obviously deeply divided. This makes good sense, but needs to be taken a good deal further. For there have always been deep divisions in the Labour Party and the labour movement and they have not stopped the Labour Party from doing a lot better than it did in 1983. The difference is that the more recent divisions have run much deeper than before and that many more activists have opposed their leaders, and also, most significant of all in my view, that the Labour leaders, unlike their predecessors since the Labour Party came into being, have not been able to maintain their ideological and political hegemony over the labour movement. Here lies the root of Labour's troubles.

In this context, too, account has to be taken of the economic decline of Britain and of the Wilson and Callaghan Governments' response to it. For just as the derelictions and betrayals and failures of these governments 'de-aligned' a mass of potential and actual Labour supporters, so did that record 'radicalise' a mass of left activists and give them a new determination to prevent a repetition of past performance. From the early seventies onwards, a new wave of activists emerged, not only more determined but better organized than the Labour Left had been earlier, and less susceptible to manipulation and seduction as well. Also, and not to be under-estimated, they found an articulate and resilient champion in Tony Benn, whose national position and place in the Labour Party gave them added strength. The Labour Left has always had problems with its parliamentary and ministerial standard bearers. Stafford Cripps was a weak and vacillating leader of the Socialist League in the thirties, and Aneurin Bevan in the post-war years was a very erratic and impulsive leader of the Bevanties, in so far as he could be said to have been their leader at all. Bevan soared above his followers, and did not really seek to mobilize support at the grassroots. Benn did. No wonder that he was so bitterly hated and reviled, by his erstwhile ministerial colleagues and fellow parliamentarians no less than by all the forces of conservatism proper.

The new activism was not homogeneous in ideological and political terms. Some small part of it – on which its enemies naturally fastened – drew its inspiration from Trotskyism. Somme of it proceeded from an unlabelled militant socialist iconoclasm, of which the most representative figure was Ken Livingstone; and most of it was probably the product of a deep but undoctrinal anger at the grassroots on the part of rank-and-file activists who were utterly fed up with the retreat by their leaders into Labour versions of Conservative policies at home and abroad.

Furthermore, the new activists rejected the view traditionally held by Labour leaders (and by much of the traditional Labour Left as well) that the political process must have the House of Commons as its main and all but exclusive focus, with grassroots activisms as playing no more than a support role for parliamentarians. On the contrary, the new activists were oriented towards work at the grassroots, and had a strong sense of the political process at local level – hence the importance they attached to what could be achieved in and through local government. Like the women's movement and the peace movement, the new generation of Labour activists (who were in any case often part of the other two movements as well) was strongly committed to extra-parliamentary pressure and did not believe that parliamentary work was so crucial as to dwarf all else: on the contrary, they saw parliamentary work as part of a larger and more important struggle in the country at large.

The new activists were, relatedly, intensely suspicious of all leaders, and notably of parliamentary leaders; and they tended to view most (but not all) left parliamentarians as being part of a 'soft left' that could not be trusted to offer sustained resistance to the retreats and compromises of the leaders of the Labour Party. In so far as this response is unstructured, it may in time fail to protect Labour left activists from appeals stemming from many diverse sources not to rock the boat, make a bad situation worse, and so on. From this point of view, the suspicion which many left activists themselves have of 'theory' is a source of real political weakness, which has very adversely affected many Labour activists in the past.

Nevertheless the General Election defeat of 1979, coming on top of the record of the Wilson and Callaghan Governments, gave a powerful impulse to activist pressures which had been building up throughout the seventies. The left in the Labour Party was able in the following years to force through major innovations in the selection of MPs and in the election of the Leader and Deputy Leader of the Labour Party. Moreover, the left was also able to achieve temporary control of the National Executive Committee and of its important sub-committees; and it was thus well placed to make a marked impact on the programme which was eventually presented in the election of 1983.

The most remarkable feature of this pressure from the left is that, even though the Labour leadership bitterly opposed it, with the vociferous encouragement of a virtually united press, it was unable to subdue it. This had in part to do with the strength of the new activism in the Labour Party and in the unions; and also with the much less solid position of that leadership. For another consequence of the failures of the Wilson and Callaghan Governments was to weaken drastically the moral and political authority of the people – drawn overwhelmingly from the Right and the Centre – who had been in charge of these governments. In any case, when one recalls the relative ease with which an earlier Labour Left was brought to heel by expulsive or the threat of expulsion, or was manipulated into submission by the kind of rhetoric and deception of which Harold Wilson was the master, the inability of the Labour leaders to crush or curb their activist opponents stands out as the really new and significant fact in recent Labour history.

However, the new activists, notwithstanding their successes, were just as unable as their predecessors to dislodge the Right and the Centre from their commanding positions in the Labour Party and the trade unions. Even when they had a majority on the NEC, they were confronted by a powerful minority of senior figures (including the Leader and the Deputy Leader) who could marshall considerable resources to block the path of the left. Also, the majority of the Parliamentary Labour Party remained under the control of the Right and the Centre, and the parliamentary left was itself badly split between the 'soft left' and the Bennites. Nor did the left have many reliable allies in the upper echelons of the trade-union hierarchy.

The high point in the activists' campaign after 1979 was the vote for the Deputy Leadership of the Labour Party by the new electoral college at the 1981 Party Conference, when Tony Been obtained 49.5 per cent of the vote, against Denis Healey's 50.4 per cent. Had Benn won, it is conceivable that the balance of forces in the Labour Party would have shifted considerably to the left, with many more people in the Parliamentary Labour Party moving over to the Social Democratic Party to which many Labour parliamentarians are in any case ideologically well attuned. But Benn did not win, and the Right and Centre remained in command, with a Leader, in the person of Michael Foot, who, for all his past Labour Left record and rhetoric, had long made his peace with the Right and the Centre. Foot had been a main pillar of the Wilson-Callaghan Government between 1974 and 1979 and a chief architect of that Government's alliance with the Liberals, and was a determined enemy of the Bennite Left.

The successes of the new activists, coupled with their failure to win a commanding position in the Labour Party, thus produced the absurd and untenable situation which is at the core of Labour's troubles: the left was able to get major items of policy adopted by Labour Party and trade-union conferences; and these items subsequently found their way into Labour's electoral programme. But the task of defending these policies was left to leaders many of whom – indeed most of whom – did not believe in them, made no secret of the fact and found many opportunities to denounce those who wanted these policies as wreckers or fools.

The full absurdity of this situation became disastrously evident in the General Election campaign. The Labour Manifesto was not the 'extreme' document which the enemies of the left, not least in the Labour Party, found it convenient to claim, then and later. It amounted for the most part to a reiteration of policies which had been put forward in the Labour Party's electoral manifestoes of the seventies and earlier. But, in addition to the pledge that a Labour government would take Britain out of the European Economic Community, it did include some proposals in the field of defence that had far-reaching implications: thus, it pledged a Labour Government to reject the deployment of Cruise and Pershing missiles on British soil and to 'begin discussions' for the removal of nuclear bases in Britain, 'to be completed within the lifetime of the Labour Government'. The document further proclaimed Labour's commitment 'to establish a non-nuclear defence policy': 'we will, after consultation, carry through in the lifetime of the next parliament our non-nuclear defence policy'. This appeared to commit a Labour Government to unilateral nuclear disarmament. But the document also said that, in addition to canceling the Trident programme, it would propose that 'Britain's Polaris force be included in the nuclear disarmament negotiations in which Britain must take part'. The obvious question, on which the Conservative and others naturally pounced, was what would happen if the negotiations failed. On this, the Labour Party spoke with uncertain and divided voices. In other words, the manifesto's attempt to square the circle had failed; and the divisions in the Labour leadership on the issue of defence made it impossibly for the Labour Party to proclaim what it was left to Enoch Powell to call the 'transparent absurdity' of the theory of nuclear deterrence, based as it was on the willingness to commit national suicide 'as a last resort'. Mrs Thatcher made the typically reckless and bombastic declaration during the election campaign that she would be perfectly ready to 'press the button': Labour was in no condition to denounce this for the degraded nonsense that it was.

VI

It is very unlikely that any major party in Britain has ever fought so inane a campaign as the Labour Party did in 1983. The basic reason for this was not incompetence and mismanagement, however much there may have been of both. These were only the manifestations of much deeper trouble, namely the division, essentially, between social reformers whose perspectives do not for all practical purposes reach beyond labourism, and socialists whose perspectives do. This age-old division has now reached a point where any attempt at accommodation only produces fudging formulas which neither satisfy nor convince anyone.

Such a situation cannot permanently endure: or at least, no party and movement can be viable in which such a situation endures. Pious references to the Labour Party being a 'broad church' which has always incorporated many different strands of thought fail to take account of a crucial fact, namely that the 'broad church' of Labour only functioned effectively in the past because one side – the Right and Centre – determined the nature of the services that were to be held, and excluded or threatened with exclusion any clergy too deviant in its dissent. Now that this can no longer be done – the clumsy and largely ineffectual attempts to banish the *Militant* Tendency confirm rather than disprove the point – the 'broad church' is unable to do its job.

The question which therefore needs to be asked is what socialists, whether they are in the Labour Party or not, should want to see by way of a resolution of this condition. The answer to that question is best considered by reference to two possibly 'scenarios'.

The first of these involves the election of a new Leader of the Labour Party able to combine a vocabulary that would please the left on the one hand with a sufficient degree of flexibility over policy on the other to reassure the Right and the Centre. The task of such a Leader might be eased somewhat by the fact that no major policy decisions have to be incorporated in an election manifesto for some time to come; and a Leader who spoke an adequately left-sounding language might hope to confuse and divide the left sufficiently to isolate its more intractable elements, and thus reduce them to a marginal position.

The realization of such a 'scenario' would restore a certain degree of coherence to the Labour Party. It would not be quite the party of Clement Attlee and Hugh Gaitskell which Mrs Thatcher was calling for during the election campaign, but it would be a recognizable version of it. Labourism, suitably embellished with some socialist phraseology (but not too much of it) would again predominate. Persuasive appeals would be made to 'unite against the common enemy', and an enticing vision of electoral victory and a Labour Government would be held out as a the reward for reasonableness and moderation.

There undoubtedly exists a considerable weight of support for such an outcome: a large majority of parliamentarians would be for it, so would a large number of trade-union leaders; so would the press and the media. It would widely be represented as a welcome sign that the Labour Party was returning to the sensible policies of old, and that it was abjuring the lunatic policies which had brought it to its present pass. Nor is there much doubt that it would meet with the approval of many Labour supporters and Labour Party members.

It is, however, a very difficult 'scenario' to realize. For its realization would represent a massive defeat for the left in the Labour Party. There is no good reason to suppose that, having got as far as it has, the left would accept such a defeat and desist from their endeavors. Inevitably, however, these endeavors maintain the Labour Party in a state of civil war.

This being the case, a realization of the 'scenario' in question requires nothing less than a thorough 'purge' of the left in the Labour Party, extending far beyond the *Militant* Tendency; and it would also need a redrawing of the constitutional rules so as to reduce drastically the increased influence which activists have been able to achieve since 1979 on such matters as the re-selection of MPs and the election of the Leader and Deputy Leader of the Labour Party. If this could be done, socialists in the Labour Party would be forced to decide whether the time had finally come to leave the Labour Party to labourism and its devotees, and to seek a realignment of the left by way of a new socialist party. However, this kind of action against the left seems well beyond the powers of any Labour leadership today.

The new activists, for their part, have proceeded from a very different 'scenario', which has not been clearly spelt out, but whose main lines are not difficult to draw. What is involved is a continuation of the struggles in which the left has been engaged, with the purpose of achieving predominance and turning the Labour Party into a socialist party free from the constrictions hitherto imposed upon it by its leaders. It must be presumed that many leading figures in the Labour Party would then want to leave it and seek new political homes elsewhere – in the Social Democratic Party, or the Liberal Party, or even the Conservative Party. In fact, it would be essential that such people *should* leave the Labour Party; for just as the left makes life difficult for a leadership which is opposed to it, so could determined Right and Centre parliamentarians make life difficult for a party in which the left had acquired predominance. No doubt, a good many other Labour Party members, at constituency level, would also leave. But these defections would be compensated by the accretion of strength which would be provided by the many people who are not now minded to join the Labour Party but might then want to do so, and be actively involved in it. It is also very likely that some, perhaps many, trade-union leaders would wish to disaffiliate from a Labour Party that had gone beyond labourism. But any such attempt would meet with stiff resistance from the left in the unions; and though the attempt might succeed in some cases, it would probably be successfully fought in others.

I must enter a personal note at this point. I have for more than ten years written that this hope of the left to transform the Labour Party – which has always been nourished by the Labour Left – was illusory, and that, far from representing a short cut to the creation of a mass socialist party in Britain (which has never existed), it was in fact a dead end in which British socialists had been trapped for many decades – in fact since the Labour Party come into being. It was this view which led me to advocate the formation of a new socialist party able to do all the work of socialist advocacy and agitation which the Labour Party had been prevented by its leaders from doing.[8]

I am far from convinced that I was mistaken. For it is by no means evident that the new activists can realize the 'scenario' I have just outlined: on the most optimistic expectations, they have a long way to go, with many large obstacles on the way. But it is obvious that I underestimated how great was the challenge which the new activists would be able to pose to their leaders; and how limited would be the capacity of these leaders to surmount the challenge. I now take it that the question whether the activists can push matters further and achieve the conquest of the Labour Party is more open than I had believed.

Rather than speculate further upon this, it may be more useful to ask what would be the prospects of a socialist Labour Party, such as the activists seek: and the same considerations would apply to a new socialist party, born from the disintegration of the Labour Party.

VII

Such a party would seek to advance purposes and policies which have long formed part of the aspirations of the socialist left. One of its main concerns would be the democratization of the whole structure of government; the abolition of anti-trade-union legislation and other repressive legislation, such as the Prevention of Terrorism Act, introduced in 1974 by Roy Jenkins, then Labour Home Secretary; the drastic curbing of police powers and the placing of the police under effective democratic control; and the end of the British military presence in Northern Ireland.

A socialist party would be pledged to the return to public ownership of the industries and services which the Conservative Government has sold off and will further have sold off; and it would take it that a major extension of public ownership under a variety of forms, and with the greatest possible measure of democratic control, was one of the indispensable conditions for the transformation of British capitalism in socialist directions, and for the dissolution of the class structure which would be one of its central aims.

In the realm of defence and foreign policy, such a party would be committed to the nuclear disarmament of Britain, as part of a radical shift in the policies followed by Labour and Conservative Governments since World War Two. A socialist party could not be true to itself if it did not include in its programme an end of British support for the world-wide counter-revolutionary crusade which the United States has been waging across the world even since the forties, and if it did not support progressive movements throughout the world struggling for national and social liberation. Such defence and foreign policies are clearly incompatible with membership of NATO.

Conventional wisdom has it that such a programme can never be endorsed by a majority of people – indeed, that it dooms the party which propounds it to marginality and irrelevance.

Two points may be made about this. The first is that there is no point in pretending that there exists a ready-made majority in the country for a socialist programme. How could there be? One of the fruits of the long predominance of labourism is precisely that the party of the working class has never carried out any sustained campaign of education and propaganda on behalf of a socialist programme; and that Labour leaders have frequently turned themselves into

fierce propagandists *against* the socialist proposals of their critics inside the
Labour Party and out, and have bent their best efforts to the task of defeating
all attempts to have the Labour Party adopt such proposals. Moreover, a vast
array of conservative forces, of the most diverse kind, are always at hand to
dissuade the working class from even thinking about the socialist ideas which
evil or foolish people are forever trying to foist upon them. This simply means
that a ceaseless battle for the 'hearts and minds' of the people is waged by the
forces of conservatism, against which have only been mobilized immeasurably
smaller socialist forces. A socialist party would seek to strengthen these forces
and to defend socialist perspectives and a socialist programme over an extended
period of time, and would accept that more than one election might have to be
held before a majority of people came to support it. In any case, a socialist party
would not only be concerned with office, but with the creation of the conditions
under which office would be more than the management of affairs on capitalist
lines. The first of these conditions is precisely a strong measure of popular support; and this support would be all the more essential, given the fierce resistance
which a socialist government seeking to apply its programme would encounter
from all the conservative forces in the land.

Ever since the Labour Party became a substantial electoral and political force,
Labour leaders have taken the view – and have persuaded many of their followers
to take the view – that government was all; and that politics is about elections: on
one side, there is power, on the other, paralysis. This is a very narrow view of the
political process. Elections are important, and no party functioning in a capital-
ist-democratic context can afford to neglect them, not least at local level. But this
is a very different matter from the view that gaining office is the sole and exclusive purpose of politics. For office, however agreeable for those who hold it, has
often meant not only impotence, but worse than impotence, namely the power
to carry out policies fundamentally at odds with the purposes for which office
was obtained. Nor is it necessarily the case that opposition means paralysis. This
has never been true of the Conservative Party and the conservative forces; and
it has only been true of the Labour Party because of the narrow ideological and
political framework in which its leaders have dwelt, and because of their concentration on electoral and parliamentary politics. But it need not be true for a
substantial working-class party. It is by no means obvious, for instance, that the
Italian Communist Party, in opposition since it was expelled from office in 1947,
has, *in socialist terms*, exercised much less influence on Italian life in this period,
than the Labour Party has exercised in government. The notion that the Labour
Party is either a 'party of government', with all the opportunistic compromises
and retreats the formulation carries, or must resign itself to being no more than
an 'ineffectual sect' may be useful propaganda for all the 'moderate' forces in the
labour movement, but it does not correspond to the real alternatives.

This relates to the second point that, while there is no popular majority for a socialist programme at present, it does not follow that there is no support for such a programme at all, and that more support for it could not be generated. This is where it is necessary to recall the fact that eight-and-a-half million people did vote Labour in 1983. There is obviously no warrant for the view that all of them consciously and deliberately supported all the items in Labour's programme, or even that they supported many of them: many such Labour voters were no doubt simply registering a vote against the Thatcher Government. But among these eight-and-a-half million voters, a large number may be taken to have voted as they did because they approved more or less strongly the general drift and many items of the Labour programme, and were not put off by the massive propaganda to which they were subjected, and which assured them that a vote for Labour was a vote for personal and national disaster. As I noted earlier, they resisted this assault just as millions of Labour voters have resisted such assaults at every election since 1945, when the Labour Party put forward a programme which its leaders had striven very hard to dilute, in the belief that its more radical proposals must inevitably lose them the election. This stubborn popular resistance to the unrelenting campaign of indoctrination to which the working class is subjected at election time and in between elections provides a basis of support on which a socialist party serious about its business can build. Much of the propaganda conducted by anti-socialist forces – Conservative, Liberal, Social Democratic and Labour – seeks to present a picture of the working class as irrevocably opposed to socialist proposals; but the propagandists would have to work much less hard if this was the case. They do have to work as hard as they do precisely because there does exist a vast degree of popular alienation from existing economic, social and political arrangements, which can be turned into support for radically different arrangements. I have called this alienation a 'state of de-subordination', as a result of which 'people who find themselves in subordinate positions, and notably the people who work in factories, mines, offices, shops, schools, hospitals and so on do what they can to mitigate, resist and transform the conditions of their subordination'.[9] Unemployment and the fear of unemployment have undoubtedly had an effect, as they were intended to do, in reducing 'de-subordination' at 'the point of production'. But this hardly means that the experience of these years of Tory Government and mass unemployment and the attack on welfare and collective provisions have generated any more popular support for existing arrangements than was previously the case. On the contrary economic decline and crisis, allied to the crying injustices generated by a grossly unequal class system, provide the ground on which socialist work can effectively proceed.

Socialist work means something different for a socialist party than the kind of political activity inscribed in the perspectives of labourism. I have noted earlier that political work, for labourism, essentially means short periods of great political activity for local and parliamentary election, with long periods of more or less routine party activity in between. Socialist work means intervention in all the many different areas of life in which class struggle occurs: for class struggle must be taken to mean not only the permanent struggle between capital and labour, crucial though that remains, but the struggle against racial and sex discrimination, the struggle against arbitrary state and police power, the struggle against the ideological hegemony of the conservative forces, and the struggle for new and radically different defence and foreign policies.

The slogan of the first Marxist organisation in Britain, the Social Democratic Federation, founded in 1884, was 'Educate, Agitate, Organise'. It is also a valid slogan for the 1980s and beyond. A socialist party could, in the coming years, give it more effective meaning than it has ever had in the past.

Notes

[1] R. Miliband, 'Moving On', in R. Miliband and J. Saville (eds), *The Socialist Register 1976*, London, Merlin Press, 1976, p.128

[2] ibid, p. 130

[3] R. Miliband, 'Socialist Advance in Britain', in R. Miliband and J. Saville (eds), *The Socialist Register 1983*, London, Merlin Press, 1983, p. 116-7

[4] ibid, p. 115

[5] ibid, p.116

[6] See for example Stuart MacIntyre, *A Proletarian Science. Marxism in Britain 1917-1933*, (1980), chapter 2

[7] See for example L. Panitch, *Social Democracy and Industrial Militancy* (1976); D. Coates, *Labour in Power?*(1980); and K. Coates, *What Went Wrong?* (1979)

[8] See 'Moving On' in *The Socialist Register 1976* and 'The future of Socialism in England', *The Socialist Register 1977*

[9] R. Miliband, 'A state of de-subordination', *British Journal of Sociology*, vol. Xxix, no. 4, December 1978, p.402

Editorial Introduction to Extract 10

The full story of the rise, special qualities and eventual defeat of the Bennite Left within the post-1979 Labour Party would not be told by scholars sympathetic to Ralph Miliband's analysis and politics until Leo Panitch and Colin Leys published *The End of Parliamentary Socialism* in 1997[1]. But many of the formative essays for that later and outstanding work first appeared in *The Socialist Register*. Of a number that could have been reproduced here, we have selected part of Leo Panitch's 1988 essay on 'Socialist Renewal and the Labour Party', in which the *Register* reported sympathetically on the character of Bennism, and its differences from traditional forms of Left Labourism.

10. SOCIALIST RENEWAL AND THE LABOUR PARTY (1988)

Leo Panitch

The Labour Party, which had always been keen to present itself as the lynchpin of political stability as well as reform in Britain, generated a new radical opposition out of the contradictions in its own practices in government and their effects on its constituencies in the 1960s and 1970s. A new Labour left began taking form long before Thatcherism had established its strength, and indeed with some perceptive anticipation of the looming possibility of such a turn to the right; and it gradually set itself the task of transforming the ideology and organization of the Labour Party as the critical means of transforming the British state and society. After the sorry experience of the 1964-70 Labour Government, reinforced by its tragic repetition from 1974-79, including the inauguration of monetarism in 1976, the Labour Party turned inward on itself to fight a battle over the very meaning of socialism and democracy and posed the question as it had never been posed with such force before in the party's history of whether a social democratic working-class party like Labour could be adapted into becoming a party directed towards socialist mobilization and change. The challenge of the new Labour left to the party's ancient structures and practices was prosecuted in an often unclear and sometimes actually confused and certainly incomplete fashion. It was also burdened with occasional but on the whole minor 'entrist' allies, such as Militant, who reflected some of the more troubling aspects, and the most easily challengeable by the forces representing the status quo, of a committed but sectarian practice. Nevertheless, the new Labour left was moving – haltingly, stumbling, taking two steps forward and one back as

must inevitably be the case when one is traversing new terrain under enemy fire
– towards a new conception of socialist party politics, one which pointed beyond
the stale and decaying practices, not only of the traditional parliamentarism of
social democracy, but also of the Leninism of the vanguard parties and the alliances between the elites of various parties that was designated as 'popular front-
ism' by the Communist parties.

As regards earlier struggles by the Labour left, it was certainly not incorrect for
critical students of the party to identify their failures with the traditional weaknesses of this left itself. Of these, the one most commonly and justifiably identified was the Labour left's 'almost total preoccupation' with parliamentarism to
the downgrading, if not the exclusion, of extra-parliamentary mobilization.[2] The
Labour left generally defended the authority of the party conference and valued
it as an expression of a collectivist, class orientation to politics which countered
the individualizing, isolation effect of bourgeois politics, wherein, as Miliband
put it in his debate with McKenzie in the 1950s, '. . . the electorate is an amorphous mass, which, at least between elections, only acquires political meaning and becomes capable of political initiative through organization, mainly
political organization'. Unless such organizational initiative was nurtured, the
result could only be 'the degradation of the business of politics. The authority
which the annual Conference of the Labour Party claims over its leaders is at
least one obstacle to that degradation."[3] But Miliband well recognized that traditionally such challenges as were initiated by the Labour left to the autonomy
of parliamentarians through the assertion of party conference supremacy did
not 'encroach very far into the political system', as Mike Rustin was to put it a
quarter of a century later. 'The idea of participation in the Labour Party has not
extended much beyond the formulation of policy and its legislative embodiment
by the State. Policies formulated democratically are to be implemented bureau-
cratically. . . Labour leftism has been a parliamentary and electoralist version,
mainly bound up with electing a Government to carry this out.'[4]

Certainly this was the case with the Bevanites in the 1950s, who were primarily a parliamentary faction, although they did have considerable support in the
constituencies. But the Bevanite organizational goals were largely limited to securing the nomination of like-minded parliamentary candidates, and within the
parliamentary framework they mainly sought no more than the right of back-
bench MPs to dissent from the collective solidarity of the Shadow Cabinet or
Cabinet. The May Day Manifesto 1968 clearly expressed the assessment of many
socialists who had turned away from the party by the late 1960s and devoted
their energies elsewhere:

> ... the traditional Labour Left has been a compromise between socialist objectives
> and the existing power structure, at the party level. It has made important efforts
> to reform this party power structure, but with the odds continually against it. . .
> it becomes of necessity involved in the same kind of machine politics, the same

manipulation of committees in the names of thousands, the same confusion of the emptying institutions of the movement with the people in whose names they are conducted, as that of the leaders and managers whom it seeks to affect or displace. It is then not only that in the game of manipulation it is always likely to lose; it is also that it is directing energy into the very machines and methods which socialists should fight ... And this has prevented the outward looking and independent long-term campaign.[5]

These words have a strong resonance in the 1980s. And they still bear a vitally important message. But it would be wrong to assimilate the project of the new Labour left with that of what went before or to forget why it emerged despite the failures of previous Labour lefts. It is important to remember that many socialists turned to the Labour Party in the context of the inability of various parties to the left of Labour to make a broad political advance in the post-1968 era; related to this was the inability of those (including the authors of the May Day Manifesto) who hoped to develop a new socialist party free of old Leninist centralist practices and insurrectionary pretensions of the Trotskyist parties, to get anything remotely like even a 'pre-party formation' off the ground. And many socialists looked again at the Labour Party, not only for these reasons, but because of the development in the Party of a new Labour left which seemed to many to have overcome the weaknesses of the past. Even as staunch a critic of the Labour Party as David Coates was writing by 1975: '... the current Labour Left, unlike any before it, is not simply or even mainly a Parliamentary force ... For it is a Left which captured control of the Party conference by mobilizing an alliance between left MPs, constituency activists, and, crucially, the votes of the delegations of the big trade unions. For the first time, the Labour Left activists in Parliament and the constituencies established a firm organizational connection, through their alliance with the leaders of the large unions, with the groundswell of industrial militancy.'[6] Coates was, if anything, portraying this alliance in too strong colours, as we shall see, although he personally remained convinced that the attempt to change the party would fail. But by the late 1970s, many people from the 1960s 'New Left' had joined the party or were at least framing their political activity within the parameters set by the new Labour left. What had happened to change their strategic and tactical perspectives? Simply this: they believed that the odds had changed. And they had – although not quite so favourably ,as some came to think. The serious socialist critique of Labourism had never been so much about 'parliamentarism versus insurrectionism' as about the kind of parliamentary strategy the Labour Party traditionally practised. Nor were most critical accounts of Labourism, such as Miliband's *Parliamentary Socialism*, premised on the attribution to it of an ahistorical 'set of "enduring reflexes"', divorced from political conjuncture, as has recently been alleged by Raphael Samuel and Gareth Stedman Jones.[7] On the contrary, they were usually based on detailed examinations of the balance of forces in different conjunctures, but tempered by an awareness of the parliamentary elite's autonomy and its enormously important role as an active agency in the construction of political discourse, not just a passive reflection of working class 'history from below'. When the odds changed, socialists who took this view were prepared to look carefully if still critically at the new balance of forces in the party. A good number of them even wanted to join the battle.

The source of the attempt to change the Labour Party is not difficult to trace. It lay in the effects which the Labour governments of 1964-70 had not only on socialists but on Labour's supporters more broadly. Recent evidence has confirmed that a new generation of working-class voters who had become voters in the 1960s were more class conscious than those who had first entered the electorate before 1929, but less class conscious than those who had become voters over the subsequent thirty years. These new voters largely opted for Labour in the mid-1960s. But it was the same new working-class voters who, in great numbers, deserted the Labour Party in the 1970 election, more than canceling out a lesser flow to Labour from among middle-class individuals. In that election the Labour Party suffered a decline in electoral support '. . . by ten times the amount we would have expected on the basis of changes in social structure. It was in that election that Labour first lost a large proportion of voters from among social groups which had previously supported the party. The loss in Labour voters from among these groups indeed continued after that date, but at very much slower rate. . . when we consider the kind of people who actually reacted against the Labour government of 1966-70. . . the largest swings away from Labour voting occurred in the solidly working-class strata."[8] It would thus appear that the critical period for understanding the electoral de-alignments that gripped the attention of psephologists with the rise of Thatcherism occurred in fact under the Wilson Government of 1966-70. It was only in 1970 that a substantial portion of the working class vote deserted Labour for the first time, with manual workers' support falling from 69 per cent in 1966 to 58 per cent in 1970 (where it stayed through 1974, and then fell further in 1979 to 50 per cent after another experience of Labour Government). As Mark Frankland has put it:

> The Parliament elected in 1966 provided the first Labour majority in fifteen years that was large enough to have a chance to build upon the achievements of 1945-50. The Parliament of 1966 thus provided the first opportunity for young voters to become disillusioned with the prospects for a socialist Britain. The same election will also have provided the first opportunity in fifteen years for the party to prove to potential supporters from middle-class backgrounds that it was content to govern a mixed society. The latter objective was the one Harold Wilson espoused. Paradoxically, his very success in achieving this objective may have been what cost the party so much support among members of the working class. Young voters may have ceased to see any class difference between the parties during this period, and so become responsive to appeals that were not class-based.[9]

Of course the Wilson government had no 'success' in actually governing a 'mixed society'. Indeed, the proof it provided that it was content to do no more than try to do so, and the fact that it failed so miserably in the attempt was no doubt its – and Labour's subsequent – electoral undoing. From this point on, Labour had to prove anew that conscious class identity in politics, at least as reflected in support for a mass party associated with the labour movement, was relevant to a large part of its own constituency. And it was hardly surprising that a great many of the activists who stayed with the party through this debacle (and even more who subsequently joined it in the 1970s) insisted that Labour could only recover if it adopted a broad range of policies of direct and manifest benefit to working people and also provided a new popular socialist practice so as to make it a relevant basis for political identification and distinguished itself from the other parties thereby.

There were two distinct extra-parliamentary forces in the party which con-verged to initiate the attempt to change the Labour Party after the 1970 defeat. The first was composed of left-wing trade union activists which reflected the radical stream of working-class tradition and catalysed the industrial mili-tancy of the time. The second was composed of an amalgam of old and new socialist party activists who stayed with the party or joined it in the early 1970s rather than having moved toward, or at least stayed long with, the revolutionary groups spawned in the late 1960s. They were quite distinctly not Maoists (as in Italy and France), by no means were most of them middle-class 'Poly-Trots' or organized entrists, and many of them were as 'organic' to the working class as Labour Party intellectuals had ever been; that is, their social origins were often working class; they often were active members in, or at least had close ties with, a union (increasingly white collar or public sector); and their political base lay in the working-class communities from which they had sprung or in which they participated as community, as well as Party, activists.

The passage of the British trade union movement from the deeply ingrained defensiveness of the post-1926 General Strike era (subsequently reinforced by the Cold War) to the militancy of the 1960s and 1970s took on many facets. But not least important was the effectiveness of a new alliance between the Labour and Marxist (especially Communist) left that became increasingly visible in challenging the predominance of the right-wing union bureaucracy. If anything laid the basis for the Labour Party's ending of its blacklist of 'Proscribed Or-ganizations' that symbolized the party's partial opening in the 1970s to old and new socialist currents, it was the preliminary development of this 'broad left' in the unions. And in the face of the disappointments of the Labour Government, there was a marked shift in the attitudes of union delegations at party confer-ences. Massive union votes for radical policy resolutions opposed by the party leadership from this point forward became a common phenomenon, and by 1979-80 it was to extend to sufficient support to see through the constitutional changes designed to limit the autonomy of the parliamentary party. As we shall see, the priority which even the left-wing union leadership continued to attach to securing that 'real partnership' between the union and party elites which Wilson had promised but not delivered on, set real limits to the project of the new Labour left. Nevertheless, throughout the 1970s the general impact of a changed climate in the union movement on the party was that it produced far greater tolerance for dissent than the parliamentary leadership would have been content to allow. And this was to have important implications for the role that a new generation of activists in the constituency parties was able to play.

By the end of the 1966-70 Labour Government, it was obvious that the Labour Party was in the throes of a severe membership crisis, which only the determination of union leaders to sustain the block membership affiliations of the unions helped to conceal. It is by no means clear that until the experience of the mid-to-late 1960s the Labour Party was in worse membership trouble than other European social democratic parties. Only the Swedish and Austrian parties showed an ability to maintain a significantly higher ratio of party membership to the total electorate throughout the post-war era.[10] But during the term of the first Wilson government individual party membership fell again by another 150,000. With regard to the party's membership crisis, as with its electoral crisis, it is obviously again the experience of the Labour Government in the 1960s that is crucial. As Seyd and Minkin put it: '... the greatest depletion took place in 1966-70, during the Wilson government ... A combination of social change, neglect and political disillusionment almost destroyed the Labour Party as a mass party. In terms of ward and committee attendance – and electoral work – activity was the lowest in individual memory.'[11]

This decline in Labour Parry membership certainly did not mean a decline in political activism in Britain. On the contrary there was a virtual explosion of extra-parliamentary activity at national and local level. Nor, it must be said, was the initial alienation of a new radical political generation entirely self-imposed. Studies of constituency parties through the 1950s and 1960s invariably show a marked exclusionary practice, particularly *vis-a-vis* left-wing activists. This was apart from the steady stream of expulsions that ran through the period. As John Palmer (who was later to play a critical role on the Greater London Councils' Enterprise Board) put it at a debate at the 1969 conference with Tribune MPs on the question of socialists working within the party: 'Whether you're in or out – that's largely a question of whether you're allowed to be in or out.'[12]

It was the massive defeats suffered by the Labour Party in the 1967 and 1968 local government elections which laid the basis for a new generation of activists to join and have an effect within the party. These defeats had undermined severely the domination of the old right-wing exclusionary cliques that had run many local party wards and branches on the basis of a small and passive membership, since their power had been based on the ability of the local machine to manipulate patronage and traditional class loyalties into large electoral majorities and the safe control of their councils. As David Blunkett, who was elected to Sheffield City Council while still a student in 1970, put it: 'Sheffield was more towards the traditional right while I was growing up – Roy Hattersley was on the Council – but gradually in the late 1960s began to swing to the left. Labour lost power in the council in 1968, [the first time since 1932-L.P.] , just for a year, but that year was traumatic. It began a shift in attitudes as well as politics.' [13]

A discernible drift towards joining the Labour Party could be seen in the early 1970s, especially among young community activists. The experience of the twelve Community Development Project teams set up under Home Office auspices in 1969 is often cited as indicative. Their inter-project report in 1974 revealed that they had moved from the social pathology approach that had led the Labour Government to call them into existence in 1969 towards an 'assumption that social problems arise from a fundamental conflict of interests between groups or classes in society. The problems are defined mainly in terms of inequalities in the distribution of power and the focus of change is thus on the centres of organized power (both private and public). The main tactic is organization and raising levels of consciousness. '[14] Most of them came to share Cynthia Cockburn's view that ' "community" belongs to capital': that participatory democracy if conceived 'apart from the arena of conflict between the dominant and the exploited class' would become 'a tournament between small groups more closely related to each other: within the working class and its near neighbours. . . they shake out as tenants, mothers, ratepayers, teenage youth, house owners, swimming enthusiasts and squatters. All are asked to compete and defend their special interests against each other, while the class with real power remains untouched and out of earshot.' [15] This did not mean that they gave up on the local state; on the contrary they saw it increasingly in terms of 'class struggles in the field of reproduction' and attempted to connect their local activities with the struggle to transform the Labour Party and through it the state at the national level.

There was thus a marked change through the 1970s on the part of the '1968 generation' in their attitude to working within the Labour Party and the broader labour movement. If there was one common ideological theme that constantly resurfaced among the new activists once they joined the party, it was their strong opposition to what Blunkett identified as 'the belief in paternalistic, parliamentary change' within the Labour Party

> We have to persuade those who are still living in the 1950s and 1960s that the way forward is to commit people from the bottom up in a jigsaw-a jigsaw that doesn't ignore national and international parameters, but relates to them. This can make it possible to mobilise people in every sense of the word at the local level, in their work, their community activity, and their commitment to the collective approach … This can only be done from the local level, because you do have to fire people's imagination and commitment. They do have to have an alternative vision of the

world, if you are going to overcome the obstacles. The idea that legislative paternalism is going to be successful has been discredited so many times that it is amaz-
ing that anyone in Parliament still believes it.[16]

Cynthia Cockburn found a similar attitude among the radical new activists
(which included Ken Livingstone) in the Norwood local party in Lambeth in the
early 1970s. They differed from traditional Labour practice in having 'a more
powerful and intrusive relationship with local popular organizations than other
Labour parties' and they were active in recruiting and fund-raising for propaganda. The agent told her that 'We get our councillors active quickly in new
street groups and tenant associations as they emerge.' Cockburn concluded that
'a relatively dynamic party. . . could afford to "use" local activists with a support
base in tenant associations, etc., to curb the strength of the councillors'.[17] This
orientation to politics laid the basis for the more visible 'municipal socialism' of
the 1980s, the central orientation of which, as a recent book on the experience
of the Greater London Council has articulated it, was to use the resources of the
state 'to extend effective democracy beyond the political franchise to increase
democratic control over the economy and economic policy'. The object of the
exercise was for political leaders, even, indeed especially, from within state,
not just to respond to voter expectations, but to centre their political practice
around 'raising expectations, encouraging people to make demands, to organize
and to have confidence in their dealings with the government they pay rates and
taxes for. . .' This was 'an end in itself, as well as a way of working on economic
policy' and it was premised on the notion that 'where popular initiative and
control grew, there was far more change than elsewhere'. The role of political
leadership, as articulated by these new activists, was to create a constituency
which would in turn pressure them to produce more effective policy: 'If that
pressure had increased, if in a sense that constituency had turned on them and
forced them to be much more responsive, then many of them would have felt
they had succeeded.'[18]

It is crucial to understand this orientation to politics on the part of the activists
who composed the new Labour left if we are to understand what the attempt to
change the Labour Party was all about at the national level. A myth has grown
up, sponsored in large part by Labour's parliamentary elite itself, that the internal party disputes over the accountability of MPs represented nothing other
than a battle conducted within a 'hermetically sealed train' by orthodox socialists wholly unconcerned with the issue of developing popular support outside
the party. The truth is actually otherwise. It was the new activists who recognized, on the basis of the experience with the Labour Government of the 1960s
and 1970s, that the traditional loyalties underlying Labour support were fraying
severely and that the only way to remedy this was not to attempt to reassert old
'parliamentary paternalism' of a social democratic welfare state in crisis, but to
turn the party into an agency of social and political mobilization. To be able to

practise the kind of politics which eventually yielded fruit in the new municipal socialism in the early 1980s, these activists had to engage in considerable intra-party conflict against the old guard at the local level. Their determination to see this through was a sign of their seriousness, of a recognition that a change of leadership was a condition of effecting the new kind of politics. A similar consideration determined the practice of the new Labour left at the national level.

Bennism

By the early 1970s the politics of the new local activists was still relatively inchoate and they had not yet thrown up any nationally recognized leaders or distinct organizational space within the party. If there is one single departure one can point to in this conjuncture, which more than any other signaled the clear initiation of the project of the new Labour left, it lies in a series of speeches made by Tony Benn in the early 1970s. These speeches displayed a depth of analysis and strategic perspective uncharacteristic of active politicians, but at the same time they manifestly reflected the attitudes and activities then current among a new generation of political and industrial activists. Benn had always been an iconoclast among both the traditional right and left groupings of the parliamentary party, a radical liberal rather than a radical socialist. But after his experience in the first Wilson Governments, he came to articulate the goals involved in changing the Labour Party with greater clarity (and as it turned out with greater commitment) than any leading party figure had ever done. It was not through his espousal of more state intervention or of 'clause four' that Benn had emerged as the spokesperson of these new activists. It was in his understanding of the limits of 'parliamentary paternalism', in his rejection of it, and in the alternative modes of political practice he tried to put on the agenda that he made his mark as 'the prominent voice' of the new Labour left.[19]

Benn's starting point in these speeches was the extra-parliamentary militancy of so many new activists at the time and the meaning it bore for democracy. He was convinced that this had been triggered not only by the heightened expectations produced by rising incomes and collective bargaining strength, post-war capitalist boom, but also by higher levels of education and training which had improved people's analytical capacities, and by the mass media revolution which gave people an unprecedented amount of information about current affairs and exposure to alternative analyses of events. He repeatedly pointed to 'the thousands of. . . pressure groups or action groups [that] have come into existence: community associations, amenity groups, shop steward's movements, consumer societies, educational campaigns, organizations to help the old, the homeless, the sick, the poor or under-developed societies, militant communal organizations, student power, noise abatement societies. . .' He saw in them 'a most important expression of human activity based on issues rather than traditional political loyalties, and [they] are often seen as more attractive, relevant and effective by new citizens than working through the party system'. But he recognized at the same time that this was only one side of the picture. He took very seriously what Heath's 'Selsdon Man' presaged, and was not wont to portray it as a throwback to an earlier type of conservatism, as were most Labour Party spokesmen on the left as well as the right. A decade later some of those commentators who discerned in Thatcher a new authoritarian populism would insistently criticize the new Labour left and Benn himself for failing to recognize its appeal. But as early as 1970 Benn in fact had anticipated them. He warned of an:

> alternative philosophy of government, now emerging everywhere on the right, (taking) as the starting point of its analysis that modern society depends on good management and that the cost of breakdowns in the system is so great that they really cannot be tolerated and that legislation to enforce greater and more effective discipline must now take priority over other issues. The new citizen is to be won over to an acceptance of this by promising him greater freedom from government, just as big business is to be promised lower taxes and less intervention and thus to be retained as a rich and powerful ally. But this new freedom to be enjoyed by big business means that it can then control the new citizen at the very same time as Government reduces its protection for him.[20]

This was a most serious reaction, Benn contended, to a situation where people were showing that by banding together collectively in a myriad of new organizations with clear objectives they could win surprising victories on given issues against large and centralized corporations and governments which were increasingly vulnerable to dislocations. The locus of decision-making power still remained in place in these 'lumbering monoliths', however, and the perpetuation of their power, increasingly enveloped with a philosophy of less state regulation of the economy but more discipline over an obstreperous citizenry, remained at the same time also intimately bound up with the traditional structures of parliamentarism:

> If the people have so much potential power why do those who enjoy privileges seem to be able to hold on to them so easily? The awful truth is this: that it is outdated concepts of parliamentary democracy accepted by too many political leaders in Parliament and on Local Authorities, which have been a major obstacle ... For too many modern political leaders have inherited an aristocratic view of parliament and their role in it ... This philosophy explains why political leaders often seem to be telling us two things: first-'there is nothing you have to do except vote for us'; and second-'If you do vote for us, we can solve your problems'. Both these statements are absolutely and demonstrably false ... A real leader will actually welcome the chance to give way to the forces that he has encouraged and mobilised by a process of education and persuasion. Legislation is thus the last process in a campaign for change... The people must be helped to understand that they will make little progress unless they are more politically self-reliant and are prepared

to organize with others, nearest to them where they work and where they live, to achieve what they want.[21]

It is important to remember that Benn continued to believe 'passionately' in parliamentary democracy, insisting that all the great achievements of the left had come about by pressures from below which made 'the parliamentary system serve the people rather than the vanity of the Parliamentarians'. He was convinced that 'the debate between extraparliamentary violence versus parliamentarism. . . is highly diversionary'. Where there was no route to democratic change there was a moral right to revolt, but where democratic popular organization and parliamentary change were not prohibited, socialist strategies could not pretend these were ephemeral, and if they did this reflected 'the pessimism of the ultra-left' which he refused to share because it served to aid the right in convincing the working class 'that whatever they did, they couldn't win'. A socialist government arriving in power through a coup would not forestall the necessity of having public support: 'when the crunch came... You would be easily overturned, because the subversion of international finance will be brought to bear with even more zest, with even more public support, if you came to power illegally. . . My criticism of those who call themselves revolutionaries is that they speak as though reform had been tried and failed. Reform hasn't been tried. . . I don't think there are any real revolutionaries in Britain. There may be dreamers, but there is nobody on the left who is actually planning and preparing themselves on the assumption that the transfer of power will come by revolution.' [22]

Nevertheless, Benn's central point was that if the Labour Party reacted defensively or with hostility to the new organizational activism that had emerged outside the party, the party would become obsolescent. 'I see it as our business so to reconstruct the Labour Party so that a Labour government will never rule again but will try to create the conditions under which it is able to act as the natural partner of a people, who really mean something more than we thought they did, when they ask for self-government.' [23] If most of the recent progressive forces had developed outside the party this had much to do with the fact that the party's 'internal democracy is also riddled with the same aristocratic ideas as deface our national democracy'. He articulated at this time many of the dimensions of reform that later became so familiar: the selection process for parliamentary candidates, the electoral base of the Leader and Deputy Leader, the accountability of Cabinet members, MPs, local Labour Groups and Councillors, and trade union delegations. It was 'not on narrow and legalistic constitutional grounds' that these issues had to be taken up, but in terms of their contribution to fostering a much broader and profound change in the party's orientation.

Tony Benn had by the early 1970s convinced himself, and certainly convinced many of those who came into the party after having rejected it in the 1960s, that 'the public will become very interested if they think we are ready to criticise our-

selves and really want to make ourselves and British politics more democratic',
and if it initiated 'a period of intense public discussion about the nature of
Parliamentary democracy and the nature of Party democracy. . . If it is thought
they are too difficult, or too dangerous or too divisive to embark on this debate
I fear we shall miss a great opportunity.' If the party just devoted itself to 'more
research to produce detailed policies which will win back public confidence in
our capacity to run a modified capitalism', it would entirely mistake the reasons it lost the 1970 election. This defeat was very largely bound up, in his view,
with the party's concentration 'on the role of Government to the exclusion of
the part that the people themselves could play in solving their own problems'.
When Benn coined the phrase in 1972 'a fundamental shift in the balance of
wealth and power in favour of working people and their families' he was in his
own mind putting the stress on power and meant by it much more than a shift
in power from capital to the state. With a characteristic optimism that inspired
many new activists but maddened many others, Benn believed that the debate he
was calling for 'is more likely to unite than divide the party – by helping it to see
its way forward to a new broader interpretation of modern popular democratic
socialism'. But he admitted that whether he was right or wrong in this judgement would depend on whether the themes the new Labour left were trying to
develop would 'command general support in the movement' and he warned
that if the party did not face the issue of democracy directly it would find itself
in a situation where other less salient differences within the party and the unions
would emerge and further weaken people's confidence in the Labour Party and
'the trend to the right would continue'. [24]

It can readily be seen that the new Labour left differed in many ways from
traditional left Labourism. The old Labour left was itself a product of the victory of 1945 and took largely for granted the near majoritarian (always over 40
per cent) electoral support that sustained the party right through the defeats
of the 1950s. The new Labour left, by contrast, was a product of the electoral
and membership crisis that surfaced during the 1964-70 Labour Governments.
Bevanism was mainly a parliamentary tendency that drew support from the
old class identities and socialist consciousnesses in the constituencies; Bennism
was more an expression of the emergence of a new generation of community
activists that understood that class identity and socialist consciousness had to
be reconstructed. The Bevanites' socialism was epitomised by 'parliamentary
paternalism': it wanted to extend the scope of nationalization and the welfare
state via legislative enactment and benign bureaucratic administration: and it
looked to the party conference as a means of sustaining that minority group of
parliamentarians who would defend such an orientation at Westminster. The
new Labour left's socialism was inflected towards the participationism of 1968:
it wanted to extend the public sphere but to the end of deploying the resources
of the state to empower people in their local and industrial communities and in

their pursuit of 'issue politics'; and it looked to the party conference as a means, not only of equipping socialist parliamentarians with socialist policies at Westminster, but of securing the accountability of parliamentarians to party activists and even more broadly of securing a redefinition of the general role of party and parliamentary political leadership.

The old and new lefts also had different understandings of class and class struggle and the meaning it bore for party and state. The old left saw the working class in more homogeneous terms and its party political project depended on a displacement of the stultifying right-wing union bureaucracy's representation of that class in the party and its replacement by left-wing union leaders who would combine with the Bevanites in Parliament to challenge the revisionists' dominance over the party. The new left saw the working class as anything but homogeneous, and although it also depended on the block vote of left-wing union delegations at party conference, its party political project involved also trying to secure space for autonomous women's and blacks' representation in the party as well as pushing for the establishment of workplace party branches. (This was in large part a generational difference, but not entirely so: the tensions that existed between the new left activists in the party and Militant had much to do with the latters' orthodox view of the homogeneity of the class and its hostility to autonomous women's and blacks' representation.) As for the relationship between class struggle and the state, a divergence in orientations was no less remarkable. Bevan's famous last speech in the House of Commons (which Harold Wilson was fond of quoting) was a lament on the difficulty of persuading working people to make sacrifices so that state economic planning might lay the basis for economic growth, a lament that saw industrial militancy as a syndicalist expression of a failure of the needs of working people to be expressed in Parliament. The new Labour left tended to look at industrial militancy more from the perspective of its potentiality for an empowerment of workers at the point of production and in the making of industrial policy. This is why Benn's encouragement (in his brief and beleagured tenure as Minister of Industry in 1974-5) of workers' co-ops and the Lucas Aerospace workers' alternate production plan became a beacon for the new Labour left and the model for industrial policy at the GLC in the 1980s.

The forces of resistance and the limits of change

It is one thing for socialists to define and articulate a project for socialist renewal; it is another thing to construct such a project and realize it. And in the latter respect the evolution and the fate of the new Labour left inevitably needs to be understood in terms of the dialectic between its goals and the resistance it faced, not only from those who had ruled the party through the 1950s and 1960s and continued to do so in the 1970s despite their terrible failure in office, but from the old left as well, whose own role in the party hardly faded from the scene in the 1970s but rather became more and more interwoven with the struggle on both sides.

As before, when the parliamentary party went over to Her Majesty's Official Opposition with their tails between their legs (and with only the partial exception of 1931), the leadership 'team' emerged largely intact and largely unchastened and unchanged by their electoral defeat. Their political vision right through the 1970s and into the 1980s remained confined to the issue of obtaining trade union wage restraint to smooth a Keynesian management of a capitalist economy under the aegis of an elitist parliamentarism. It was a leadership that remained not only content to try to govern in this fashion but determined to do so. This mentality was perhaps best epitomized by Anthony Crosland, who as the theoretical author of the revisionism of the 1950s was the one leading Labour figure who could really claim any distinction as a strategic and economic thinker. In a Fabian lecture in 1970. he drew an explicit contrast between 'the position today' and the 1950s when in light of full employment and the welfare state 'a fundamental rethinking was required'. There was no need for another such departure in the 1970s, he claimed, 'and the evidence is the lack of any furious ideological ferment within the party'. This astonishing lack of awareness and comprehension of what was already taking place within the party, let alone outside it, was matched by an equal blindness to the deep contradictions that had beset modern capitalism and which were on the verge of ushering in an end to the post-war boom. Even by 1974, when Crosland acknowledged a revival of Marxist economic analysis and prescription (which he insisted, however, was only confined to Britain), he was still convinced that 'if we examine the western world as a whole we cannot detect signs of a new and fundamental crisis. . . full employment is maintained; economic growth continues; world trade expands. . .' The 'one possible exception' to this was Britain, and if this now made him take note of the 'Marxist revival' there, it only confirmed its general irrelevance. This explains the obsession of the old revisionists with Common Market entry. It derived from their belief that riding on the coat-tails of an allegedly crisis-free European capitalism would be a political as well as economic prophylactic for continuing to govern Britain along the lines 'of a clear commitment to the agreed ideals of the 1950s'.[25]

The very success that the National Executive (increasingly reflecting in its composition a shift to both the old and new left among constituency and union activists) had in advancing radical economic policies at party conferences in the early 1970s reflected the enormous vacuum in economic thinking among the parliamentary leadership. Yet it is important to stress that in so far as this turn to the left is understood only in terms of policies that promised a greater extension of the state's role in the economy, this was not in itself a new phenomenon nor did it address the severity of the party's crisis. The common view that the really significant departure from the norm for the Labour Party in the 1970s concerned the development of such policies is flawed. It was certainly the most visible; it was where the left initially made most inroads amidst the very radical rhetoric that could be heard on all sides at party conferences, but it was not the most salient aspect of what was just then emerging as a challenge to party tradition. The heady debates among socialist economists concerning the ambiguous nature of Planning Agreements, the National Enterprise Board and the import and exchange controls advanced under the Alternative Economic Strategy missed the main point. For in so far as the policy changes were directed at merely electing a Labour Government to carry them through from on high, they portended in themselves little indeed. For they did not by themselves address the central political question of the structural changes in party and parliamentary politics, as well as in the ideological orientations of the leadership, that could open the means to their implementation. The main question was not only whether a Labour Government would have either the will or the courage to go ahead with the enunciated policy once it became clear what else it would involve, but how they could transform their own managerialist practices to mobilizing ones so as to retain their popular mandate even if they could be elected on this basis.

The parliamentary leadership discovered after 1970 that they no longer had the same unchallenged initiative in policy formation within the party as they had in the early 1 960s, but they certainly retained the veto power that went with the continuing independence of the parliamentary party and the strength of its appeal to party unity on narrow electoralist grounds. Harold Lever, who was to play an important role in the 1970s in articulating the 'realistic' policy posture of the parliamentary leadership in the face of the radical policies being advanced by NEC and the conference, perhaps expressed the parliamentary leadership's philosophy most clearly:

> Clause four or no clause four, Labour's leadership plainly believes in a mixed economy,... [it] knows as well as any businessman that an engine which runs on profit cannot be made to run faster without extra fuel ... For their part, businessmen should show less sensitivity and more sense. It is time they realized that a ringing political slogan is often used as a sop to party diehards or as an anaesthetic while doctrinal surgery is being carried out.[26]

It was precisely for this reason that it was the bringing the question of the adequacy of the vehicle, not just the adequacy of the policy on to the Labour Party's agenda, that stamped the new Labour left with a truly original and strategically salient mark. By the late 1960s a number of constituency parties were already submitting resolutions and amendments to Labour Party conferences related to this question. In 1968 there was one calling for a constitutional commission, whose mandate for overcoming the popular 'frustration and apathy to such an extent that democracy itself is endangered' ought to include such changes to encourage full participation in the party by its members as a wider mechanism for the election of the Leader. Another called for disciplinary measures against MPs who 'act against the principles and policies determined by National Conference'. [27] The Wilson Government's consistent flaunting of conference decisions could not but be a central issue at this time. But it was remarkable how many of the speeches at conferences at this time went beyond mere recrimination and raised more strategic concerns. One CLP delegate argued: 'How can we go to the pressure groups and say, "If you join us perhaps we can say to you that your policies will be accepted and implemented?" We cannot.' Unless the participation that had been strangled in the party was renewed, the party itself was no more than an ineffectual pressure group. She insisted that the leadership should not insult the delegates by going back to the old argument about day-to-day decisions having to be made by parliamentary representatives: the delegates from the constituency parties and the trade unions operated and well understood the relationship between them and their Labour Groups, GMCs, and union executives. Jack Jones, the leader of Britain's largest union, the TGWU went further. He argued that if the Party's view of socialism were to be made relevant to 'the things that were worrying ordinary people today' this involved going back to the social ownership of the means of production, distribution and exchange as 'the essential base – and I mean Clause Four'. But 'in order to achieve that we have got to start to build genuine democracy in Britain instead of the sham democracy which exists at the present time. . . we have a great barrier of custom and practice in our Parliament which acts as a keep out notice to the man in the street and too many Parliamentarians love that. . . For too long the idea has been that an MP was just a representative, and not a delegate. That idea had been reinforced with such a snobbish view that decisions have been the exclusive prerogative of a few, and in so many cases the MP has not even been a representative.' The issue, he insisted, was not only that of eliminating the House of Lords and making MPs accountable to CLPs: to meet the demands that citizens' groups by the dozens were making on the corridors of power, it would be necessary to set up such things as 'representative conferences' through which MPs would be required continually to consult with community organizations.[28]

Given the extent of the underlying crisis, the imperative condition for the success of the new Labour left's strategy was to win over the party quickly so that the kind of outward looking mobilization could be inaugurated. Where this was accomplished in local parties and in the unions, significant changes in the representative role of local councillors and union officials was registered, although their policies and mobilizing capacities were inevitably highly constrained in so far as a transformation of the party at the national level did not take place. But such a rapid turnabout in the orientation of the parliamentary party was simply not on the cards. The intransigence of the 'parliamentary paternalists' could not defeat the new Labour left, but it could turn its struggle inward and thus deny its potential for effecting the broader strategy it had articulated. Despite the difference in the strategic orientation of the new Labour left from the old, the dilemma outlined by the May Day Manifesto still obtained. The problem is simply stated. The new Labour left, with substantial and growing support in the extra-parliamentary party, was trying to get its leadership to develop a socialist strategy, not only in terms of programme but of mobilization. But the preponderant part of the leadership was not interested in developing a socialist strategy; it did not believe in it; it considered it irrelevant, or actually harmful, to the Labour Party's and to Britain's problems. Roy Jenkins told the party conference in the early 1970s that 'socialism is just a slogan'. One local councillor (later an MP closely associated with Benn) retorted that missed the very point that the new activists were trying to make: there was 'a crying need' for the party 'to translate the abstractions of economic control into concepts that people can understand. . . and to translate them in such a way that makes them not just moonshine, but something which is eminently and imminently practical' .[29] The dilemma for the new Labour left, however, was how it could turn the party into a socialist party without purging itself of its leadership – without lopping off its own head, so to speak. This dilemma was reinforced as the PLP, even after the shift to the left in the extra-parliamentary party became unmistakably clear, and even while the Tribune Group of MPs (composed of both old and new left figures) grew to upwards of 70 members, brazenly continued to elect a shadow cabinet dominated by the centre-right through the 1970s and into the 1980s. It was not the fetishization of intra-party democracy, but the attempt to provide an answer to this dilemma that led to the pressures for constitutional reform.

And in this respect, the National Executive of the party, and the union-dominated Conference Arrangements Committee, was much less ready to be moved than on radical policy resolutions. The issue of constitutional reform was largely kept off the agenda of the party conference in the early 1970s and thereafter any resolution of it was postponed until after the 1979 election. A critical role in this respect was played by the old parliamentary left itself, above all by its leading spokesman, Michael Foot. The main thrust of most of the Tribune MPs after the 1970 election defeat was to raise again the issue of public ownership. They returned, in other words, to reviving the terms of the stale debate over more or less nationalization. Michael Foot wrote that 'what is needed is a strong shift leftwards... the Party in Parliament ought to start that process, but if it won't the party conference will have to do it for them.[30] But in so far as the Tribune MPs were determined to make the key issue that of more public ownership, the question was not about the numbers of firms targeted for public ownership in conference resolutions, but of how Foot's promise that the conference would force the PLP to 'do it' could be realized.

A Tribune Group pamphlet in 1972 did take up the issue of the accountability of Labour representatives at all levels '[31] but Foot's name was conspicuous by its absence from the list of 38 MPs who endorsed the pamphlet. Indeed, Foot was already in the process of acting as a buffer for the parliamentary leadership. He strongly opposed an inquest after 1970 into the mistakes of the Labour Government. As he explained in 1972: 'It was a dangerous moment. The Left within the Labour Party could have demanded a grand inquest on all the delinquencies of 1964-70, could have mounted a furious attack on the leadership'.[32] From 1972, when he became Shadow Leader of the House and was elected to the NEC at the top of the constituency section, his role became that of recementing the frayed bonds of trust among and between the parliamentary and trade union elites. His primary goal was to avoid dissension within the party so as to present a united parliamentary face against Heath's Government, which he saw then in much the same terms as he later saw Thatcher's, as the 'most hard-faced Conservative Government since Neville Chamberlain', rather than as Benn saw it, as presaging a far more populist and hence dangerous new conservatism. The overarching concern of Foot (and later, of his annointed successor, Kinnock) with party unity determined that he would play a dampening and ultimately oppositional role to the forces trying to change the party. In so far as his shadow cabinet parliamentary colleagues were as opposed to the radical economic policies as they were to broader changes in the party, the logic of his position led him by 1973 to supporting Wilson in making as vague as possible the leadership's commitments to party conference in this regard. A year later, after Labour had stumbled back into office in the wake of Heath's confrontation with the unions, he came to play a key role in the Cabinet against Benn's attempt to mobilize popular support for and implement those policies as Minister of Industry. Much of this took place behind the scenes in closed NEC and cabinet meetings, however, and this contributed to Foot's retaining the loyalty of many constituency party activists. The centre-right parliamentarians could not obtain such support on their own; Foot was a critical intermediary, therefore, and the role he played was of real consequence to slowing the progress of the new Labour left in the extra-parliamentary party.

Of even greater consequence was the fact that Foot enjoyed the support of, and in turn had a strong political influence on, the left-wing union leadership. Despite the shift to the left in the unions, the actual political meaning of this for the Labour Party remained almost as ambiguous in socialist terms as the political meaning of the party's vast trade union membership had ever been. The number of indirectly affiliated union members to the party had doubled from 2,500,000 to almost 5 million with the 1945 Government's introduction of the provision for trade unionists having individually to 'contract out' of paying a political levy as part of their dues. It then stayed virtually constant right through to the mid-1970s hovering around five-and-a-half million (thereafter rising to near six million as union membership in the late 1970s grew apace). But while this made the union financial clout in the party and their block votes at party conferences ever more important, this still only reflected the steadiness of the unions' organizational link with the party and concealed any trends in trade union membership support for or activity in the party. In the late 1960s, it was common to see reports of branches voting to disaffiliate from the party, which were always explained in terms of the actions of the Labour Government. Union journals and conferences were replete with appeals from leaders to their members and branches not to show their displeasure in this negative fashion. They tried to protect Labour by calling for workers to vote for it and above all by continuing to finance the party, but they entered into conflict with the Labour Government through 'direct action' industrial militancy. It was a mark of their political desperation.

Some of the union's anger was directed at trade union-sponsored MPs who had supported the Government's policies, and, as we have seen, a deeper concern with the nature of parliamentary representation was raised at this time by Jack Jones. Although this was indeed a portent of the eventual support the left-wing unions were to give to the constitutional changes, the fact that this support took until after the 1979 election defeat to materialize in sufficient numbers to see the reforms through was taken by many on the new Labour left as a sad indication of just how slowly the old union cart horse moves. But the main reason for this, in fact, was that democratization never really stood at the forefront of even the left-wing union's political approach to resolving their difficulties with the party leadership. They saw the main way forward primarily in terms of insisting on a more effective 'elite accommodation' between the industrial and parliamentary leadership. This insistence, most strongly voiced by Jack Jones himself, came to be institutionalized in the 'social contract' and in the creation in January 1972 of the TUC-Labour Party Liaison Committee which became from then on the effective final arbiter of party policy (although, as the Labour Government of 1974-79 showed, the effective final arbiter of Labour Government policy remained the Treasury). It was also this insistence which also gave Michael Foot his new prominence in the Labour leadership. Foot's retention of the politically crucial role of intermediary with the left union leadership into the 1980s, alongside the high personal regard for him in the constituencies, proved crucial to slowing, and ultimately to defeating, the attempt to change the Labour Party.

There were two further elements that played an important role in the complex array of forces that determined this outcome. One of these was located deep in the bowels of the party organization – its permanent officials; the other was external to the party but had a constant impact upon it – the British media. The new Labour left's strategy of opening the party to new currents of community and issue politics and turning it outward toward socialist education and mobilization obviously required a major reform of party organization. This especially applied to the role of its agents and regional organizers who usually played a policing role against left-wing influence in the constituencies. Yet despite the NEC's selection of General Secretaries after 1972 who were not only close to the Tribune left, but broadly sympathetic with the new Labour left's project, they proved unable to escape the traditional role of the General Secretary as a protective buffer between the party conference and the parliamentary leadership. This involved calling for tolerance on all sides, but increasingly striving for a form of party unity that would maintain stability as far as possible. This meant deflecting the thrust of constitutional change, but no less important it also meant setting aside any serious consideration of the sweeping changes that were needed in the party's organization. While many of the most creative new left activists increasingly found employment with left-led Labour Councils or unions, the one place where they were most needed for the change in the party to succeed – in the party's national organization – was the place where they were least likely to be hired. To have done so would have inflamed even further the party leadership. And as the centre-right parliamentarians responded to challenges in the constituencies to deselect anti-socialist MPs with a vociferous campaign against alleged 'extremists' in the party, the General Secretaries were drawn into appeasing this by overseeing right-wing inspired party inquiries into Militant's operation as an organized entrist group in the party.

Militant was not the main source of the intra-party conflict and everyone knew it. It was an easy target, as a sectarian cadre organization, which the right in the party, and increasingly the forces that grouped around Foot, employed to taint the much broader and non-sectarian new Labour left in the party. Roy Hattersley was, for once, candid about this at the climax of the intra-party crisis in 1981: 'The problem is not Militant, about whom we always talk, because Militant is so easily identifiable and so unpleasant that most people are prepared to squash it. . . the problem is those organizations which talk the language of democratic socialism'. [33] The National Executive after 1970 tried to establish a more tolerant and open party to socialist ideas and currents, but their attempt to mollify the right in the party by going along with the attack on Militant, had the effect of fanning the flames, as the right and their supporters in the media, constantly upped the ante to attack radical local government leaders, the advocates of feminist reforms and of black sections in the party, let alone Marxists of any stripe in the party, as 'kindred pestilences' (Michael Foot's own unfortunate phrase).[34] In the name of party unity against the capitalist forces of reaction, the forces of party conservatism and of compromise fed the media in creating a powerful public impression that the main source of anti-democratic pressures in Britain lay inside the Labour Party. What this amounted to was a decade-long exercise in establishing the illegitimacy, not only of Militant, but of the democratic aspirations and thrust of the new Labour left.

The role of the media had hardly been ignored by the new Labour left, especially by Benn, who took the view as early as 1973 that the 'bias of the media against working people' could no longer be ignored by the party leadership as a long-term strategic issue.[35] The main point was not about the media's treatment of party policies and Labour leaders had enough access to the media so they 'are able to look after themselves'. Labour's problem with the media indeed went much deeper and ultimately rested on the fact that the media closed off the possibility of revealing what broad popular support might exist or be developed for the social forces that underlay radical change. 'The greatest complaint against the media is that its power is used to dominate the community, that it excludes ordinary people and that it is not accountable in any way, save the crude test of market success. The main victims are the trade unions whose motives are regularly distorted, whose members are insulted and ignored, and who are presented in a way that denies them the opportunity to describe their work and interests properly.' Government censorship would be 'totally wrong and unacceptable'; and so would industrial action 'arbitrarily exercised by anyone in the production chain who took exception to something that was being printed and transmitted'. What he proposed was that the unions should demand a Code of Conduct be agreed with the broadcasting media for equality of treatment in the handling of industrial disputes and they should demand that the TUC be allocated a certain number of hours per year, like the parties, to present their policies and explain the position of member unions. More fundamentally, unions in the media, who concentrated too narrowly on the traditional issues of collective bargaining, ought to be encouraged to form a federation and bargain for the establishment in each newspaper or broadcasting unit of a council, elected by the whole labour force, which would be responsible for receiving, discussing and issuing published reports on complaints against bias or victimization of journalists for what they had said or written. This would not encumber the daily process of producing news, but 'accountability afterwards is perfectly practicable and would influence future action'. It was a typical 'Bennite' proposal, concentrating less on what a Labour Government could do legislatively to counter media bias, but on what it could do to encourage those directly involved to act in a political and strategic way themselves.

For a party with a very different leadership and with less of an institutionalized division of labour between political and industrial action, this kind of thinking might have been very potent strategically. For the Labour Party, it ran directly against the grain, and was in fact used opportunistically by the centre-right Labour parliamentarians to discredit Benn. Benn was certainly highly media-conscious – he has always seemed to believe that the most dangerous thing for his style of political leadership was to be ignored by the press. This may have been a fatal error, since by the early 1970s the media already began treating 'Bennism' as a metaphor not only for a mendacious ultra-leftism, but for a 'loony' brand thereof: 'Benn became a four-letter word which fitted comfortably into a single column in the largest type-face and symbolised the leftward shift in the party. "Bennery" was coined and assumed to be synonymous with demogoguery, populism, public ownership, syndicalism and workers' control. Yet the prejudicial approach toward his often tentative, exploratory, restless views blinded many to what he was seeking.' [36] The British press not only demonstrated in this respect its partisan guardianship of a narrow interpretation of parliamentary democracy and its extreme defensiveness against Benn's criticisms of the systemic structural biases of the media. It also showed that when it came to discrediting prominent political dissidents – and especially those who were 'traitors to their class' – by labelling them as psychologically unstable, they could teach the Soviets a thing or two. Holding the 'fool' up to public ridicule has always been an effective alternative means of exclusion to that of institutional incarceration. The social democrats in the parliamentary party not only played up to this grotesque fault in the primary organs of opinion formation – they actually fed it and encouraged it, using their close relations with mainstream journalists as a means of demonstrating the inherent unpopularity of the new Labour left's ideas and thus bringing pressure on the party to resist and defeat them. Yet at the same time their hands trembled, as they opened their copies of *The Times* or even *The Guardian*, lest they discover another example of what Benn had allegedly said the night before that might have tarnished their respectability. ('Was Benn speaking for the Labour Party?' was the question the press was always implicitly and often explicitly asking.) Their solution to this contradiction was increasingly to use the media as a powerful weapon on their side in the intra-party debate. Unless 'Bennery' was defeated, the party would also suffer the same fate of not being treated seriously by received opinion. As is often the case with contradictions, this produced less a resolution of the problem (since 'Bennism' did have a strong base in the party) than a vicious circle.

But it also posed a real contradiction for Benn, and given his role as the most prominent spokesperson of the new Labour left, for the whole project of changing the Labour Party. He kept an annual tally of the hundreds of meetings at which he spoke, and it seemed that he partly judged his success as a politician in terms of how extensively his accompanying press releases were taken up by the media nationally. This was consistent with the role of motivator and educator, rather than legislator and decision-maker, that he now ascribed to political leadership. Many on the new Labour left were not uncritical of this approach, feeling that he might well spend less time delivering speeches and preparing press releases and more time organizing. It was indeed remarkable that he did not through the 1970s try to establish around himself a disciplined intra-party faction. He still did not join the Tribune Group (although they put him on their slate for the PLP's Shadow Cabinet elections from 1970 onwards), and even when the Campaign for Labour Party Democracy formed in 1973, he kept aloof

from it. Given that he was burning his bridges with most of the PLP by the positions he was taking, and that Foot was emerging as the trade union voice in the
party hierarchy, it is ironic indeed that a sizeable proportion of the old left in the
party fell in with and fed media cynicism about Benn's motivations, ascribing
them to personal ambition alone – a transparent bid for the party leadership.
This especially applies to Foot, who increasingly insisted on treating 'Bennism'
almost exclusively in this light, although he had always been scathingly dismiss-
ive of the same charges when they were earlier made against Bevan.

In fact, Benn did remarkably little to trim his sails so as to increase his accept-
ability to the majority of MPs (wherein the choice of the Leader resided until
1981) or even to the majority of union leaders, despite the fact that the unions,
together with the MPs, were sure to dominate any electoral college for leadership
election of the kind he had advanced as early as 1971. (Addressing the 1972 TUC
congress, he had insisted the unions were insufficiently democratic themselves;
had made no serious effort to explain their work even to the wives and families
of union members, let alone to the broader public; and failed to support enough
other movements of legitimate protest by women, the poor and others. All this
allowed them to be portrayed as if they 'actively favoured the conservative philosophy of acquisitiveness'. Above all, Benn repeatedly challenged the unions to
stop waiting for Labour Governments to install industrial democracy and make
this the centre-piece of collective bargaining, including using the strike weapon
to achieve it.[37]) For Benn to have become leader on the basis of the kind of principles he was espousing and the new forces he was encouraging would indeed
have given him a mandate for radical transformation of the party. As attached
to this goal, on which he never wavered, his leadership ambitions were hardly to
his discredit – indeed realizing this ambition probably constituted one crucial
ingredient for altering the unfavourable odds against a successful attempt to
change the party. The fact that most of his parliamentary colleagues sought to
demean what he was saying and doing by constantly pointing to his leadership
aspirations may say more about their own narrow conception of Labour Party
politics as a personality contest.

It was in the context of this complex array of pressures against change that
party activists increasingly turned towards supporting the Campaign for Labour
Party Democracy's attempt to concentrate the intra-party forces for change
around winning precise constitutional reforms designed to break the hold of the
centre-right parliamentarians over the party. (The catalyst for the formation of
the CLPD by an initially small group of activists was Wilson's veto of the NEC's
decision in 1973 to specify in the party manifesto that twenty leading manufacturing companies, one of the major banks, and two or three leading insurance
companies would be brought into the public domain under the aegis of the
NEB. The specification of 25 companies was not aimed at the electorate, but at
the leadership, and seen as means of requiring them to comply with the general

direction of policy already established by the party conference. Wilson's veto presaged for many activists the trajectory of the Labour Government elected in 1974, and compounded their discomfort at slogging away through two election campaigns in a year for sitting MPs who were in no sense representative of the activists' own political orientations.) During the course of the 1974-79 Government, the activists did not abandon the party in the wake of the Government's showing itself to be primarily accountable to the Treasury and the IMF and to anonymous international financial markets. Rather they mobilized behind the CLPD's proposals for constitutional change, while continuing their work at the local level.

Constituency delegates were traditionally an 'amorphous mass' at party conference and trade union delegates generally met only with their own delegations to decide how they would cast their block votes. By 1979, the CLPD had effected a dramatic change in this pattern both by lobbying constituencies in advance of the conference in relation to the resolutions they advanced, and by bringing union and constituency delegates together at massive meetings on the eve of conference to plan tactics to get those resolutions on the agenda and to secure their passage in the face of opposition from the platform. There is no doubt that most activists saw the constitutional reforms in instrumental terms: taking the election of the leader and deputy leader out of the exclusive hands of MPs and passing it to the party conference would, they expected, mean that Foot and Benn would take the leadership; requiring a competitive reselection process for MPs in their constituencies would at least force MPs generally to be more mindful of their activists' political goals. But the increasing sense of urgency with which they organized to accomplish this, reflected their recognition that the issue of the autonomy of parliamentarians was not just about whether they were free to make decisions inside the state. It was at the same time about the autonomy the Labour leadership's vaunted position of 'government' at the pinnacle of the state gave them from the task of renewing class identity and undertaking socialist mobilization in the face of an ever more visible and explicit right-wing populist threat. Despite the fact that Labour came to office in 1974 with less than 40 per cent of the vote (37 per cent in the February election and 39 per cent in October) for the first time since the 1920s, Wilson had proclaimed that his third and fourth victories in five successive elections proved that 'Labour is now the natural party of Government.' Most party activists had been far less triumphalist in 1974, and as Labour's electoral fate in 1979 and afterwards was foreshadowed in opinion poll findings and local election defeats during the term of this Government, they appeared ever more strongly placed to force a resolution of the challenge to the party which the new Labour left had raised.

Breaking the Mould?

'Breaking the mould': this was a central motif of political discourse as Britain entered the 1980s. Paradoxically, it applied least of all to the party from which the term itself emanated. The Social Democratic Party which emerged in 1981 out of the Labour Party's conflicts primarily represented an attempt to shift the practices which had actually dominated the Conservative and Labour parties for decades towards the institutional terrain of a new party of the centre, once it became apparent that the two major parties were abandoning, or at least finding it increasingly difficult to sustain, their old political way of life. Thus even if the creation of a new party with some immediate electoral appeal amidst massive media support was itself novel, what this party represented programmatically and ideologically was not a new but a very old political practice.

In so far as 'breaking the mould' was – beyond the most superficial conceptions – the object of party politics, developments in the Conservative and Labour parties really reflected this. Mrs Thatcher's 'market populism' had catalyzed a back-bench, upper-middle class revolt in the Tory party against the Keynesianism and corporatism to which the Heath Government had quickly attempted to return after its own brief flirtation with the individualist 'Selsdon Man' in 1970. The objects of this revolt were almost as much the established Tory defenders of the welfare state, corporatist industrial relations, and Foreign Office pragmatism as anyone else. The fact that Edward Heath's (temporary) individualist appeal in 1970 and the more committed and virulent Thatcherite 'market populist' appeal in 1979 managed to win support among the skilled working class already represented a more decisive rupture with pre-existing electoral and ideological patterns than anything that the SDP subsequently attempted or achieved.

But, as we have seen, the crisis of Keynesianism and corporatism that produced Thatcherism had also produced another challenge to the mould of British politics. Immediately after the Labour Government's defeat in 1979, the Labour Party finally had the great debate on democracy that Benn and the new Labour left had called for almost a decade before. The Labour Party now turned inward on itself to fight a battle over the very meaning of socialism and democracy and posed the question, as it had never been posed with such force before in the party's history, of whether a social democratic working-class party like Labour could be adapted into becoming a party directed towards socialist mobilization and change.

Although it scarcely seems credible today, it was only some six years ago that there was a widespread impression inside Britain and out, and ranging over the whole political spectrum, that something approaching a fundamental transformation of the Labour Parry was in train. The CLPD's organizing efforts and the parliamentary leadership's cynical manipulation of union loyalties to obtain their support for years of wage restraint, finally yielded sufficient support for the constitutional reforms to have them carried through at party conferences in 1980 and 1981. A book on *The Battle for the Labour Party*, published shortly after the 1981 party conference, began with these words: 'The Labour Party has undergone cataclysmic change. The power of the traditional leadership has been broken.'[38] Robert McKenzie, in his last published article before his death, returned to his defence of the British constitution with a new sense of urgency, and criticized the party leadership for paying lip service to the ideal of intra-party democracy and failing to make it clear 'that political parties are unique among political organizations in that their leaders must escape control of their followers if they are to fulfill their broader role in the political community'.[39] Those who looked at the question of parliamentary representation from the point of view of the management of the existing social order, and who obfuscated the dominance of capital amidst the 'other interest group volitions and demands' a government had to balance apart from those of its own party activists, were aghast at the rather moderate constitutional reforms the party had effected. Those who looked at it from the point of view of whether socialists could turn the Labour Party towards trying to mobilize a majority constituency in favour of a transition to socialism and marry parliamentary representation with such mobilization so as to effect this peacefully, took heart.

To be sure, observers on the left were generally more sober regarding what had transpired in the Labour Party. They recognized that most social democratic parties (and many bourgeois parties) elected their leaders at conference and required a competitive reselection process for sitting parliamentarians. What mattered was whether the inauguration of these reforms in the Labour Party would sustain the momentum of the new Labour left so that its much broader strategic perspective, as we have outlined it above, now became dominant in the party. This was still to be tested in Benn's campaign for the deputy leadership under the new electoral college in 1981; in the fate of further proposals for constitutional reform being advanced to open space for enhanced women's and blacks' representation in the party; in the national party's degree of support for the new experiments in municipal socialism; above all, in the kind of leadership they provided for extra-parliamentary struggles against Thatcherism. But it was certainly striking how many on the British left now felt the need to reassess long-standing views on the possibility of changing the party. Ralph Miliband's position perhaps epitomized the views of socialists who had right through the rise of the new Labour left in the 1970s still thought, as he had, that the 'hope of the left to transform the Labour Party was illusory, and that far from representing a short cut to the creation of a mass socialist party in Britain (which has never existed), it was in fact a dead end in which British socialists had been trapped for many decades – in fact since the Labour Party came into being'. Writing in 1983, he was still 'far from convinced that I was mistaken ... on the most optimistic expectations [the new activists] have a long way to go, with many obstacles in their way. But it is obvious that I underestimated how great was the challenge which the new activists would be able to pose to their leaders; and how limited would be the capacity of those leaders to surmount the challenge. I now take it that the question whether the activists can push matters further and achieve the conquest of the Labour Party is more open than I thought."[40]

It was in fact less open than he, and many others, thought. The deep intransigence of the bulk of the party leadership even to having the debate, let alone to seriously trying to refashion Labour's conventional interpretation of democracy, proved to be the determining factor in ensuring that the intra-party debate on democracy (which was itself unstoppable) produced not unity but continuing division and abrasiveness on all sides. It had taken over ten years of struggle by the new Labour left to effect two quite moderate constitutional changes. By this time Thatcher was in power and was effecting a counter-revolution against the welfare state. And by this time, as well, before the ink was even dry on Labour's constitutional changes, a counter-revolution was in effect in the party led by those still convinced that reproducing Labour's traditional image as an alternative parliamentary 'team' was the way to restore its ever more severe electoral problems. The balance in the party had temporarily shifted far enough to the left to yield the new Labour left with a momentary victory. But it had not shifted far enough to sustain their momentum in the face of both of these counter-revolutions.

This is not to say that those who came to recognize the novelty and significance of the new Labour left's challenge were mistaken in doing so. Those who, in the debates of the early 1980s, still insisted on the impossibility of changing the Labour Party were indeed proved correct. But the reasons for this did not primarily lie, as for instance David Coates now tended to insist, on the new Labour left reflecting 'the traditional limits of Left Labourism[41] . On the contrary, what was so remarkable about the new Labour left, as I have tried to show in this essay, was that in important respects it transcended those limits. On the other hand, the limits of the old Labour left, epitomized by Foot, and of the limits of the union leadership, who still gave top priority to striking a better partnership with the leadership 'next time', were indeed crucial in the defeat of the attempt to change the party. Foot's election as Leader by the PLP in 1980 (Callaghan's resignation being timed to avoid the possibility of Benn being elected when the new electoral college came into force) reflected a recognition on the part of enough MPs that only a Leader traditionally associated with the parliamentary left could command sufficient support in the unions and constituencies to contain and deflect the new Labour left's momentum. This entailed real costs in policy terms for the centre-right parliamentarians, and those who left to form the SDP were not prepared to sustain these costs, since Foot's occupancy of the leadership at least guaranteed that Party policy would finally incorporate unilateral nuclear disarmament. But Foot's continuing commitment to NATO, together with the fact that the centre-right continued to dominate shadow cabinet elections, left considerable space for manoeuvre for the vast majority of social democratic parliamentarians who opted to stay with Labour. And their staying was bound up with, and indeed was conditional upon, Foot and later Kinnock proving that the constitutional changes could be contained and rendered innocuous in terms of their implication for the autonomy of the parliamentary party; and relatedly, that the new Labour left could be defeated and marginalized.

What became clear during 1981, as Foot joined with the centre-right in a campaign in the media against Benn's very decision to put the electoral college to the test by challenging Dennis Healey for the deputy leadership, was that if unity had to be achieved on the basis of realizing the new Labour left's strategic vision, of which the constitutional changes were only a necessary but hardly sufficient part, then there would be no unity. With the Rank and File Mobilizing Committee providing Benn with an organizational cadre for the first time, Benn succeeded in winning the vast majority of the constituency votes. The RFMC's political meetings at trade union conferences also marked an important break with traditional boundaries between the two wings of the movement. But the outcome of membership ballots undertaken by a number of unions, where Healey generally did better than Benn, indicated not only the effects of a heavily biased, indeed virtually hysterial, media; it also indicated the costs to the new Labour left of its having devoted its energies to effect the intra-party constitutional campaign to the detriment of conducting a broader political campaign. In the end, the trade union vote was narrowly split, while the PLP vote was overwhelmingly for Healey. It took the abstention of only 19 Tribune MPs, led by Kinnock (who thereby proved his 'trustworthiness' to the centre-right in the party) to defeat Benn. It was a watershed in the attempt to change the party and the centre-right immediately pushed its advantage. A group of centre-right trade unionists which had the year before engineered an important change in the make-up of the TUC General Council now turned their efforts to the party and effected a parallel change in the composition of the NEC, and swept the left from the control of key party committees. At the same time, the right wing in the unions and the PLP, and to some extent Foot himself, led the media in a vociferous public opposition against any attempt in the constituencies to actually reselect an MP, against demands by women and blacks for strengthening their representation, and against the GLC's 'loony left' municipal socialism.

Right through the intra-party struggle on the constitutional reforms, until early 1981, Labour had run well ahead of Thatcher in the opinion polls. This, together with the elections in France and Greece of parties whose programmes were even more radical than Labour's, and the new Labour left's taking control of the Greater London Council, emboldened the forces for change in the party. But a combination of factors rapidly undermined such confidence. The SDP's emergence as the first media-created party in Britain's history showed immediate potential for capturing a sizeable portion of Labour's vote; the Falklands war established, on the basis of a recrudescent chauvinism (tragically connived in by Foot himself), Thatcher's image as Britannia incarnate; and the effect of the international capitalist recession, as well as domestic austerity policies, had the effect of reducing inflation, which produced a rise in real wages for those sectors of the working class not immediately touched by the massive rise in unemployment. It suddenly became clear that Thatcherism might not be a temporary interregnum. The new Labour left had long understood that only a long-term campaign of mobilization and education to refashion and reconstruct working class and socialist identities could restore securely Labour's electoral base. But they had also expected that this might still be accomplished through scraping back into state office as Labour had done in 1974 (and was still doing at the local level in the 1980s) and using state resources to empower popular forces. What now became all too clear was that the new Labour left's balancing act, between changing a party fundamentally while relying on an anti-government vote to sustain in the meanwhile the viability of the party's claim to office, was no longer sustainable itself. The choice between a long-term campaign and immediate even if unstable electoral viability became a stark one after 1981. The attempt to change the Labour Party at that point ran up against the most intractable barrier that stands in the way of changing an electoralist party: that is, that trying to change it in as fundamental a way as the new Labour left proposed involves continual, not temporary, disunity within it, and a visibly disunified party cannot win elections. And winning elections appeared ever more important if only as a defensive mechanism against the depredations of Thatcherism.

Yet such was the severity of Labour's failure over the previous decades in government as well as in sustaining the party as a counter-hegemonic community, that despite the marginalization of the left at the national level before the 1983 election campaign, and even more so under Kinnock's leadership thereafter, Labour's parliamentary team has failed miserably to restore Labour's electoral fortunes. The one accomplishment that can be claimed is that voiced by Austin Mitchell MP after the 1987 election campaign: 'The Labour Party has now moved back to the middle ground... It is not the Labour Party of 1981. It has reverted to the historic mould'.[42]

If Benn's defeat at the 1981 conference marked the crucial watershed in the attempt to change the party, it was Neil Kinnock's attack on Militant and the National Union of Mineworker's leadership at the 1985 party conference after the miner's strike that marked the patching of the old party mould. The unparalleled support for the miners at the base of the party, in strong contrast with the party leadership's visible lack of enthusiasm (to put it mildly) for the strike, had shown that the struggle within the party was also a struggle about the very nature of the labour movement in Britain. It involved thereby far more than party 'factionalism', but concerned fundamental differences over collective bargaining strategies no less than differences over ideological or constitutional ones. The miners' strike signified an old fact about the Labour Party: that class struggles are not only represented by it or restrained by it, but appear within it and often divide it. And it revealed very clearly what was the most important aspect of the struggle inside the party, i.e., that it concerned the question of whether the Labour Party leadership was to seek office – and conduct itself once in office – on the basis of distancing itself from class struggles, and indeed other popular extra-parliamentary struggles. This was the absolutely central issue raised in the attempt to change the Labour Party.

Neil Kinnock's attack on the NUM and Militant at the 1985 Conference represented, and was intended to represent, far more than a distancing of the party from what he derisorily called 'the generals of gesture' and 'the tendency tacticians' of the 'hard left'. And it was more than a particularly impassioned assertion of the theme that had brought him to the leadership and governed his behaviour in it, i.e. that the task of winning the next election had to stand as an 'unavoidable and total precondition' over any other consideration. This had all been asserted before, by Foot no less than Kinnock, and it actually had dominated the party's practice since two years before the 1983 election. Kinnock's speech was, above all, a full redeclaration of independence for the parliamentary party. And it was successful because it was premised on four years during which the left had suffered more defeats than victories in the party. Until the 1983 election, however, particularly as seen in the imaginative and popular initiatives of a number of local Labour councils, the possibility of developing a novel socialist practice which would garner rather than lose votes had by no means been effaced yet in the party. But in the immediate aftermath of the terrible defeat it suffered in the June 1983 general election, most of the Labour Party became as transfixed by a conservative appeal of unity as it was by the demand for change after the 1979 election. The concern with party unity as a possible means of quickly restoring Labour's electoral viability was not surprising given the extent of the defeat, but given the form this unity took it rendered quite secondary any serious attempt to revive the attempt to transform the Labour Party. The popularity of the Kinnock/Hattersley 'dream ticket' at the 1983 Conference, the massive vote at that conference in favour of the Militant expulsions, the marginalization of Tony Benn and the absorption of a large number of his erstwhile supporters into the Kinnock 'team', the election of a shadow cabinet with many new faces but still dominated numerically by the centre-right of the parliamentary party – all this represented a series of severe defeats for those forces which had been at the centre of the thrust for change after 1979. It confirmed the passing of the initiative within the party precisely to those elements, by no means any longer confined to the traditional centre-right, who attributed a great deal of the blame for the election defeat to the process of change having gone 'too far', and who looked to policy 'moderation' as the basis for both the new unity and for electoral success.

The miners' strike temporarily threw this tack off course. On its success depended, as the party leadership wrung their hands on the side-lines, not only the fate of the mining communities, but the regaining of the initiative by the new Labour left in the party. The Thatcher Government's 'counterrevolution' against the Keynesian/welfare state had produced such mass unemployment, destitution, alienation and conflict that the maintenance of public order had come to depend, paradoxically in light of the claims of the new Conservatism, not on less state but on more state – and indeed on the most coercive elements of the state. Since the confrontations at the pits, no less than the confrontations in the inner cities, involved important segments of Labour's class and ethnic constituencies, this had brought the Labour Party face to face with the question of whether to counsel moderation on the traditional Labour principles of obeying and respecting the law and the police, or whether to mobilize support for the struggles, including by coming out full square against the government's blatantly coercive tactics and against the bias of the police and the judiciary. This is a wrenching question for a party whose politics is premised on the values of social harmony and moderation. The Labour Party's raison d'etre has been to hasten a process of gradual reform which it believed was natural and inevitable: it contained no ready made consensus on what to do in the face of state reaction on the one side, and on the other a stubborn refusal on the part of a substantial section of the party's own constituency to back down in the face of it. Although its parliamentary leaders knew what they were supposed to say, that is, counsel compromise and look to the next election, the question was whether they could say it without recreating a damaging scission within the party. Kinnock's equivocations while the strike was at its height, condemning violence on all sides without taking sides, could only be replaced by his bravado at the 1985 Conference once Mrs Thatcher and the full strength of the police, the judicial system and the media had done their work.

Labour Party conferences, with the saturation media coverage they attract, are as much public displays of the balance of forces in the party as they are venues for policy resolution. As Labour Leaders had done so often in the past, but with far greater effect than usual given recent Party history, Kinnock spoke as much over the heads of the delegates as he spoke to them. He was effectively saying, to the media, to the Tories and the Alliance, and not least to the social democrats who still dominated the PLP: You may say that the Party is beholden to the unions, you may say the constituencies are dominated by extremists, but you can't pin that tab on me. And since within the British constitutional framework what matters once a party is elected is not so much what the party does or says as what the Prime Minister does and says, this was indeed the message they all wanted to hear.

Significantly, the delegates in their great majority gave Kinnock a prolonged standing ovation. Only the cynic could ascribe this wholly to the delegates playing their allotted role before the television cameras in the spectacle that is the Leader's speech to Conference. Many of the same 1,800 people who attended a Labour Herald rally the night before to hear and cheer Benn and Scargill were on their feet applauding Kinnock. This political schizophrenia is not surprising if it is recognized that it has less to do with deference to the Leader than to the fact that Kinnock, like Foot before him, retained a substantial base among the rank-and-file of the party of a kind that right-wing parliamentarians have never had, in good part because of his position on unilateralism and his defence of the welfare state. And however much the delegates might have preferred, and indeed continued to vote for, left-wing resolutions and national executive candidates, they also badly wanted to win the next election, to get Thatcher out at all costs. There was a strong pull to accept the argument that this meant bending to the media's prejudices and the shadow cabinet's conventionalism to give the appearance of party unity behind Kinnock's 'moderation'.

The trouble with this, of course, was that it closed off the possibility of constructing out of the current crisis anything resembling a socialist alternative to Thatcherism within the given party system. Conference commitments on unilateralism remained intact but they sat uncomfortably with a renewed commitment to NATO and increased expenditure on conventional defence within it. Kinnock's attack on the use of Marxist rhetoric did not mean that he was abandoning rhetoric himself, but reasserting the primacy of social democratic rhetoric in the hope of recovering the good old pre-Thatcherite days when the use of such rhetoric was so familiar it was invisible. Nevertheless, the strength and depth of the socialist mobilization in the party that preceded this was such that there was no smooth passage to presenting a unified face to the electorate through the rhetorical swamp of social democratic verbiage. In the current crises of capitalism and of American global hegemony, there is no clear road back to the nostrums of Atlanticism in foreign policy and Keynesianism and corporatism in domestic policy. It was in good part because of this that the challenge from the left was far more profound and still has deeper resonance in the party than anything that went before. Under these circumstances the exorcism of the left could be a one-off event, and this made the leadership's strategy not a little problematic. For the danger in a strategy that depended on the Labour leadership proving it was worthy to govern by its attacks on the left was that there can never really be sufficient proof that will make the strategy credible. Despite the expulsions that preceded the 1983 election, despite such unimpeachably respectable figures as Dennis Healey and Peter Shore presiding over the daily press conferences at party headquarters during the campaign, Mrs Thatcher was still able to make a leading theme of her campaign the choice this 'historic election' offered between 'two totally different ways of life', with the prize to be fought for being 'no less than the chance to banish from our land the dark, divisive clouds of Marxist Socialism'. And David Steel could still allege that Labour was drawing its inspiration from 'the decaying bones of Karl Marx in Highgate Cemetery'. Given what transpired in the party after 1983, the Labour leadership hoped that continuing McCarthyism of this sort would sound unfair. Yet, despite Kinnock's attack on Militant and the NUM, *The Times* immediately turned its attention to women and black activists: '… the face of the Labour Party has not stabilized. What is offered to the voters in Brent, Haringey or Hackney is not Mr Kinnock's emollience but Miss Abbott's rhetoric of class struggle and skin-colour consciousness and the insurrectionary talk of Mr Bernie Grant. In a party with no boundaries, in a church with no catechism beyond the nullity of Clause Four, they have as good a claim to speak for "socialism" as he does. Exit (perhaps) Mr Mulhearn, Mr Hatton and sundry other followers of the Fourth International; enter – with no one to bar their way – class and race warriors in thrall to the same Marxist doctrine.' [43]

The tendency to blatant distortion of the socialist left, in all its diversity, is based on the most crude presumptions of what the term 'Marxism' is attached to in the eyes of those who subscribe to such ideas in the party. Indeed, it is probably not even in the broadest terms accurate to identify most of the women and black activists as Marxist at all. But this very crudity derives from an a priori passion finally to write finis, albeit some two decades later than it was supposed to happen, to 'the end of (socialist) ideology'. This passion is not much less strong among those in the Labour Party who long for an end to Thatcherism than it is in the opinion *The Times* represents. For instance, the right-wing Solidarity Group of MPs labelled as 'Stalinist' a Campaign Group of MPs' (formed around Benn after 1981) questionnaire to the candidates for Labour Chief Whip in 1985. The questionnaire asked whether they favoured recorded votes for PLP elections and meetings; party conference control over PLP rules; election of the shadow cabinet by the electoral college that elects the leaders; black sections in the constituencies; a strengthened role for the women's conference of the party; inclusion of at least one woman and one black on all constituency short lists for parliamentary candidates; withdrawal from the Common Market; and expulsion of people giving any support to the Militant Tendency.[44] That a questionnaire designed to reveal the political positions of candidates for party office should have been construed as Stalinist, of all things, presumably implying some ultra-centralist organizational practice rather than the antithesis of it, as is patently the case, is worthy of Ronald Reagan's designation of the Samoza Contras in Nicaragua as 'freedom fighters'. But it is the function of such political rhetoric, not its accuracy, that counts. The function of the rhetoric hinges on establishing the illegitimacy of the very attempt to change the Labour Party on the basis of the political principles that the left had actually taken up in the 1970s, i.e. denying the complete autonomy of Parliamentarians between elections, advancing the common ownership of the means of production as a relevant goal, and conceiving strategic questions in terms of class and popular struggles. The notion that these principles are inherently totalitarian, or the claim that they are catechisms of a dead church, can only be taken seriously if they are seen for what they really are: ideological aids in the struggle to consolidate the old parliamentarist mould.

If the new Labour left was 'unrealistic', as has so often been alleged, it was mainly in that it severely *underestimated* the sheer breadth and depth of the parliamentary leadership's commitment to the old parliamentarism and the sheer weight of conventional wisdom and bourgeois opinion they could call to their side in defense of it. It also *overestimated* the commitment of the left union leadership to the new labour left's struggle and the staying power of the collective instrumentalism of industrial militancy under conditions of capitalist restructuring, mass unemployment and state reaction. In the face of this, as is so often the case in history, some of the new Labour left's original activists, and even more of the commentators who watched from the sidelines, initially with some sympathy, became themselves dispirited and confused about what had been the point of the thing all along. Many of them succumbed to the illusion that Labour's electoral disintegration was caused by the intra-party debate, forgetting that this debate was itself but a symptom of the failures of parliamentary paternalism. And some began to bend to the views of the social democrats inside and outside the party regarding a further redefinition of the intraparty democracy. After most of the parliamentarians had fought tooth and nail to prevent anyone but MPs from electing the leader and declared that the reselection of MPs sounded the death-knell of democracy, they suddenly switched to the view that these new rights should be passed over to a ballot of all party members. The reason was entirely tactical. They hoped thereby that an 'amorphous mass' would now save them from the initiative that political organization within party structures had raised up. To be sure, the constitutional reforms that had been effected inevitably and properly brought forward critical questions regarding whether the constituency party structures, and especially those in the unions, were conducive to allowing all those who wanted to participate to do so. But this involved further reforms to encourage participation and accountability at party meetings, as many on the left and especially Benn had long insisted, not an incorporation within the party of the plebiscitory principles that governed elections between parliamentary teams at the level of the state.

Under the impact of Thatcher's ever more bold attacks on municipal socialism and class struggle trade unionism, and the Labour leadership's attack on Militant and others inside the party, the new Labour left grew increasingly fractious and indeed fractured. As the proponents of the parliamentary paternalism renewed themselves and once again powerfully asserted their control over the party, segments of the new Labour left fell in with the view that the fortunes of the party could only be restored if the parliamentary 'team' were allowed to get on with it. Some of them joined that team. This is a sad thing. But it speaks more to the factors that rendered the Labour Party incapable of transformation than to the objectives of the new Labour left.

The new Labour left never claimed that there was a ready-made majority constituency in Britain that was just waiting for the opportunity to elect a socialist government, once the Labour Party sorted itself out. On the contrary, its development was characterized by the concern to turn the Labour Party into the kind of party that might at least attempt to mobilize such support. Those who are opposed to the socialist project, or those who study politics as allegedly neutral commentators, will be little concerned with this objective. Most socialists will be rather less content to merely accept the defeat of the attempt to change the Labour Party and join with Labour's parliamentary team in an attempt to win back support by appealing for votes on the individualist grounds that Thatcherism has prepared. Nor will most of them, it may be hoped, be content to sit back and wait for the economy to unfold with the stock market. Since the 1987 election, there have been attempts to chart a new way forward as seen in the large socialist conference held in Benn's constituency in October 1987, attended by two thousand socialists inside and outside the Labour Party, and including representatives of the Greens and the Welsh Nationalists. Enduring sectarian blinkers of parts of the extra-Labour left endanger such initiatives: there must be an appreciation of the new Labour left's project of broadening democracy and making it more amenable to popular struggles. But new attempts at socialist renewal of that project will have to concentrate less on reforming the Labour Party and more on building a long-term independent campaign for a democratic socialism that transcends the limits of parliamentary paternalism.

Notes

[1] L. Panitch and C. Leys, *The End of Parliamentary Socialism: From New Left to New Labour*, London, Verso, 1997

[2] D. Coates, *The Labour Party and the Struggle for Socialism*, Cambridge 1975, p.178

[3] R. Miliband, 'Party Democracy and Parliamentary Government', *Political Studies*, Vol. VI, 1958, pp. 176-82.

[4] M. Rustin, 'Labour's Constitutional Crisis', *New Left Review*, 126, March-April 1981, p. 25.

[5] Raymond Williams (ed.), *The May Day Manifesto* 1968, Harmondsworth, 1968, pp. 173-4.

[6] Coates, p. 209.

[7] 'The Labour Party and Social Democracy', in Samuel and Stedman Jones,(eds.), *Culture, Ideology and Politics: Essays for Eric Hobsbawm*, History Workshop Series, London 1982, pp. 320-9.

[8] M. Franklin, *The Decline in Class Voting in Britain*, Oxford 1985, pp. 153, 161.

[9] Ibid, p.174

[10] S. Barolini, 'The membership of mass parties: the Social Democratic experience 1889-1978', in H. Daalder and P.Main *Western European Party Systems: Continuity and Change*, London, 1983, p.188

[11] 'The Labour Party and its members', *New Society*, September 20, 1979, p. 613.

[12] Fringe meeting debate between the Tribune Group and the International Socialists at 1969 Labour Party Conference.

[13] D. Blunkett, 'Why I am a Socialist: Sheffield Steel', *New Socialist*, NovemberDecember 19$2, p.

56.

[14] Quoted in C. Cockburn, *The Local State*, London 1977, p. 126.

[15] Ibid, pp. 118, 159-61.

[16] Interview with David Blunkett, in M. Boddy and C. Fudge, *Local Socialism*, London 1984, pp. 244-5.

[17] Cockburn, p. 90.

[18] M. Mackintosh and H. Wainwright, A Taste of Power: The Politics of Local Economics, London 1987, p. 399.

[19] The term is Minkin's: The Labour Party Conference, London 1978, p. 329.

[20] T. Benn, *The New Politics: a socialist reconnaissance*, Fabian Tract 402. September 1970, pp. 8-9, 12.

[21] Speeches by Tony Benn, Nottingham 1974, pp. 277-9.

[22] Interview with Tony Benn in A. Freeman, *The Benn Heresy*, London 1982, pp. 174-5.

[23] Speeches, pp. 223-4.

[24] See Speeches, pp. 275, 281, 285, 287-8; and *The New Politics*, p. 28. .

[25] A. Crosland, *Socialism Now and other essays*, London 1974, esp. pp. 27, 72.

[26] Quoted in *The Observer, April 3 1966*

[27] . Agenda for the 67th annual conference of the Labour Party, Blackpool 1968, pp. 31-2

[28] Labour Party Conference Report, 1970, pp. 176, 182-4.

[29] Labour Party Conference Report, 1971, p. 236.

[30] Quoted in M. Hatfield, *The House the Left Built*, London 1978, pp. 36. 41.

[31] *Labour: Party or Puppet?*, July 1972.

[32] Quoted in Hatfield, p. 114

[33] Interview with Roy Hattersley in D. Kogan and M. Kogan, *The Battle for the Labour Party*, London 1982, p. 37.

[34] Letter to *The Times*, December 11, 1985.

[35] T. Benn, Speeches, pp. 164-75

[36] Hatfield, p. 68.

[37] See TUC Report 1972, pp. 401-2; and Benn, Speeches, pp. 188-95, 16-25, 285.

[38] Kogan and Kogan, p. 10.

[39] R. McKenzie, 'Power in the Labour Party: the issue of intra-party democracy', in D. Kavanagh (ed.), *The Politics of the Labour Party*, London 1982, pp. 196-7.

[40] R. Miliband, 'Socialist Advance in Britain', *The Socialist Register 1983*, pp. 116-7.

[41] See his 'Labour's New Reformism' and 'The Limits of the Labour Left' in *New Left Review* 129 (September-October 1981) and 135 (September-October 1982).

[42] Quoted in Tribune, September 11, 1987.

[43] *The Times*, December 10, 1985.

[44] 'Whips refuse "Stalinist" questions', *The Times*, October 21, 1985.

Editorial Introduction to Extract 11

The other current feeding into *The End of Parliamentary Socialism* has been the scholarship of Colin Leys. Picking up the story in his 1996 *Socialist Register* essay from the point at which it was left in the Panitch essay of 1988, Leys traced the transition of policy – away from the programmes of the Left – first under the leadership of Neil Kinnock and then of Tony Blair, noting as he did so the particular role played by a new generation of Party intellectuals and speech writers. The result for Leys, as for Panitch, has been one of closure: that with the dominance of the Blairites within the Party, we had reached that point at which the leadership no longer even pretended that the Party was engaged on the project of parliamentary socialism. As they put it in the opening of the first edition of *The End of Parliamentary Socialism*, 'For almost a century the Labour Party was committed to "parliamentary socialism", with all its limitations; with the 1997 election, that commitment was finally abandoned.'[1]. In this way, with the publication of their 1997 volume, significantly modelled in its title as well as in its argument on the original Miliband study, Panitch and Leys brought the 1961 Miliband history to its conclusion: arguing with some force that Ralph Miliband's persistent sense – that the Labour Party was not a vehicle for the achievement of socialism, and never could be – had been vindicated by events, and made relevant again by that vindication.

11. THE BRITISH LABOUR PARTY'S TRANSITION FROM SOCIALISM TO CAPITALISM (1996)

Colin Leys

... each age, even each decade, has its little cant word coiled up inside real discourse like a tiny grub in the middle of an apple. Each age, even each decade, is overly impressed for a little while by half-way bright youngish men on the make who adeptly manipulate the current terminology at precisely the right moment to make precisely the right impression on those who are a little older, a little less intelligent and considerably less alert.[2]

Dennis Potter wrote these words in 1993, about the way the BBC was being denatured and commercialised in the name of 'management'. In the case of the Labour Party, the 'little cant word' is 'modernisation' (although a strong dose of 'management' comes with it).[3] In its name, a new kind of party, more and more removed from what is left of the labour movement and from its active membership in the constituencies, is being constructed. And the means used to accomplish this – an unprecedented concentration of power in the hands of the party leader – has also elevated him in relation to back-bench Labour MPs, and perhaps even, to a greater extent than in the past, his Shadow Cabinet colleagues.

The aim has been to allow the leader to determine party policy with at most the nominal approval of the party outside parliament, i.e. both its trade union wing and its constituency activists – and to be seen by the media to do so. But the process also means that for the first time in the party's history the leader is also almost completely free from the influence of the party's traditional ethos – the mix of values and practices, evolved over some 150 years of collective political effort, which has hitherto defined the priorities and principles underlying party policy.

By no means everything in this ethos was admirable – as Henry Drucker pointed out in 1979, it contained a great deal that was archaic, anti-intellectual, and so on;[4] but it also comprised the most egalitarian, humanistic, unselfish, internationalist and brave elements of progressive British culture. Previous party leaders were influenced by this ethos in different ways and to different degrees: but none has been as untouched by it as Tony Blair, either before he became leader in July 1994 or since.[5] Not only is he not someone formed by the party's ethos, or much constrained by it in his day to day work as party leader; in the Leader's Office (i.e. official parliamentary office of the Leader of the Opposition), and in his most intimate circle of political friends, he operates in a milieu based on a different ethos, an ethos of professional politics based on higher education management skills, and the culture of the communications industry. Some of the chief exponents of this ethos more or less openly despise that of the old labour movement, and while they may, like Blair, sometimes call themselves socialists, they no longer think of socialism as an alternative social and economic system to capitalism.

The Labour Party was, to be sure, not formed as a political party dedicated to replacing capitalism with socialism, but as a parliamentary voice for wage workers. But electoral success led to the evolution of the LRC into a mass political party which by 1944, when the 1930s depression had been followed by the social mobilisation of the second world war, led it to adopt and then implement a programme of reforms which in 1945 leaders were happy to call socialist: including a commitment to full employment, the nationalisation of 20 percent of the economy, and the establishment of a comprehensive system of state-provided social security health and other social services.

By 1995 all this had been abandoned as party policy, and the word 'socialism' now figured in party literature and the leader's speeches rather rarely, and always in carefully circumscribed language, usually emphasizing the degree to which it is not socialism as it used to be understood. Socialism, for Blair in particular, refers to an ethical ideal: and for him 'modernising' Labour policy means dropping all previous ideas about the application of that ideal; i.e., not just 'old Labour' ideas about public ownership or the welfare state, but also, if not even more so, all the 'new left's' thinking and practice about participative democracy in the 1970s.

In this discourse, the one thing that is clearly modern is global capitalism; fundamentally, 'modernisation' means adapting to it. As a highly public token of this, soon after his election as leader Blair set himself the task of getting rid of the party's commitment to the principle of common ownership of the means of production, embodied in Clause Four of the party constitution, and replacing it with a portmanteau commitment to a range of values (a dynamic economy, a just society, an open democracy and a healthy environment) – including, crucially for the media, an endorsement of 'the enterprise of the market and the rigour of competition' and 'a thriving private sector'[6] After a two-month campaign of regional meetings with Labour Party members Blair secured a two thirds majority for this change at a special party conference in April 1995. In the vote, 90 percent of the constituency parties' votes were cast in favour of the change, compared with only 54 percent of the trade union votes (though given that all that was needed was to drop a ballot paper in the letter box the constituency 'turnout' – or 'response rate' – was notably low); this reversal in the balance of forces – the constituency vote having previously been an activists' vote, and on the whole more left-leaning than the unions' – is a key measure of the change that has occurred.

Meantime the leadership also dissociated itself from almost any previous policy that the media had chosen to dub 'socialist': repudiating, for the future, increased taxation (even though Britain had become distinctly under-taxed by the standards of other European countries), all state 'intervention' in the economy, and the restoration of trade union rights (not to mention any idea of requiring companies to be as internally democratic as unions); even disavowing any idea of reducing the tax privileges of private schools.

The transition under Kinnock, 1983-1992

The origins of this transformation lie in the party's divided response to the crisis of British social democracy in the 1970s, when the country's industrial weaknesses caught up with it. Chronic balance of payments difficulties forced a choice between two strategies: deflating the economy, allowing unemployment to rise, letting average real wages fall and hoping that private investment would restore competitiveness; or extending public control and forcing the pace through public investment. A majority of party activists, and the leadership of some of the biggest unions affiliated to the party, favoured the second option, while the Labour government in office from 1974 to 1979 pursued, in effect, the

first. The result was a successful internal party campaign, whose most prominent champion was the former Industry minister Tony Benn, to change the party's constitution so as to make the leader and the Parliamentary Labour Party
(PLP) more responsive to the views of the party outside parliament. Leaders
were in future to be chosen by an electoral college drawn from the unions and
constituency parties as well as the PLP; sitting Labour MPs had to submit themselves for reselection as candidates by their constituency parties before elections;
and election manifestos had to be agreed between the Shadow Cabinet and the
party's National Executive Committee (NEC), These changes were bitterly resisted and led to (or were the pretext for) the defection in 1981-82 of 27 MPs to
form a new party, the Social Democratic Party. When Labour then proceeded
to lose the 1983 election disastrously, the predominantly right-wing leadership
and PLP blamed, not the defectors, but those who had spearheaded the constitutional changes, and who had also championed a strengthened public sector
and other left inclined policies which, they said, the result showed that voters
did not want.

In reality, Labour's 1983 campaign was dominated by the right wing of the
leadership, who conducted all the media events while the left kept a low profile.
And there are several important alternative explanations for the defeat, from
the continuing opinion-poll effect of the 'Falklands factor' in favour of Mrs
Thatcher, to Michael Foot's vacillating and uninspiring leadership, the accelerat-
ing consumer boom (for those in work) led by Reagan's spending programmes,
and so on. But faced by a tabloid press plumbing new depths of malevolence
against the left, the right, supported by the unions, decided to renounce it.

The party leader, Michael Foot, resigned immediately after the election and the
new leadership electoral college overwhelmingly endorsed the so called 'dream
ticket' candidatures of Neil Kinnock as leader and Roy Hattersley as deputy[7].
Kinnock, although perceived as a 'soft' (i.e. anti-Benn) left-winger, responded
to the party's predicament by establishing an altogether novel degree of personal
control over it. Several circumstance allowed him to do this. First, the severity
of the 1983 defeat created a mood of 'recovery at any price' in most sectors of
the party. Second, 'coming from the left, he [Kinnock] did not alienate the constituency parties [which were still largely Bennite in outlook] in the way Wilson
and Callaghan had'.[8] Third, Kinnock had been elected as leader by overwhelming majorities in all three sections of the new electoral college and so enjoyed a
new kind of legitimacy. Fourth, the Office of the Leader of the Opposition now
disposed of far more resources than ever before, thanks to a new funding policy
introduced by Edward Short as Leader of the House of Commons in 1974. By
1983 the Labour front bench had at its disposal £440,000, and by 1988, £839,000,
for research and assistance; and the trade unions even added a further £100,000
per annum for the free use of the Leader.[9]

Kinnock immediately set about removing effective policy-making control from where the party constitution appeared to locate it, i.e. in the National Executive Committee (NEC) and the annual party Conference. As seen by Seyd and Whiteley, academic observers not unsympathetic to Kinnock, the party had become unpopular with the electorate because its policies reflected the views of its radical activists in the constituencies and the trade unions, who were unrepresentative of the electorate. Therefore

> The party leadership's first task ... was to reduce the activists' powers. It could not afford just to ignore them, because of their possession of significant constitutional powers. Yet it was electorally inexpedient for the leadership to rely on the block votes of certain trade union leaders to maintain its position at the patty conference, because of the trade unions general unpopularity, even among their own members.[10]

Kinnock's solution was to create a new system of Joint Policy Committees composed equally of NEC members and MPs. These effectively superseded the NEC's Home Policy and International Committees with their myriad subcommittees of mainly co-opted experts drawn from the party's membership; and although the joint policy committees were chaired by NEC members, and assisted by secretaries drawn from both the party headquarters and PLP staff, effective control of their agendas and outcomes passed gradually into the hands of the leader and his professional advisers. Lewis Minkin, a seasoned and meticulous researcher on the party, commented that

> ... one must note the growing confidence, increasing resources and, at times, ruthless assertiveness of the PLP leaders, as they took full advantage of the mood change brough about by the defeat of 1983. From the first, the key Jobs and Industry Joint Committee was colonised by co-opted supporters of the Shadow Chancellor and Deputy Leader. Key subcommittee chairs were taken by the Front Bench. An economic strategy emerged not only from the committee but in public speeches by Hattersley, in which the new direction was charted and new policy departures sometimes announced before they were taken into the Party's procedures. Through his political and policy advisers, the new Leader was able to exercise a selective but broad-ranging oversight... the Leader's assistants sat in on policy committees, formal and informal, taking initiatives, 'fighting fires', and letting others in the unions know 'what Neil wants'.[11]

The old tripartite NEC-PLP-TUC 'Liaison Committee', through which the NEC had formerly operated to secure pre-conference agreement of policy issues, was gradually sidelined. What now became dominant was the office of the Leader.

Kinnock also deployed his power directly against the party's so-called 'hard' left in other ways. He denounced the Trotskyist Militant Tendency and oversaw a series of measures to delegitimise it; he conspicuously dissociated himself from the mineworkers in their epic confrontation with the government over pit closures in 1984-85; he closed the party's mildly left-of-centre New Socialist magazine; and he successfully marginalised leading left-wing MPs such as Tony Benn and Eric Heffer in the party's inner councils.

Then in 1987 came the further shock of the party's third successive election defeat. A slick media-oriented campaign had failed to do more than beat back the challenge of the Liberal-SDP Alliance; the Conservatives returned with another large parliamentary majority. Now instead of merely trying to reduce the visibility and influence of the left wing of the party, Kinnock initiated a more radical change in party policy and a more radical loosening of the links tying the leadership to the party outside parliament.

The new overall 'Policy Review' set in motion by Kinnock after the 1987 defeat consisted of seven 'policy groups', each jointly chaired by member of the NEC and a member of the Labour front bench. By now what was at stake was how far the party should go in accepting the legacy of Thatcherism as a new 'settlement', as the Conservatives had one accepted that of 1945-51. In the end, the answer was mixed. 'The market' was accepted, as a potentially neutral means of allocating resources: but emphasis continued to be laid on the need to redistribute wealth for more equal opportunities in the market. The state's role in industrial policy, environmental regulation, regional policy, training, competition, and control of natural monopolies, continued to be stressed, and public ownership was not renounced, although employee share ownership schemes, cooperatives and the public ownership of individual firms rather than whole industries were endorsed. On industrial relations, a return to the pre-Thatcher system was ruled out, though trade unions were to get new rights under a new, specialised system of industrial relations courts.

The results of the Policy Review registered the balance of forces and opinions in the party's NEC down to 1989. Of perhaps greater significance in the long run were a number of organisational changes that would eventually drastically reduce the significance of the NEC and indeed the whole extra-parliamentary party. One was the creation in 1985 of 'Communications and Campaign Directorate' (CCD), directed by Peter Mandelson, which at its peak in 1986-87 had an annual budget of £300,000 and operated in close collaboration with the leader's office and with virtually total autonomy from the administrative hierarchy in the rest of the party headquarters. Mandelson also set up a 'Shadow Communications Agency' (SCA), coordinated by a professional market research and advertising specialist, Philip Gould, and relying on changing groups of sympathetic volunteers from the same milieu to provide information about the electorate and recommend ways of appealing to it. Mandelson took the power of the media as a given and devoted himself to getting the party to present itself in ways that the media would report positively. Gould provided 'interpretations' of the opinions and attitudes of voters.

Much has been written about the influence of Mandelson and the SCE. In retrospect what seems most significant is that they were taken very seriously by Kinnock and that they reinforced three salient tendencies. First, to treat the electors primarily as consumers of party programme: with already-given attitudes and interests, rather than as people who can be persuaded to find their needs and aspirations met in the party's project for social change. Second, to treat editors and journalists as the arbiters of what is sensible or acceptable, in a way that party members, or even national executive members, are not. Third, to treat professional interpreters of the electors' attitudes as authoritative.

The first tendency – treating voters as consumers with pre-given wishes – was noted and resisted by many in the party's senior leadership, yet followed logically enough from defining the party's one and only task as that of winning the next election: even if the leader had been a thinker of vision, with a body of new philosophy and practical thinking to draw on, winning electoral support for it would have required much more time (and propitious circumstances) than was afforded by the interval between two elections. As for accepting the power of editors and journalists to define what is sound and sensible and what is not, this too is defensible if their power to damage the party's short-term electoral prospects is once taken for granted. Acceptance of the authority of opinion researchers was more problematic, especially since the methods used by the Shadow Communications Agency involved a great deal of 'interpretation' and presentational slant, the aim of which seems to have been largely to jolt senior party personnel into recognising that even Labour voters were mostly uninterested in existing Labour politics, or even opposed to them. Using the same methods a team interested in finding the bases for a new long-term socialist strategy would undoubtedly have been able to do so, and to illustrate their findings with quotations just as evocative as 'it's nice to have a social conscience but it's your family that counts' and other Thatcherite-sounding statements quoted with such effect by the SCA in one of its first presentations, 'Society and Self';[12] for, contrary to the opinion of Hughes and Wintour, two commentators very close to Mandelson, the results of opinion research are never truly 'unequivocal'.[13] Meanwhile, as the role assigned to 'communications' expanded, the role of party members was symbolically downgraded by the curious exercise called 'Labour Listens', mounted by the party's national headquarters in 1988-89. Meetings were organised throughout the country at which members of the public were invited to tell the party what they thought. The process was barely serious. There was no concern for the representativeness of the meetings, nor were any mechanisms put in place to ensure that what people said was fed into the Policy Review[14]. The one thing that was clear was that the meetings were not for listening to Labour activists. It was clearly an effort, however misconceived or even fraudulent, to link the party to the public over the heads of its active members, and to be seen to be doing so.

The grip of the leader's office on policy-making thus became more and more detailed and exclusive, and through Mandelson's management of press relations the leader's views gradually came to be treated as party policy by the media:

> Again and again the Leader would let it be known through his private office what would and would not be Labour Party policy. The press grew accustomed to this and gave far more weight to these unattributable briefings than to the decisions of the annual Labour Party Conference. The Walworth Road [party headquarters] policy directorate became an irrelevance.[15]

In addition to keeping tight control over policy formation in the short run, Kinnock also pursued two linked strategies designed to reduce the long-term influence of both the unions and active party members. First, under the slogan 'one member one vote', all individual party members would be able to vote in elections for the party leader, the selection of candidates for parliament, and delegates to annual conferences; balloting would be done by post. Kinnock and his advisers assumed (rightly, as the 1995 Clause Four vote was to prove), that this would reduce the influent of activists who attended meetings. On the basis that this gave more power to individual members Kinnock argued that more people would want to be members, envisaging a doubling of the membership from the then level of about 250,000 (at one time Kinnock rashly set a target of one million). Second, as individual membership rose, Kinnock proposed that the weigh of the trade union block vote at annual conferences should be reduced.

These proposals addressed real problems. Party activists were indeed unrepresentative of the opinions of Labour supporters and voters (in fact in pre-Thatcher days surveys regularly showed the latter supporting Conservative policy planks more than Labour ones). Party leaders have always relied on the block votes of 'affiliated' trade union members to outvote the constituency-based activists at annual conferences, so that conference policy decisions produced what they saw as potentially winning election platforms. But this was increasingly indefensible, as trade union leaders cast millions of votes for members who were less and less politically involved. Enlarging the party's individual membership was in every way desirable. On the other hand dropping the need for members to attend any meetings in order to vote on policies, combined with the leadership's espousal of policies beamed so exclusively at 'middle England', gave the change a specific political meaning. What it seemed to portend was a North American-style party of professional politicians supported by a membership who were essentially donors and election helpers, not active participants in party policy formation.

These changes were not achieved by Kinnock, but by his successor John Smith (leader from 1992 to his premature death in 1994). 'One member one vote' (or OMOV, as the new system was called) was agreed at the 1993 Conference, and in the same year the unions agreed to a reduction of their joint weight in conference votes to 70 per cent, and in candidate and delegate selection at constituency level to 40 per cent; and also, in principle, to a future lowering of their collective voting power at annual conferences to 50 per cent once individual membership surpassed 300,000. And building on this, Smith's successor Tony Blair sought still further reductions in the influence of the trade unions, ending union sponsorship of MPs and floating the idea of a still greater reduction in the weight of the union vote at conferences; he was also thought likely to put pressure on the unions to move towards balloting their members on policy issues before conference votes, on OMOV lines.[16] And in a further centralising move Blair persuaded the PLP to let the leader select the party's Chief Whip in the House of Commons.[17]

Apart from the OMOV issue, John Smith's leadership saw a halt to the centralising process and a notable reopening of policy debate, at least within the PLP. Mandelson had already left the Communications and Campaigns Directorate in 1989 to become MP for Hartlepool; the Directorate was now wound up, while Patricia Hewitt, Kinnock's former Press Secretary and a key architect of his centralisation measures, after overseeing the Policy Review, moved to a new Labour-oriented think-tank, the Institute for Public Policy Research, and thence to a high-powered job in the private sector. A more traditional style of leadership was re-established.

'New Labour': the modernisation project of Tony Blair

With Blair's election as leader in 1994, however, the Kinnock regime was revived, with the young staffers from the Leader's Office once more omnipresent, policy documents handed to members of the NEC at the door to be signed for and returned at the end of the meeting, and shadow cabinet members required to clear all their speeches with the Leader's Office in advance. Key players in Kinnock's team also reappeared. Mandelson returned to centre stage, after a celebrated 'secret' role as Blair's campaign manager in the leadership contest, as one of the new leader's closest advisers. He was appointed a junior whip, and in July 1995 was given charge of running a by-election campaign (in Littleborough and Saddleworth) which gained instant notoriety for appealing to right-wing authoritarianism and anti-tax attitudes, and for its use of negative personal attacks on the ultimately successful Liberal Democrat candidate; in October he was appointed to the front bench in the Deputy Leader's office. Hewitt remained in the private sector but returned to the inner circle as a member of an unofficial group of policy-makers run by Mandelson for Blair.[18]

The OMOV strategy now began to show quite dramatic results. By mid-1995, according to Labour's General Secretary Tom Sawyer, 113,000 new members had joined since Blair became leader and the party's total membership had risen to 350,000. On the other hand, there was a corresponding loss of enthusiasm among activists, and in the same period 38,000 members had left. This was a serious exodus, but a price the leadership was evidently prepared to pay; an interesting example, in fact, of a government dismissing an unpopular electorate and choosing one it likes better.[19] The question was how far others in the PLP or the trade unions, whose support for the leadership remained, in spite of everything, electorally important – if only in not giving rise to displays of party disunity – would acquiesce. Signs accumulated that their toleration was wearing thin, but complaints were muted out of a desire to give the new leader the benefit of every doubt, particularly given the party's unprecedented opinion poll ratings throughout his first year. A demand from Bill Morris, the leader of the Transport and General Workers Union, that there should be a pause in the 'modernisation' process after the special Clause Four conference, was disregarded, but party agents and workers reported that constituency party General Council meetings, once the focus of rank and file participation, were increasingly inquorate. Finally three events broke the issue open: Blair's decision to accept an invitation to address a conference of Rupert Murdoch's News International group in Australia, Peter Mandelson's conduct of the Littleborough and Saddleworth by-election, and Blair's announcement that he wanted an early end to trade union sponsorship of MPs.

Murdoch's newspapers had vilified Labour throughout the Thatcher years with unremitting lack of scruple (it was of Murdoch that Dennis Potter said, in his blistering final television interview with Melvyn Brag, 'There is no one person more responsible for the pollution of what was already a fairly polluted press');[20] and Blair's willingness to fly to Australia, as his guest was of a piece with Mandelson's ruthless pursuit of votes at the Littleborough and Saddleworth by-election. Both exercises had the mark of Mandelson's famous 'unsentimentality', and both stuck in the gullets of many party activists. The issue of trade union sponsorship of MPs was a slower-burning fuse, but in the context of the impending reduction of union voting strength at party conferences, and hints that Blair would call for further reductions in future, the fact that Blair chose also to call for the end of union sponsorship was seen as further evidence of the London-based middle-class orientation of the leader and his Office. Open resentment was eventually triggered by an article in the *New Statesman* in July 1995 by a mildly left-wing backbench MP, Richard Burden, in which he criticised the 'amorality' of the by-election campaign as a manifestation of 'New Labour's' top-down, centralised power structure, and of a party 'desperate to be elected as representative of mainstream opinion, and yet with its own inner sanctum holding a virtual monopoly on defining what such mainstream opinion consists of'.[21] This was followed by a short outburst of articles and statements also voicing what had previously been said publicly only by the party's left wing.[22]

What really united all the critics was pinpointed by Roy Hattersley, who had been deputy leader under Kinnock and a militant member of the party's right wing. 'As always', he said, the complaints have been directed at a series of surrogate targets – the arrogance of the young men and women in the leader's office, the increasing detachment from the trade unions, and the most wizened of old chestnuts, 'the lack of democracy in policy making'…

A formulation calculated to remind Blair that Hattersley himself had always staunchly resisted calls for democracy when these came from the party's left wing with its base in the old constituency parties. The real problem, Hattersley asserted, was a concern about policy; the present leadership had abandoned ideology so completely, and was so preoccupied with winning middle class support, that its commitment to the fundamental needs of the 'disadvantaged' was no longer clear. 'Ideology', he declared

> is what keeps parties consistent and credible as well as honest. In the long term, the party's public esteem would be protected by a robust statement of fundamental intention. Socialism – which is proclaimed in the New Clause IV – requires the bedrock of principle to be the redistribution of power and wealth… When the going gets rough, it is not the new recruits from the SDP who will stay at his [Tony Blair's] side. They will jump ship as soon as they realise that he is not the reincarnation of David Owen [the former SDP leader, now Lord Owen]. The necessary support will come from members of the real Labour Party who, rightly, think he shares their basic beliefs. He ought to confirm their optimism now and bring to an end the nonsense of last week [i.e. the sudden spate of criticism].[23]

Hattersley's intervention was a good indication of how far the leadership had moved away from the party's historic ethos. People like Hattersley had fought against the left on the basis of a counter-ideology – 'labourism' – no less powerful for being implicit in the labour movement's practices and traditions, rather than explicitly formulated in any body of doctrine. But 'New Labour' was rapidly abandoning that ideology or ethos too. Blair's response was predictable:

> [He] pledged to continue with his wide-ranging 'modernisation' of the Labour Party in order to ensure victory in the general election, making it clear that he was undeterred by criticism of his leadership style… election victory could only be gained by shaking off old-fashioned links and building up voters' trust in the new-style party … But [people] need to be sure of Labour, they will only be sure of Labour if we show that we have learned the lessons of the past and are a party true to our principles but applying them in the modem world'[24]

Retreat was excluded by the logic of his sustained effort to woo 'middle England', and by his agreement with the media that his claim to be able to rid the Labour Party of its last vestiges of anti-capitalism was the acid test of his merits as a leader. Hattersley's 'real Labour' members might be alienated, but catering at all significantly to them would be pilloried by the media and could jeopardise the party's electoral prospects, which were currently strong (a Labour opinion poll lead over the Conservatives of almost 30 percent) precisely to the extent that 'old Labour' had been so publicly dethroned.[25] The new recruits (wherever they came from) might indeed prove fickle, but the party's capacity to attract them was an index of its ability to win an election with the votes of the kind of people they represented. Thereafter, perhaps with the aid of state funding for parties (advocated by Denis Healey, the former Deputy Leader, among others), party members might become as relatively unimportant as they are in the Conservative Party or any other bourgeois political party endowed with funds sufficient to fight election campaigns, which are in any case increasingly decided in the media.

'New Labour' policy

What has been described so far is primarily a change – sympathisers call it a revolution – of organisation and practice, though with obvious policy implications. Now something more needs to be said about the policy content of what Blair's team habitually call 'the project', even though this is made difficult by the project's nature: a distinctive kind of utopianism, presented as 'realism'. The 'realism' consists essentially of the assertion that global capitalism is a permanent and irremovable fact of life, not an inhuman and ultimately self-destructive system: correspondingly, politics is the art of living with it, not a vocation to overcome it. It is not clear that most 'New Labour' evangelists (a term often used on account of Blair's religious faith and zealous speaking style) are particularly concerned about the truth-value of this founding assumption; another characteristic of their writing and speeches is to proceed by denigrating any unwelcome idea as the product of 'old' Labour thinking, rather than arguing for the validity of what is offered in its place. There is perhaps also a vaguely postmodern assumption at work that no such general characterisation of something like global capitalism is really possible; 'grand narratives' are also out of date. The flavour was well summarised by Henry Porter in a very favourable survey of Blair's first year as leader: 'Nothing seems the same as it was; even the old distinctions between left and right no longer matter as much as generational differences appear to.' And what is distinctive about the new generation? Porter quotes 'a close political ally' of Blair:

> Tony had been thinking along these lines long before he was made leader. In fact he was impatient under John Smith to reform the Labour Party. He understood that a whole new generation of people in their thirties and forties had arrived and that they had attitudes and a whole culture which are light years away from the old Labour Party. Intellectually they accept the restrictions in responsible policy-making that now exist.[26]

It is worth noting, in passing, that speaking in terms of 'whole generations', or even 'people' in general, without drawing distinctions between employed or unemployed, rich and poor – in a word, between class conditions – is a marked characteristic of 'New Labour' discourse: Seyd and Whiteley's survey of Labour members actually found the strongest leftwing views among people in their thirties and forties.[27] The thirty and forty-somethings Blair's ally had in mind no doubt exist, but they are evidently a particular social category within their age group – people like Blair himself, perhaps. Be that as it may, Blair, says Porter, 'has realised that things are not as clear as they appeared to be in the eighties and that many of the new homeowners and new parents – in his words, "the moderate middle-income majority" – are also consumers of Murdochs's various media products. They are... concerned with social and economic issues... but perhaps the emphasis is more on the good management of a society than on fairness or compassion. And this is exactly the direction Tony Blair has taken Labour, arguing that a compassionate society is firstly a competently run and prosperous society …' – and so on. Or as Blair put it, in the soundbite language of 'modernisation':

> What we are about is a partnership between the public and the private sectors, rather than a battle between the two. We are about reforming the welfare state, making it a platform of opportunity. Tough on crime and tough on the causes of crime. Rolling back the quango state. It is extremely important to make sure before you start getting lost in the thicket of policy that the public has really got the big picture.[28]

Perhaps what has already been said is enough to convey some of the substance as well as the flavour of 'New Labour's' Project: i.e. it offers an optimistic prospect of a more rational, somewhat fairer, more efficiently run society, in which however nothing will be done that seriously offends the sensibilities or interests of the middle classes, or invites penalties from the markets. This is consistent with Labour's perceived electoral task (i.e., to break out of its old working class base), as well as being realistic about where economic power is seen to lie.

In terms of specific policies this has meant a drastic narrowing of the gap between the Thatcher legacy and what Labour proposes. For instance, 'reforming the welfare state, making it a platform of opportunity' means cutting it, while worrying about the 'poverty trap'; 'tough on crime and tough on the causes of crime' translates roughly into not opposing the 1994 Criminal Justice Act (which drastically reduced individual rights vis a vis the police), speaking critically about single parents, and promising jail sentences for people who persistently harass their neighbours, while also implying that better government under Labour will create more jobs and provide more housing and better child care and other services that evidently have a bearing on the level of crime.

On education, Blair has retreated from the party's previous commitment to return to control by elected local authorities schools that have 'opted out' (to be run by boards of governors responsible to the central government) under Thatcher's legislation.[29] On the economy, he has called for macro-economic policies of the strictest fiscal and monetary orthodoxy, not complemented by any firm commitment to reform the operations of the City or secure a significant increase in industrial investment. On health, he has endorsed only limited changes in the 'internal market' imposed by the Conservatives on the National Health Service, laying emphasis on the need to minimise further organisational disruption. On the constitution, he has endorsed the party's commitment to abolishing the hereditary element in the House of Lords and creating Scottish and Welsh Assemblies and though with an unconcealed lack of enthusiasm – the commitment to hold a referendum on proportional representation; and he has retreated from the commitment to establish regional assemblies in England, proposing instead to submit the idea to regional referenda.

Except on the constitution, Porter comments, 'each statement constitutes a synthesis between the Thatcherite reforms of the early eighties and communitarian politics.[30] And the same could really be said of the new Clause Four, which effectively ruled out any reversal of Conservative privatisations. Speaking generally, 'New Labour' policy is to accept most of Thatcher's legislative and administrative legacy in almost all spheres. The list of points on which change is promised is not long.

Lest this leave an impression of purely pragmatic adjustment to perceived electoral necessities, let us conclude this section with a quotation from one of Blair's speeches which paints the kind of broader picture that he favours (what Porter, perhaps unkindly, calls 'political cinemascope'). Celebrating the fiftieth anniversary of the 1945 Labour government, which he identified as having drawn its strength from a broad national consensus, Blair declared: 'I passionately want to lead a party which once again embodies and leads the national mood for change and renewal'. He concluded:

> Socialists have to be both moralists and empiricists. Values are fundamental. But socialism has to be made real in the world as it is and not as we would like it to be. Our commitment to a different vision of society stands intact. But the ways of achieving it must change. Those should and will cross the old boundaries between left and right, progressive and conservative. They did in 1945. What marks us out are the objectives and the sense of unity and purpose by which we are driven. Our task now is nothing less than national renewal. Rebuilding our country as a strong and active civil society. We should gain confidence from the government of 1945; confidence in our values, in our insights and in our ability to deliver change. The generation of 1945 has set us an example which it is an honour to follow.[31]

This kind of rhetoric has a forerunner, but it is the rhetoric of Ramsay MacDonald, not Clement Attlee. Of course MacDonald's style belonged to the days of platform oratory, and audiences that were still used to sermons; Blair's is attuned to the production of quotable quotes in fifteen-second soundbites. But what they have in common is the theme of class conciliation, wrapped in misty appeals to social bonds that transcend class divisions. Where MacDonald spoke of 'all practical men and women' Blair talks about 'a strong and active civil society'. Both constantly invoke 'the nation'. Both have their eyes fixed on the middle-class voter.[32]

In 1945 Attlee did not need this kind of rhetoric, for a simple reason: thanks to the slump and the war, the ideas and policies for which the party had campaigned for over a decade had already become hegemonic within a large part of the middle class, so that a spade could be called a spade. Nationalisation, whether of the mines or the Bank of England, could be called nationalisation, and nothing could have been more specific than universal social security, a free health service, and full employment. But unlike Attlee, and like MacDonald, 'New Labour' is far from having propounded policies capable of bringing about 'national renewal', let alone made them hegemonic. This is why Blair's rhetoric has the MacDonaldite flavour it has.

Intellectuals and 'New Labour'

Much of what Blair has accomplished was begun by Kinnock. Their projects are separated, however, by more than John Smith's brief interregnum. There is a different rhetoric, symbolised by the 'New Labour' label adopted (in imitation of Bill Clinton's self-description as a 'New Democrat') by the Blair leadership, and it has different intellectual roots.[33] Some of these lie in Blair's own formation as a Christian socialist at Oxford, but there are other contributions that need to be taken into account, even if this can be done only in a tentative and sketchy way here.

One contribution of intellectuals to the project of the 'modernisers' is that mainstream commentators have been remarkably uncritical; whether because his interlocutors are impressed by his rhetoric, or because they tacitly yearn for a change of government, or even hope to influence it, is impossible to say. The closest Henry Porter, in the interview already cited, came to a criticism was to note Blair's unconvincing reply to the question, how he envisaged Britain after two years of a Labour government; 'it was the least fluent answer, and petered out in a series of headings.[34] Criticism from the left of the Labour party has been dismissed (and not reported) as old-fashioned and irrelevant, though with occasional condescending acknowledgements of its 'sincerity' (or even, in the case of Tony Benn, its 'authority'; and criticism from the right, however perceptive, is seen as purely partisan.[35] One of the very few mainstream commentators to raise appropriate doubts has been the former SDP theorist David Marquand. The buzzwords of neoliberalism – 'flexibility', 'dynamism', 'enterprise' and 'competitiveness' – are now seen to be

> merely code words for harder work for longer hours, with less protection against
> more powerful bosses. But when we try to tell our rulers that... we face a blank wall
> of patronising management-speak ...New Labour speaks a different dialect from
> the Government's, but not a different language... On the central question now
> facing the political economies of western Europe, new Labour and the new right
> are one.[36]

Television interviewers, however, have rarely confronted the Labour leader with
this palpable truth. The absence of serious intellectual criticism in the mainstream media has surely played a part in the modernisers' advance.

Of course, the other side of this phenomenon has been 'New Labour's' own
heavy investment in media management. Peter Mandelson, in his role as director
of the Communications and Campaigns Directorate in the late 1980s, became
Labour's answer to Mrs Thatcher's Press Secretary Bernard Ingham, tirelessly
'managing' news and tempting, cajoling or bullying journalists and editors to
give favourable treatment to the Labour leadership. According to Bryan Gould
and others, Mandelson also emulates Ingham's notorious 'black briefings',
putting out unattributable negative comments on individual colleagues;[37] and
he has been widely credited with doing the same, in an unofficial capacity, on
behalf of Tony Blair.[38]

However Mandelson's role should not be seen in a purely practical light, nor
should Blair's alleged comment that 'my project will be complete when the
Labour Party learns to love Peter Mandelson' be seen as merely provocative.[39]
Mandelson attracts hostility for a reason that goes deeper than his alleged devi-
ousness: he accepts the electoral logic of social democracy in the age of global
capitalism with a consistency and wholeheartedness of which most Labour MPs,
let alone rank and file members, are incapable.[40] He takes it as given that globalisation imposes very severe limits on all social and economic policies, so that the
only ones worth promoting are those that capital – 'the market' – will accept;
and he includes in this the power of the increasingly globally-owned media,
and is determined to do whatever it takes – including getting Blair to make his
highly symbolic visit to the annual meeting in Australia of Murdoch's world-
wide media executives – to win whatever political leeway this situation affords
(such as a less venomously hostile treatment by the one-third of British national
newspaper circulation controlled by Murdoch than was given to Kinnock). In
his view, to oppose this is sentimental self-indulgence which the party cannot
afford; his notorious alleged remarks about the party conference or the unions
being dispensable are deliberate provocations to those who resist this logic.[41]
What most profoundly upsets many of his critics, one suspects, is that they do
not really see a way of staying in the electoral game without adopting in practice
what Mandelson makes into a point of principle, including accepting the media

as they are. They know that any serious proposal to bring the media under control, to de-commodify them and recreate a genuinely open medium for political debate, would attract the massed opposition of all the media, in the name – so far has the ideological pass already been sold – of the principle of 'free speech'. Mandelson's chief fault is, then, to act openly on a logic that in practice they accept, but have trouble acknowledging. It is hard to deny that in doing so he does the party the significant intellectual service of challenging hypocrisy.

But if Mandelson is the Labour Party's intellectual 'bad cop', there are others who aspire to be good ones, to equip the party with ideas and policies which on their merits will win the party a succession of elections and allow it to refashion British society. These intellectuals have operated largely, if not exclusively, through various new 'think tanks' which have proliferated in the later years of Labour's prolonged exile from office. This no doubt partly reflects the exhaustion of the Labourist tradition, embodied in the Fabian Society and discredited by the crisis of social democracy in the 1970s, although other factors are undoubtedly also involved, including the example of the role played by right-wing think tanks in the evolution of 'Thatcherism'.[42] Think-tanks also act as screening-mechanisms, putting into the public arena only work that conforms to their respective ideological orientations, for party leaders to take or leave; this may also have simplified the Blair team's task in avoiding the kind of intellectuals they felt unsympathetic towards.[43] At all events, by the end of the 1980s at least three significant left-of-centre policy study centres were in business: the Institute of Public Policy Research (IPPR), Charter 88, and Demos.

Of these only the IPPR, founded in 1988, was specifically designed to help the Labour Party. Although it was formally a non-party institution, its first director (Baroness Blackstone) and deputy director (Patricia Hewitt, fresh from supervising Labour's Policy Review) were both prominent Labour figures, and its task was to provide Labour, following its purge of old policies, with a body of solidly-researched policy documents of a calibre which the party's own 'policy directorate' did not have the resources to produce. Its publications, and most notably the much-publicised report of the Borrie Commission on Social Justice, established on the initiative of John Smith as Labour leader, have a characteristic blend of 'realistic' (in the 'modernisers" sense) assumptions about the permanence of global capitalism, and well-documented analyses of economic and social problems and suggestions for their amelioration within the limits of the possible;[44] where the Fabians' motto was, 'When I strike, I strike hard', the IPPR's might be, 'We can't strike, but we'll try pushing'. Blair's thinking undoubtedly draws on the work of the IPPR (and David Miliband, his political adviser, was secretary to the Borrie Commission), although it is not the main source of his inspiration.

Even less central to Blair's thinking, perhaps, is Charter 88, a non-party organisation also established in 1988, which focusses on issues of democratic rights and liberties. Although its substantial work on issues like devolution and Quangos has undoubtedly contributed both to Labour thinking and to building public support for constitutional reform, its advocacy of proportional representation and a written constitution, both dear to the Liberal-Democrats and both unpopular with Blair and his team, makes it a tainted source.[45]

But the case is very different with Demos, the youngest of the three think-tanks in question, launched in early 1993. Geoff Mulgan, its founder-director, was formerly adviser to Gordon Brown, Blair's Shadow Chancellor of the Exchequer, and felt that 'public policy and politic thinking' had 'become too short-term, partisan and out of touch':

> In the past creative thinking often came from within the traditional institutions of parliament and parties, and from within the main political ideologies. But these are no longer able to keep up with the pace of change in society, the economy, technology and culture. Society has become more porous and complex, as old traditions and hierarchies have broken down. Demos is a response to this new situation. It draws on ideas from outside the political mainstream ... the main focus is on long-term issues rather than the immediate programmatic needs of parties and government. In addition, Demos has two broader aims: one is to help modernise our political culture, to make it more relevant more international and more at ease with the future. The other is to point the way to new forms of democracy and governance fit for the 21st century.[46]

There is no space here to do justice to the range and vitality of Demos's publications in the first two and a half years of its life. Mulgan's intellectual verve and energy are stamped on the whole enterprise, not only in the choice of topics and authors for research projects and publications, but also in the form of a series of impressive lead articles co-authored by him in Demos Quarterly, the organisation's theme-oriented journal: these include 'The End of Unemployment', 'Back to Greece: the Scope for Direct Democracy', and 'Well-being and Time'.[47] These articles have distinctive merits and shortcomings; all that is possible here is to indicate certain characteristics of Mulgan's work, reflected broadly in the output of Demos generally, that are also evident in the speeches of Tony Blair.

First, there is a distinctive kind of utopianism, springing from the almost complete lack of any serious attention to political economy. Mulgan acknowledges that Demos has neglected political economy; this is deliberate, inasmuch as he thinks political economy is a 'weak' field.[48] Paradoxically, the resulting utopianism is presented as 'realism'. The question posed is predominantly one of what shall we do about various trends that are inexorably working themselves out through the dynamics of modern capitalism and the technological changes it brings – this is the 'realism' part. What is utopian is that no particular constraints accompany the options considered, and no agents of change are specified; we are often in a world of social science fiction. Mulgan seems able to envisage things which seem prima facie absurd, such as a world of totally 'flexible' employment, in which no one has a job, but only short-term contracts casual labour in modern dress;[49] perhaps this is what 'making our political culture more relevant' (to what, exactly?) means. Sometimes, though not always, he subsequently raises doubts about these implausible futures, but by no means always feels compelled to make a final judgement between the thesis and its antithesis. For instance, on work 'flexibility', he also recognises that 'a fluid, disordered world will leave the majority miserable', so that 'alongside speed and flexibility we also need to remember the importance of balance: of mechanisms for finding useful activity for those [the majority?] left out by change; of public spaces for quiet and reflection, like parks and churches where time stands still; of home life as well as work life.'[50] But who the 'we' are, who should remember this, and what obstacles the dynamics of capitalism may place in the way of our doing anything about it, are not specified.

Second, there is a constant stress on complexity, differentiation, pluralism and choice. Partly this is code for abandoning analysis in terms of classes. Partly it seems to be a postmodern embrace of difference and particularity (which goes with a rejection of 'grand narratives', of which critical political economy is one). But whatever its sources, Mulgan's approach to the allegedly new degree of 'diversity' in contemporary capitalist societies leads him to make eclecticism into a virtue. No great effort is made to bring into any kind of systematic unity the topics, concepts, analyses and perceptions that he draws from so many diverse fields, or even to ask how far they are all compatible. There is a kaleidoscopic effect, analogous to the 'cinemascopic' character of Blair's speeches.

A third characteristic feature of Mulgan's work is a fascination with the new, especially if it comes from the USA.[51] This was well represented by Demos's sponsorship of a visit to the UK by the American 'communitarian' theorist Amitai Etzioni in March 1995, and the publication of his views on the 'parenting deficit' as a Demos pamphlet – views which accord well with the 'community oriented' Christianity that Blair adopted at Oxford; and immediately after Etzioni's visit Blair delivered a lecture in which he stressed the duties people owe to society and called for the prosecution of the parents of chronically truant schoolchildren, and action against noisy and abusive neighbours.[52] But it is not just new thinkers, so much as novelty itself, that is the key leitmotif of Mulgan's work. For him, what is wrong with past socialist thought is above all that it is 'out of touch' with the 'pace of change'; being 'in touch' is the supreme virtue. It is a virtue mainly found in the younger generation (a preoccupation with generational differences is one of Mulgan's favourite themes), but it is also something which even a middle-aged 'New Labour' standard-bearer can easily hold onto under pressure. When criticism of Blair's style of 'modernisation' finally surfaced in mid-1995, for instance, the once-radical 'old Labour' leader of Sheffield City Council, David Blunkett, now Shadow education spokesman, defended his vacationing leader in the following terms: 'The rapidity of change is such that if we don't stay ahead of the game, and are there speaking about the new world in a new situation, we will allow the election to slip away from us again.'[53]

I am not making any claim about the extent of Demos's influence on 'New Labour', in spite of Mulgan's close links to both Brown and Blair[54]. But if one were looking for the intellectual inspiration for what is most distinctive in the modernisation rhetoric of 'New Labour', this would have to be the place to start: 'realism' about (sc. acceptance of) global capitalism; a utopian approach to the discussion of responses to it, justified by the alleged incapacity of political economy to analyse it; the celebration of diversity and choice; the fetishism of change and novelty; the systematic rejection of analysis in terms of social class.

It is, as Tony Blair remarked, 'liberating' to cut free from the bonds of what he called a 'too narrow view of democratic socialism'[55], and 'New Labour's' young speechwriters, liberated from both the labour movement's past ethos and any particular intellectual discipline, may be able to deploy the buzzwords of 'modernisation' to good short-term electoral effect. But whether any serious project for social change, let alone one that can sincerely be called socialist, can be constructed on such foundations, is another question.

Conclusion

This is not to say that Tony Blair and his team are not serious about social change. They were undoubtedly right to think that change in the party was called for by much more than the need – however desperate that was – to win the next election. Even if the Conservative Party and the popular press had not persuaded a majority of voters that 'nationalisation' was inefficient, and the state 'too large', it would still have been essential for Labour to 'modernise' its policies and its structures in face of the multiple changes that have occurred over the last twenty years. The question is only what kind of modernisation is called for.

The most obvious criticism to be made of 'New Labour's' version is that it accepts the market uncritically, and substitutes elite centralism for democracy within the party. Labour's historic mission has been to counter-pose social need to the selfishness of the market and its socially destructive effects. Now the market's true character and destructive long-term effects are once again becoming plain for all to see – in the shape of chronic unemployment and growing job insecurity, growing inequality, social tensions and welfare dependency, a grossly neglected infrastructure and declining international competitiveness. It is by no means obvious that if the Labour Party firmly declared its opposition to a market-driven society (as opposed to one that accepts but seriously regulates markets) this would in the long run hurt it electorally, as the Thatcher years are exposed, week by week, as years of cruel illusion and deception. But a serious critique of the market is what 'New Labour', in its paralytic fear of seeming anticapitalist, above all abjures. 'New Labour' runs the risk, in fact, of achieving office – though not real power – on the basis of 'realistically' accepting the market just as its ultimate unacceptability, as the motor and arbiter of social life, is once again becoming clear.

Labour also has a rich pool of popular democratic experience and ideas, developed in the 1970s in reaction against the state-socialism of the postwar years, which could be drawn upon to help build a popular consensus for a new socialist project. But this too is treated by 'New Labour' as at best an irrelevance, and at worst a contamination. Centralisation of power in the party remains the order of the day.[56] Internal party debate has been reduced to a historic minimum. Policy is now 'revealed' at the party's annual conference, not decided there. 'New Labour' has, in effect, finally broken with any idea of the party as a vehicle for the aspirations and ideas of a social movement, the expression of any kind of collective will. From now on it will frankly be run by professional politicians with at most an occasional plebiscitary relationship with its members.

Notes

[1] L. Panitch and C. Leys, *The End of Parliamentary Socialism: From New Left to New Labour*, London, Verso, 1997, p. xiv

[2] Dennis Potter, *Seeing the Blossom* (London: Faber and Faber, 1994) p. 47.

[3] In an extraordinarily revealing interview the party's General Secretary, Tom Sawyer, said that 'he favoured management consultants to help inject new thinking into the party's targeting of new members, including judgements on whether members are best recruited in marginals or heartlands, to raise funds or to be active. Different marketing techniques will be used for different goals... The General Secretary has also taken members of the national executive to Cranfield Institute of Management to discuss the role of the committee.' (Guardian August 8 1995).

[4] Henry M. Drucker, *Doctrine and Ethos it: the Labour Party* (London: Allen and Unwin, 1979).

[5] Part of the reason for this is that Blair joined the Labour Party in London in 1975 as it was entering into a period of bitter internal conflict, and when the labour movement was ceasing to be as representative of the whole working class as it had once felt and, in some respects, been. At the same time, in his early years in the party he seems to have been peculiarly cut off from what was still positive and morally compelling in the old party ethos; see John Rentoul, *Tony Blair* (London: Little, Brown, 1995), especially chapters 3-4.

[6] The new Clause Four of the party constitution pledges the party to work for 'a just society' which 'nurtures families', but does not pledge it to make women equal with men or blacks with whites.

[7] Foot had been chosen as leader by the parliamentary party in 1979 when Callaghan resigned as a means of forestalling the possible election of the left-wing Tony Benn under the new leadership election system which had been adopted at the 1979 party conference, but which was not due to come into operation until 1980.

[8] Martin J. Smith, 'A Return to Revisionism? The Labour Party's Policy Review' in M.J. Smith and Joanna Spear (eds.), *The Changing Labour Party* (London: Routledge, 1992), p. 19.

[9] 'There were now, for the first time in party history, resources for a sizeable advisory staff available to the PLP leadership.' Lewis Minkin, *The Contentious Alliance: Trade Unions and the Labour Party* (Edinburgh: Edinburgh University Press, 1991), p. 400.

[10] Patrick Seyd and Paul Whiteley, 'Labour's Renewal Strategy', in Smith and Spear op. cit., p. 31.

[11] Minkin, op. cit., p. 409.

[12] Quoted in Richard Heffernan and Mike Marqusee, *Defeat from the Jaws of Victory, Inside*

Kinnock's Labour Party (London: Verso, 1992), p. 211. According to Colin Hughes and Patrick Wintour in *Labour Rebuilt: The New Model Party* (London: Fourth Estate, 1990) pp. 60-b1, the crucial document of this kind was 'Labour and Britain in the 1990s', presented to the NEC and Shadow Cabinet in November 1987.

[13] Hughes and Wintour, ibid., p. 153.

[14] One of the points on which all commentators seem to agree is the uselessness of 'Labour Listens', however high-minded its original intentions. See, e.g., Hughes and Wintour, op. cit., pp. 98-103, and Heffernan and Marqusee, op. cit., pp. 215-16.

[15] Heffernan and Marqusee, op. cit., p. 115. These authors are hostile witnesses, but the consequences of the phenomenon they correctly report in this passage were forcibly apparent following Tony Blair's election as leader in 1994. The press wanted to know from Blair's speeches what party policy would now be; the old discourse of how a new leader's personal views would sit with those of the majority in the national executive, let alone the annual conference, was completely absent. When Roland Wales, head of the party's Policy Directorate, finally resigned in October 1995, barely disguising the fact that it was because his job had become pointless, it was treated by the press as barely newsworthy.

[16] This idea was widely canvassed in the aftermath of the party's special conference in April 1995, at which some big unions cast votes against the change to a new Clause Four without having balloted their members, while the votes of those which had were cast in favour of the change. The non-balloting unions cited the expense involved – estimated at over £15 million – as a decisive objection, although several leaders were said to agree that some further democratisation of their policy-making procedures was now needed.

[17] The PLP agreed in July 1995 to allow the Chief Whip to be chosen by the leader from among the members of the Labour shadow cabinet (itself chosen by the PLP), rather than being directly elected to the post by the PLP, as the existing rules prescribed: the existing Chief Whip simultaneously agreed to stand down in October 1995 in return for a senior role in opposition and in a future Labour government, allowing Blair to appoint someone of his choice (Donald Dewar). It was also widely expected that Blair would eventually propose a name change for the party. Significantly, Blair announced at the April 1995 special conference on Clause Four that 'the name was not going to change' (i.e. from Labour to 'New Labour', as the party was now called on all its publications) – thus denying the rumour while simultaneously implying that it lay within his power to get it changed if he chose to.

[18] Besides Mandelson and Hewitt the group included Roger Liddle (a former adviser to Bill Rodgers, one of the SDP's founding figures); Geoff Mulgan, the founder and director of Demos, a non-party think-tank; Derek Scott, a City-based economist amd former adviser to Denis Healey as Chancellor of the Exchequer in the 1970s; and Sir Nicholas Monck, a former permanent secretary at the Department of Employment. As the press noted, none of Blair's shadow cabinet colleagues, nor the Deputy Leader, were included in the group, which was said to meet at Westminster on alternate Fridays (Michael White in *The Guardian* July 15 1995). A spokesman for Blair's office maintained that these were merely some individuals who had offered assistance on an ad hoc basis to 'write sections of speeches and background papers' (*The Guardian* July 17 1995). Patricia Hewitt said their function was to help write speeches and 'bounce ideas' (interview, August 2 1995). Given the freedom that the leader had by then acquired to make policy it would be naive to imagine that any group that had close and regular policy discussions with him was not influential.

[19] This process did not originate with Blair's election as leader. Already under Kinnock, according to Heffernan and Marqusee, 'For rank and file Party members... attending meetings came to seem pointless since the decisions had clearly already been taken at the top' (Heffernan and Marqusee, op. cit., p. 213).

[20] Dennis Potter, op. cit., p. 14.

[21] *New Statesman and Society*, August 11 1995. Burden was subsequently said to have realised too late that the article would create a lot of trouble and tried unsuccessfully to withdraw it, a claim which he later denied; if so, it is an interesting example of spindoctor disinformation.

[22] For example in Socialist Campaign News and Labour Briefing. The new public critics included John Edmonds, leader of the large General Municipal and Boilermakers union, and Roy Hattersley, the former Deputy Leader under Neil Kinnock, neither of whom was left-wing. According to Patrick Wintour (*The Guardian*, August 11 1995), 'Blairites argue that given the helter-skelter pace of his reform programme it is surprising that there have only been rumblings, rather than an earthquake. But much of the backstage criticism of Mr Blair is not directed at his reforms, but [sic] fears of what he may do, and the lack of consultation. Two recent deputations, one from the NEC and another from union sponsored MPs, went to complain about the threat to union sponsorship.

[23] Roy Hattersley, 'Why Labour is stumbling', *The Independent* August 12 1995.

[24] *The Guardian* September 5 1995. In the same interview Blair was also quoted as saying that 'the party had no plans to reduce the trade unions' block vote to below 50 per cent', which the paper called 'a conciliatory gesture to the unions'. The trade unions might be forgiven for being irritated rather than conciliated by this statement, since it was not for the leader to say what plans 'the party' had on this matter (compare note 16 above, with respect to changing the party's name).

[25] The 'adjusted' figure, i.e. adjusted by allocating the undecideds in the light of past voting patterns, was more like 17 percent-still a very large lead.

[26] Henry Porter, 'Zealous Moderate', *The Guardian*, July 18 1995

[27] Seyd and Whiteley, op. cit., p. 37.

[28] Ibid. One of the hallmarks of Blair's speaking style which may also well be a generational difference is his apparent comfort with this kind of language that the Shadow Communications Agency worked so hard to teach the Shadow Cabinet in the 1980s. Hughes and Wintour record how in 1988 Robin Cook and Harriet Harman were taught to say 'cash before care', instead of whatever they originally thought of saying in criticism of a leaked White Paper on health, and how this was worth £2m. of political advertising (op. cit. p. 59). A 'quango' is a 'quasi non-governmental organisation', appointive and largely unaccountable bodies whose number and membership (consisting largely of Conservative supporters) increased dramatically under the Thatcher years, to the point where they had many more members than the total of the country's elected councillors, and were responsible for spending roughly as much money.

[29] Education policy has been an instructive example of the changed locus of policy-making. In late 1994 David Blunkett, the shadow education minister, made a speech suggesting the possibility of removing the tax privileges enjoyed by private schools. This was immediately repudiated by the leader's office in an obvious effort at 'fire-fighting' – i.e. heading off a predictable attack from the Conservatives to the effect that Labour was still a party of class envy. Subsequently, after Blair's decision to send his own son to a distinctly elitist grant-maintained school (the London Oratory School) – a decision much resented by many inside the party, which was then committed to end grant-maintained status – Blunkett announced a new policy on these schools, proposing to put them on the same financial footing as local authority-controlled schools, but to leave them free from local authority control, relabelled as 'foundation schools'. Two aspects of this decision were noteworthy, in addition to its acceptance of the new social hierarchy that the Conservatives had thus created within the state education sector. One was that the press treated the new policy document 'Diversity and Excellence', produced by Blunkett in close collaboration with Blair's office, as 'Labour's new policy'. The other was Blunkett's comment on it: 'I think I have squared the circle' (*The Guardian* June 23 1995).

[30] Henry Porter, 'Rampaging with Charm', *The Guardian* July 17 1995.

[31] Tony Blair, 'The Flavour of Success', based on a speech made on July 5 1995 to the Fabian Society, *The Guardian* July 6,1995

[32] For a discussion of MacDonald's socialism and the context that governed it see David Marquand, *Ramsay MacDonald* (London: Jonathan Cape, 1977), especially pp. 88-92, 245 56 and 279. It is sobering to note that while much of Marquand's analysis applies very closely to Blair, there is a fundamental difference: throughout the twenties MacDonald opposed the market and accorded priority to the interests of the working class and the unemployed.

[33] For the visit of Tony Blair and Gordon Brown to Clinton's 'transition team' after the Presidential election of 1992 see John Rentoul, *Tony Blair* (London: Little Brown, 1995), Ch. 13. Much of the visit was arranged by the Political Secretary at the Washington embassy, Jonathan Powell; in 1995 he left the foreign service to become Blair's 'head of private office'. One of Powell's brothers, Chris, ran an advertising agency which had the Labour Party's account. Another brother, Charles, had been Thatcher's Private Secretary.

[34] 'The main changes will be a strong attack on long-term unemployment, the problems of getting people back to work; a proper modern industrial policy, preparing this country for the global market; education and schools; help for small businesses; economic regeneration; science and technology...' ('Rampaging With Charm', op. cit.).

[35] The former Conservative Minister for Defence, Alan Clark, criticising the intellectual positions of both parties in early 1995, wrote provocatively: 'Here is this great Labour movement, rooted in a noble ethic... Now they are quite deliberately choosing to discard the whole of that tradition... 'New Labour' is no more than a bunch of people who want to win an election... Simply an alternative cluster of suits who, marginally more "likeable", will administer virtually identical policies... You can anaesthetise great parties, for short periods, by the prospect of power as a reward for "good behaviour". But lobotomies are different.' (*The Guardian*, March 17 1995).

[36] David Marquand, 'Political babble', *The Guardian* June 5 1995.

[37] Bryan Gould, 'The party with no bottle', an extract from his autobiography *Goodbye To All That* (London: Macmillan, forthcoming 1995) in *The Guardian* August 19 1995.

[38] According to Porter, he provided Blair with 'both manipulative expertise and certain covert services with which the leader should not be too visibly associated' ('Zealous Moderate', op. cit.). One could speculate that these services included covert help to Jack Dromney, the challenger in 1995 for the leadership of the Transport and General Workers' Union favoured by Blair, and similar interventions in candidate selection; including, perhaps, Blair's announcement in August 1995, on his own authority, that women-only shortlists, which the party had agreed to apply to candidate selection in half Labour's vacant seats and which were unpopular with many of the male members of the constituency patties concerned, would be dropped after the next election.

[39] Quoted in Seumas Milne, 'The Leader's Little Helper', *The Guardian* February 11, 1995.

[40] One is reminded of the opprobrium heaped on Edward Bernstein for spelling out the principles of the German Social Democrats' reformist practice in his *Evolutionary Socialism*. His friend Ignaz Auer wrote protestingly: 'My dear Ede, you don't talk about it, you just do it!' (quoted in Peter Gay, *The Dilemma of Democratic Socialism* (New York: Columbia University Press, 1952, p. 267).

[41] According to Heffernan and Marqusee, Mandelson once said it would be nice to abolish the party conference, but it was not worth the trouble (op. cit., p. 209), and that in private he 'made it clear that as far as he was concerned the unions were a nuisance and the sooner they were expelled from Labour headquarters the better' (p. 218).

[42] Radhika Desai summarises the most commonly adduced factors as follows: 'the institutionalisation of intellectual life in the Academy, its consequent isolation from wider social currents and its attendant disciplinary specialisation; the domination of intellectual life by the media; the substitution of market-driven decisions for any independent judgement intellectuals have had in culture and politics; and the replacement of a generally educated public, interested in social and political ideas, by a plurality of more specialised and disparate audiences' (Radhika Desai, *Intellectuals and Socialism: 'Social Democrats' and the Labour Party* (London: Lawrence and Wishari, 1994), p. 27). Whatever the mix of causes, it is striking that by 1994 it was hard to find a significant intellectual making a sustained left-wing public argument for a particular line of policy outside the framework of the think-tanks. Exceptions within the PLP would include Tony Benn and Alan Simpson in the Socialist Campaign Group of MPs, and Frank Field, an independent thinker on a wide range of social issues; outside parliament the chief exception was Will Hutton, the Guardian's assistant editor and columnist, arguing for a more radical set of 'social market' reforms than anything the Labour leadership was likely to countenance. Occasional commentators from the universities, such as David Marquand and Andrew Gamble at Sheffield, or John Gray at Oxford and William

Wallace at the LSE, did not so much argue for a particular line of policy as comment critically on the shortcomings of current Labour and Conservative policies and ideas.

[43] Numerous highly competent left intellectuals, very aware of the need for a radical rethinking of the socialist project and uninterested in Labour's shibboleths, were more than ready to work for the new leadership, but were not welcomed, let alone sought after. A study of those who were welcomed would make interesting reading. One of the striking features of Blair's immediate entourage was how many people it included who were formerly non-political or had SDP or Liberal-Democrat ties.

[44] The Bowie Report, *Social Justice: Strategies for National Renewal* (London: Vintage, 1994), is actually a comprehensive programme of economic and social reform for national competitiveness.

[45] The key text on Quangos is Stuart Weir and Wendy Hall (eds.), *Ego Trip: Extra-governmental organizations in the United Kingdom and their accountability* (London: The Democratic Audit of the United Kingdom and Charier 88, 1994). See also Anthony Barnett's persuasively argued *The Defining Moment* (Charter 88, 1995), setting out the constitutional issues at stake for the Labour Party in the next general election. The striking level of support for a bill of rights, proportional representation and other constitutional reforms, which have been advocated by the Liberal Democrats but not the Labour Party, must owe something to the publicity and mobilising efforts of Charter 88.

[46] From the statement, 'Why Demos?', in Demos's brochure.

[47] In Demos 2, 1994, pp. 4-14; Demos 3 1994, pp. 2-9; and Demos 5 1995, pp. 2-11.

[48] Interview, August 11, 1995. Mulgan has also written that 'Marx may have had an unequalled grasp of the dynamics of capitalism but he is not much use for a world of derivatives trading' (*The Guardian* January 14 1995). Demos intends to undertake work in political economy in the future.

[49] Or a world of 'twin economies' in which those who can't earn incomes in the main economy operate in a separate quasi-barter economy with state support, such as free access for market stalls on derelict land and ultra-cheap building accommodation (Geoff Mulgan, 'Creating a twin economy', *Demos Quarterly* 2/1994, p. 29). Mulgan's capacity to think positively about this sort of future has something in common with Mandelson's famous 'unsentimental' approach to politics. It marks them both off decisively from the ethos of the labour movement, including its past intellectual wing.

[50] Geoff Mulgan and Helen Wilkinson, 'Well-being and Time', Demos Quarterly 5/1995, p. 11.

[51] In an interview 1 put it to Geoff Mulgan that his preoccupation with introducing American thinkers to the British public had a parallel with the New Left Review's efforts to introduce European Marxism to Britain in the late 1960s and early 1970s. He dissented to the extent that he had no specific line of thought to promote, and turned to the USA only as a major source of high-calibre and varied thought relevant to the fast-changing real world.

[52] Criticism of the communitarian discourse of Blair's Spectator lecture was an exception to the mainstream's general tolerance of his political rhetoric; in *The Guardian* John Gray,Will Hutton, Bea Campbell, Martin Walker and Suzanne Moore all devoted space to thoughtful critiques.

[53] *The Guardian* August 21 1995. Blunkett was responding specifically to the charge by Alan Simpson MP, the secretary of the Socialist Campaign group, that under Blair the party was becoming indistinguishable from the old SDP Perhaps, if Mulgan read Blunkett's statement, he experienced the kind of feelings teachers have when they read in them students' essays unconscious and sometimes embarassingly revealing parodies of then own ideas.

[54] Mulgan was a member of the previously-mentioned so-called 'secret committee of trusted moderates' set up to meet fortnightly with Blair at Westminster.

[55] Tony Blair, 'The flavour of success', op. cit.

[56] A further instance was the rejection by the National Executive Committee of Liz Davies as a prospective parliamentary candidate for Leeds East just before the annual Conference in October 1995. Ms Davies, a barrister, had been adopted by a substantial majority of the local party from a women-only shortlist. Her real crime, it was clear, was her advocacy of left-wing views.

Editorial Introduction to Extract 12

This section concludes with my 1996 essay on 'old constraints and new parameters'. Written ahead of the arrival of New Labour in power, it has much in common with the pieces reproduced earlier from *The Socialist Register*. Its argument reflects the long-term influence – sometimes direct, sometimes more mediated – of Miliband's work on the Labour Party and the Labour Left. The central thesis of this piece, originally published in *New Left Review,* is that New Labour was not quite as new as it persistently claimed – that in truth much of what was presented as novel by the Blairites had recognizable antecedents in earlier periods of Labour Party history. The point of setting New Labour in that longer time frame was to underscore the likelihood that, once in office, old patterns of Labour Government conservatism would also reappear. The essay undoubtedly bent the stick too far against the grain of New Labour claims in making its central assertion– playing down to an erroneous degree the extent to which New Labour had actually entirely abandoned any attempt to realize the reformist project of earlier Labour administrations. It also, with the wisdom of hindsight, failed adequately to anticipate the depth of the Tory implosion, and the associated length of time New Labour would enjoy in power without serious political opposition. But its emphasis on continuities was (and is) important still – not least as a counterweight to that view of the past (as somehow qualitative different, and either better or worse, depending on your contemporary politics) that creeps into both Blairite justifications of why the party had to change and Labour Left arguments that it ought not to have done so. In its sensitivity to the limitations of past Labour Party practice, and its pessimism about the possibilities of any left-wing party transformation, the essay stands fully within the Miliband tradition; and brings us, as with Colin Leys' essay, to the very moment of New Labour's arrival in power.

12. LABOUR GOVERNMENTS: OLD CONSTRAINTS AND NEW PARAMETERS (1996)

David Coates

It is good to be able to explore again the pattern of constraints likely to beset a Labour Government. For a long time now, such concerns have been definitely off our collective agendas because of the string of heavy electoral defeats for Labour. The bulk of the UK Left spent the 1980s discussing not how to use power but how to win it: how to create a bloc of electoral forces sufficient large to bring an end to Thatcherism. We all read Eric Hobsbawm, struggled with the possibility that the *Forward March of Labour* had well and truly *Halted*, and contemplated the politics of electoral pacts. Yet that seems for the moment now to be behind us. It seems that realistically we can begin to anticipate again the arrival of Labour in power; and, because we can, it is time to go back to literatures and arguments prevalent on the Left in the 1960s and 1970s, literatures concerned with the aspirations of incoming Labour governments and with the barriers likely to be erected in their path. Of course, here as elsewhere, the past is never a perfect guide to the future. Some at least of the barriers awaiting a Blair government will be new ones – in form certainly, even in basic character – but I suspect that most will not. For in a very real sense we already know much of what will constrain an incoming Labour Government, because we also know what constrained Labour governments in the past. So in order not to be overly surprised when the constraints come, and in order to avoid the temptation then to re-invent the wheel, this is an opportune moment to look back, and to consider again what happens to Labour governments whenever they try to rule UK capital.

Electoral and Governmental Continuities

Looking back at the record of the Labour Party as a political force in the UK since 1900, the over-riding impression that we need to keep before us is that of weakness and fragility. We need to remember how regularly hopes have been created only to be dashed, promises made only to be broken, agendas set never to be sustained. We need to remember how previous generations of Labour politicians – both in opposition and in power – tended to fall short of even the most modest aims of the people sustaining them; and we need to contemplate at least the possibility that a Blair-led Labour government will disappoint its supporters in a similar way. Amid the understandable pleasure, for many on the Left, at the prospect of a Conservative electoral defeat at last, we need to keep a very tight grip on any creeping sense of euphoria. For there are very good reasons to anticipate that the performance of New Labour in power will actually be poorer even than that of the Labour governments which preceded it. These reasons are rooted ultimately in underlying continuities in Labour politics which the term 'New Labour' serves only to obscure. Such continuities are, at one and the same time, electoral and governmental in character.

In electoral terms, it is striking how much assistance from external events and forces the Labour Party has always needed to create an electoral bloc sufficiently substantial to give it parliamentary power. It is also striking just how quickly that bloc has then eroded. After all, it took two world wars and a massive capitalist depression to wean sufficiently large numbers of UK workers away from an electoral loyalty to Liberalism and Conservatism, to give Labour its first (and still its largest) parliamentary majority in 1945. It then took another thirteen years of Conservative mismanagement and anachronistic fustiness to enable Harold Wilson fleetingly to reconstitute the width of that electoral bloc in 1966; and in neither instance did Labour manage to retain over the long term the majority it had so gratuitously won.

For in each case Labour was largely the passive recipient of electoral swings. Its own politics never normally possessed sufficient magnetic force to redraw the shape of electoral Britain by the power of its own programme and possibilities alone. The forces shaping that electoral map were largely external to Labour and beyond its control. They came (and the Labour Party flourished); they went (and the Labour Party was unable to prevent their going). It is true, of course, that the Labour Party, did slowly build up its core vote by its own organizational and ideological efforts: defeating the Communist Party for the loyalty (by 1945) of the majority of unionized workers. But its capacity as a party to sweep up the bulk of the unorganized working class (in 1945) and of the new white collar and managerial strata in the private sector (in 1966), was largely not of its doing. Admittedly, it promised full employment and welfare to woo the first in 1945; and it promised industrial modernization to woo the second in 1966. But in each case Labour was incapable of preventing the erosion of its electoral support beyond a reliable core; and since 1966 (and especially 1979), as we know to our cost, the Party has also seen its core vote dramatically erode. Labour is now the party of public-sector workers (both proletarian and semi-professional), not of the organized working class in total, and is having to win back the vote of skilled workers in private industry – votes that, between 1945 and 1966, it briefly but unambiguously came to think of as its own.

This electoral fragility was, on the surface, the product of a particular pattern of performance in government. But it was also, in a deeper way the product of the relationship that Labour politicians habitually establish with their own electorate, whether in government or not. Labour has never established what we could call – in a Gramscian sense – a hegemonic relationship with its own

electoral base; and it certainly is not doing so now. Even in its heyday the Labour
Party never created a extensive and sophisticated socialist universe – of newspapers, clubs, communities and institutions – within which to fuse itself to its people. It never created a labour movement in anything other than name. Instead
of consolidating a strong class movement behind it, to sustain its radicalism in
office, the Labour Party in the past was satisfied merely to establish an episodic
and ephemeral relationship between itself and its people, a relationship wholly
mediated through the pursuit and registering of the vote. And, even as an electoral machine, the Party's presence at grass-roots level has lain (and continues to
lie) dormant between elections, only swinging into frenetic activity in the run-
up to election day. In those moments it has always insisted – certainly by implication and often explicitly – that the whole task of the Left should be reduced to
door-knocking and vote-catching. But the very fact that the Labour Party in the
vast majority of its constituencies has not crossed any doors since the last election, tends to mean that fewer doors open to it, and that doors open to it with
increasing indifference, except in circumstances of Tory crisis that the Labour
Party itself can do little to precipitate. Not surprisingly then, Labour majorities
when they come tend to be accidental rather than created, and invariably prove
to be as tenuous as they are fortuitous.

I will return to the question of hegemonic politics – to the issue of the stability,
commitment and meaning of the Labour vote – in the last section of this article;
but let me add now that the electoral fragility of Labour since 1966 has been
massively reinforced by the under-performance of Labour in power. Labour
Governments hitherto – even when they have had parliamentary majorities –
have fallen into a regular and a depressing mould; and indeed have done so on a
declining trajectory – in the sense that the performance of each majority Labour
government to date has been, in retrospect, less satisfactory than the one before.
A brief resume of the overall performance of each post-war Labour government
makes that very clear.

The Attlee Government – inheriting as it did an extensive wartime planning
machine and a culture of cooperation and planning, and facing a momentarily
discredited (and briefly less self-confident) capitalist class – did extend public
ownership, create welfare institutions and maintain full-employment. However,
even it was blown off course by financial crises from 1947. It retreated rapidly
from planning and controls towards the end of its tenure in office, and experienced growing difficulties with wage restraint and incomes policy by 1951. But
at least Attlee left office with the Party's massive popular vote intact, robbed of
power in the end, not by the defection of supporters, but by the vagaries of the
UK electoral system.

Not so the first Wilson governments, which had started with such promise
(Tony Blair please note) of a New Britain – which would be scientific, dynamic,
competitive and socially just. The first Wilson governments fell after a prolonged

period of tension with the trade unions, and after the first mini-winter of discontent (by 1970 the brief flirtation of sections of the private-sector middle class
with Labour was already over, though its trade union electoral base remained
intact, if by then largely inert and unenthusiastic). Then in the 1970s the story
repeated itself with a louder drum roll and more awesome consequences. For
though it was forced into radicalism by trade union pressure between 1970 and
1974, and entered office against the backcloth of unprecedented industrial militancy and working-class self-confidence, the last Wilson government quickly
made a turn to the right, under financial pressure and eventually IMF instruc-
tion, at the cost eventually (for Callaghan, if not for Wilson) of a massive winter
of discontent and heavy electoral hemorrhaging. As we now know, 1979 was a
great watershed. It marked the beginning of the loss of the votes of skilled workers, particularly the votes of skilled workers in the South, workers antagonized
by four years of pay restraint. (It was in this respect both ironic and significant
that the first Cabinet casualty of that erosion should have been Shirley Williams,
defeated in Dagenham in 1979 by the defection of car workers.) From 1979 the
Labour Party began to turn itself from the party of the organized working class
into the party of the old northern working class. The electoral loyalty of its
southern proletarian base was progressively eroded.

The underlying problem was and is very clear. If those Labour governments
had wanted, as they said they wanted, to run a successful welfare capitalism in
a socially progressive way, they each needed to put together a bloc of social
forces – a governmental bloc-built (if the Swedish model is any guide) primarily
around an organic relationship between the party and the unions. But, as we
have seen, only twice, and then only briefly, have previous Labour governments
possessed such a bloc. What is striking about the first of those periods was how
quickly the Attlee Government retreated from the orchestration of such a bloc
– abandoning both radicalism and modernization – under the impact of external pressures, primarily from the US, pressures fed directly into the power-
equation through sterling crises and dollar shortages. Yet the Attlee retreat was
at least largely *imposed*, unlike that of the Wilson government a generation later,
when the retreat was far more internally triggered and *voluntary*. The last Wilson
government retreated from interventionism (for both radical and modernizing
ends) as quickly as it could, after being given what the bulk of its leading members took to be a more conservative mandate by the EC referendum result in
1975. So never in this party's by now long history has its leadership consciously,
deliberately and over a long period of time sought to construct such a progressive modernizing bloc; and it is not doing so now. Even in opposition, the Party
under Tony Blair is not prepared to be seen in close proximity to the unions;
and the unions are so weakened as no longer to be insisting on such proximity. Rather, both are conscious of the electoral price of creating such a bloc in
the short time before the next election; and in that sense both the Party and the

unions are now immobilized by the legacy of Labour's wasted years: when the Party (and particularly the leadership) did nothing effectively to resist the strident anti-unionism of the dominant liberal-conservative culture.

The pattern of past Labour governments is clear: initial high hopes and grand promises rapidly giving way – via poor performance – to great disappointments and voter alienation. So far at least, Labour has never managed to hold on to power for more than one parliament and a bit; and no Labour government (not even Attlee's) has yet managed to sustain its initial policy stance. Rather, and in every case, Labour's policy shift when in power has invariably been from initial radicalism to eventual moderation at the cost ultimately (with the possible exception of the Attlee governments) of an industrial and electoral confrontation with at least sections of Labour's own proletarian base. Promising much and delivering little, Labour has never yet managed to establish itself as the governing party; and because it has not, the question we must face is whether an incoming Blair administration can do any better.

Back to the Future

Blairite optimism that things will be different this time round is currently very high. Supporters of the present Labour leadership would no doubt treat the story I have just told as the story of 'Old Labour', and insist that theirs will be the story of 'New Labour'. Not for them the heady promises of radical change. They will disappoint less by promising less; and by delivering on their more modest promises. As Mandelson and Liddle put it:

> New Labour ... in giving renewed expression to the Party's founding beliefs ... is a deliberate move forward from ... the postwar Labour Party of Wilson and Callaghan ... Modernization is about more than developing a package of attractive propositions that can win Labour power. It is about working through a credible strategy for successful government that avoids the failures of the past.[1]

Yet not all of us are convinced of the viability of this claim, or even that there is very much that is actually new in 'New Labour'. Of course, New Labour likes to present itself as qualitatively different from Old Labour[2], and it is true that the internal story of the Labour Party since 1983 has been one of a retreat from Bennite radicalism, from the Alternative Economic Strategy and from nuclear disarmament. But the degree of retreat (which is marked, and which is indeed the basis of New Labour's claim to be new) actually tells us more about the degree of leftward shift that occurred between 1979 and 1983 than it does about the novelty of New Labour. In many ways New Labour is working its way back to the Party's conventional understanding of how to trigger economic growth through the construction of a close and collaborative relationship with the owners of private capital. It is all very well for Mandelson and Liddle to posit an alternative policy package from the past – of 'centralized planning and state control'[3]-as the epitome of Old Labour. It is all very well for them to contrast the view of 'past Labour governments' on the mixed economy and New Labour's commitment to the rigour of the dynamic market.' That may work for short-term rhetorical and electoral purposes; but it cannot stand as an accurate picture of what previous Labour governments actually did. What previous Labour governments actually did was work with the grain of market forces, in a collaborative relationship with senior managers in major companies, to trigger privately-generated economic growth; and that, of course, is precisely what New Labour is saying that it intends to do as well.

Perhaps one reason why New Labour does not recognize its own place in the actual continuity of Labour politics is that the Blairites' own historical memory seems remarkably short. New Labour obviously has a PR reason for asserting its newness: but it is worrying to see its leading apologists so persuaded by their own public relations. That, in its turn, may have something to do with the fact that so many of the leading New Labourites are very young (in actual years and in years of party service) and that it is now so long since Labour was last in power. New Labour is certainly new in generational terms. Its leading figures will come to government – if they do – without any direct personal involvement in Labour's last governmental failure; and in that rather trivial sense New Labour does represent a sharp rupture with even the Party's recent past. But any political party out of office for so long has to be 'new' in this way, as one generation of politicians gives way to another, and the Labour Party has certainly gone through such generational shifts on a number of occasions in the past (after 1931, after 1951, and again since 1979). The more important question is whether such a generational shift marks an equivalent rupture in the underlying policy orientations that otherwise link these generations of leaders one to another. The important question is not whether the personalities are new, but whether the arrival of a new set of leading players also signals a qualitative break with the Party's underlying continuities and traditions.

New Labour likes to present itself as just such a qualitative break and many of the Party's left-wing critics are currently treating Blairite party reforms and policy retreats in equally cosmic terms. So – amid the hype now surrounding the impending arrival of the Blair-led Party in power – it is worth bending the stick the other way: to emphasize the persistence of party traditions, and to place current developments in the context of Labour's underlying policy continuities. It is worth reminding ourselves that the Labour Party has always been a broad coalition of two main groupings, two projects, two political universes: a coalition of *social reformists* (keen to subordinate the power of private capital to progressive social ends) and *bourgeois radicals* (keen to modernize the local industrial base). It is worth reminding ourselves, that is, that in a very real sense *there has always been Old Labour and New Labour.*

The politics of Labour's social reformists have always focused on redistributing power (and resources) from the privileged to the poor. The politics of Labour's bourgeois radicals have always focused on strengthening the competitiveness of local capital, from which to glean surpluses for welfare provision without major policies of income redistribution. What is new about New Labour is not that the general economic policy stance of the Blairites is fundamentally novel: on the contrary, as I say, in general terms it is simply that into which Labour governments in the past have quickly and consistently settled. What is new in New Labour is that the forces of Old Labour are so weak. It is the *dominance and self-confidence* of the modernizers, not their novelty, which distinguishes the Blair party from its predecessors; and since what Blair calls 'new' has been the dominant policy stance of every Labour government after its brief flirtation with radicalism – since every Labour government has tried to do what Blair says he is trying to do – the fate of earlier Labour administrations does have a relevance for the future of a Labour government led by him.

In the past, when many of us spent our time examining Labour governments, it was the defeat of their radical ambitions, the defeat of social reformism, that tended to hold our attention. Certainly looking back over my writing, that is definitely the case.[4] And when exploring that – when asking why Left Labourism did not succeed, even when it had the upper hand within the Party (as it did between 1970 and 1975) – what emerged was a picture of fierce and deeply embedded constraints on radical politics. The quickest way to picture those constraints is to imagine a pebble dropped into a pond, with ripples flowing out in ever widening circles. If you put 'Old Labour' in the middle of the circles – let it be the pebble dropped into the encircling constraints – then you can move out, making a list of where the barriers lay. In the 1970s they lay firstly within the Labour Cabinet (with the modernizers themselves), then with the civil service, then with sections of organized business (the press and the CBI in particular), then with multinational companies, then with international financial agencies. Those were the old constraints on Labour radicalism; and were Labour to be radical again they would all rapidly reappear.

But Tony Blair is a modernizer. His constraints lie elsewhere – and were not studied much by many of us in the 1970s. We were so angry at Wilson's backsliding from radicalism that we failed to see how inept at economic modernization his governments had turned out to be. Indeed, having revisited the Wilson years with that set of concerns in mind, I think I need to admit to a certain revisionism of my own. As a modernizer, the first Wilson government was not that bad. It certainly tried to create the instruments of state-triggered private-sector regeneration: originally the ineffectual Department of Economic Affairs, and subsequently the much more potent Ministry of Technology – headed, of course, by Tony Benn in his technocratic incarnation as Anthony Wedgewood-Benn. Even the second Wilson government created the National Enterprise

Board and took another group of moribund industries and (this time also) firms into public ownership; and in this sense both Wilson governments did at least attempt to modernize the local industrial base. But those attempts were not in the end in any way successful. The Wilson governments both tried and failed to modernize the UK's industrial base. They failed, in part, because the concerns of macro-economic policy (particularly concerns about inflation and sterling) took precedence over investment and growth (as will doubtless happen again); but they also failed because the bloc of social forces and governmental institutions that could have modernized UK industry in the 1960s and 1970s did not exist, and was not called into being by them.

Tony Blair has recently positioned himself in relation to Wilson modernization in the following way:

> Today's Labour Party – 'New Labour' – is the heir to a proud tradition in the Party's history. The 1945 government combined practicality and idealism in equal measure. It changed Britain in a way that was relevant to the postwar world. It was 'new' Labour. In 1964, Harold Wilson was a modernizer, as his speeches and programmes demonstrate. But, despite the considerable achievements of that government, he was unable to carry through his project in full. The Wilson government did not fully succeed in modernizing the economy or establishing Labour as the natural party of government. Without change within the Party there was bound to be a tension between what he wanted to do and the culture and politics of the Party that had to do it. The modernizing edge was blunted. In the 1990s, a renewed Labour Party is in a much stronger position to lead national renewal.[5]

Of course, the implication of that reading of Labour's recent past is that the chief barrier to successful modernization lay within the Labour Party itself: hence presumably the Blairite preoccupation with internal party reform. Yet in reality it was not an unreformed party that blocked Wilson's modernization, but an unreformed state. What the Wilson governments, as modernizing governments, lacked more than anything else was a state structure able to trigger private industrial growth, and a coalition of social forces dedicated to the support of that state. Indeed for these purposes, it is useful to think of the UK state as a triangle with the Treasury, the Ministry of Defence and the Department of Trade and Industry at its points. A state equipped to trigger industrial growth needs a strong DTI, sustained by powerful interest groups and social forces. What the Wilson governments inherited – and sustained – was a state dominated by the Treasury and its attendant social forces and institutions (in the City) and by the MoD and its military-industrial complex. Labour in the 1960s and 1970s never put together a strong industry ministry; and it never forged a strong coalition of support for such a ministry from either the organized labour movement (on the Scandinavian model) or from private civilian industry (as in Japan). In fact private civilian industry in the UK (that is, local UK manufacturing capital) was – and is – profoundly anti-statist and anti-Labour. It is deeply liberal in it economics and Conservative in its politics. It was in the 1970s. It is now. We are not in Germany, nor Japan. And no matter how many cocktail offensives the Blairites launch, they will never pull UK private capital round just by the force of arguments alone. Old Labour had a way – in theory at least – of effecting a degree of support from private capital: public ownership and planning agreements. Tony Blair has eschewed such vulgar class politics, explicitly promising the UK business community that the involvement of a future Labour government in British industry would be 'limited and specific'. But charm is no substitute for power – and because it is not, Blair the modernizer is likely to be no more successful than was Wilson before him.

So on both the social-reformist and bourgeois-radical elements of the. Labour coalition, old constraints abound. The general interests of capital have not gone away. On the contrary, the strength and self-confidence of the local capitalist class has been steadily enhanced by nearly two decades of Conservative rule. The present generation of owners and senior managers have an arrogance (and a fat cat mentality) unprecedented since the war. If Old Labour was in charge, the Cedric Browns of this world would be giving Labour radicalism a very hard run for its money. Yet, as we know, New Labour is in charge – keener to modernize rather than reform. But such modernizing aspirations still face the unreformed features of UK capital as a system. They face a financial sector dominated by short-termism. They face UK-based transnationals geared to global accumulation strategies. They face a local business class imbued with liberal economic ideas, and they face a state dominated by Treasury thinking. Old constraints have not gone away: and because they have not, both wings of the Labour coalition would do well to remember Tawney's old adage about social democracy and the tiger: that 'you can peel an onion leaf by leaf, but you cannot strip a tiger claw by claw. Vivisection is its trade and it will do the clawing first.' Previous Labour Governments have been clawed to death by the opposition of organized capital; and all the indications are that a Blair government will experience a similar fate. Tony Blair may have beaten Old Labour into silence in order to win power but he cannot, just by that achievement, escape the truth of Old Labour's argument about the constraints on the use of power once won. New Labour might not like it; but Old Labour is right to insist that radical social reform is a prerequisite of industrial modernization, and not its antithesis.

New Labour, New Constraints

If that were not enough, a future Blair-led Labour Government faces two new constraints as well: one externally-imposed, one more self-inflicted.

To take the external one first: namely, changes in the international political economy, and in the positioning of the UK within that political economy. The degree of globalization now underway, and the resulting capacity of the nation state to manage its local economy, is of course currently a matter of great academic and political debate. However, for our purposes, it is enough to notice what is broadly agreed between all the major participants in the UK version of that debate: that increased international mobility of capital (and the intensification of international competition) on the one side, and the associated emergence of a new international division of labour (and the resulting slippage of the UK down international competitive league tables) on the other, have actually squeezed the space available in the UK for autonomous state action. This affects both the 'radical bourgeois' and the 'social reformist' project, both modernizers and socialists in the Labour coalition. And since the Labour Party was never very good at pursuing either of those projects in power even when the space was greater, it is hard to see why it will be any more effective when the space is less. Labour did not effect significant social reform, or industrial transformation, even in the 1960s when the UK was still the second most successful capitalist economy in the world system. It is hard to see it doing any better now it faces a globalized financial system, a hollowed-out UK manufacturing base, and a new international orthodoxy of neo-liberalism.

The internal constraint just adds to Labour's difficulties. New Labour prides itself on not being Old Labour, but in the process it has shed some of Old Labour's residual strengths. Old Labour was no great shakes, but – as we saw earlier – it did at least stay close to the unions when it could. It did at least recognize the need for a class base, both for its electoral coalition and for its governmental one. And Old Labour certainly was aware that Labour governments needed to create new agencies of state management if they were to achieve their modernizing goal. New Labour is currently buying none of that. That is why Mandelson and Liddle are right to emphasize the gap between New Labour economic plans and Old Labour's willingness to involve national trade union leaders in their design: to that degree, New Labour is qualitatively different from the party even in the immediate past.[6] It is also why Roy Hattersley and others are right to emphasize how little of the Croslandite programme of social reform has been taken on board by those closest to the new Labour leadership.[7]

Tony Blair seems determined to establish Labour's electoral credentials by demonstrating the Party's distance from the unions, and by eschewing any vestigial class appeal. His rhetoric of stakeholder capitalism allows no space for the creation of new state institutions of planning and control, and puts him well to the right, not simply of Will Hutton but even of a former Social Democrat like David Marquand.'[8] The Labour front bench under Tony Blair operates wholly within the dominant enthusiasms for (at most) only lightly regulated markets (which is but coded language, of course, for leaving private capital to do whatever it will); and has reset its dominant economic project to one of restoring supply-side competitiveness to UK-based firms. As Noel Thompsom put it in an earlier *NLR*, 'since the late 1980s, the Labour Party has advanced a supply-side socialism which aims to increase the flow, enhance the quality and improve the use of factor inputs; the primary objective being to increase productive efficiency, reduce unit costs and crucially, enhance Britain's international competitiveness'.[9] The Labour Party under Tony Blair is setting itself to go down the route of Clintonite economics, and is already having some difficulty in establishing any clear political water between itself and Michael Heseltine. By buying in so heavily to the dominant neo-liberal paradigm, the leaders of New Labour are ensuring that an incoming Blair government will be even less effective than were either the Wilson or the Attlee governments before it: less effective not simply as an instrument of social reform (where really the Blairites seem to have very few ambitions) but also as an instrument of economic modernization. The new internal constraint on Labour is one of a self-inflicted and deeply immobilizing feebleness.

New Labour and Hegemonic Politics

In pulling the argument together, and looking forward, let me link the new Blairite feebleness to my earlier comments on the need for strong electoral and governmental blocs: on the need, that is, for a genuinely hegemonic politics of the Left. That need – to my mind – is underscored by the manner in which we are now beginning to emerge from a quite remarkable period of right-wing hegemonic politics. For whatever else Margaret Thatcher was, she was genuinely a politician in the Gramscian mode. In the heyday of her dominance, Thatcherism re-established the link between values and policies in UK public life, made ideas (and ideology) central to political leadership, and required of its supporters, not only that they believed its central tenets, but that they lived and applied them to the full. Like all successful political forces in democratic societies, Thatcherism took many of the central values and aspirations held by us all (values of liberty and individual rights, aspirations for prosperity and progress), tied them to a series of operating principles (in her case, overwhelmingly the principle of the unfettered market), and then steadily, resolutely and with great self-confidence, applied that operating principle, in the pursuit of those values and aspirations, to policy area after policy area. In the Thatcherite litany, the 1970s was the critical decade – the time in which the electorate's lived and shared experience of the bankruptcy of social democracy created the political space that Thatcherite liberalism could (and did) fill. Out of the years of failed Labour governments, Thatcherism emerged to win the electoral battle, first by capturing the moral high ground, then the policy agenda, and finally political power itself. But Thatcherism was – as our experience of it in power has shown – a profoundly flawed project. Its values were narrow and self-seeking. Its central organizing principle was incapable of delivering sustained economic renaissance, and the policies it engendered were productive only of weak industry, impoverished social services and a divided and scarred society. With the steady dawning of reality over promise, the Thatcherite vision has gone, and with it – at long last – the moral authority of its advocates.

So, in an important sense, we are back to where we were in the late 1970s – with a discredited government, and in need of a fundamental change of direction and leadership. The moral authority of an entire political project – and not just of the government which espouses it – is eroding. Larger and larger sections of the electorate are open to a new vision, new leadership, alternative policies, even a different moral authority. This is why the Labour Party is – at long last – faced with the real prospect of power again.[10] But to realize that prospect – and when realized, to have the moral and social force to use it effectively and to use it well – the Labour Party needs to turn in these last precious months of opposition to the creation of its own hegemonic project. But it actually is not doing that – except in a very weak and limited way. The shadow cabinet is spending more time scaling down aspirations and restraining policy promises than it is in laying out a coherent programmatic alternative. It is making itself 'virtually fireproof against Tory attacks'[11] at the cost of a progressive and debilitating timidity. In its limpness, the Blair Labour Party stands fully in the tradition of earlier generations of the Party. This limpness (and the corresponding need for strength) were very clear even to a relatively moderate socialist like R.H. Tawney when, reacting to the fiasco of 1931, he wrote this;

> The great weakness of British Labour … is its lack of a creed. The Labour Party is hesitant in action because divided in mind. It does not achieve what it could because it does not know what it wants. It frets out of office and fumbles in it … If the Labour Party is to tackle its job with some hope of success, it must mobilize behind it a body of conviction as resolute and informed as the opposition in front of it … The way to create [this], and the way, when created, for it to set about its task is not to promise smooth things: support won by such methods is a reed shaken by every wind … The function of the Party is not to offer the largest possible number of carrots to the largest possible number of donkeys … To kick over an idol, you must first get off your knees.'[12]

Such a Tawneyian – not to say a Gramscian – reading of the nature of modern politics would give a set of distinct and difficult tasks to a Blair-led Labour Party keen to push back the barriers to its effective creation of first an electoral and then a governmental bloc, tasks that the Blair Party seems remarkably reluctant to undertake.

On the electoral and ideological front, it would commit the Party to an out-and-out assault on the contemporary enthusiasm for market-led economic growth. The Party would need to say that the whole liberal-based growth paradigm does not work. It does not work in its own terms, in that it does not provide a mechanism for breaking out of circles of cumulative decline – markets in that sense do not clear. More importantly, it does not work in social and human terms. Its outcomes are just not morally acceptable at the individual level, where its down-sizing and intensification of work processes are producing massive degrees of job insecurity and historically unprecedented levels of personal stress. Nor are its outcomes acceptable at the national level, where it is producing unemployment, the intensification of poverty, a shrinking base for welfare provision and a part-time, under-skilled labour force on low wages.

Since the whole liberal project falls foul of well-known deficiencies in neo-classical growth theory, and is simply an excuse for private capitalist excess, it needs to be completely broken with, and a whole new language of socially-determined growth targets and practices presented as a viable alternative .... Now there have been moments when New Labour has looked as though it was poised to commit itself to at least a watered-down version of these new growth strategies – particularly when Will Hutton was taking his country walks with Robin Cook, or when Tony Blair first announced his conversion to the big idea of stakeholding. But then he explained to Sir David Frost just how little substance that conversion had,[13] Robin Cook was replaced as industrial spokesperson, industrial policy was incrementally de-radicalized, and all the time Gordon Brown remained firmly the Treasury's man. Which means, I think, if I am not blinded by too many historical parallels, that the best we can hope for from the ultra-orthodox economics underpinning New Labour is a re-run of the1960s defeat of George Brown by James Callaghan, or of the 1970s drubbing of Tony Benn by Denis Healey; and even that will require a tougher stance by the John Prescotts of the Party than has currently been evident. Certainly the present deployment of personnel on Labour's front bench means that New Labour's ability to articulate a distinctive and progressive political economy has already fallen foul of its prior determination to appease nervous and conservative financial markets. Labour is not yet in power; but as far as I can tell, the Treasury has already won.

So ideologically (and therefore electorally) New Labour is not articulating a clearly different political vision. And, even if it were, it would in power have to carry that vision into practice by forming a radical bloc of social forces behind its modernizing and reforming zeal: and that too, as we have already seen, would oblige it to do something that no Labour Government has yet managed to do and sustain over any length of time. It would have to say to local business and banking leaders that private capital has not and will not act as the adequate custodian of the long-term interests of the UK's industrial base, or of the concerns and needs of those who work in or depend upon it. It would have to say that if those concerns and needs are to be serviced, responsibility for the specification and pursuit of long-term goals will have to be shifted and reset: shifted initially into a partnership between private capital, the trade union movement and a democratized state; and ultimately reset, through the creation of a genuine industrial democracy. But the problem is that Tony Blair does not give such a radical meaning to the notion of stakeholder capitalism. Even more fundamentally, the trouble is that the Labour Party under Tony Blair does not seem to think in even Tawneyian, let alone in Gramscian terms. It does not seem to think in terms of hegemonic domination and the consolidation of social blocs of support, and it certainly does not think in class terms when charting either its immediate electoral prerequisites or its future governmental allies.

New Labour, New Danger – A Revived New Right

There is a crucial imbalance here, for Labour's conservative opponents certainly do think and act in such terms, and they always have. Of course, it is slightly easier for Conservative politicians to grasp this vital point about power in a capitalist system. Since they charge themselves primarily with the task of running a dominant system, it is normal quite easy for them to identify with dominant classes. But Labour has always tried to run and to reform the system simultaneously: triggered into reforming it by the impact of the unreformed system on the poor and disadvantaged, but obliged to run the system in a cooperative relationship with the rich and privileged. In consequence, the Party power has never quite worked out with which bloc of social forces it ought primarily to identify.

I have occasionally drawn on R.H. Tawney's writings from the 1930s in building the argument of this article. That is because the choice of social forces was much starker and more blatant in the 1930s than it is now. Yet even then the Labour Party in power very easily lost its way. Nye Bevan wrote a very telling passage on the politics of Ramsay MacDonald that still have much to say about the constraints (and the choices) facing an incoming Labour administration. It is a passage I have quoted before, but it bears repeating.[14]

> In opposition, the Labour Party is compelled, by the nature of the class struggle, to take up an alignment which hamstrings it when in office. A party climbing to power by articulating the demands of the dispossessed must always wear a predatory visage to the property-owning class ... although all the time its heart is tender with the promise of peaceful gradualism. It knows that the limited vision of the workers will behold only its outward appearance, but it hopes that the gods of private enterprise will look upon its heart. In either case, one must be deceived. To satisfy the workers the Labour Party must fulfill the threat of its face, and so destroy the political conditions necessary to economic gradualism. To calm the fears of private enterprise it must betray its promises to the workers, and so lose their support.[15]

The Blair leadership would do well to ponder that dilemma, to recognize it, and to see its force. They would do well to re-read their Tawney and their Bevan. They like to discount such old-fashioned class analysis, and focus instead on their own modernizing agenda. But if, as writers like Will Hutton have argued, the barriers to economic modernization are intimately related to the barriers to radicalism, then the real problem the Blairites face is that only a high level of social radicalism will actual dismantle the barriers to the economic modernization which is so vital to their long-term survival in office. Of course, a Blair-led Labour Government might shift a few political barriers: it might reform the House of Lords, go for devolution, perhaps settle the Irish question to a degree (though on even this agenda the noises from the Leader's Office the days suggest caution and moderation). In other words, an incoming Blair Government might complete Gladstone's reform programme a century late, if it really applied itself. Yet even that would be simply moving the deck chairs on the Titanic unless that modernization of state structures was quickly accompanied by a challenge to the wider pattern of class power – in economy and society – that both preserve social privilege and undermine economic competitiveness. It is this wider challenge for which the Blairite Labour Party seems to be preparing neither itself nor its supporters.

Yet if the next Labour Government does not extend itself in that way – if it does not grasp the bigger nettle, as I fear that it will not – then the long term prospects for the Left in the UK are very bleak. For the great danger looming before us as the Tories temporarily implode is that, in the wake of a weak and ineffective Blair government, history will repeat itself. That just as Attlee prepared the way for a Keynesian Conservatism, and Wilson triggered first Selsdon man and then Thatcher woman, so such a Blair Government would pave the way for a revitalized and really unpleasant right-wing Conservatism…. Tony Blair is too like a Francois Mitterrand or a Felipe Gonzalez for my liking – and where such social-democratic modernizers tread, the collective history of the twentieth century European Left suggests that a rekindled Conservatism inexorably follows.

Notes

[1] P. Mandelson and R. Liddle, *The Blair Revolution; Can New Labour Deliver?* London 1996, pp, vii-viii.

[2] Royden Harrison counted the word 'new' used 37 times in the hour-long speech by Tony Blair to the Labour Party conference in 1995, of which 13 were references to New Labour! R. Harrison, *New Labour as Past History*, Nottingham 1996, p. 2.

[3] Mandelson and Liddle, op.cit, p.21

[4] See in particular, *The Labour Party and the Struggle for Socialism*, Cambridge 1975, and *Labour in Power? A Study of the Labour Government 1974-79*, London 1980.

[5] Tony Blair, 'My Vision for Britain', in G. Radice, ed., *What Needs to Change: New Visions for Britain*, London 1995. p.10

[6] There is a definite streak of anti-trade unionism in the Mandelson and Liddle version of *The Blair Revolution*; and plenty of early signs of an unwillingness by the Blair leadership to undo the legal framework imposed on the trade unions by the Thatcher government. One example of the tone and content of that anti-unionism can be found on pages 12-13 of Mandelson and Liddle: 'British industrial relations has been changed for the better, and its basic legal framework which the Conservatives established will remain in place.'

Mandelson and Liddle certainly tie Old Labour to the unions, and want no part of that connection for New Labour. As they put it, 'whereas the old Left saw its job as to represent trade unions, pressure groups and the working class, and the Right saw its role to protect the rich together with powerful corporate interests, New Labour stands for the ordinary families who work hard and play by the rules' (p. 18). Presumably, on this understanding of trade unions, they are full of people who do not work hard, play by the rules or come from ordinary families!

[7] The Hattersley irritation with Mandelson and Liddle is well captured in his 'Bubble Squeak' article in *The Guardian*, 27 February 1996. His disquiet with Blairite education policy has been widely reported and documented.

[8] For Marquand's unease, see his 'Elusive visions', *The Guardian*, 24 June 1996, p.14

[9] N. Thompson, 'Supply-side socialism: the political economy of New Labour', *New Left Review*, 216, p. 39

[10] How else are we to understand the quite remarkable popularity of Will Hutton's *The State We're In*, except as a clear indication of a deep-seated and widespread hunger in many sections of UK society for a new and radical politics based on a clear critique of the evils of Thatcherism and the inadequacy of free-market capitalism.

[11] 'A Mighty Whimper at his Enemies', *The Independent on Sunday*, 7 July 1996.

[12] R.H. Tawney, 'The Choice Before the Labour Party', *Political Quarterly* 1932, reproduced in W. A. Robson, ed., *The Political Quarterly in the 1930s*, London 1971, pp 96,105, Others, too, have seen shades of Ramsay MacDonald in the rhetoric of Tony Blair. Colin Leys, for example, argued that what both have in common 'is the theme of class conciliation, wrapped in misty appeals to social bonds that transcend class divisions. When MacDonald spoke of "all practical men and women" Blair talks about "a strong and active civil society". Both constantly invoke "the nation". Both have their eyes fixed on the middle-class voter.' C. Leys,' The British Labour Party's Transition....', p. 20.

[13] For details of the Frost interview with Tony Blair on stakeholding, see N. Thompson, Supply-side Socialism', p. 38.

[14] See earlier in this collection, the essay 'The failure of the socialist promise' (1975)

[15] Cited in M. Foot, *Aneurin Bevan*, vol. 1, London, 1962, pp. 130-1

Part 3: Moving On

Editorial Introduction to Extracts 13 and 14

If the Labour Party is to be rejected as a vehicle for socialist politics in the UK, and its form of parliamentarianism criticized as inadequate for the creation of popular support for socialist politics, then the issue arises of what alternative form/forms of political organization and activity should be pursued if the Left in Britain is ever to 'move on'. That question was first posed in the pages of the *Socialist Register* by Ralph Miliband in a much discussed article in 1976. In that 'Moving On' essay, he argued the case for a new political formation for the Left, and did so by assessing and discounting the capacity of either the British Community Party or the then leading Trostskyist groupings adequately to fulfill that role. So accurate was his sense of their long-term impotence that, were that essay to be reproduced here, it would read as a dialogue with the already gone; which is why it seems more appropriate to close this collection with two fines essays written by Hilary Wainwright two decades later, essays that reflect upon and go beyond Miliband's 1976 call for the British Left to move past the Labour Party.

Between the Miliband and the Wainwright 'moments' in this debate, the *Socialist Register* produced a series of essays (some already reproduced in this collection) on the possibility of advancing the cause of socialism in Britain by organizing within the Labour Party or outside it. Invariably these essays ended with a call for movement on at least three fronts. The first was for the formation of a political bloc crossing the boundaries of the Labour Party, a unity of Left Labourites and the extra-parliamentary Left, on the premise 'that the socialist cause needs political articulation, and that this political articulation, though not exclusively provided by parties, does nevertheless require the agency of party'.[1] The second was for that party to develop programmatic positions 'of course concerned with immediate issues, grievances and demands; but... also, beyond this, concerned with the effective dissolution of the structures of power of capitalist society and their replacement by a fundamentally different social order, based on the social ownership and control of the main means of economic activity, and governed by principles of co-operation, civic freedom, egalitarianism, and democratic arrangements far superior to the narrow class-bound arrangements of capitalist democracy'[2]. And the third was a call for that political bloc to grow by immersing itself in – and connecting it politics to – industrial struggles and social movements of an oppositional and progressive kind: a call for the Left to 'move on' by sinking itself into the 'daily life and struggles of working people'[3] – in an immersion in popular struggles built on the recognition that capitalism also cripples working people's emancipatory capacities, making it essential that the Left develop strategies that lead to an accumulation of democratic socialist capacities rather than the accumulation of capital[4].

The two essays from the *Register* reproduced here make those calls fully, and in the process re-state, in a new time and for a new generation, the clear and by now traditional Miliband-inspired call for a new political formation on the Left, one that is independent of, and to the left of, what Hilary Wainwright here calls a Labour Party now transformed 'into a party of modern capitalist management'. The first of the two essays (written in 1995) re-examined the 1976 arguments for 'Moving On', and applied them to a Labour Party newly under the leadership of Tony Blair. The second, a year later, defended the need to move on against the arguments of Barry Winter that the place for the Left was still within the Labour Party. Together the two pieces represent the clearest case now available within the pages of recent *Socialist Registers* on the need for, and the way to attain, a new socialist political formation in Britain.

The collection ends with a retrospective essay, initially prepared for the 2001 PSA Labour Movement Study Group conference on Labour Party historiography, in which Leo Panitch and I argue strongly for the continued relevance of the Milibandian perspective.

13. ONCE MORE MOVING ON: SOCIAL MOVEMENT, POLITICAL REPRESENTATION AND THE FUTURE OF THE RADICAL LEFT (1995)

Hilary Wainwright

Introduction

A paradox highlights the problem facing the radical left in Britain today. Historically the British working class movement has been one of Europe s strongest: the earliest, the most densely organized, one of the most militant and associated throughout its history with a rich variety of wider democratic movements and co-operative experiment. Yet the British state has remained one of the most un-democratic in Europe, retaining close protective bonds with the financial heart of British capitalism. It is as if some resilient, invisible membrane has separated the labour and other democratic social movements from unsettling the real centers of economic power in Britain. No doubt the membrane has many con-stituents but one is certainly the highly mediated, indirect way in which extra-parliamentary radicalism is represented – but in effect diffused – by the Labour Party. The membrane is held in place by the majoritarian, first-past-the-post electoral system which makes it very difficult for minorities on the left, reflecting radical social forces to thrive and gain a voice of their own.

The problem of how to create such a voice; how, in other words, to establish a socialist organization in Britain able to attract a substantial measure of support and hold out genuine promise of further growth ,[5] was one of Ralph Miliband s theoretical and practical preoccupations. It was one I shared with him. The idea was not and is not some grandiose fantasy of replacing the Labour Party. The aim is rather to create an independent, insubordinate challenge and spur to the left of Labour.

In 'Moving On' in *Socialist Register 1976* Ralph looks back over the period since 1956. He concludes that in the intervening twenty years the radical left in Britain made no progress towards establishing such an effective political formation. A lot has happened in the Labour movement in these years, and much of this has been positive. But, he insists: in organizational and programmatic terms there has been no advance. [6] Ralph had a rare ability to see and report the left's weaknesses with cool clarity and without despair. In 'Moving On' as in all his political writings, he addressed these difficulties all the better to overcome them.

He analyzed the enormous problem posed by the Labour Party. Electorally it is the party of the majority of the working class and the only left party with any mass membership; yet at the same time it is irretrievably tied to the reproduction of British capitalism, albeit in an ameliorated form. Ralph describes how this difficulty is compounded by the debilitating but deeply and widely held illusion which imprisons the left of the party in permanent subordination.

He then describes the predicament of the Communist Party of Great Britain with its significant base in the trade unions, but its inability to gain any electoral representation. He challenges its defensive acceptance of the Labour Party's irrevocable domination of the labour movement. He is contemptuous of its attempts to inflect the Labour Party leftwards while at the same time denying any belief that 'the Labour Party will be transformed into the kind of socialist organization required to assume the leadership of socialist advance in Britain.'[7] The CPGB was a party doomed to remain marginal.

Finally, Ralph addresses the question of why the groups on the radical left – most notably at that time, the International Socialists and the International Marxist Group – whose growth was in part a response to exactly the failings he had analyzed in the Labour and Communist Parties, had not fared better. As he remarks, a good deal depends on the answer. After considering the explanations the groups themselves suggest – ruling class hegemony, the reformism of existing working-class parties and their leaders – or the explanations which highlight the sectarian, internally rigid organization of these groups, he focuses on the inappropriateness of their Bolshevik perspective. It is this which produces their isolation and what he describes earlier as their lack of implantation. (And this isolation in turn disposes them to a dogmatic and sectarian style.) By Bolshevik he means an underlying understanding of socialist change based on a revolutionary seizure of power on the Bolshevik model of 1917. He argues that in the context of a parliamentary bourgeois democratic regime, a strategy of socialist advance has to include a real measure of electoral legitimation.

So his essay ends with a statement of the need for a new kind of party: one which aims to achieve representation within existing political institutions but which is also involved in many different forms of action, pressure and struggle. He does not in this essay emphasize or explore the distinctiveness of such a party, with its strategic perspectives fitting into neither the parliamentary nor the Bolshevik models that have underlain the division within the socialist movement over the last 50 years. He returns to this theme in his last book *Socialism for a Sceptical Age* in ways which I will discuss below.

In 1995, nearly a further 20 years on from Ralph s survey, has the radical left in Britain moved on? Has it come nearer to defining the kind of political formation that could be effective for a strategy for socialist transformation in Britain in the 21st century? Has it begun to prepare at least the elements that might constitute it?

Twenty years of change

Four very different kinds of changes have occurred in the past twenty years which influence both the character and the potential for a political organization to the left of the Labour Party, a political formation with both parliamentary representation and a significant active base in society. At the risk of opening a Pandora s Box of questions, which I have no chance of answering in this essay, I want to emphasize that these changes have also influenced the vision and perspectives of the radical left.

First, there has been the rise of new social movements on the left – indeed several waves of them. These have been an expression of thoroughgoing frustration with the existing parties and political system. There is nothing unique to the past twenty five years or so in the mere fact of movements forming around new issues of social justice, emancipation, democracy and peace. What has been distinctive about the movements which have waxed and waned repeatedly since the late 60s is their sense of themselves as more than protest movements or efforts to extend the agenda of mainstream parties. I am thinking of the student, feminist, lesbian and gay, ecological, peace and solidarity movements and also many community-based groups, alternative or counter-cultural projects and networks, organizations of ethnic minorities and radically-minded parts of the trade union movement. They have in common an explicit sense of themselves as direct agencies of social and political transformation, with their own methods and understandings of political power. From their origins they have turned their backs on the politics of passing the buck: in other words asking others, MPs, councilors, parties, to act on their behalf or take their problem to the relevant authorities. Instead they have experimented with a politics of doing it themselves. In the course of their struggles they may make a variety of alliances with conventional political parties, but in doing so they are usually assertive of their autonomy and their distinct sources of power and knowledge.

The historical timing of these movements is significant here: they emerged at a time when Labour and Social Democratic Parties – the expression of earlier movements – faith in the power of the vote and parliamentary representation were in office and had had several previous periods in office. Thus the new radicalism of these movements has been shaped more or less explicitly by experience of both the benefits and the limits of social changes which earlier reformers had believed could be achieved by social democratic governments and their benevolent experts.

Secondly and at the same time, processes of international economic competition and political realignment have meant that both political power and political culture have become increasingly international, and for Britain, European. This has steadily, sometimes imperceptibly, eroded the sovereignty of the British nation state and the foundations of all its peculiarities – for example its centralized character and its disproportional, first-past-the-post electoral system. The external forces of erosion have been periodically hastened by internal pressures from the nations and regions of the United Kingdom. This internationalization and regionalization has also widened the horizons of the radical left in Britain. Strategic thinking is influenced increasingly by a growing awareness of the paths pursued by the left on the continent. Also, as the importance of Britain and Europe diminished on a global scale with the industrialization of the East and South, experiments in the industrial South, most notably in South Africa and Brazil, are providing new models – precarious and tentative – of the role of popular movements in social transformation and in producing innovative forms of radical political agency.

Thirdly, profound changes have taken place in the Labour Party which are likely to alter radically the way the Labour left, who had hoped that the party would one day be theirs, see their future. Some of these changes are common to social democratic parties throughout Western Europe, for instance the promotion, even in opposition, of an explicitly market-led economic strategy and a weakening of previous commitments to public expenditure and intervention. Some of the changes are specific or at any rate particularly marked, in the British circumstances of four successive election defeats. The strategic thinking of the party's leadership even since the second of these defeats has been premised on the notion that the trades unions and the Party's left are to blame for Mrs Thatcher's first and second general election victories, in 1979 and '83. Hence, the logic goes, Labour s comeback as a party of government depends on establishing the party's independence from the unions and eliminating from the party all trace of the radical left. While loyalty to the party and its recently elected leader, Tony Blair, as the only alternative to the Tories is strong, dissent over this particular project of supposed modernization is widespread. It is not restricted to the left itself but also includes party members who, whatever their own beliefs, are loyal to the

Labour Party's founding claim to be a broad church. For the time being, at a moment when getting rid of the Tories provides a unifying discipline, this dissent is subdued. But a sign of this instability behind the Labour Party avocado stage sets has been the hostile response to the leadership's rewriting of the party's aims and objectives, followed by a debate in which Tony Blair has been given wary and conditional support. The expression of this pent up dissent in the event of a Labour government will be a central factor influencing the future of the left.

Fourthly, the collapse of the Soviet bloc produced a final crisis in the already confused and divided Communist Party of Great Britain, leading to the demolition of what had proved to be, in spirit of its merits in particular struggles, a dead end for activists, especially trade union activists, committed to building a left independent of Labour. The end of the Cold War and the way it ended, has had wider reverberations for the radical left. Amongst this left that believes in change that goes to the roots of capitalist society, there has long been an underlying divide. There are those for whom socialism was a project brought about from above, an elitist project carried out by a leadership with the support of the people, on behalf of the people, to meet their needs in a rational way. Such a vision has been most closely associated with the Communist Party: Eric Hobsbawm s *Age of Extremes*[8] expresses its character and faces up to its failure with a breathtaking historical sweep. But it also has had a variety of champions on the Labour left.

On the other hand is the tradition of socialism from below, a prolonged and uneven process of collective self-emancipation in which democratic state power would play a role that was framing and supporting more direct forms of economic and community democracy and self-management. Throughout the 20th century this tradition has been subordinate, though with moments of heroic expression and daring experiment. These range from the writing and political leadership of Rosa Luxemburg, through the workers councils of 1920s Northern Italy, to the workers councils of Hungary in 1956 and many of the activities of the student revolutionaries of Paris 1968 and more mundanely, the experiments of Ken Livingstone's Greater London Council in the 1980s. Subordination has also allowed this tradition to survive on a somewhat vague promise. It has inspired many cooperative and decentralized initiatives, but in general it has not had to address in a sustained manner the problems of its faith in the capacities of the majority of people and its objectives of eliminating injustice and oppression of ruthless and powerful enemies. The end of the Soviet bloc and the patent failure of socialism as social engineering from above required exponents and practitioners of this tradition to face up to the realities of dealing with power.

In this process they will be aided by a further consequence of the end of the Cold War. Political debate is slowly releasing itself from sterile polarities: reform versus revolution, parliamentary versus extra-parliamentary – and related to this, reform of the state and constitution versus popular struggle, individual versus collective, state versus market. A shift from such polarities had already begun under the impact of social movements, especially feminism.

I will argue that these changes are producing a conjuncture in which the radical left can move on and is tentatively doing so. Moreover, an arduous and sometimes apparently futile process of preparation has been going on over the last twenty years, trying not so much to found a new organization, but to create and maintain connections of solidarity and intellectual engagement amongst those on the left whose political commitment does not end with the Labour Party. It has been and continues to be a process which does not lay down the form that a popularly based organization of the radical left might take. Rather it has modestly helped to gather, and nurture, practical and intellectual resources to grasp the opportunities to create such an organization when they arise[9]. This process has built on the work of the old new left in the previous twenty years.[10] Ralph was a central figure in both phases. In the course of this essay, I will attempt to draw some lessons from my own involvement in the work of the last twenty years.

New movements and old parties

The foundational change affecting prospects for a new political agency for the left has been the emergence of social movements with a strong sense of themselves as bringing about radical social change through directly challenging the institutions they experience as oppressive. The signs of this were apparent as Ralph wrote, but their significance only became clear in Britain in the eighties – and even now it is a little hazy. Their organizational forms do not have the visibility, formality or longevity of the traditional organizations of the left with which Ralph's 1976 survey was concerned. They are fluid, diverse and often highly localized. I am not assuming that these movements are in their entirety on the left. But a left has been shaped by them and, in Britain, seeks change through them rather than through any of the parties of the left. Moreover in Britain at any rate, this is not a phenomena limited to a single generation or two: the class of '68 for example. The movements of squatters, ravers, anti-road protesters, travelers and organizations of the unemployed that have coalesced with others on the left against the Criminal Justice Bill, now meet regularly to develop what they explicitly describe as a Do-It-Yourself (DIY) politics .

Before reflecting on their distinctiveness and on how far they do represent a moving on, it is important to clarify that the description 'new' does not imply that these movements are counter-posed or invariably separate from workers organizations originating in earlier decades. In Britain a complex lattice work of connections has grown up in which feminists, eco-, peace or anti-racist activists, for example, have had considerable influence on both the policies and ways of organizing of the trade unions and vice versa. This process has been uneven and primarily at a local and regional level, but its significance is that the politics of the social movement left is backed by some of the sources of power of the old labour movement; and on the other hand the labour movement has, through the work of these new movement activists, reached constituencies beyond the scope of its traditional, often inflexible and inward-looking, procedures.

One example of these interconnections is the tradition of women's support groups in strikes of mainly male workers. It started with feminists and pro-trade union women in the communities surrounding the Oxford car factories in the early 1970s who organized to counter right-wing housewives seeking to undermine the strikes of car workers resisting new more exploitative work systems. It reached a peak with the extra-ordinary alliance of women in the mining communities, urban feminists, lesbian and gay activists, black groups and rank-and-file Labour Party and trade union activists, that came together to support the miners in 1984/85. Other examples are the ways in which socialist feminists have worked with trade unions like the shopworkers union USDAW, parts of the textile unions, and the T&GWU to reach out to home workers, especially women, who are best reached through community organizing. Further connections include the links the peace movement made and continues to make with some workers in the arms industry; the links between radical scientists and trade unionists over health and safety and the environment, and more recently, local trades councils in towns like Coventry working with animal rights activists against the export of live animals.

In his last book *Socialism For a Sceptical Age* Ralph did address the emergence of new social movements. He recognized that many on the left in the past 25 years or so have found involvement in social movements to be both far more politically effective and more personally satisfying that life in existing political parties. Moreover he acknowledged that movement criticisms of left parties were generally valid and that new movements had been highly successful in forcing upon these parties questions they had in an earlier epoch tended to relegate to the periphery of their concerns, or to ignore altogether. [11] But he insists that, be this as it may, parties of the Left do remain of primary importance as a potential, if not actual, instrument of socialist advance. In defence of this conclusion, he notes the ways that movements wane when the issues that brought them to the fore lose their mobilizing force. He points to the experience of the US, a country without a socialist party where, even though there is no shortage of grass roots movements, conservatism holds sway and has been hugely successful in warding off any serious challenge from the left.

After an assessment of the present state and future potential of left parties and movements in the post-Cold War world, he concludes that the radical left's best hope lies with strengthening the left in social democratic parties. He says: Ultimately, the best that the left can hope for in the relevant future in advanced capitalist countries (and for that matter elsewhere as well) is the strengthening of left reformism as a current of thought and policy in social democratic parties[12].

This appears to represent quite a significant shift from the position he arrived at in the conclusion to the second edition of *Parliamentary Socialism* in 1972. Here he analyzed how the lack 'at present' of any effective challenge to an overwhelming preponderance of the Labour Party as the party of the left helps to explain why so many socialists at the grass roots of the party, the trade unions and even the Communist Party, cling to the belief that the Labour party will eventually be radically transformed. He ends sternly with both a reprimand and a prescription: But the absence of a viable socialist alternative is no reason for resigned acceptance or the perpetuation of hopes which have no basis in political reality. One the contrary, what is required is to begin preparing the ground for the coming into being of such alternative.[13]

I don't think his argument in *Socialism For a Sceptical Age* is in fact a rejection of this earlier position. It is a particular way of addressing practical and immediate questions of governmental power – a pressing problem after 16 years of brutal Conservative rule. But it can still incorporate the idea of an independent party of the radical left. Ralph's notion of strengthening left reformism depends on the vitality of the left outside Social Democratic Parties as well as, perhaps even more than, inside them. Indeed Ralph notes that the emergence of new socialist parties in many countries is one of the notable features of the present time. Their growth is essential if the left is to prosper. [14] He was thinking presumably of the Socialist People's Party which regularly wins between 12 and 17 per cent of the vote in Denmark; the Left Socialists in Norway, a decisive influence in the campaign for a 'no' vote in the referendum on membership of the European Union; the United Left in Spain, formed out of parts of the defunct Spanish Communist Party, the left of the nationalist movements and the independent left from the 1980s to campaign against Spain's membership of NATO; the Green Left in Holland, another product of several left parties, working in close alliance with a variety transatlantically of the Workers Party of Brazil, a relatively new party based on the militant workers, peasant and urban social movements of modern Brazil: a party which fights and sometimes wins elections at every level (with the exception, after high hopes, of the top elective job of President) but whose driving strategy for social change rests on grass roots organization amongst the movements that are its base.[15]

The notion of alliances and coalitions is essential to these new left formations. Their implicit conception of alliances works in two directions: first, sideways, as it were, to other political parties and secondly, outwards to autonomous movements and campaigns. First, an element in their strategy as parliamentary parties involved alliances with – or conditional support for – other parliamentary parties, most notably Social Democratic Parties, to pursue legislative support and gain public resources for radical policies often initiated by movements outside conventional politics. As Ralph says, these parties are not likely to supplant Social Democratic Parties but to act as a spur and a challenge.

In Northern Europe, under proportional electoral systems, it is often the case that Social Democratic Parties have depended on the support of either liberal or center right parties in order to govern. There is growing pressure on them, to look to their left and consider a federal coalition – already a reality in several regions with the party on their left, for instance in Germany, the Greens. Similarly in Holland and Denmark at a local level there are many examples of the radical left governing in coalition or giving conditional support to a social democratic majority.

An important example of a relatively open and publicly valued process of negotiated and conditional alliance between a party of the socialist left and a social democratic government is emerging in South Africa in the relation between the South African Communist Party (SACP) and the moderate leadership of the ANC. The relationship no doubt is fraught with tensions and is probably dependent for whatever stability it has on the many decades of common struggle through which all those involved have come. Nevertheless its development could provide important lessons for the North. Central to the SACP s influence is its base in the ANC and trade union movements that became so powerful in South Africa society in the course of the struggle against apartheid.

Here too Ralph recognized a new possibility, an opportunity for moving on. In Marxist thought, he reminds us, dual power has always been taken to mean an adversary relation between a revolutionary movement operating in a revolutionary situation, and a bourgeois government under challenge from that movement. It is, however, possible to think of dual power in different terms: as a partnership between socialist government on the one hand and a variety of grassroots agencies on the other. [16]

To be effective such a partnership could not be one that was formed the day after an election victory. Consequently this idea must apply to the relation between socialist parties and grass roots movements long before the former achieved office. The exemplary case of such partnership would be the Brazilian Workers Party and its close relation with a variety of autonomous movements and campaigns including the radical trade union movement (CUT).

These two conceptions of alliances (both with other political parties and with autonomous social movements) are implicit in the activities of new left parties in Western Europe. They point to a form of party that is modeled on neither existing Social Democratic or Labour Parties nor of Communist Parties of the past. Certainly, when I talk here of moving on towards an organization of the radical left in Britain, I am imagining a party which, though in part born out of struggles within these traditional parties and the lessons drawn from their failures, has a distinctive character that is greatly influenced by both the agendas and the implicit methodology of the new movements – the feminist green, anti-racist and the 1980s peace/anti-Cold War movements in particular.

Questions of political methodology

The influence of these movements on the programmes of all parties on the left, old as well as new, is well known. Less analyzed but equally important is the question of methodology: principles of organization, approaches to power, views of knowledge and of whose knowledge matters. In Britain, where the space for the new left to develop politically has been notably cramped, the explicit development of a new political methodology is a vital condition for moving on. So I will summarize my own assessment of important elements of the methodological differences.

My argument is that in practice, though not yet in any systematic theory, these movements from the late sixties onwards have been pioneering a new and distinct form of political agency in often instinctive revolt at the pompous irrelevance of conventional politics to the problems of everyday life. It is not that everything they do is entirely novel or notably coherent. It is rather that across the movements that have developed independently of established political parties, certain common themes can be identified in the ways that they organize, develop policies and more generally mobilize new sources of power. These themes seem to me to come from a common experience of both the limits of government in parliamentary democracies (and the state that ruled in the name of socialism in the East) and the personal and environmental costs of an overarching emphasis on the priority of economic growth – whether under private ownership or public.

The theme on which I will elaborate, because of its fundamental character it is not of course the only methodological theme – concerns the character and organization of knowledge. Discussions about knowledge are not normally the stuff of politics. But state and party institutions are underpinned by presuppositions about the character of knowledge and its organization, for example what constitutes valid knowledge; what knowledge matters to political decisions; who carries or holds politically significant knowledge. Normally these presuppositions are just part of the culture of an institution that people inherit and duly reproduce or more or less unconsciously modify. But when these institutions fail to live up to the expectations of significant numbers of people and/or break down, and when people organize radically to transform them, a counter culture emerges, and the old presuppositions are laid bare. Thus as the traditional parties of the left (the main subjects of Ralph's 1976 survey) failed adequately to respond to the new and radical demands of feminism, ecology, sexual liberation, radical trade unionism and the anti-Cold War politics of the peace movement, competing conceptions of knowledge became important in political debate. This is one aspect of the widespread interest among movement and left activists, at different times, in the critical theory of Marcuse and Habermas, in the post-

modernism of Foucault and Derrida and more recently the critical realism of
Bhaskar. Unfortunately, however, these philosophical debates have rarely been
explicitly anchored in questions of political agency. Indeed some tendencies of
post-modernism have in effect denied the efficacy of purposeful political activity.[17] Without entering into these debates on this occasion[18] I will indicate the
importance of the challenge of recent social movements to presumptions of
traditional parties of the left to be able to centralize and codify the knowledge
necessary for social change. I will also highlight the importance of this for questions of political organization.

The old methods of Social Democratic Labour Parties on the one hand and
Communist parties on the other differ in important ways, and historically there
are many varieties of each. But they share similar roots which have produced
features common to both. Both kinds of parties, for instance, have traditionally
tended either to take social movements under their wing: 'our womens/peace/
tenants movement', 'This Great Movement of Ours' or, if the movement is too
stroppy to be embraced, to give them leper status and treat them as 'outside
our/the movement' and presumably irrelevant and doomed. Their underlying
assumption is that power for change lies overwhelmingly through steering the
nation state, in the case of social democratic parties, or in effect, becoming the
state in the case of Communist Parties.

My purpose is to highlight the way that a common focus on the nation state
(i.e. a single focus of popular sovereignty) and with it, the party, as a single focus
of the power to transform, has been underpinned by assumptions about the
character of social and economic knowledge. The understanding of knowledge
that shaped state action and especially the use to which social reformers desired
to put the state was based on the model of the natural sciences. It was an understanding which first developed alongside the ideal of the nation state in the
18th and 19th centuries. This model aspired to formulate general laws describing
regular conjunctions of events of phenomena. These laws then provided the
premises from which social as well as natural science was thought to be able to
make certain predictions and gain evermore perfect knowledge as the discovery
of further generalizations progressed. Historically this positivistic model had a
progressive impact, countering the reactionary influence of religious faith and
superstition on medical, physical and social intervention. It has now been criticized and surpassed in many different ways. For my concern with the politics
of knowledge the crucial point is that when applied to the study and reform
of society, it assumed that general scientific laws were the only valid form of
knowledge, hence dismissing the practical, often tacit, uncodified and sometimes uncodifiable knowledge of the majority of people. This in turn favoured a
social engineering approach to the process of social change: change from above
by those who know the mechanics of society.

In the early 1980s in Britain and in more sweeping form in the former Soviet bloc in the early 90s, free-market ideology rose from the intellectual grave to challenge this from the right. The theoretical case for the free-market elaborated and propounded most effectively by Frederick Hayek throughout his long life, challenged the possibility of democratic collective intervention in the market. This attack on what Hayek saw as invariably a disastrous social engineering was based on a theory of the economic uses of knowledge which celebrated the intimate knowledge of the individual consumer or entrepreneur. My argument concerning the importance of recent democratic social movements is that in their practice they hold out an alternative to the engineering model of social change – and all the mechanistic ways of organizing and intervening which flow from it – from the left. Hence a critical theorization of the innovatory features of their practice provides tools for a more convincing reply to the right than could be made in the past. Their practice combines both a striving towards purposefully bringing about an intended social outcome, with a recognition of the practical, sometimes uncodifiable and hence non-predictive character of much socially and politically important knowledge. Their forms of organization are frequently shaped specifically for the purpose of socializing, sharing the kinds of inside knowledge unavailable to centralized state and party institutions. It is collective and not individualistic.

This does not imply an uncritical acceptance of whatever practical knowledge is offered by a movement's membership on the spurious grounds that knowledge from experience has its own inherent truth, I am a woman; the knowledge that comes from my experience as a woman is valid; therefore whatever I say about women's oppression must be true. But central to the debates in these movements has been the problem of collectively arriving at some agreed solution that is based on taking seriously, without critically accepting, everyone's practical knowledge and drawing on appropriate historical and theoretical knowledge. The methodology developed from this gives the lie to the right s presumption that the choice is between state and market; the fantasy of a central brain versus the pragmatic reality of atomized economic man.

Robert Michels in formulating his 'the iron law of oligarchy' provides, albeit unintentionally, the best description of how the social engineering model of social scientific knowledge underpinned the methods of the traditional parties of the left. Writing about the Social Democratic Party in Germany before World War I, he formulated his law before the founding of the Third International. But much of what he says about the parties of the Second International is apposite to the Third. He believes that in any political organization, however formally democratic, there is an unavoidable degree of specialized expertise owned by a professional elite which, whatever the procedures for accountability, becomes autonomous from the masses , grass roots or base. These, as the term 'the masses' implied, are understood as undifferentiated in their interests and passive in their knowledge. Michels assumes that they are capable only of knowing with which elite their interests lie, and lack the expertise to know, even partially, how those interests might be met.

Michels took as a given – in accord with the philosophical orthodoxy of his time – the exclusive importance of scientific or professional knowledge and the incompetence or ignorance of the masses. In all the affairs of management for whose decision there is requisite specialized knowledge a measure of despotism must be allowed and thereby a deviation from the principles of pure democracy. From the democratic point of view this is perhaps an evil, but it is a necessary evil. Socialism does not signify everything by the people, but everything for the people .[19] Several important assumptions lead Michels to this conclusion. First is the idea that the only knowledge relevant to the efficacy of the party is a techni-cal, positivistically construed scientific knowledge that is inaccessible to the or-dinary members and, once learnt by an official of the party, sets him or her apart from the members. Possession of knowledge in Michels term emancipates (the officers) from the masses and makes them independent of their control.

Second, there is the assumption that facts and values are entirely separate; that the members are capable simply of establishing the party's values. The party then appoints or elects an official to collect the appropriate facts, which is a purely technical matter and depends on specialized knowledge. Parties based on these assumptions have structures for involving the members in taking decisions of principle – assumed to be entirely separate from questions of implementa-tion. They also have an extensive staff which works with the executive to imple-ment and elaborate these policies. A gulf develops between the members and the leadership because the former have little basis on which to judge the appropri-ateness of the executive's work from the standpoint of the principles in which they believe. Where they believe the executive to be wrong they have little basis on which to argue for an alternative. They are in effect politically deskilled.

Michels also assumed that a socialist party's energies must unavoidably be fixed on a single goal, around a single locus of power: the goal of capturing the wheel of state power to steer it towards socialism. Organization, it was assumed, is the only means for the creation of a collective will. And organization, accord-ing to Michels, is based on the principle of least effort, that is to say, upon the greatest possible economy of energy. The metaphors for the kind of party this produced were, not surprisingly, military and mechanical: the party is divided into the rank and file and the officers – an efficient party is also an effective electoral machine. Michels' client party is also an effective electoral machine. Michels remarks, from his observations, that there is hardly one expression of military tactics and strategy, hardly a phrase of barrack slang which does not recur again and again in the leading articles of the socialist press. Efficiency in capturing state power required that the specialized elite ruled as standardized an organization as possible. Concerns of autonomous activity undermined the party. Centralization made for economies of effort.

Given the underlying political culture which he describes, the iron law of oligarchy does indeed hold. He was writing, however, from within this culture. Having the perspicacity of a trained sceptic he identified its fundamental features, of which many a party cadre, believing the party s democratic rhetoric, would hardly have been conscious. He treats these features as the unavoidable givens of socialist political agency.

Existing new left parties in Europe illustrate radically distinct principles from those of traditional Communist or Social Democratic Parties on all these issues of underlying methodology. First, there is a recognition of sources of knowledge of social needs and possible solutions not encompassed by the kinds of scientific – or top down – knowledge available to a state or party leadership. The second principle involves a recognition of diverse sources of power to change. This stems from the understanding which activists in recent movements have of the power to bring about social change; a view based on an alertness to their own complicity in reproducing and therefore potentially in transforming social institutions. As a result they have identified spheres of everyday life – sexual and familial relations, food consumption and distribution, housing arrangements, transport, work – where non-compliance or experimentation with alternatives can be a source, however limited, of political power, especially if it is exercised in combination with more traditional sources – strike action, political representation, demonstrations. This leads at best to a recognition of quite different political functions requiring quite distinct ways of organizing: the organizing necessary to build and spread a grass roots movement or to sustain a co-operative business alongside for example, the organizing necessary to achieve political representation. So for instance in the Dutch Green Left, the obligations of party membership are based on the assumption that many party members are active in movements that are autonomous of the party, something the party supports. Moreover, on the party's election list and among their MPs are people who are known mainly as leaders of local movements rather than as party spokespeople, thought they support the party's aims.

Knowledge and power are closely related instruments for any effective agency or process of social change. These parties have experimented with new methods of organizing which recognize that they have no monopoly of the knowledge and power necessary for changes they desire. The newer parties such as the German Greens (1979) and the Dutch Green Left (1989) see themselves as political voices for movements which are independent but in close association with the party.

Crucial to these new ways of organizing is the influence of the movements themselves – including a degree of learning from their failures and limitations. This is why, of all the various changes over the last two decades, I consider the emergence of the new movements as fundamental to the possibilities of moving on. When Ralph wrote in 1976, the old models had reached an impasse, but no new principles of political organization had emerged. One still cannot talk about a clear and proven new model of left political agency anywhere, least of all in Britain. On the continent, especially Northern countries, the new left parties are an accepted part of public political debate. But even there the impact of the new politics is not assured. Its development depends on the strength of movements outside the political systems. Old methods have a subtle, unconscious pulling power, drawing supposedly innovating organizations back into well established grooves, especially when the objectives of these organizations include public office. This has been a recurrent source of division in the German Greens for instance. They introduced a variety of measures, for example that people should only hold positions of leadership for a limited period (the principle of rotation); that there should always be several spokespeople; that all leading bodies should be made up of at least 50% women. The old methods appear to present the easiest route, especially when, as with West Germany s parliamentary state, they are backed by enormous recourses; or as in Britain, where in the past beguiling short cuts to office via taking over sometimes hollow structures of the Labour Party, tempt social movement radicals to devote themselves to committee room manoeuvring. On the other hand occasionally, for example in London in the late 70s and early 80s, it was of great importance for the whole of the radical left that some activists were prepared to devote several years to the plotting and manoeu-vring – as well as some very creative policy work – necessary to win control of the London Labour Party and hence the Greater London Council. Perhaps this will be a permanent tension, inherent in the very nature of political organizations whose course of radicalism rests on the knowledge and power of grass roots movements but whose stability and lasting, cumulative political impact requires at least a foothold within the existing political system.

Challenges to national sovereignty; openings for the left

But national state institutions and the parties that cleave to them, particularly those of the British state, are being shaken by economic globalization and politi-cal reconfiguration. In the case of Britain, this is an erosion taking place from Europe and from the nations and regions of the UK; it is taking place through institutional changes from above and cultural shifts and organizational innova-tions from below. Over the past twenty years or so these international develop-ments have stimulated ambitious initiatives from movements on a European scale, whether of an economic kind: workplace trade union leaders developing organized links with equivalent leaders on the continent in industries as diverse as pharmaceuticals, cars and chocolate; or involving previously unorganized workers like the European network of homeworkers; or of a directly political kind, for instance the powerfully pan-European peace movement of the 1980s. Moreover the regional, national and continental challenges to the unitary and centralized British state are opening opportunities by which these movements and other radical social forces could gain more radical political representation.

As processes of globalization have become apparent, movement forms of organization have proved more able to mobilize effective kinds of international knowledge and power than political parties whose strategies for change have been exclusively focused on national state power. This comparison should not be exaggerated, because the overwhelming political reality that has accompanied globalization is the victory of neo-liberalism. Those challenges that have in any way dented the right, however, owe much to the distinctive organizational reach of recent social movements.

A good example of the ability that radical movements have developed to think and organize strategically on an international scale is the peace movement of the early 80s. For a brief but vital moment it influenced the course of European history, in particular the way the Cold War ended. My argument here is not that this movement brought about the end of the Cold War. It was the process of implosion and conscious democratic reform in Gorbachev's Soviet Union that was the prime historic moving force which led eventually to the fall of the wall. But if the hawks in the Western alliance has been unchallenged in the period when Gorbachev called Reagan's bluff and responded to the West's Zero Option – exchanging the scrapping of cruise for that of SS20s – with his offer to dismantle SS20s and negotiate a nuclear free Europe, perestroika and glasnost would probably not have had the time and space to gather the momentum they did. The pan-European peace movement, with its East-West networks; its ability to mobilize simultaneously across Western capitals; its ability to gather, piece together and publicize strategic intelligence on NATO, had an impact on West European public opinion which politicians could not ignore. The West's initial offer of the 'Zero Option' was itself an attempt to defuse the popular anxiety about the sitting of cruise missiles across Western Europe. It was made in ignorance of the changes taking place in the Soviet bureaucracy and on the assumption that the Soviet response would be inadequate. The peace movement knew differently. Their contacts gave them an inside knowledge some would say also a little influence – which gave them greater insight into the momentous processes that were underway.[20]

They did not pack up the camps that surrounded the missile sites, or lift their pressure on all political parties to see the Zero Option through. The result was that the NATO powers, contrary to the initial personal preferences of Thatcher and Reagan, responded favourably to Gorbachev and entered into serious negotiations one of whose by-products was the precarious and unstable path of perestroika. If the peace movement had been powerless and the hawks had had their way, Gorbachev would probably have been rebuffed. As a result, the ending of the Soviet bloc would very likely have been much longer and more drawn out and marked by the kind of violence and state resistance that suppressed the students at Tienanmen Square. In this sense the European peace movement of the 80s influenced history in a way that no national party was able to. Its full goals – the dismantling of Cold War institutions in the West as well as the East – are as yet unfulfilled, but its distinctive political capacities helped to create the international conditions that favoured the generally peaceful way in which the people of the Soviet Union and Eastern and Central Europe brought down their side of the Iron Curtain.

In any cool assessment of the importance of recent grass roots movements for socialist change, these periods of sustained activity and partial success must be balanced by a recognition of how quickly movements can lose their breath, disperse and all but disappear. It is also important to remember how at times of visibility movements have often depended on representatives within the political system, either from movement parties or supporters in traditional parties. For instance, the Dutch and German peace movements – the strength of both of which had a decisive impact on NATO – were significantly aided by the parliamentary work and voices of the Greens, the Dutch Left and left MPs in the social democratic parties of both countries.

The problem of political visibility

Why should representation matter? After all, the strength and persistence of the peace movement in the 1980s shows that some modern social movements have many of the advantages of political organization that one associates with a party: continuity, memory, cumulative understanding and resources, sustained visibility. The quick-footedness, self-confidence and political maturity of the 1980s peace movement, for instance, owes something to the lasting roots which earlier movements, of feminists, students, anti-nuclear, radical trade union activists had put down. Significant groupings of people who became politically active in the 60s and 70s and who in earlier generations would have been the cadre of Communist or Social Democratic Parties instead devoted their political energies to long term if sporadic independent organizing, educating and agitating. Even their personal networks provided a kind of framework for passing on traditions.

A major contribution to this continuity was provided by the infrastructure and communication network of CND. Although CND was only one part of this very widely based movement, its longevity across generations of the radical left and its political visibility make a revealing study in any discussion of the problems of visibility and sustainability facing any notion of an organization to the left of the Labour Party.

CND was founded in the late 50s in response to the agreement of the then Conservative government to allow US nuclear missiles (the Thor missile) to be sited around the country. It is still going strong with 50,000 members in 1995.

Periodically it has brought together the predominantly middle class non-conformist British left, regardless of party. In doing so it has acted as a form of political displacement for a limited but significant section of the British left, a political home for many of the disaffected. It has much of the infrastructure of a party – hundreds of branches; a centre which briefs and informs the members; an annual conference; frequently high profile leaders and something of a common culture. It has even managed to gain political representation and the visibility that flows from it, by making sure that MPs who supported it were very closely identified with the cause, Michael Foot in his early political days being the classic example. At the same time as unintentionally and informally serving a wider political function for the disaffected left, it very strictly limited its formal concerns to nuclear disarmament. This is probably a factor in its longevity and its high visibility. Different parts of the left came together because they agreed one central issue: banning the bomb. The intense ideological debated took place in the pub and on the demonstrations. Also, under Britain s present political system it is probably only by being, or presenting itself, as a single issue campaign that a movement can gain sustained political representation and hence visibility.

In these ways CND is the exception that proves the rule that without parliamentary representation a social movement can easily become invisible. Normally a left movement that has broad political goals has no direct access to the political system. Not only does it therefore lack political visibility but it tends to become abstract and overly propagandistic in its appeal. Political representation acts as a focus and a pressure on an organization to translate its aspirations into specific proposals about the exercise of power. Moreover the experience of trying (whether though the New Left Clubs of the 1950s or the Socialist Society in the 1980s and the Socialist Movement in the 1990s) shows the difficulties of establishing lasting local, regional structures amongst the independent activists of the radical left in Britain, where such structures cannot feed into a political organization with a national public presence able to reach out and gain popular support.

Organization on a purely extra-parliamentary basis is extremely difficult to sustain. Given the fact that the media reflect the parliamentary and majoritarian definition of politics in Britain, an extra-parliamentary left, even with a few sympathetic Labour MPs, is in effect organizing in the dark. It takes a great effort of will to keep up one's own forms of communication when the movement gains little validation from the wider society. An example would be the fate of the left that came together during the 1884-85 miners strike and later led to the creation of the Socialist Movement. During the strike there was a tremendously active and creative coalition involving, especially at local level, just about every social and trade union movement and almost all the organizations of the left. Efforts were made to build something from this: for example a Socialist Conference attended by nearly 2,000 people was held in Chesterfield in 1986 attracting significant national publicity. These conferences have continued, and a movement bas been partially institutionalized, even to the extent of launching an independent magazine for the wider left, *Red Pepper*, Moreover, in most towns and cities there is an active radical left that comes together across party and organizational boundaries around major issues of the day. It is tempting to think of this network of disparate activists as a party in waiting; in reality it is a coalition of the disenfranchised with as yet no very clear definition of its future. Moreover, involvement in these and other somewhat precarious projects of the radical left is far far smaller than on the continent where it has its own political presence. In sum, the marginal fate of the radical left in Britain is a telling witness to the limits of extra-parliamentary movements in parliamentary democracies.

In recent years, however, both the internal and external challenges to the existing British state have increased the possibilities of direct political representation for the radical left.

Already in Scotland the level of political debate and negotiation provides something of an inspiration and encouragement to democrats and pluralist socialists south of the border. All parties bar the Tories have highly developed proposals for a Scottish Parliament involving proportional representation and positive discrimination to remedy the disadvantages facing women. The Labour Party in Scotland, reluctantly and still with a few laggards, has had to accept that it cannot rule the roost of the left. A left exists independently and in electoral competition with Labour. Such a left is in part represented by the Scottish National Party (SNP), a party whose present leadership and the majority of its membership are well to the left of Labour, thought it is first and foremost a nationalist party. Scottish Militant, a small but very active party formed, as its name implies by Scottish members of the Trotskyist, entrist group Militant when they were expelled from the party, has also built a small electoral base through the leading role it played in the campaign against the poll tax and on to the problems facing working class communities in Scotland.

Development in Irelands also shake the status quo of Britain s unwritten codes of oligarchic rule. Although there is unlikely to be any lasting democratic settlement until after the next general election, debate and negotiations are driving towards a written constitution. The associated constitutional issues of bills of rights, electoral systems, degrees of decentralization and the ending of the hold of Westminster are all becoming central to public debate. The cultural and information flows between Eire, Northern Ireland, Scotland, England and Wales make it impossible to inoculate the English mainland against the democracy bug, especially, when the mainland carries independent campaigns like Charter 88, Liberty and the Electoral Reform Society or politically allied groups like the Labour Campaign for Electoral Reform.

The pressure for electoral reform is strongly reinforced from Europe. Membership of the European Union requires Britain to introduce a proportional electoral system for the European elections by 1996. Constitutional conservatives in both major parties will have great difficulty presenting such a reform from attracting public interest and spreading to the elections for Westminster, especially with the all-party – bar the Tory minority – agreement for a proportional system in the Scottish Parliament, to whose creation the Labour leadership is committed. The extent of public disaffection with existing political parties, and the general sense of not being represented – both well-documented in opinion polls – is also likely to lead to a spread of interest in a more proportional electoral system once people have had a taste of the extended choices for which it can allow.

A further institutional pressure stemming from Europe is (paradoxically, given the concern over the democratic deficit in Brussels) the way that it provides an alternative source of resources and political platform to Westminster. It thus strengthens decentralizing pressures against party leaderships seeking to tighten central control and helps to pluralize British politics. An example of the former is the way that radical employment, social or ecological projects in many British cities – previously funded by left wing local authorities – have been able to get money from the European Commission which is not available from the government. This experience has helped to nurture the seeds of regional consciousness and militancy in different regions of the UK as well as fueling national consciousness in Scotland and Wales.[21]

Another pluralizing mechanism can be seen in the way that the emergence of the European Parliament as an increasingly serious political platform upsets the ultimately centralized character of the Labour Party (the power of the parliamentary leadership through its extensive capacities for patronage). Members of the Labour Groups of the European Parliament, which increasingly offers a career structure of its own, are not beholden in any way to the Westminster leadership. Neither does Walworth Road, the Labour Party s HQ, have anything like as much influence over the choice of candidates for European constituencies. They have the independence to develop their own line. A recent example was when nearly half of the Labour MEPs publicly challenged Tony Blair's attempts to eliminate a commitment to common ownership from the Party's constitution. Several of them, most notably Ken Coates, went on to argue the relevance of common ownership for a European economy. Such a rebellion would be unthinkable among MPs. It gave a considerable fillip of confidence to activists in the constituencies and unions who wanted to challenge the direction of the new leadership.

Another source of the political intellectual confidence of the left MEPs is the fact they have allies to their left in votes and campaigns in the European Parliament. The experience of working with the new left parties on the continent has begun to break down the fear of such parties that has long been a feature for the political monoculture of the British labour movement – in which any talk of left alternatives to Labour is viewed as a betrayal. It has enabled left Labour MEPs to observe that the existence of an electoral and extra-parliamentary competitor to the left of social democracy usually strengthens the hand of the left inside these social democratic parties and more generally adds to critical and left influences on the whole political culture. Such thoughts have historically been inimical to Labour Party thinking. Labourism involved a political logic which transfers, inappropriately and indiscriminately, the imperatives of industrial unity – one out all out; the importance of unity for the effectiveness of strike action – to politics, a sphere where a more pluralist ethos would be more appropriate to the lively political culture of the left. Here Tony Blair's leadership – despite his claim to modernize – deploys this anti-pluralist ethic of old Labour as a bulwark to the leadership's power. In this organizational sense he is just the latest chip off old Labour's block.

How might the break up of Labour s monoculture develop and allow democratic expression of the views and activities of the radical left?

Labour's options and the end of the left's illusions

The former Cambridge economist and advisor to Labour in the 1960s, Nicholas Kaldor, once remarked that if post-war regulations over the movement and conduct of finance were lifted there would never again be a Labour government. What he did not anticipate was Labour learning to live with financial deregulation and operating monetarist policies along with some mild social reforms. The Spanish and French Socialist Parties responded to the mobility of capital in this way, and Tony Blair's Labour Party shows every indication of governing in the same way.

Its rhetoric proclaims a passionate and no doubt sincere concern with social justice and the righting of sixteen years of Tory wrongs. Labour's new leadership is determined, however, not to make specific policy commitments beyond those that have been proved by the opinion polls to be uncontroversial. This is not inertia or unconscious cowardice but electoral strategy. It hopes to glide into office on fair winds released by the collapse of the Major government, steering according to the lights of middle England. Any specific commitment of which the public is yet to be convinced is a hostage to fortune, an electoral gaffe. At times this can made Labour spokespeople appear evasive and totally unconvincing. If it were not for the extent of the failure, the corruption and the divided state of the government, one would seriously doubt the tactical wisdom – not to mention deeper strategic disagreements – of this approach.

My purpose here, however, is not to second-guess Labour's electoral advisors but to explore the likely dynamic of Labour politics in the event of a Labour government – either a Labour majority or a coalition with the Liberal Democrats. To consider likely developments in depth we need to ask a question to which many loyal but independent minded activists have assumed, as they gave support to Tony Blair, that there is a positive answer. Is there any possibility that the softly, softly, no commitments tactics are simply that: tactics to get into government? Once in government will Tony Blair implement a programme of radical reform on which his research team has been working discreetly in the meantime?

Certainly there is no lack of alternative policies which are quite compatible with the modernization of Labour. The most coherent are provided by Will Hutton, *The Guardian*'s Economic Editor, in his latest book *The State We're In*.[22] This is in effect a manifesto for modernizing British capitalism. Hutton argues that the economic weakness of British capitalism lies in its financial system with its high profit targets and its short-term horizons. He also argues that this has been sustained by and has symbiotically reinforced Britain's unmodernized, undemocratic political system. He argues for a radical, republican overhaul of the City and industry which would involve a regionalized Bank of England, a German model of workers rights vis-à-vis management and regulatory measures to ensure the greater availability of finance for long term and socially useful investment. He also argues for a thoroughgoing democratization of every state institution aimed at the sharing of sovereignty between local, regional, national and continental levels of government and civic associations, and at the dethroning of the executive and particularly the Treasury. He further urges that Britain should play a leading role in establishing stable democratic international economic institutions. It is not socialism, but, if it were to be implemented by Labour, it would be very widely supported within the party.

The problem, however, for a party that has gained office by stealth as Labour seems intent on doing, is that it will not have built a public awareness, the groundswell of popular pressure that would put the City and similar entrenched interests on the defensive. Putting Will Hutton in the Cabinet or employing him as an advisor would not be a solution. For the problem is not simply of devising the reforms but, given their challenging character, the current condition is winning public understanding and confidence in the reforms. This requires a pre-election campaign of persuasion and consciousness- raising which at the time of writing Tony Blair seems to be avoiding like the plague.

In the absence of a strong public campaign on these kind of reforming economic and social policies, a majority or even more so, a minority Labour government is likely to come into serious conflict with many of its own supporters in the trade unions, in parliament and amongst the public more generally – people will expect that a Labour government will mean the end of the absolute rule of the market and a noticeable improvement in the lives of millions of people. These are the kinds of circumstances in which Left Labour MPs are likely to vote against the party whip and ally themselves with extra-parliamentary campaigns rather than fall in behind government action.

In fact, in the event of a minority Labour government, a well organized, politically coherent band of Left MPs could have as much bargaining power as the Liberal Democrats. The Socialist Campaign Group of MPs (the most organized group of left MPs) has not been notable for its coherence in the past five years or so. But recent new recruits from the 1992 election appear to be joining with others to make it a more effective body. However, the variables involved in the event of some kind of Labour government make it too complex to predict the form that divisions in the party, and most significantly the unions, might take.

But several points can be made with certainty which return us to some of the reasons behind Ralph's conclusion that by 1976 the left had not moved on. First, most radical socialist members of the Labour Party, including MPs, have few if any illusions about turning it into a socialist party, whether with one, two or three more heaves. That does not mean they will walk away from it in disgust when a Labour government fails to introduce radical economic reform – though some certainly will. They feel the party or at least parts of it are as much, if not more, their party as the leadership's – and they will fight for their right to remain in the party on their own terms. The constitutional reforms in the late 1970s and early 1980s, especially mandatory reselection of MPs, has had the effect of strengthening the bond between effective and conscientious MPs and their constituency party. Most of the Campaign Group MPs fit into the category. Before any rebellious stand they will work to bring significant sections of the party with them. But they too are under no illusions about where power in the party lies.

The late Richard Crossman, left of center member of Labour Cabinets in the 1960s, political diarist and political theorist, once made a classic comparison between the dignified elements of Britain's unwritten constitution disguising the realities of power and a similar mystification in the structure of the Labour Party. In order to maintain the enthusiasm of party militants to do the organizing work for which the Conservative Party pays a vast army of workers, argues Crossman, a constitution was needed which apparently created a full party democracy while excluding (these militants) from power.[23] With the constitutional reforms of the late 70s and early 80s these militants, with support from thousands of trade unionists, threatened to intrude into the party's centers of power. Some accommodated to this power; others have been rudely pushed back. But many of them have seen through the constitution's dignified appearance and become fully aware of their position. They know that they may have a power base in the party but that this is not realistically a spring board for the centers of party power. More likely it is a way outwards and sideways to the left and movements outside the party and a platform to communicate to the wider public. This is how they use it.

The other notable way in which the left in the Labour Party have moved on from the state of affairs that Ralph described in 1976 is that they no longer conduct themselves as subordinates. In terms of the power structure of the party they are under no illusion that they are in a subordinate position, but they have no hesitation in drawing on other sources of power to win political victories independently of Labour s front bench. Tony Benn sets the example. He constantly runs his own campaign on matters of government abuses of power regardless of the Party leadership. On the basis of considerable popularity, reluctant respect and interest from the media he sometimes wins and almost always strikes a noticeably insubordinate note of opposition. Other MPs, Jeremy Corbyn and Chris Mullin for instance, are associated with impressive victories in the Courts over the appalling miscarriages of justice and helped free the wrongfully convicted Birmingham Six and Guildford Four, where the powerful opposition came from a persistent extra-parliamentary campaign.

These features of the radical Labour Left also reveal something about the left outside Westminster and frequently outside the Labour Party: that diffuse though it is, it has the potential to provide a power base of its own. Whether on the issue of cruise missiles in the 80s, the Gulf War in the 90s; over the poll tax, education, hospital closures, the rights of the disabled, or the Criminal Justice Act, movements have been organized independently of the Labour Party – or of any party. Most of the activists who come together in these movements and regularly participate in local networks of the left are in no hurry to join or form a party. Whether Labourist or Leninist, parties do not have a good record as far as most of the left in Britain is concerned. But this does not mean these activists limit themselves to single issue politics. Amongst many of them there is a strong desire to make connections across issues and localities and to define a shared vision based on common wealth, common land, equality, justice, sustainability and do-it-yourself politics.

A minority of left activists have joined the Green Party. And in recent years, following a split with the more parliamentarist – moderate – group of well known personalities, this party is open to close collaboration with others on the radical left, inviting left Labour MPs and independent socialists to speak at their conference and collaborate in their campaigns. A smaller minority has joined the Socialist Workers Party, which though energetic and persistent has not, for all its longevity, managed seriously to grow or extend its impact beyond the campuses and occasional workplaces and union branches. It includes many serious effective socialists, and it is likely to grow as individuals leave a Labour Party whose leadership intends to drop the party's founding socialist commitment. But as an organization it has not early moved on from the isolated and often sectarian position Ralph describes in his 1976 survey.

In sum then, and trying with difficulty to be as cool in my assessment as Ralph was in his, I would argue that there has been progress in the last twenty years towards 'an effective political formation' of the radical left. But it has been uneven and incomplete. It cannot be measured by membership cards, numbers of branches, election victories or the size of the troops on the ground. The progress has been in the growth of a self-confident left without illusions about Labour (inside as well as outside the Labour Party) and able to reach out to and ally with movements independent of Labour; in the methodological foundations for a political organization that is rooted in the daily life and struggles of working people but has representatives in the political system; in creating coalitions of likeminded radical leftists across formal party divides. It is too early to tell how these changes will combine with others to produce the political agency we need. After all, it has been done successfully elsewhere in Western Europe. The British left, more particularly the English left, tends to be a little slow. But with the British state, the symbol and part cause of our inertia, under pressure from all sides, and with the chance to add to that pressure ourselves if and when Labour is in office, we might catch up. Perhaps too, if we are attentive to the experiences and lessons of others, we can gain from being late.

Notes

[1] R. Miliband and M. Liebman, (Beyond Social Democracy', in R. Miliband, J. Saville, M.Liebman and L. Panitch (eds), *Social Democracy and After: The Socialist Regiter 1985/6*, London, Merlin Press, 1986, p.488

[2] Ibid

[3] H. Wainwright, 'Once more moving on: social movements, political representation and the Left', in L. Panitch (ed), *Why Not Capitalism: The Socialist Register 1995*, London, Merlin Press, 1995, p.100

[4] L. Panitch and S. Gindin, 'Transcending Pessimism: Rekindling Socialist Imagination', in L. Panitch and C. Leys (eds), (2000), *Necessary and Unnecesary Utopias: The Socialist Register 2000*, London, Merlin Press, 2000

[5] See Ralph Miliband, Moving On , *Socialist Register1976*, ed. Ralph Miliband and John Saville. Merlin Press, London p.128

[6] Ibid.

[7] Ibid. pp. 133 & 134

[8] Eric Hobsbawm, *The Age of Extremes*, Michael Joseph, London 1994

[9] For myself this is a process which began by attending the Conferences of the Institute for Workers Control in the late 60s and early 70s, usually in Birmingham, Nottingham or Sheffield. These brought together from all over the country local left wing working class leaders of an independent turn of mind, those intellectuals from the old new left engaged with grass roots politics, and activists from the new student movement and even the emerging women's movement. Then in 1981 came the 2,000 strong conference following the publication of *Beyond the Fragments* which I co-authored with Sheila Rowbotham and Lynne Segal. Following this, in 1982, came the foundation of the Socialist Society committed to socialist education, research and propaganda of a radical kind, independent of party. In 1986, in the aftermath of the miners strike, when there was the strong pressure for the left movement that was not tied to the increasingly hostile inner life of the Labour Party but on the other hand did not involve withdrawal from the party, the Society jointly with the Campaign Group of Labour MPs to organize a Socialist Conference in Chesterfield. This became an annual event and led to the formation of the Socialist Movement, which in 1994 helped to launch Red Pepper as an independent magazine for the radical left.

[10] For example the New Left Clubs in the late 1950s and early 1960s associated with the Universities and Left Review. Then in 1967, the Convention of the Left organized by Raymond Williams

[11] Ralph Miliband, *Socialism for a Sceptical Age*, Polity Press, Cambridge 1994, p.148

[12] Ibid, p,148

[13] R. Miliband, *Parliamentary Socialism*, Merlin Press London 1972

[14] *Socialism for a Sceptical Age*, p. 148

[15] For the history of the Workers Party see M. Keck, *Workers Party and Democracy in Brazil*, London 1991.

[16] *Socialism for a Sceptical Age*, p. 184

[17] Critical theory, especially the work of Marcuse, was especially influential with the student movements of Germany, Britain and the US in the late 60s. Critical theory s focus on themes such as bureaucracy, authoritarianism, information technology and sexual repression resonated with the movement's own interests. In the 1980s post-moderism, with its focus on the symbolic, was a strong influence on many people associated with for example, feminism and sexual liberation, many of whose activities were also concerned with the symbolic, as well as the material. However, the denial by many post-modern theorists of any reality beyond discourse, could not resonate with those social movements activists who collective effort was aimed at transforming power structures that existed independently of themselves. Here critical realism, a philosophically development influences by the movements as well seeking to act as an 'underlabourer' for their politics, is closer to the movements methods. It can sustain philosophically the presumption of most social movement activists of a real world independent of their knowledge of it – the object of their efforts of transformation. But in contrast to many forms of positivism and crude determinism, it does not reduce this reality to one structure or one level of reality. For useful commentaries on these different traditions see W. Outhwaite *New Philosophies of Social Science*, London, 1987 and *Jurgen Habermas*, Polity Press, Cambridge 1994; D. Harvey *The Condition of Postmodernity*, Blackwells, Oxford 1990 and R. Braidotti, *Patterns of Dissonance*; A. Sayer, *An Introduction to Critical Realism* Verso, London 1994 and R. Bhaskar, *Reclaiming Reality*, Verso, London 1991.

[18] In *Arguments for a New Left; Answering the Free Market* I do assess central contributions to these debates from the point of view of strategies for democratic social change.

[19] Robert Michels, *Political Parties*, Dover Publications, New York 1959.

[20] For the full story see Chapter 8 of my *Arguments for a New Left*, Blackwells, Oxford. 1994. And also for the views of many of the leading participants, East and West wee M. Kaldor ed. *Europe From Below*, Verso. London 1991

[21] Looking ahead to the days when such regional and city autonomy exists in Britain: strong city and regional layers of government provide favourable conditions for parties of the new left – on the continent it is at these levels that new left parties are strongest. Another lesson from these continental experiences is that it is at this level that the partnership between political representatives of the left and democratic civic activity has strongest day-to-day reality. Also, it seems that at a local level voters are more prepared to experiment with choosing a party to the left of the mainstream.

[22] Will Hutton, *The State We're In*, Jonathan Cape, London 1995.

[23] In his introduction to Bagehot's *The English Constitution*, Fontana, 1963.

14. BUILDING NEW PARTIES FOR A DIFFERENT KIND OF SOCIALISM: A RESPONSE (1996)

Hilary Wainwright

Barry Winter and I share a common starting point: a common concern with how the left can connect and communicate with the majority of people.

He believes that the most effective strategy for socialists to reach the people is primarily through the Labour Party and through building the left within it. This conclusion rests on the idea that the left will not get a hearing unless it is positioned in 'the political mainstream' – and he tends to see such a location as being the Labour Party. Political activity outside the Labour party, he describes, though not totally dismissively, as 'the fringe'.

His argument also depends on the idea that, after all, most of the people in the Labour Party are pretty representative of the wider population and if we can communicate effectively inside the party we are 'on the way to connecting' with this wider population. He believes that failures of the Labour left to achieve this wider influence are a result of major tactical blunders and anti-democratic behaviour rather than due to deeper limits on change built into the Party's institutions – which in turn, I will argue, shape, though not justify, some of the Labour left's undoubted mistakes.

I believe, by contrast, that the left's position inside the Labour Party has changed from being the opportunity it arguably was in the past into an imprisonment, which actually distorts and constrains the left's ability to convince the people of the relevance of radical socialist politics. The implication of my argument is that any section of the left which restricts its political location to the Labour Party and refuses seriously to consider the prospect of a party to the left of Labour, isolates itself from the people. It will make itself marginal, 'on the fringe' of political debate. My case is that in the long or even medium run, the most effective way for the radical left in the UK to engage with the political mainstream, as in most other West European countries, is with a political voice to the left of social democracy. This is not to say that working through such a party is an exclusive option; there would still be a significant left working mainly within the Labour party as, for example, in Denmark, Germany, Norway, Holland and Spain where there is a significant social democratic left, strengthened by the existence of a political competitor to social democracy's left. (Incidentally, Ralph Miliband explicitly assumes the influence of such radical sources of electoral as well as social pressure when he argues that the radical left's best medium term hope lies in strengthening the left in social democratic parties. He still held to his analysis of the limits of working from a permanently subordinate position within these parties).

This fundamental difference in strategy towards a shared goal influences our understandings of the importance of social movements, the political ramifications of the collapse of Soviet Communism, the decline of social democracy and the pressures of Europe and Scotland on Britain's unwritten constitution – the further points of disagreement itemised in Winter's critique. I will dwell first on the source of the strategic difference and secondly set out the case for seriously preparing for parties of the radical left which present an electoral challenge to Labour (I put it in the plural because such preparations for an electoral – as well as extra-parliamentary – coalition are already underway in Scotland).

In the Labour Party's early years, the structure of the party, based on trade union affiliations as well as the affiliation of political societies and parties did provide for the left a captive audience of politically alert listeners. There were several reasons for this, both to do with the character of trade unions in that period and the early structure of the trade union/ party alliance. First, trade union membership then was a much more conscious commitment, a commitment to collective resistance to the employers and more often than not, the state. Although one should be wary of generalising, it was a commitment against the grain of majority opinion, and often taken at some risk. As a result trade union branches and the structures built up from them, trades councils, district committees and so on, were generally lively and well-attended, real live centres of debate, discussion and action about the needs of working class people. This in turn influenced the character of union participation in the Labour Party, especially at a local level. After all, Trades Councils were 'Trades and Labour Councils' affiliated to the Labour Party. Left activists could with real justification assume that the trade union affiliates with whom they were working and arguing as they built the Labour Party were a live connection between socialists and the wider public.

In the last 60 years, changes in the character of the unions and in the structure of party-union relations have turned this captive activist audience into something nearer the dead souls of Tom Nairn's famous description of the block vote. Ironically, the very success of the Labour Representation Committee's original project, to establish the trade unions as a legitimate estate of the realm, weakened the role of Labour's union affiliates as a live connection between the left in the Labour Party and the public outside. Moreover it made the block basis of affiliation and representation open to abuse, by left and right, since the union delegates casting votes in highly politicised discussions, were representing a membership which, except in rare periods of mass industrial action, or on issues directly affecting their interests, were politically apathetic.

Since the 1960s, ever since trade unions had the almost habitual, indeed with the check-off system, automatic, support of over 30% of the population rather than a small, class conscious minority, the left in the Labour Party has faced a serious dilemma: to win any serious influence in the Labour Party and to do so on a sustainable and democratic basis, the left had to convince a significant section of this mass trade union membership to support left socialist policies. Such a task itself requires a political party, with its own press, campaigns and education, able to reach beyond the fulltime and lay officials representing the membership in the forums of the Party. In other words to move Labour to the left, the left needed their own organisation with equivalant functions – other than electoral – to a party.

In its heyday in the 1920s, this is what the Independent Labour Party was, a left party within the larger federated structure of the Labour Party. The Communist Party also tried to play this role, first by attempting to affiliate to the party then by acting in effect as the industrial wing of the Labour left. Apart from the limits of the Communist party as an advocate of democratic socialism, the Labour Party became increasingly centralised, losing many features of its genuinely federal political character, making any kind of dual membership or lasting alliance with another political party – even one which abstained from independent electoral activity – virtually impossible. One reaction to this and to Labour's dramatic turn to the right under Ramsey MacDonald, was a split in the ILP with an initially significant section leaving to form their own electoral party. At that stage, without a proportional electoral system and without any trade union support, such a move did not solve the dilemma (though those who tried to maintain the ILP's existence inside the party were no more able to overcome the dilemma than those outside).

There have been moments of course, when industrial and political develop-ments have radicalised the mass of trade unionists, without the midwife of a socialist party. The mid-1970s, with the miners' strike bringing down Prime Minister Edward Heath was such a moment. This produced the move to the left in the trade unions which gave the Bennite left its hope of victory. But the ultimate defeat of Bennism illustrates the dilemma of the left described above. The 'Bennite' left did not have the sort of organisation – in effect a campaigning, educational political party which could have worked at the base of the unions to build on the organic militancy of that period and turn it into a sustained shift in consciousness. They had an organisation that could lobby trade union representatives, at many different levels; but beyond activist newsletters, local rallies and conference fringe meetings, it could do little more. In tactical terms it was an impressive organisational effort. As such it was able to harvest the conse-quences of an earlier shift in consciousness but it could not sustain and deepen that radicalisation. All too often, as Winter implies, it accepted the undemo-cratic mechanisms of the block vote because they worked in the left's favour. On the other hand, there were occasions when the campaign for constitutional change and for Benn to be leader did open up debate in the unions to a remark-able degree. Where they were successful, however, they could not maintain the commitment. They often ended up controlling structures where there was no sustained base of support for their position. This is one factor behind the relative ease of Tony Blair's rout of the left.

Sometimes the left was able to use control of the institutions, however hollow their initial popular content, to built popular support. Ken Livingstone's radical but immensely popular GLC would be a case in point. But more often than not the necessity to defend or win control over structures in which political partici-pation is low has tied up the energies of Labour left activists in inward-looking wrangles. Thus while there are many critical lessons to be drawn about the tac-tics of the Labour left in the 1980s, I would argue that what dragged them down was the structures they inhabited of which they were insufficiently critical.

The only solution to the left's dilemma within our present electoral and party system would be the possibility of dual membership of Labour as a coalition party, with other political parties of the left. The (unique) relationship between the ANC and the South African Communist Party illustrates the possibility; a relationship with many similarities to the ILP's relationship to the Labour Party in its early days. But even to make the comparison, highlights how radically the Labour Party has changed since the fluidity of those early years. The process of making itself electable on the terms set by the British establishment, has led the party to mirror the establishment's view of the left and treat it as an embarrassment, something to be hidden, camouflaged and otherwise side-lined. Frosts from the Cold War at different periods have stiffened this anti-pluralist ethic.

This ditching of pluralism for reasons of electoral expediency has become extreme in reaction to four successive defeats, all blamed to various degrees on the left. It is this which has created a felt need on the left for their own political voice.

My case for such an independent voice does not rest on optimism as Winter implies. On the contrary it is because of the serious difficulties facing the left that such a political initiative needs to be prepared, through careful negotiation. In particular, there is a growing awareness of the need to work now to prepare a positive focus for the disillusion that will set in under what we might as well call 'Blatcherism'. People remember that as disillusion set in under Callaghan and the first moves towards monetarism, there was an ominous growth in electoral support for the far right. Racism and xenophobia are now more firmly entrenched in the Conservative party than ever before, as indicated by the resignations and growing disaffection of its 'Christian democrats'. A left that simply continues with a 'business as usual' routine in the Labour Party, however hard-working, cannot create the confident alternative that will be necessary to prevent Portillo and his crew from sailing to power on the demoralisation created by Blair.

It is because this need for new directions – diffuse and inchoate though these presently may be – is widely felt that the basis for new political initiatives exists. My examples of a new confidence amongst some leading left MPs, for instance, were intended not to imply some revival of the Labour left but to illustrate how when some left MPs made common cause with campaigns outside the Labour Party and helped these movements gain a popular platform they had a real impact, bridging that chasm between socialists and the rest of society. This is leading to a detached co-habitation between many on the Labour left and the leadership of the party. They inhabit the same home but even more than before follow entirely different political lives.

Similarly my focus on recent progressive social movements was not driven by some naive presumption that they could give virgin birth to a new political party. It is rather that in their practice, influenced as it was and is by the failure both of social democracy and Soviet communism, they have been testing out new methods of organising, new understandings of social change, and in particular the connections that link individual consciousness self-awareness, practical knowledge and skill to the collective capacity and the collective power to transform structures. A critical development of these insights needs to be central to the left's future initiatives if they are not to be dogged by past failures.

Barry Winter says that for me the past does not weigh heavily. In one sense that is true. But it is not because I have taken the social movement escapism pill. Rather it is because as someone who became a socialist in opposition to the actual experience of both Soviet Communism and social democracy, I have sought since their collapse and demise, to think through why and how the libertarian left with which I have identified is different. This does not mean that I now believe that the libertarian left, influenced as it is by involvement in social and radical trade union movements, has a clear programme and strategy. But it does mean I have a clear, methodological, as well as substantive sense of why the socialism for which, with many others, I am working, is different; why in a certain sense the past in so far as it is the past of regimes and governments that ruled in the name of socialism, is not my past.

In elaborating a different kind of socialism we need to learn from the past and especially to discover socialist traditions that have been suppressed and marginalised. But with perspectives clarified by an understanding of history and a knowledge of previously hidden continuities, a modern vision of socialism can best be made practical through focusing reflective attention, with an international lens, on present and future experiments in social co-operation, public ownership and democratic participation.

While Barry Winter may consider that I am cavalier towards the past, I find that for Barry the present does not sufficiently impinge. In particular the present state of decay of the British state and the pressures it is under from within – most notably Scotland, but also the implosion of the royal establishment, the revelations of the Scott inquiry, the rebellions of the young and poor whose city councils can no longer provide public services – and from without, the steady encroachment of European integration. Barry Winter rather begrudgingly admits that the unstoppable pressure for constitutional reform is likely to lead to electoral reform. This, he says, might give scope to the forces of the right. Indeed it might. In fact constitutional reform of itself is never automatically progressive. That is why the left needs to be well ahead of the process, not just predicting that change might happen and that the picture is complex and dangerous. We need to spell out what kind of electoral reform, what kind of bill of rights, what powers for local and regional government, what kind of republic. And knowing that electoral reform at Westminster is almost unavoidable as the pressure surrounds this archaic citadel on all sides, we need to prepare to make the most of it to give political expression to the millions of people who presently feel disenfranchised.

If anything is going to play into the hands of the right, it is to imagine that the 'inside left' can change the Labour Party to provide an adequate voice for the generations of disaffected voters it has alienated in the past.

I detect in Barry Winter's writing an effort to maintain a taboo. A taboo on serious discussion of what is part of the political scene in virtually every West European political system: a party to the left of social democracy, trying with varying degrees of success to rethink socialism, but with a continuing commitment to a different economic and social system. In effect it is a taboo, prevalent in England at least, on openly imagining what possibilities might emerge under democratic constitutional arrangements as if the left had some vested interest in the existing unwritten constitution and should not think beyond it.

At the end of 1995 Arthur Scargill had the confidence – born of frustration and a touch of arrogance perhaps- to break the taboo. Scargill's virtue is his ability to identify an injustice and insist publicly on action to right the wrong – whether the government's pit closure plans or the political injustice of the radical left's exclusion from political representation. His flaw, in my opinion, is his voluntaristic presumption that others might follow his lead despite the absence of the prior process of coalition building that could produce a more strategically effective initiative. It is up to others who share some elements of his long term goal to respond to his initiative and turn it into a far reaching debate that may well end up with outcomes different from that which Scargill presently proposes. At the time of writing it appears unlikely that this will be possible. It is likely that others on the left with different timetables and more inclusive ways of organising will need to pursue their own discussions (for instance left organisations from within the Green party, the Labour party, the Democratic Left and independent socialists in the Socialist Movement and Red-Green network are already engaged in a process of convergences).

The problem of left political representation which he addresses is too important to leave to Scargill. It is not just a crisis of representation for his particular brand of socialism but for all those – left greens, for example who believe in a socialisation of wealth and a transformation rather than mere amelioration of capitalist political economy. Now that the Mandleson/Blair leadership is following to its practical conclusion the view that everything associated with the left's influence in the early 1980s has to be exorcised, it has become an urgent issue. Many long-term Labour activists have made the painful decision to leave the party: others have made the equally painful decision to hang on for the time being. Many politically active citizens are homeless or lodging in temporary accommodation.

But the silencing of the left is not just a matter of frustrated activists. A small, but significant number of voters also feel that their views no longer have a legitimate voice in the political system. It's not just the anecdotal evidence of local left activists who have told me about how they have been rung up by people who want details of Scargill's new party, or indeed of the reports from his office of hundreds of requests, especially from trade unionists, for party cards. Opinions polls show significant minorities with views on taxation, public spending, privatisation and public ownership to the left of New Labour's. There is also the question of the marginalisation of what Fenner Brockway called the 'outside left' for the wider political culture. The suppression of this left by the current Labour machine is an extreme response to the way in which the electoral system makes the floating voter the magnet to which the main parties are drawn. There is an inbuilt pressure on Labour to look over its right shoulder which can only be countered by pressures in the party bolstering up the left against short-term electoral imperatives – a diminishing possibility after four electoral defeats – or by an electoral competitor to labour's left, which is not a serious possibility until there is real momentum towards the introduction of a proportional electoral system.

As the transformation of Labour into a party of modern capitalist management proceeds apace, however, the refusal of many Labour Party socialists seriously to discuss even the long term prospects and conditions for a new party will become a seal on their own subordination. Their timidity in providing an intellectual and campaigning alternative focus – if not an electoral one – increases the humiliating phenomenon of grown men and women slavishly obeying a leader who is intellectually vacuous, however tactically brilliant he and his team may be.

The case for a left electoral challenge to Labour and hence for proportional representation is a perfectly respectable one which could quite legitimately be supported by people within the party. A left electoral challenge under a proportionate electoral system would overcome the bias towards the centre; it would provide both a left ally for and pressure on Labour in government – opening up, formalising and in effect making democratic the coalition that the labour movement claims to be. None of this case adds up to the kind of 'betrayal' of which some Labour socialists accuse anyone who advocates even serious debate about a left party.

Moreover, there are a variety of ways short of an electoral challenge to Labour, in which the left inside and outside the Party could work together campaigning and refining shared socialist policies in the build-up to the election and in opposition to many of the policies that a new Labour government will pursue. The exact timing of an electoral challenge could then be open, to wait for conditions in which such a challenge would gain mass support, rather than lost deposits.

But what are the conditions for left party, parties or an electoral alliance to come into being as an effective political force? The experience of northern Europe where left parties have between 8 and 18% of the vote points to two conditions: first the existence of a proportional electoral system and secondly the occurrence of a major split in a Communist or social democratic party or both. In New Zealand, working with the colonial legacy of a Westminster first-past-the-post system, a split from the Labour Party there in response to the Thatcherite economic policies pursued by a Labour government led to the creation of a new left breakaway led by Jim Anderton, which, in coalition with an already-established Green Party and radical Maori party, has proved not only a serious electoral challenge to Labour but also a decisive factor in overturning the electoral system. But the breakaway was equivalent to Tony Benn, Ken Livingstone and Peter Hain, if not Robin Cook and Michael Meacher, splitting from British Labour.

In Britain, the historical lack of a strong communist party, the demise of the Independent Labour Party and Labour's monopoly of labour movement political representation – partly thanks to an electoral system designed to protect the establishment – has denied the left a base from which a challenge to Labour might grow organically. In this context, a few sustained campaigning movements, notably CND, have periodically acted as a convivial shelter for the politically homeless.

Discussion of the prospects for a new left party or electoral alliance in Britain needs to take account of very different national dynamics, especially in Scotland and England. In Scotland, as already mentioned, there is, in preparation for a Scottish parliament, work under way for a left electoral alliance. One of the possible components, Scottish Militant Labour, has already a small number of local government seats. The Scottish National Party is itself, on present policies, a left electoral challenge to Labour. In England, too, the emphasis has to be on preparations. After all, there is much to prepare for: the strong possibility of a real momentum towards electoral reform, assuming the Lib Dems are in a strong position after the election; the strong likelihood of policies proposed by a Labour government for which many left MPs will find it impossible to vote.

There are also many preparatory problems to consider – for example, problems of structure that determine how one approaches questions of programme and policy. Scargill's proposal extols the original constitution of Labour, with its coalition-like character. Moreover, he stresses that 'radical opposition in Britain is symbolised not by the Labour and trade union movement, but by the groupings such as those which defeated the poll tax, the anti-motorway and animal rights bodies, Greenpeace and other anti-nuclear campaigners, and those fighting against open-cast mining'. But the structure he proposes, 'a simple socialist constitution', does not allow for the diversity and flexibility that a coalition of left political organisations and a closer relation with these new movements would require.

Then there is the question of electoral intervention. If the preparations followed the Scottish model, then there could conceivably be a selective and realistic electoral intervention even at the next election. It could involve support for socialist Labour MPs, Green Party candidates and the left of Plaid Cymru in

Wales, plus one or two high-profile challenges in safe Labour seats with leading New Labour MPs or safe Tory seats – if there are such things.

Finally, there is the question of policy. Again, given the fissiparous state of the left, it would be more realistic if the coalition of electoral-alliance model were followed and an agreed platform of economic, constitutional, social and international themes drawn up instead of a detailed party manifesto. A green socialist alliance of this kind would not be exclusively electoral. It would provide a platform and information exchange for the variety of trade union and green campaigns now emerging. Even during the election campaign, it could organise for policies and support for extraparliamentary campaigns where it did not back a particular candidate.

A vacuum has been steadily opening up in British politics to which Scargill has now responded, without any of the political sensitivity needed effectively to begin to fill it. If the radically minded left inside the Labour Party is to help to renew the left, it will not suffice to scoff at the idea of a new left. The possibility is irreversibly on the agenda, the debate is about what kind, when, following what preparations, negotiations, period of nonparty coalition. For this, the left in Britain needs to learn from the successes and failures of the radical left across the world. Just as the British establishment, Labour as well as Conservative, can no longer cling on to the political cosiness of a two party monopoly, so the British left can no longer plead 'British peculiarities' and retreat into inner Labour Party obscurity. It has to learn, drawing on international experiences, how to take its message to the people, independently, no longer under the cover of Labour.

15. THE CONTINUING RELEVANCE OF THE MILIBANDIAN PERSPECTIVE

David Coates and Leo Panitch

The belief in the effective transformation of the Labour Party into an instrument of socialist politics is the most crippling of illusions to which socialists in Britain have been prone ….To say that the Labour Party is the party of the working class is … important … but it affords no answer to the point at issue, namely that a socialist party is needed in Britain, and that the Labour Party is not it, and it will not be turned into it. To say that it is a party of the working class is, on this view, to open the discussion, not to conclude it. It might be otherwise if there was any likelihood that the Labour Party could be turned into a socialist formation; but that is precisely the premise which must, on a realistic view, be precluded.[1]

The legacy of Ralph Miliband's own writings on the Labour Party has been, and remains, both an important and a controversial one. It is one which is often caricatured by critics unfamiliar with (and apparently reluctant to spend the time to become familiar with) its central theses. Indeed one of the reasons why this book of essays may be of lasting value is that it brings together a collection that, among other things, show how ridiculous (and indeed sloppy) it is to simply dismiss the work of Ralph Miliband (and the other writers whose work is reproduced here) as 'what Ben Pimlott calls the "we wuz robbed" school of party history, which includes writers such as Ralph Miliband, David Coates, James Hinton and John Saville'[2]. Indeed in that same collection of essays, sanctified as they were by a Tony Blair foreword and a Michael Foot preface, Robert Taylor, reporting on the writings of Miliband, Saville, Coates and this time Tom Nairn, told his readers that in our work 'trade unions were portrayed as a formidable, defensive barrier to Labour's Socialist advance, supposedly holding back the masses from commitment to a militant socialism, less inhibited by the inevitable constraints imposed on the opportunities for political action by reformist parliamentary politics and industrial relations voluntarism'[3]. No such thing. He would have been far more accurate to say instead that the cumulative effect of Ralph Miliband's work, within the literature on what the Blairite wing of the Labour Party would now call 'Old Labour', was the presence of a set of arguments which included the following:

(a) The centrality of parliamentarianism to the theory and practice of Labour Party politics, and its deleterious consequences for the Party's capacity to act as a successfully reformist party when in office.

(b) The functionality of the Labour Party's periodically radical rhetoric to the long-term stability of the UK class structure, and its deleterious consequences for the creation and consolidation of a radicalized proletariat in the UK.

(c) The inability of socialists within the Labour Party to do more than briefly (and episodically) radicalize the rhetoric and policy commitments of the party in opposition, and its deleterious consequences for the creation of a genuinely potent socialist party in the UK.

Critics would also have done well to observe that Ralph Miliband's later writings were not predominantly focused on the Labour Party: that, from 1969, when Miliband published *The State in Capitalist Society*, the focus of his work shifted to state theory: a shift which – beginning with his famous debate with Poulantzas – made him one of the most internationally recognized intellectual figures in political science and sociology not only within but well beyond the English speaking world. In that change of focus and status, it was not that the original positions were abandoned so much as generalized. The Miliband thesis in *The State* book was the by now standard one for the 'school' as a whole: that democratic politics in advanced capitalist societies operate within powerful class constraints; and that these are constraints structured into the political domain through the conservatism of the state bureaucracy, the pressure of business and financial interests, and the ideological pressure of capitalist values in the mass media. Social democratic parties of the Labour Party variety were not entirely ignored in this analysis: but they appeared there only in less prominent roles. They were mentioned as orchestrators of capitalist legitimation and working class demobilization, as part of the political processes that accommodate democratic aspirations to capitalist power structures, and as 'singularly weak agencies of mass education in socialist principles and purposes'[4]. What in *Parliamentary Socialism* had been presented as a vulnerability to parliamentary socialization now reappeared in *The State in Capitalist Society* as an inadequate capacity for counter-hegemonic politics: 'the ideological defenses' of Labour leaders being singled out there as 'generally not … of nearly sufficient strength to enable them to resist with any great measure of success conservative pressure, intimidation and enticement'[5].

Yet British politics were never far from Miliband's mind and what was presented in general terms in *The State* book also reappeared later as very much a UK phenomenon. In Miliband's *Capitalist Democracy in Britain*, the compatibility of capitalism with democracy in Britain, now explained in neo-Gramscian terms, was seen as a consequence of 'the hegemony exercised by the dominant class and its conservative forces'[6]. And the capacity of that hegemony to survive unscathed was, in Miliband's 1982 book, still seen in considerable measure as a product of past Labour Party policy. He was clear on this when critiquing the arguments of his mentor, Harold Laski:

'The whole political scene would indeed have been transformed had the Labour Party in the inter-war years been the socialist party which he wanted it to be, or at least believed that it must soon become. But one of the most significant facts about the British political scene was precisely that the Labour Party was not then, and was not on the way to becoming, such a party. This gave Laski's argument a certain air of unreality, which the passage of time has made even more pronounced. This is a great pity because the argument itself is right: the political system would be fundamentally affected if the Labour Party (or any other party) did become a major force for socialist change; even more so if it was able to form a government and sought to implement a programme of socialist policies. But the fact is that the political system has never had to face such a situation. This of course is something which itself requires explanation.'[7]

Key to that explanation for Miliband, in 1982 as much as in 1961, was the Labour Party's own exposure to (and enthusiasm for) the rules and institutions of parliamentarism as these were generally understood among the British political class. 'Nothing', he wrote,

has weighed more heavily upon labour politics in Britain than the existence of a strong framework of representation: however inadequate and undemocratic it might be, there did exist, it was believed, a solid proven structure that could be made more adequate and democratic, that had already undergone reform, and that in due course could be used to serve whatever purpose a majority might desire, including the creation of a socialist order.'[8]

Parliamentarism of this kind worked, according to Miliband, by co-option and incorporation. 'It simultaneously enshrines the principle of popular *inclusion* and that of popular *exclusion*'[9]: co-opting and incorporating the working class as an electorate, their more radical parliamentary representatives, and their trade union leaderships. The British parliamentary state has sustained the private rule of capital in the UK by drawing all these potentially oppositional social forces and political institutions into a form of democratic politics that still leaves elected governments subject to the constraints of a conservative state apparatus and a well-entrenched business and financial class, and that still leaves their electorate subject to heavy ideological pressure from schools, churches and the media. And, Miliband continued to argue, the Labour Party leadership had long been an active player in that process of political socialization and incorporation: training early generations in the rules of parliamentary politics (especially in the 1920s the illegitimacy of the use by Labour of industrial power for political ends); and repressing (until challenged by the Bennite internal party reforms of the early 1980s) internal party democracy so that MPs could remain free of effective pressure from constituency activists and Labour Cabinets free of party control when in office. [10]

It should hardly need saying that the Miliband and Saville did not subscribe to some 'sell out' theory of British Labour, some notion that the British working class was inherently socialist but persistently betrayed by its moderate political leadership. That is a criticism occasionally leveled against them; and it is unwarranted. The Milibandian understanding of the relationship between Labour as a political party, the working class as a social force, and socialism as a body of ideas has always been far more complex than that. As Marxists they always believed that the contradictory relationship between capital and labour in a capitalist society did (and does) preclude an effective long term realization of working class interests without a major resetting of property relationships. They did not apologize for perpetually raising the socialist question, seeing it still a legitimate issue to discuss when exploring left-wing political formations. But Miliband's critique of British Labour was not that an already existing socialist working class requires better political leadership. Such a claim constituted, in his view, what in 1977 he termed

> a second and related misjudgment, namely the gross overestimation of the strength of the socialist forces in the Labour Party and in the labour movement at large. The whole argument is often conducted as if large and powerful socialist armies were already assembled, and only waiting for new and resolute commanders in place of the old ones to move to the assault of capitalism. But this is obviously nonsense.[11]

Or again, half a decade later:

> There is no point pretending that there exists a ready-made majority in the country for a socialist programme. How could there be? One of the fruits of the long predominance of labourism is precisely that the party of the working class has never carried out any sustained campaign of education and propaganda on behalf of a socialist programme; and that Labour leaders have frequently turned themselves into fierce propagandists against the socialist proposal of their critics inside the Labour Party and out, and have bent their best efforts to the task of defeating all attempts to have the Labour Party adopt such proposals. Moreover, a vast array of conservative forces, of the most diverse kind, are always at hand to dissuade the working class from even thinking about ... socialist ideas ... a ceaseless battle for the "hearts and minds" of the people is waged by the forces of conservatism, against which have only been mobilized immeasurably smaller socialist forces.[12]

The Milibandian thesis was never that an inherently socialist working class was periodically betrayed by Labour Party moderation. It was rather that the possibility of such a radicalized class has been blocked by, among other things, the presence of a party committed to Labourism rather than socialism, and by the periodic left-ward shift in rhetoric made by the Labour Party whenever working class militancy intensified. The argument was always that the emergence of such a working class was extraordinarily difficult to trigger with the Labour Party

in the way; but it was also that the creation of mass support for socialist programmes was both possible and necessary. The whole thrust of the Milibandian
argument on the working class and socialism was that the fusion between the
two was one that had to be *created*; and that such a creation required clear and
unambiguous political leadership of the kind that the Labour Party systematically declined to offer. As Miliband and Liebman put it in 1986:

> 'The notion that very large parts of "the electorate", and notably the working class,
> is bound to reject radical programmes is a convenient alibi, but little else. The real
> point, which is crucial, is that such programmes and policies need to be defended
> and propagated with the utmost determination and vigour by leaders totally con-
> vinced of the justice of their cause. It is this which is always lacking: infirmity of
> purpose and the fear of radical measures lies not with the working class but with
> the social democratic leaders themselves.'[13]

Careless critics have therefore moved too quickly to condemn those who take
this perspective for misunderstanding the Labour Party's project as something
other (and more radical) than it was. Not so. They always understood that
project (in all its moderation and episodic radicalism) well enough. They simply
found it wanting both when measured against its own promises and when set on
the wider map of European and global working class politics.

II

To dwell as we have thus far on Ralph Miliband's contribution to studying the
Labour Party minimizes the great effect of the broader role he played in founding a creative new current of Marxist political analysis. The remit of his *Marxism
and Politics*, arguably his greatest book, was the need to show clearly

> ... what a Marxist political theory specifically involves; and to indicate how far it
> may serve to illuminate any particular aspect of historical or contemporary reality.
> For this pupose, the developments in Marxist political thinking in recent years have
> obviously been of great value, not least because the constricting 'triumphalism' of
> an earlier period has been strongly challenged and the challenge has produced a
> much greater awareness among Marxists that Marxism, in this as much as in other
> realms, is full of questions to be asked and – no less important – of answers to be
> questioned. Many hitherto neglected or underestimated problems have attracted
> greater attention; and many old problems have been perceived in better light. As
> a result, the beginnings have been made of a political theorization in the Marxist
> mode. But these are only beginnings ...'[14]

It was this broader perspective, this invitation to go beyond the old Marxist
paradigm and create a new and richer one that excited a new generation of intellectuals and scholars, the two of us among them. Unconnected with each other

in any way, we eagerly took up many of the themes that Miliband (and Saville) had already sounded in the study of labourism, seeking not only to extend the account of the contemporary party's history beyond where *Parliamentary Socialism* had left off, but to develop further the conceptual apparatus for doing so. Like Miliband, we also sought to go beyond the Labour Party in this respect and to contribute to the development of Marxist political theory in general. And unlike Miliband himself (who once privately admitted to being bored by economics) we also sought to engage on this basis with the new Marxist political economy. Thus while we took up writing accounts of the Labour Party from the 1960s to the 1990s from a Marxist perspective, standing on Miliband's shoulders so to speak, we also departed from him in various ways from the beginning, not least by telling the history of policy and intra-party conflict in more detail and using more original research materials than he did, but above all by concentrating much more on economic policy and having in general a greater concern with political economy.

Miliband was therefore not alone in making a turn from the focused analysis of one political party to a more general political sociology of social democracy and the state. So too did a number of academics heavily influenced by him and by his writings. By the mid-1970s Leo Panitch had already contributed to founding the international debate on corporatism and followed this not only with further interventions into that debate but also with his initial contributions to the new Marxist work on the state[15]. After *Labour in Power?* Coates's own Gramscian turn then produced *The Context of British Politics*[16] and *Running the Country*[17]; both of which sit alongside Colin Leys' *Politics in Britain*[18] as major attempts to produce a general assessment of the parameters of Labour politics in the manner of Miliband's writings on the state. We then went the further inch – into intellectual territory that Ralph Miliband did not explore – rounding out this Marxist political sociology with a series of studies in international and comparative political economy: Panitch encouraging (and developing himself) a new approach to democratic state administration and a distinctive *Socialist Register* position on the relationship of globalization to the state[19]; and Coates producing first a detailed survey of UK economic under-performance[20] and then a comparative study of *Models of Capitalism*[21]. This work produced new frameworks for analyzing developments in Labour politics: not only exploring the limits of Old Labour politics through a discussion of 'corporatism', but also the limits of New Labour through notions of 'progressive competitiveness'. In this way, a Milibandian perspective was brought to the analysis of New Labour, armed with a range of concepts and arguments which went beyond those available to it in the first phase of its work on the Labour Party.

The first moves in that direction had come in response to the experience of Labour in power between 1974 and 1979. Through his intervention in the famous profits squeeze debate of the 1970s, Panitch[22] stressed the centrality of class conflict to understanding the crisis of the British economy. In a study initially designed as an update of *The Labour Party and the Struggle for Socialism,* Coates developed what was an early attempt at Milibandian political economy to explain Labour's dismal performance in office. In *Labour in Power?* Coates argued that, though vital as a first step, it was no longer enough merely to list the range of powerful interests constraining Labour governments, because to do only that was to imply that those interests were in control of their world even if Labour was not in control of its. What was needed instead was the recognition that 'neither private elites nor public figures either understood or were in complete control of the main processes which shaped the world economy over which they presided', and that it was the *capitalist* nature of that world economy that ultimately held the key to the failure of this Labour Government and to the growing estrangement of trade unionists from it. 'To understand the events of the 1970s,' Coates argued, 'to assess the true impact of elite constraints, to place the power of British trade unionism, and to discuss the future of the Left in Britain, the question of capitalism had to be faced, and its impact on British politics fully understood'[23].

The question, of course, was how; and one answer to that question came from a systematic examination of the class constraints eroding the viability of corporatism. Panitch defined corporatism as 'a political structure within advanced capitalism which integrates organized socio-economic producer groups through a system of representation and co-operative mutual interaction at the leadership level and of mobilization and social control at the mass level' [24]; and he emphasized its inherent instability with the presence of strong social democratic labour movements. The class parameters surrounding even the corporatist version of the capitalist state, he argued, and the resulting policy outputs reflecting 'capitalist class dominance', had eventually to draw unions out of corporatist structures, or had at least to oblige them 'to abstain from accommodative behaviour if they were not to be repudiated by their rank and file membership'[25]. This explanation of the propensity of Labour governments to succumb to winters of discontent of the 1979 variety was also one that Coates's later writings on this last example of Old Labour in power began to echo. 'What the Labour Party understood as socialism'

> was more properly understood as a mild form of corporatism, the sharing of political power with bureaucratized trade union leadership and corporate capital. Yet … this power sharing was itself a major barrier to capital accumulation, and so proved destructive of the very economic growth that Labour governments sought to extract from the mixed economy …. For even on such favourable political and industrial terrain corporatism proved to be extraordinarily brittle. Anaesthetizing rather than removing the basic cleavage of interest between capital and labour, by pushing that tension down to lower levels of decision-making, corporatist structures … in the end fell victim to the contradictions they were supposed to suppress. [26]

This repositioning of the study of the Labour Party on the wider canvass of state theory and corporatist political practice moved the center of gravity of our studies away from the detail of Labour Party political developments into a more general analysis of capitalism and the contemporary state. That move was accentuated through the course of the 1980s and 1990s by further emphasis on questions of political economy. The long years of Thatcherism imposed their own imperative. While Coates probed the adequacy of Thatcherite claims about the adverse *economic* consequences of a strong labour movement, and argued against the low-wage, low-welfare growth strategy that the Conservatives were then pursuing, Panitch, followed Greg Albo, his colleague at York University in Toronto, in theorizing that strategy as one of 'competitive austerity' and contrasted it to the emerging center-left enthusiasm for strategies of 'progressive competitiveness;'[27] and developed arguments about the inadequacies of each.[28] As New Labour repositioned the Party's economic policies – away not simply from the statism of the Bennite AES but also from the corporatism of Old Labour – Panitch began to see parallels between Labour's growing enthusiasm for labour reskilling as the key to industrial modernization and the whole thrust of 'Clintonomics', and to warn the Left about both. 'The two centuries-old search for a cross-class "producer" alliance between labour and national capital as an alternative to class struggle', he wrote in 1994, ' has taken shape in recent years in the form of the progressive competitiveness strategy, but its weaknesses have been very quickly revealed in the context of the globalization of capital' [29]. Similar arguments were by then appearing sequentially in Coates' 1990s writings on the UK economy: first in the form of a critique of Thatcherite low wage growth strategies in *The Question of UK Decline* (1994), and later as critiques of New Labour's emerging political economy[30] and of contemporary social democratic growth strategies of the Swedish [31] or Clinton/Reich variety[32]. By the time *Models of Capitalism* (2000) was published towards the end of New Labour's first term, those following a Milibandian perspective had equipped themselves with a set of *political economy* theses that both illuminated central weaknesses in New Labour's economic strategy and rounded out what had hitherto been an approach to the politics of Labour more narrowly anchored on the terrain of history and sociology.[33]

Between the earlier 1980s writings on the limits of Old Labour's corporatism and the later 1990s writings on the dangers of New Labour's enthusiasm for 'progressive competitiveness' – there was also a further refining and deepening of some of the older strands of the Milibandian approach to Labour Party politics: particularly the inability of the Labour Party to transform itself into an effective counter-hegemonic force in contemporary UK society, and the inability of the Labour Left, however well endowed, to transform the Labor Party into a socialist one. The argument on the link between Labour's electoral politics and its weakness as a hegemonic force occurs in a number of places in Coates's work.[34] On each occasion Labour's electoral fragility was linked to its inability/ refusal to forge more than an episodic and limited electoral relationship with its mass base. In 1996, Coates noted the high 'degree of assistance from external events and forces the Labour Party has always needed to create an electoral bloc sufficiently substantial to give it parliamentary power', and its long-established failure to establish any of the institutions –'newspapers, clubs, communities and institutions' of a fully functioning labour movement. Restricting itself to a vote-getting relationship with its working class base, so the argument went, and mobilizing even that relationship only episodically, Labour left the formulation of mass opinion to more conservative sources of values and policy in the privately owned media; so marooning itself largely as the 'passive recipient of electoral swings', with its own politics never normally in possession of 'sufficient magnetic force to redraw the shape of electoral Britain by the power of its own programme and possibilities alone'. No wonder then, Coates argued, that majorities so gratuitously won were easily lost, or that 'Labour majorities when they come tend to be accidental rather than created, and invariably prove to be as tenuous as they are fortuitous'. [35]

So although the general move away from Labour Party studies to more general work on political sociology and political economy has been the main feature of our work over the last two decades, it would not be correct to say that those who adopted a Milibandian view have been silent on the detail of Labour Party developments in the long years of Opposition after 1979. On the contrary, they played a full part in the debates triggered by the 1983 electoral defeat: arguing in particular against the 'move to the right' logic of Hobsbawm's *The Forward March of Labour Halted*[36] while also chronicling and commenting upon the Party's policy trajectory after 1983.[37] And Panitch and Leys *The End of Parliamentary Socialism* (1997/2001),[38] dedicated as it was to Miliband's memory, direcly spoke to the continuing relevance and importance of the approach he pioneered to the understanding of the detailed internal development of the Labour Party. Ever since *Parliamentary Socialism,* the Milibandian argument for socialist politics had engaged with successive generations of the Labour Left; but not until *The End of Parliamentary Socialism* had any of the academics closely associated with Miliband addressed themselves in a detailed, focused and sympathetic way to Left Labour politics. That omission was now addressed, with the post-1970 Labour Left treated as a *new* Left sensitive to the weaknesses of its predecessors, above all in terms of its understanding that what would first of all have to be involved in making the Labour Party socialist would entail a *break* with party tradition rather than the constant romanticizing of it, as was the wont of the traditional Labour left. No less important, as against the statism of that traditional Labour left, the new left in the party recognized that democratizing the party would be the first step needed for a more extensive democratization of the British state. *The End of Parliamentary Socialism* offered a detailed guide to the conflict within the party from 1970 to 1983, covering the radical democratic character, as well as the weaknesses, of Bennism, the Campaign for Labour Party Democracy and the Alternative Economic Strategy – and the role of the union leadership and the old left played in their ultimate defeat – and then went on to analyse the process of policy reformulation and the disempowerment of activism within the Labour Party up to the end of the century.

The end result of this intellectual journey, we believe, has been the creation of a distinct Milibandian voice in the current set of debates on the nature and potential of New Labour. Though as concerned as other scholars and commentators to isolate what is new is New Labour's 'third way' [39], the Milibandian voice in the burgeoning literature triggered by the 1997 victory has been distinctive in at least three ways.

- It is distinctive partly because of its propensity to combine its recognition of novelty with an emphasis on continuities in the politics of New Labour: underlying continuities (with Old Labour) in the Party's continuing enthusiasm for a co-operative relationship with the business community; continuities with Gaitskellite revisionism from the 1950s; and continuities (between New Labour and the Major Government which preceded it) in basic industrial and employment policy [40]. There is still, that is, more than an echo of Miliband's propensity to see Labour leaderships of whatever stripe as a political force which acts 'as a safe alternative government for the British establishment'. [41]

- It is distinctive too in the persistence of its focus on New Labour's economic and social policy. Not much store was set on the radicalism of New Labour's constitutional agenda, hence the preference to address the policy (and ultimately electoral) consequences of New Labour's enthusiasm for 'new growth theory'. This focus definitely reflects our post-1980 shift away from Labour Party studies mentioned earlier, a shift which ironically and by a quite circuitous route left us well-positioned to explain the constraints on New Labour when the revamped Labour Party returned in power. For by moving the focus of our work into international and comparative political economy, those of us who earlier had been influenced so heavily by Miliband's work on the Labour Party found that, when we came back to writing about New Labour, we were better positioned to write about the Blairite *economic* project than were many of the scholars whose work had remained sharply focused on party politics and party issues alone, as ours broadly speaking had not.

- A third feature of our work on New Labour in power is its propensity still to measure New Labour's performance – as once we measured Old

Labour's – against various kinds of socialist yardsticks. By those tests, the party led by Tony Blair is far less a party of social reform even than was that led by Harold Wilson; and of course the Blair-led government is light years away from the reformist party long sought by the Labour Left – the one briefly brought into view again by Bennite pressure between 1970 and 1983 before being 'modernized' away by Kinnock and Blair. As Colin Leys (who joined Panitch as co-editor of *The Socialist Register* in 1977) argued before New Labour came to power, this was not to deny that policy modernization was necessary to win victory after nearly two decades in opposition. What concerned him however, even before they came to office, was whether, as New Labour deployed 'the buzzword of "modernization" to good short-term electoral effect … any serious project for social change, let alone one that can seriously be called socialist, can be constructed on such a foundation'.[42] In keeping with the Milibandian perspective as a whole, he proved correct in thinking that the answer to that concern would soon be given with a resounding 'No'.

The development of such arguments – over the two decades since Old Labour left office – then enables and obliges us to add to the original set of arguments listed in Section I of this essay, the following new elements defining of the Milibandian perspective on the Labour Party.

d) The centrality of corporatism to the politics of Old Labour, and the particular inappropriateness of that form of politics to parties of social reform in an economy with so weak a manufacturing base and so globally-focused a set of financial institutions.

e) The peculiarly electoralist nature of the Labour Party's relationship with its potential mass base, and the particularly inappropriate nature of that relationship for a party requiring to consolidate a counter-hegemonic presence.

f) The attractiveness of the Bennite attempt to reset Labour Party politics, and the necessary limits of that attempt.

g) The centrality of strategies of 'progressive competitiveness' to the New Labour project, and the particular inappropriateness of those strategies for a party seeking both a prolonged period of majority electoral support and a strengthened industrial base from which to finance social provision.

III

Complex and extensive bodies of argument require careful reading, but such readings take time – time that many critics of the Milibandian perspective have not always afforded it. As we noted at the start of this essay, too often the whole corpus has been dismissed as merely criticizing the Labour Party for not being a socialist party when in truth it never set out to be one; as though that was the argument being offered in *Parliamentary Socialism* and in the scholarship inspired by it. But that was never the Milbandian view of the Labour Party. The Labour Party has always been understood from within this perspective – even at moments of the party's greatest radicalism – as at most a *reformist party*, and moreover one less seeking to transform capitalism into socialism by parliamentary means than as at most a *party of social reform*, one within which reformists and more moderate reformers battled for dominance (with the latter invariably in the ascendancy). The whole focus has been not on the politics of Labour as a party that betrays its own socialist goals and its already socialist working class constituency, but on the politics of labourism and its consequences: on the manner in which a party, moderate in its fundamental aims even when these were articulated in some form of socialist discourse and possessed of 'a narrow interpretation of parliamentary democracy'[43] , locked itself onto a trajectory of increasing conservatism, a trajectory which arguably has now repositioned the party to the right of any programmatic position that could be described as even progressive, let alone socialist, in intent. We have always conceded the presence within the Labour Party of individuals and programmes of a socialist/progressive kind; but what we have always insisted upon is that socialists within the Party have never enjoyed more than a minority and subordinate presence.

A Labour Party that embraces capitalist globalization rather than denouncing it, and treats the working class as one interest group among many amidst an overarching commitment to the idea that 'business must lead', may appear to be one no longer capable of being understood in terms of the concept of parliamentary socialism. The transformation from Old Labour to New Labour, in the sense of displacing the representation of class and of any socialist discourse altogether from the center of the party system, is designed to make many of contractions of parliamentary socialism disappear, so that all that will be left of parliamentary socialism, then, will be a unidimentional parliamentarism. But it seems to us that the political tragedy this entails will not go uncontested in a world where the social divisions of class, far from disappearing, are reasserting themselves in new forms. Nor will serious students of British politics, if they are to understand the historical trajectory to this political tragedy, and consider what is now to be done about it, be able to do without the conceptual apparatus, as well as the rich historical accounts, furnished from the Milibandian perspective. In this sense, at least, the Miliband legacy remains as relevant as ever.

But what *is now* to be done? The frustration which more moderate commentators on Labour matters have had with Miliband's and our own writings down the years seem to have been created in part by the fact that the concept of 'socialism', used as a yardstick against which to judge New and well as Old Labour, appears insufficiently defined. In defence we would simply say that this frustration ignores those writings in the Milibandian genre that offer varying degrees of specification of what may be meant by socialism today [44]. It is not that there is a single Miliband-inspired definition of an alternative order. Such a specification would have an arbitrariness that would render it valueless. It is rather than we can point to various moves to specify part of what that socialism might be, to put some flesh on what the 2000 *Socialist* Register called *Necessary Utopias* with contributions by such luminaries as Terry Eagleton, Diane Elson, Norman Geras, Kate Soper, among others, to what Gindin and Panitch in that volume call 'rekindling the socialist imagination'. If this work is not read by scholars of the Labour Party, it already says something significant – and sad – about their own lack of interest in answering the question of what is socialism, rather than just in posing it in a negative fashion.

The Milibandian argument has always been, in that sense, an argument addressed only to part of the audience interested in the Labour Party. It has been (and it remains) an argument – a set of theses about labour and its possibilities – addressed primarily to the concerns of socialists – those inside the Labour Party itself and those beyond. 'Is activity within the Party a precursor of the creation of a mass base for socialist politics, or a debilitating distraction from that creation?' This is the central Miliband question. Those who take that perspective have always been keen to ally with the Labour Left and to support its growth;[45] but ultimately they have also been, as Hilary Wainwright once called herself, 'obstinate refusniks'.[46] And they have always recognised that the creation of a socialist working class in the UK was a task that would take a long time, which is one reason why they have argued that the Labour Party's short-term electoral concerns so obviously predisposed the Party against any attempt to undertake it.

A final word on the importance of Ralph Miliband himself. Because time is passing since his death, and because his major writings from the late 1960s were not directly focused on the Labour Party per se, there is a danger that new generations of Labour Party scholars will discount his importance. That would be a great loss to left-wing scholarship in the UK. We have separately recorded our own personal debts to him and his work;[47] but the debt (and the importance) runs wider than that. Ralph Miliband was a member of that generation of socialist intellectual giants who, by the sheer force of their personalities, the charisma of their teaching and the quality of their scholarship, created a huge (and more or less safe) intellectual space within UK universities for radical students to pursue radical research. Before them, the range of the tolerable (and the tolerated) in the study of British Labour was narrow and arcane. We have the freedom to react to them now, to decide how much to take from their work as our own, because they won for us a width and a quality of scholarship missing in their youth. This intellectual space has not yet been completely expunged in the cold winter of post-Thatcherite, neo-liberal orthodoxies, and of New Labour's – and social democracy's in general – embrace of so many of them. But we badly need intellectuals of such stature back again to fill that space, and to build on it anew.

Notes

[1] R. Miliband, 'Moving On', in R. Miliband and J. Saville (eds), *The Socialist Register* 1976, London, Merlin Press, 1976, pp. 128, 130

[2] K. Jefferys, 'The Attlee Years, 1935-55', in B. Brivati and R. Heffernan (eds), *The Labour Party: A Centenary History*, London, Macmillan, 2000, p. 68

[3] Robert Taylor, 'The Trade Unions and the Formation of the Labour Party', in Brivati and Heffernan, op.cit., p. 10

[4] R. Miliband, R., *The State in Capitalist Society*, London, Weidenfeld and Nicolson, 1969, p.196

[5] Ibid, p.195

[6] R. Miliband, R., *Capitalist Democracy in Britain*, Oxford, Oxford University Press, 1982, p.15

[7] Ibid, p.16

[8] Ibid, p.23

[9] Ibid, p.38

[10] Ibid, pp. 68-76

[11] R. Miliband, 'The future of socialism in England', in R. Miliband and J. Saville (eds), *The Socialist Register* 1977, Merlin Press, p.47

[12] R. Miliband, *Class Power and State Power*, London, Verso,1983, pp. 304-5

[13] R. Miliband, and M. Liebman, 'Beyond Social Democracy', in R. Miliband, J. Saville, M.Liebman and L. Panitch (eds), *Social Democracy and After: The Socialist Register 1985/6*, London, Merlin Press 1986, p. 481

[14] R. Miliband, *Marxism and Politics*, Oxford, Oxford University Press 1977, p.14

[15] L. Panitch, 'The Development of Corporatism in Liberal Democracies', *Comparative Political Studies*, vol. 10, no. 1, 1977; 'Recent theorizations of Corporatism: Reflections on a Growth Industry', *British Journal of Sociology*, vol. 31, no. 2, June 1980; 'The limits of corporatism: trade unions and the capitalist state', *New Left Review* 125, January/February 1981, pp. 21-44; 'The State and the Future of Socialism', *Capital and Class* no. 11, Summer 1980. All these are collected in his *Working Class Politics in Crisis: Essays on Labour and the State* London, Verso, 1986. See also the Conclusion to his *Social Democracy and Industrial Militancy* Cambridge, Cambridge University Press, 1976; the introductory chapter to his edited collection, *The Canadian State: Political Economy and Political Power* Toronto, Toronto University Press, 1977; and his comparative survey of the social democratic state and corporatism in Germany, Sweden, Austria and Britain, 'The Tripartite experience', in K. Banting (ed), *The State and Economic Interests*, vol. 32, Royal Commission on the Economic Union and Development Prospects for Canada, Toronto, University of Toronto Press 1986, pp. 37-118

[16] D. Coates, *The Context of British Politics* , London, Hutchinson, 1984

[17] D. Coates, *Running the Country*, London, Hodder and Stoughton 1990/1995

[18] C. Leys, *Politics in Britain*, Toronto, University of Toronto Press 1983

[19] G. Albo, D. Langille and L. Panitch (eds), *A Different Kind of State: Popular Power and Democratic Administration*, Toronto, Oxford University Press, 1993; L. Panitch, 'Globalization and the State', in R. miliband and J. Saville (eds), *Between Globalism and Nationalism: The Socialist Register 1994*, London, Merlin Press, pp. 60-93

[20] D.Coates, *The Question of UK Decline*, London, Harvester, 1994

[21] D. Coates, *Models of Capitalism: Growth and Stagnation in the Contemporary Era*, Cambridge, Polity Press, 2000

[22] L. Panitch, 'Profits and Politics: Labour and the Crisis of British Capitalism', *Politics and Society*, vol. 7, no. 4, December 1977

[23] D. Coates, *Labour in Power? A Study of the Labour Government 1974-79*, London, Longman, 1980,pp. 160-161

[24] L. Panitch, 'The development of corporatism in liberal democracies', op.cit., p.66

[25] ibid, pp. 83-7

[26] D. Coates, D. *The Context of British Politics*, London, Hutchinson, 1984, p.258; D. Coates, 'Corporatism and the state in theory and practice', in M. Harrison (ed), *Corporatism and the Welfare State*, Aldershot, Gower, 1984, pp. 131

[27] G. Albo, 'Competitive austerity and the impasse of capitalist employment policy', in R. Miliband and L. Panitch (eds), *Between Globalism and Nationalism: The Socialist Register 1994*, London, Merlin Press, pp. 144-170; G. Albo, 'A world market of opportunities? Capitalist obstacles and Left economic policy', in L. Panitch (eds), *Ruthless Criticism of All that Exists: The Socialist Register 1997*, London, Merlin Press, pp. 1-43; L. Panitch, 'Globalisation and the State', in R. Miliband and L. Panitch (eds), *Between Globalism and Nationalism: The Socialist Register 1994*, London, Merlin Press, pp.60-93 [Add also LP 98,2000]

[28] The relevance of this analysis to a contemporary understanding of the fundamental weakness of New Labour's economic and political strategy, even though it has nothing directly to say about the detail of Labour Party policy per se, is hard to miss. This is Albo on the neo-liberal alternative. 'Neo-liberal policies of keeping wage increases below productivity growth and pushing down domestic costs has led to an unstable vicious circle of competitive austerity:' each country reduce domestic demand and adopts an export-oriented strategy of dumping its surplus production, for which there are fewer consumers in its national economy given the decrease in workers' living standards and productivity gains all going to the capitalist, in the world market. This has created a global demand crisis and the growth of surplus capacity across the business cycle'. On the 'progressive competitiveness' alternative initially canvassed by Clinton Democrats and the Ontario NDP, Panitch wrote: . "It presents a programme of vast economic readjustment for both labour and capital, with blithe regard for how, in the interim, the logic of competitive austerity could be avoided: it presumes that mass unemployment is primarily a problem of skills adjustment to technological change rather than one aspect of a crisis of overproduction; it fosters an illusion of a rate of employment growth in high tech sectors sufficient to offset the rate of unemployment growth in other sectors; it either even more unrealistically assumes a rate of growth of world markets massive enough to accommodate all those adopting this strategy, or it blithely ignores the issues associated with exporting unemployment to those who don't succeed at this strategy under conditions of unlimited demand (and with the attendant consequences this would have for sustaining demand); it ignores the reality that capital can also adapt leading technologies in low wage economies, and the competitive pressures on capital in this context to push down wages even in high tech sectors and limit the costs to it of the social wage and adjustment policies so central to the whole strategy's progressive logic in the first place.'

[29] L. Panitch, 'Globalisation and the State', in R. Miliband and L. Panitch (eds), *Between Globalism and Nationalism: The Socialist Register 1994*, London, Merlin Press, p.87

[30] D. Coates, ' Model of capitalism in the new world order: the British case', *Political Studies*, vol. 47, no. 4, 1999, pp. 643-660

[31] D. Coates, 'Labour Power and International Competitiveness: a critique of ruling orthodoxies', in L. Panitch and C. Leys (eds), *Global Capitalism versus Democracy, The Socialist Register 1999*, London, Merlin Press, pp. 108-141

[32] D. Coates, *Models of Capitalism*, Cambridge UK, Polity Press, 2000

[33] This is *Models of Capitalism* on the limits of a growth strategy that uses education and training policy as a substitute for industrial policy: 'Center-left theorists have… to recognize the poverty of the vision of the world created by the reduction of the state's role to that of investment in human capital. What 're-skilling labour' as a growth strategy does is leave investment as a 'Dutch auction' in which local labour forces (and local states) bid…for the favours of mobile capital. Such a strategy is equally predicated on leaving capital unregulated as is its neo-liberal alternative; and in both cases lacks the capacity to lift any particular economy on to a high growth path without at the same time pushing an alternative economy on to a lower one. That may be electorally popular within the successful economy, but it is neither socially progressive at the level of the world

economy as a whole, nor free of its own internal propensity to be undermined by similar initiatives elsewhere, whose cumulative effect is to leave individual economies persistently prone to the crises of competitiveness, unemployment and social retrenchment which re-skilling was meant to avoid. You cannot get off the treadmill simply by running faster. All you can do by that mechanism is temporarily pass others, until they respond by running faster too, with the long-term consequence of having the whole field increase their speed just to stand still. The victor in such a race is not the runner, but the treadmill.' (254)

[34]D. Coates, 'The Labour Party and the Future of the Left', in R. Miliband and J. Saville (eds), *The Socialist Register* 1983, London, Merlin Press, p. 98; 'Social democracy and the logic of political traditions', *Economy and Society*, vol. 15, no. 3, 1986. p.423; *The Crisis of Labour*, Oxford, Philip Allan, 1989, pp. 103-3; 'Labour governments: old constraints and new parameters', *New Left Review* 219,1996, pp.63-4

[35] Ibid, pp. 63-4

[36] L. Panitch, 'The Impasse of Social Democratic Politics' in R. Miliband et al, *Social Democracy and After: The Socialist Register 1985/6'*, London, Merlin Press, pp. 50-97 (Chapter 1 of his *Working Class Politics in Crisis*, London, Verso, 1986)

[37] H. Wainwright, *Labour: A Tale of Two Parties*, London, Hogarth Press, 1987; L. Panitch, 'The Impasse of Social Democratic Politics' in R. Miliband et al, *Social Democracy and After: The Socialist Register 1985/6'*, London, Merlin Press, pp. 50-97; C. Leys, 'The British Labour Party's transition from socialism to capitalism', in L. Panitch (ed), *Are There Alternatives; The Socialist Register* 1996, London, Merlin Press, pp. 7-32; D. Coates, 'Labour governments: old constraints and new parameters', *New Left Review* 219, 1996, pp. 62-78

[38] L. Panitch and C. Leys, *The End of Parliamentary Socialism: From New Left to New Labour*, London, Verso (first edition 1997; second, with an epilogue co-written with D. Coates, 2001)

[39] ibid, pp. 237-261; D. Coates,, 'The character of New Labour', in D. Coates and P. Lawler (eds), *New Labour in Power*, Manchester, Manchester University Press, 2000, pp. 1-15

[40] D. Coates, 'New Labour's industrial and employment policy', in D. Coates and P. Lawler (eds), *New Labour in Power*, op cit., pp. 122-135;

[41] L. Panitch, and C. Leys, *The End of Parliamentary Socialism: From New Left to New Labour*, op.cit, p.218

[42] C. Leys, 'The British Labour Party's transition from socialism to capitalism', in L. Panitch (ed), *Are There Alternatives; The Socialist Register* 1996, London, Merlin Press, p.26

[43] L. Panitch, L., 'Socialist Renewal and the Labour Party', in R. Miliband, L. Panitch and J. Saville (eds), *Problems of Socialist Renewal East and West: The Socialist Register* 1988, London, Merlin Press, pp. 349

[44] See for example, R. Miliband, R. *Marxism and Politics*, Oxford, Oxford University Press 1977, and *Socialism for a Skeptical Age*, Cambridge, Polity Press, 1994; T. Burden, H. Breitenbach, H., and D. Coates, *Features of a Viable Socialism*, London, Harvester Wheatsheaf, l990; L. Panitch, 'The State and the Future of Socialism", *Capital and Class*, no. 11, Summer 1980, and 'Transcending Pessimism: Rekindling Socialist Imagination', (with S. Gindin), in L. Panitch and C. Leys (eds), *Necessary and Unnecessary Utopias: The Socialist Register 2000*, London, Merlin Press, 1999, as well as Panitch's recent book, *Renewing Socialism: Democracy, Strategy and Imagination*, Boulder, Westview, 2001. See also H. Wainwright, *Arguments for a New Left*, London, Oxford, Basil Blackwell, 1994: G. Albo, D. Langille and L. Panitch, *A Different Kind of State*, Toronto, Oxford University Press, 1993, and G. Albo, 'A world market of opportunities? Capitalist obstacles and Left economic policy', in L. Panitch (eds), *Ruthless Criticism of All that Exists: The Socialist Register 1997*, London, Merlin Press, pp. 1-43; and C. Leys, 'The public sphere and the media', in L. Panitch and C. Leys (eds), *Global Capitalism Versus Democracy: The Socialist Register 1999*, London, Merlin, 1999.

[45] L. Panitch, L. and C. Leys, *The End of Parliamentary Socialism: From New Left to New Labour*, London, Verso, 1997, pp. 268ff

[46] H. Wainwright, *Labour: A Tale of Two Parties*, London, Hogarth Press, 1987, p.6

[47] L. Panitch, L. 'Ralph Miliband: Socialist Intellectual 1924-1994' in L. Panitch (ed), *Why Not Capitalism: The Socialist Register 1995*, London, Merlin Press, pp. 1-21; D. Coates, 'The View at Half-Time: Politics and UK Economic Under-Performance', *University of Leeds Review*, vol. 38, 1996, pp. 37-55